BARRON'S

W9-ANX-584

HOW TO PREPARE FOR
REAL ESTATE LICENSING EXAMINATIONS

SALESPERSON AND BROKER

THIRD EDITION

by
J. Bruce Lindeman, Ph.D.
Professor of Real Estate
University of Arkansas
at Little Rock

Jack P. Friedman, Ph.D.
Laguarta Professor of Real Estate
Department of Finance/Real Estate Research Center
Texas A&M University

Barron's Educational Series, Inc. • New York • London • Toronto • Sydney

All inquiries should be addressed to:
Barron's Educational Series, Inc.
250 Wireless Boulevard
Hauppauge, New York 11788

Library of Congress Catalog Card No. 87-15758

International Standard Book No. 0-8120-2996-8

Library of Congress Cataloging in Publication Data
Lindeman, J. Bruce (John Bruce)
  Barron's how to prepare for real estate licensing
examinations: sales person and broker / by J. Bruce
Lindeman, Jack P. Friedman. — 3rd ed.
      p.   cm.
  ISBN 0-8120-2996-8
  1. Real estate business—Law and legislation—
United States—Examinations, questions, etc.   2. Real
property—United States—Examinations, questions, etc.
3. Real estate business—Licenses—United States.
I. Friedman, Jack P.   II. Title.   III Title: How to
prepare for real estate licensing examinations.
KF2042.R4L56   1987
346.7304′37—dc19   87-15758
[347.306437]   CIP

PRINTED IN THE U.S.A.

CONTENTS

Illustrations

Tables

PREFACE

During the past decade, legal, social, economic, and financial matters affecting real estate have become more complex, creating greater educational needs for those who are engaged in the real estate business. In today's environment, a salesperson cannot survive solely on a pleasant disposition and a neat appearance. He or she must be aware of and obey federal, state, and local regulations. He or she needs in-depth knowledge of the property being brokered, including its physical surroundings and its economic, legal, social, and political environment.

In recognition of these needs, most states have adopted more stringent standards for the licensure of real estate brokers and salespersons. These standards include more education, more rigorous examinations, or both. Population mobility, the need for licensure reciprocity, increased federal regulation, and greater communication and cooperation between state license law officials have all led to more uniformity in real estate licensing standards. Most states presently use examinations prepared by just two organizations, instead of each state's preparing exams independently, as before.

This book was written as an introduction to real estate, taking into consideration real estate complexities, the need for more knowledge, and the trend toward uniformity among states. It is primarily intended to serve those seeking to meet licensure requirements but it may also satisfy the needs of those wanting to know more about real property law, contracts, finance, brokerage, ethics, leasing, appraisal, mathematics, fair housing, truth in lending, and other such topics. For the person just wanting to buy or sell a home, the glossary may serve as a reference for greater understanding of the transactions. It alone can prevent misunderstandings that are costly in terms of time and money.

A careful reading of any document is crucial to understanding it. Many people have unfortunately lost money by failing to read and understand contracts before signing them. Similarly, a careful reading of this book will be helpful toward understanding the complex subject it concerns. Tests have been included at the end of each chapter and comprehensive exams at the end of the book so that you can test yourself for understanding of the material presented, both chapter by chapter and at the end. Though your instructor can be of valuable assistance, the knowledge that you gain will approximate the effort that you expend.

Should you become actively engaged in the real estate business, we wish you much success. We hope that all your dealings will be honest and fair. Only in this way can the real estate business become recognized as a profession.

We thank the many people who have aided us in preparing this book, including Suzanne Barnhill, Irene Koby, Bob Ritchie, and Brenda Wagner. We thank our families for their patience and dedicate this book to them.

J. Bruce Lindeman
Jack P. Friedman

Examination Timetable*

Uniform Real Estate Licensing Examination: Salesperson/Broker
(administered by Educational Testing Service—ETS)

About 20% of the questions in salesperson and broker examinations require math.

Salesperson 4.5 hours	Broker 4.5 hours
Uniform Examination — 80 questions on: Real estate contracts (13%); financing (24%); real estate ownership (22%); real estate brokerage (24%); real estate valuation (17%). State Portion — 30-50 questions on state law & practice, license law.	Uniform Examination — 80 questions on: Real estate brokerage (35%); contracts and other legal aspects (27%); pricing and valuation (15%); finance and investment (23%). State Portion — 30-50 questions on state law & practice, license law.

National Real Estate Examination
(administered by The American College Testing Program—ACT

About 10% of the questions in salesperson and broker examinations require math.

Salesperson 3 to 4 hours	Broker 3 to 4 hours
National Exam — 100 questions on: Property ownership, transfer and use (36%); brokerage and laws of agency (30%); finance (17%); valuation and economics (17%). State Portion — 30-50 questions on state law & practice, license law.	National Exam — 100 questions on: Property ownership, transfer and use (25%); brokerage and laws of agency (30%); valuation and economics (25%); finance (20%). State Portion — 30-50 questions on state law & practice, license law.

Real Estate Assessment for Licensure
(administered by Assessment Systems, Inc.—ASI)

About 20% of the questions in salesperson and broker examinations require math.

Salesperson 3 to 4 hours	Broker 3 to 4 hours
General Exam — 80 questions on: Real estate law (30%); property ownership, transfer (20%); brokerage / agency (20%); finance (20%); appraisal (10%). State Portion — 30-50 questions on state law & practice, license law.	General Exam — 80 questions on: Real estate law (15%); property ownership / transfer (25%); brokerage / agency (25%); appraisal (15%); finance (20%). State Portion — 30-50 questions on state law & practice, license law.

Individual State Examination for Salesperson or Broker
(format varies with state)

---

*Format and time limits subject to change.

PART I: INTRODUCTION TO REAL ESTATE

Chapter 1/*How To Use This Book*

If you are reading this book, it is probably because you are interested in employment in the real estate field. Real estate is a fast-growing, exciting field that offers almost unlimited income potential to someone who is willing to work hard and to learn the special features of this very interesting business.

In order to enter most areas of the real estate business it is necessary to take and pass a licensing examination. This book is designed to help you *succeed* in taking that first step. To fulfill that purpose, this book contains a number of special features designed to improve its usefulness to you:

1. This book can be used to study for any licensing examination offered in the real estate field by any state. It covers all three nationally distributed examinations (ETS, ACT and ASI) as well as those given in states that prepare their own examinations. No matter where you live, this is the book you need. To determine which test you would take, see the Nationwide Testing Schedule (Table 1-1).

2. Special emphasis is given to those topics that license applicants find most troublesome on examinations:
   a. Arithmetic and Real Estate Math
   b. Contracts
   c. Closing Statements (for broker applicants)

3. Hundreds of sample questions are included in the text, covering all the materials discussed.

4. Seven complete examinations are included for practice. There are facsimiles of both salesperson and broker examinations for all three national examinations (ETS, ACT and ASI) and a special examination for states which administer their own examinations. Also included are several supplemental examinations for specific specialized topic areas that are examined in some, but not all states. All in all, nearly 1,500 practice questions are provided in the text and examinations combined!

5. A full and complete glossary is included, along with instructions as to the best study strategy for getting the most out of it.

6. The final chapter before the model tests concerns the *strategy* and *techniques* of taking examinations so that you can be sure to get every point possible.

TOPICS

This book is divided into 23 chapters, the sample examinations, and one appendix. Each chapter covers a specific topic. Some are long; some are short. However, it should be remembered that the material in most of the chapters complements the material in the others. This would be especially so in Part III, "Real Estate Contracts." The first chapter of Part III (Chapter 7, "Introduction to Contracts") is a long one; it discusses all the generally

Table 1-1.
NATIONWIDE TESTING SCHEDULE: Examinations Used By Each State*

	Own Exam	ACT	ETS	ASI		Own Exam	ACT	ETS	ASI
Alabama		•			Montana			•	
Alaska			•		Nebraska			•	
Arizona				•	Nevada		•		
Arkansas				•	New Hampshire			•	
California	•				New Jersey				•
Colorado			•		New Mexico		•		
Connecticut			•		New York	•			
Delaware			•		North Carolina			•	
District of Columbia				•	North Dakota			•	
Florida	•				Ohio	•			
Georgia		•			Oklahoma	•			
Hawaii			•		Oregon			•	
Idaho				•	Pennsylvania			•	
Illinois			•		Rhode Island			•	
Indiana				•	South Carolina	•			
Iowa		•			South Dakota			•	
Kansas				•	Tennessee			•	
Kentucky				•	Texas	•			
Louisiana				•	Utah				•
Maine			•		Vermont			•	
Maryland				•	Virginia		•		
Massachusetts				•	Washington		•		
Michigan			•		West Virginia	•			
Minnesota	•				Wisconsin		•		
Mississippi	•				Wyoming			•	
Missouri		•							

*This listing is subject to change, as states adopt a national exam, or occasionally switch to another. For the latest information on your state's procedures, check with your state real estate licensing office (addresses included in the Appendix).

relevant things you should know that apply to all of the separate contracts you have to know about. Each of the other chapters in Part III is devoted to one or more types or parts of real estate contracts. For each of these chapters, remember that all the general material in Chapter 7 applies to what you are learning. Chapter 8 discusses land description; Chapters 9 through 13 serve to point out the specific characteristics of each of the real estate contracts; these characteristics are in addition to all those mentioned in Chapter 7.

SAMPLE QUESTIONS

Most chapters are followed by sample questions concerning the material contained in the chapter. You can use these questions to test yourself on what you have read; also note that these questions are written in the format most frequently encountered on licensing examinations. When you have finished studying the material in the book, you can take the three sample final examinations that follow Chapter 23. These will enable you to check on your retention of the material you have read and will give you some experience in taking real estate examinations in a format similar to the licensing examination. Each model examination has a three-hour time limit.

You should not take all three examinations at once. Rather, take the first one, and then correct it, using the key that appears in Chapter 26. The questions you got wrong will pinpoint the areas in which you need further study. Do this additional studying, and then take the second examination. Once again, use the questions you may have missed to guide you to still further study. Try to understand why you missed each question you got wrong; that way you can be sure you won't make that mistake again. Finally, take the third examination, once again using the few questions you miss as guides for final study before taking the licensing examination itself.

If you are applying for a broker's license, you also will find supplemental examinations on closing statements (settlement statements), and on contracts.

REAL ESTATE ARITHMETIC

A great many license applicants feel they will have trouble with the mathematical portions of the examinations. Therefore, we have included in this book mathematical study aids not normally found in real estate books. Chapter 17, "Arithmetic Review," is unique to this book; it is a *complete* and *thorough* review of *all* the arithmetic techniques you will have to know to pass the licensing examination's mathematics questions. Many applicants have not had to use the arithmetic skills they learned in school and, so, have become rusty at them. If you feel that this might be your problem, be sure to go over Chapter 17 *before* you read Chapter 18, "Real Estate Mathematics and Problem Solving." In fact, even if you feel confident of your mathematical ability, it would be wise to look through Chapter 17 and do a few of the problems in each of the problem sets. This way you'll be absolutely sure of your ability and certain that you haven't overlooked some particular aspect of arithmetic you may have forgotten.

Once you are sure of your arithmetic ability, Chapter 18 will show you how that ability is used in solving arithmetic problems that involve real estate situations. Chapter 17, then, discusses working with fractions, decimals, percents, areas, volumes, and the like. Chapter 18 discusses rates of interest, commissions, profit rates, subdivision, prorating charges, calculating taxes, etc. Chapter 19, "Closing Statements," considers the particular problem of preparation of closing statements; this area usually is reserved for brokerage examinations in most states. Therefore, if you are applying for a salesperson's license, skip Chapter 19.

TAKING EXAMINATIONS

Chapters 22 and 23 have been specially prepared to give you all the knowledge available concerning the *techniques* of taking examinations. These chapters will tell you all you must know about how to approach an examination, and how to make sure that you get the highest score possible. *Be sure to read these chapters!* They will give you valuable guidelines for taking the licensing examination and will introduce you to the kind of examination you can expect to encounter.

STUDY STRATEGY

You should approach your study of the materials you must know in a systematic and sensible way in order to get the most out of it. Therefore, we have provided the following study strategy.

1. First, you must find out everything you can about the licensing examination offered by your state, including where and when it is given, how much it costs, and how to apply. See the section called "Preparing for the Examination" in Chapter 22 for a full checklist of the things you should find out. Remember one thing: when you need some information, it is best usually to TELEPHONE. Even if it's a long-distance call to your state's real estate licensing office, the cost is very slight compared to what the information is worth to you. Even if you make several calls, you are not likely to spend more than $10 on them, much less than you probably will have to spend on examination and licensing fees. If you can find out some needed fact right away, you are that much ahead of the game. Also, people are usually more willing to give

attention to calls than to letters; if you write for information your letter may languish on a desk for days, but if you call and point out that you're on long distance, you often will get immediate attention.

2. Your next step is to assemble all the study materials you will need. They include:
    a. This book
    b. Your state's Real Estate License Law
    c. Any study materials *specifically* recommended or required by your state. Most particularly, this includes *all* study materials provided by your state's real estate licensing agency; these will tell you what you must know about the special features of your state's laws and practices.

3. Now you begin studying. Start with Chapter 2 in this book, the glossary of real estate terms. Read it carefully, making sure you take note of all the terms. Don't try to understand them all at this point; just become slightly familiar with them.

4. Proceed through the chapters in the order they appear in the book. When you get to Chapter 5 ("Real Estate License Law"), have your copy of your state's license law handy to refer to.

5. When you have read through Chapter 23 and have answered all the questions at the end of each chapter, take the first sample examination and correct it. Note your weak areas, to be concentrated upon in your later study.

6. At this point you should read all the study materials provided by your state, and compare your state's practices and laws to those outlined in this book. You will have noted a number of places in this book where you should fill in your state's practice on a particular point — now is the time to do that.

7. Now you have covered general real estate principles and your state's special materials. Take the second Practice Examination.

8. Go over this book again, as well as your state's provided materials and license law. Pay particular attention to those problem areas pointed out by the questions you missed on the first two sample examinations. Take the third examination.

9. Now you should be ready to take, and PASS, your state's Real Estate License Examination. Be sure to schedule your studying so that you finish up only a day or two prior to the actual licensing examination; in this way, all the material you have learned will be fresh in your mind.

Chapter 2/*Definitions of Real Estate Terms*

On the next few pages is a glossary of real estate terminology. It is quite extensive and probably covers all the terms you might be expected to be familiar with when you take a licensing examination. We suggest that you begin your preparation for the examination by carefully reading over this glossary. It may seem a boring and tedious thing to do, but it will have many advantages. The main thing is that it will acquaint you with some important terminology used in the real estate business. Once you have studied these terms, your study of the remaining material in this book will be much easier for you; most of what you read about you will already have at least a minimal familiarity with. In fact, the purpose of the rest of the book is to show you how all these many things relate to one another in the real estate business.

The best way to study the glossary is to go over it once fairly quickly. Don't skip anything, but don't study it intensely, either. A while later, begin to go over the terms much more carefully, devoting a lot of attention to absorbing the definition as it is given to you. Make sure not to skip over anything: a lot of real estate terms may look familiar because they are composed of familiar words. More likely than not, however, you will find that the *real estate meaning* is *not* the one you are used to. This is one of the more important problems that a lot of people have with the real estate licensing examinations: you must learn terminology and be prepared to use the special meanings that many words have when they are used in a real estate context.

Once you have spent a good amount of time on the terminology, go on through the rest of the book. Use the glossary for reference whenever you need to, when you are studying further along in the book. Later, as the time for the examination approaches, you will find it very fruitful to go over the glossary again. It will be a sort of special thumbnail review for you to read the terms once again, after you have studied the rest of the book, and will be of considerable help in your final preparation for the examination. This is especially so since you will often encounter strictly definitional questions (such as, "The term *fee simple* means most nearly _____ .").

Glossary

ABSTRACT OF TITLE / A summary of all of the recorded instruments and proceedings that affect the title to property.

ACCELERATION CLAUSE / A provision in a loan giving the lender the right to declare the entire amount immediately due and payable upon the violation of a different loan provision, such as failure to make payments on time.

ACCEPTANCE / The act of agreeing to accept an offer.

ACCESS RIGHT / The right of an owner to get to and from his property.

ACCRETION / The addition to land through processes of nature, such as deposits of soil carried by streams.

ACCRUED INTEREST / Interest that has been earned but not paid. If 6 percent interest is earned on a $100 deposit, then $6 of interest has accrued to the depositor.

ACKNOWLEDGMENT / A declaration by a person who has signed a document that such signature is his voluntary act, made before a duly authorized person or officer.

ACRE / A measure of land equaling 160 square rods, 10 square chains, 4840 square yards, or 43,560 square feet.

ADJACENT / Lying near to but not necessarily in actual contact with.

ADJOINING / Contiguous; attaching; in actual contact with.

ADJUSTABLE RATE MORTGAGE (ARM) / A mortgage loan which has an interest rate which is allowed to vary during the life of the loan; usually there are *caps* on the amounts by which the interest rate can change annually and over the life of the loan.

ADMINISTRATOR / A person appointed by a court to administer the estate of a deceased person who left no will.

ADMINISTRATOR'S DEED / A deed conveying the property of one who died without a will (intestate).

ADULT / One who has attained the age of majority.

AD VALOREM / According to valuation.

AD VALOREM TAX / A tax based on the value of the thing being taxed. **Example:** If the effective tax rate is 1 percent, the tax would be $1 per $100 of property value.

ADVERSE POSSESSION / A means of acquiring title to real estate where an occupant has been in actual, open, notorious, exclusive, and continuous occupancy of property for the period required by state law.

AFFIDAVIT / A statement or declaration in writing, sworn to or affirmed before some officer who is authorized to administer an oath or affirmation.

AFFIRM / To confirm; to ratify; to verify.

AGENCY / The legal relationship between a principal and his agent arising from a contract in which the principal employs the agent to perform certain acts on his (the principal's) behalf.

AGENT / One who undertakes to transact some business or to manage some affair for another, with the authority of the latter. **Example:** An owner employs a broker to act as his agent in selling real property; the broker in turn employs salespersons to act as his agents to sell the same property.

AGREEMENT OF SALE / A written agreement between seller and purchaser in which the purchaser agrees to buy certain real estate and the seller agrees to sell upon terms and conditions of the agreement. Also called *offer and acceptance, contract of sale.*

AIR RIGHTS / The right to use, control, or occupy the space above a designated property. **Example:** The Pan Am Building in New York City is built on air rights above the Grand Central Railroad Station.

ALIENATION / Transferring property to another, as the transfer of property and possession of lands, by gift or by sale, from one person to another.

ALLUVIUM (or ALLUVION) / Soil deposited by accretion. Usually considered to belong to the owner of the land to which it is added.

AMENITIES / In appraising, the nonmonetary benefits derived from property ownership. **Example:** pride of home ownership.

AMORTIZATION / A gradual paying off of a debt by periodic installments.

ANNUITY / A series of equal or nearly equal periodic payments or receipts. **Example:** The receipt of $100 per year for the next five years constitutes a $100 five-year annuity.

APPRAISAL / An opinion or estimate of the value of a property.

APPRAISAL APPROACH / One of three methods used in estimating the value of property: Income Approach, Market Comparison Approach, and Cost Approach. See each.

APPRAISAL BY SUMMATION / See "Cost Approach."

APPRAISER / One qualified to estimate the value of real property.

APPRECIATION / An increase in the value of property.

APPURTENANCE / Something that is outside the property itself but is considered a part of the property and adds to its greater enjoyment, such as the right to cross another's land (i.e., *right-of-way* or *easement*).

ARM / See "Adjustable Rate Mortgage".

ASSESSED VALUATION / A valuation placed upon property by a public officer or a board, as a basis for taxation.

ASSESSMENT / A charge against real estate made by a government to cover the cost of an improvement such as a street or sewer line. (See also "Assessed Valuation.")

ASSESSMENT RATIO / The ratio of assessed value to market value. **Example:** A county requires a 40 percent assessment ratio on all property to be taxed. Property with a $10,000 value is therefore assessed at $4000 (40 percent of $10,000), and the tax rate is applied to $4000.

ASSESSOR / An official who has the responsibility of placing an assessed value on property.

ASSIGNEE / The person to whom an agreement or contract is sold or transferred.

ASSIGNMENT / The method or manner by which a right or contract is transferred from one person to another.

ASSIGNOR / A party who assigns or transfers an agreement or contract to another.

ASSUMPTION OF MORTGAGE / The purchase of mortgaged property whereby the buyer accepts liability for the debt that continues to exist. The seller remains liable to the lender unless the lender agrees to release him.

ATTACHMENT / Legal seizure of property to force payment of a debt.

ATTEST / To witness to; to witness by observation and signature.

ATTORNEY IN FACT / One who is authorized to act for another under a power of attorney, which may be general or limited in scope.

AVULSION / The sudden removal of land from one owner to another, when a river abruptly changes its channel.

BACKFILL / The replacement of excavated earth into a hole or against a structure.

BALLOON PAYMENT / The final payment on a loan, when that payment is greater than the preceding installment payments and pays the note in full. **Example:** A debt requires interest-only payments annually for five years, at the end of which time the principal balance (a balloon payment) is due.

BARGAIN AND SALE DEED / A deed that conveys real estate, generally lacking a warranty. The grantor will thus claim to have ownership but will not defend against all claims.

BASE AND MERIDIAN / Imaginary lines used by surveyors to find and describe the location of land.

BASE LINE / Part of the Rectangular Survey or Government Survey method of land description. The base line is the major east-west line to which all north-south measurements refer.

BENEFICIARY / The person who receives or is to receive the benefits resulting from certain acts.

BEQUEATH / To give or hand down personal property by a will.

BEQUEST / That personal property which is given by the terms of a will.

BILL OF ASSURANCE / Recorded restrictions affecting a subdivision and a part of all deeds to lots therein.

BILL OF SALE / A written instrument given to pass title of personal property from a seller to a buyer. Used when furniture and portable appliances are sold.

BINDER / An agreement, accompanied by a deposit, for the purchase of real estate, to evidence good faith on the part of the purchaser.

BLANKET MORTGAGE / A single mortgage that includes more than one parcel of real estate as security.

BONA FIDE / In good faith, without fraud.

BOND / A certificate that serves as evidence of a debt.

BROKER / One who is licensed by a state to act for property owners in real estate transactions, within the scope of state law.

BROKERAGE / The business of being a broker.

BUILDING CODES / Regulations established by local governments describing the minimum structural requirements for buildings; includes foundation, roofing, plumbing, electrical, and other specifications for safety and sanitation.

BUILDING LINE / A line fixed at a certain distance from the front and/or sides of a lot, beyond which the building may not project.

BUILDING LOAN AGREEMENT / An agreement whereby the lender lends money to an owner with loan advances at certain stages of construction, i.e., upon completion of the foundation, framing, etc.

BUNDLE OF RIGHTS THEORY / The theory that ownership of realty implies rights such as occupancy, use and enjoyment, and the right to sell, bequeath, give, or lease all or part of these rights.

BUYDOWN / Payment of discount points at loan origination in order to secure a lower interest rate; rate may be "bought down" for only a few years or for the life of the loan.

CANCELLATION CLAUSE / A provision in a contract that gives the right to terminate obligations upon the occurrence of certain specified conditions or events. **Example:** A cancellation clause in a lease may allow the landlord to break the lease upon sale of the building.

CAP / The limit by which the interest rate on an adjustable rate mortgage may be changed; usually there are annual caps and lifetime caps.

CAPITALIZATION / A process whereby anticipated future income is converted to one lump sum capital value.

CAPITALIZATION RATE / A rate of return used to convert anticipated future income into a capital value.

CARRYING CHARGES / Expenses necessary for holding property, such as taxes and interest on idle property or property under construction.

CAVEAT EMPTOR / "Let the buyer beware." The buyer must examine the goods or property and buy at his own risk.

CERTIFICATE OF NO DEFENSE / See "Estoppel Certificate."

CERTIFIED COMMERCIAL INVESTMENT MEMBER (CCIM) / A designation awarded by the Realtors National Marketing Institute, which is affiliated with the National Association of REALTORS®.

CERTIFIED PROPERTY MANAGER (CPM) / A member of the Institute of Real Property Management, an organization affiliated with the National Association of REALTORS®.

CERTIFIED RESIDENTIAL BROKER (CRB) / A designation awarded by the Realtors National Marketing Institute, which is affiliated with the National Association of REALTORS®.

CHAIN / A unit of land measurement: 66 feet in length.

CHAIN OF TITLE / A history of conveyances and encumbrances affecting a title from the time the original patent was granted, or as far back as records are available. See "Abstract of Title."

CHATTEL / Personal property, including autos and household goods and fixtures.

CHATTEL MORTGAGE / A pledge of personal property as security for a debt.

CLEAR TITLE / A title free and clear of all encumbrances.

CLIENT / The one who employs a broker, lawyer, accountant, appraiser, etc.

CLOSING DATE / The date on which the seller delivers the deed and the buyer pays for the property.

CLOSING STATEMENT / An accounting of funds from a real estate sale, made to both the seller and the buyer separately. Most states require the broker to furnish accurate closing statements to all parties to the transaction in which he is an agent.

CLOUD ON THE TITLE / An outstanding claim or encumbrance that, if valid, would affect or impair the owner's title. **Example:** A dies and in his will leaves land to B. A's widow, Mrs. A, is contesting the validity of A's will. During this period there is a cloud on B's title to the land.

COLOR OF TITLE / That which appears to be good title but is not. **Example:** A gives B a deed to land that he has never actually owned; B farms the land under a color of title.

COMMERCIAL PROPERTY / Property designed for use by retail, wholesale, office, hotel, and service users.

COMMINGLE / To mingle or mix, such as the deposit of another's money in a broker's personal account.

COMMISSION / An amount earned by a real estate broker for his services. Also, the official body that enforces real estate license laws.

COMMITMENT / A pledge or promise; a firm agreement.

COMMON LAW / The body of law that has grown out of legal customs and practices that developed in England. "Common Law" prevails unless superseded by other law.

COMMON PROPERTY / Land or a tract of land considered to be the property of the public in which all persons enjoy rights.

COMMUNITY PROPERTY / Property accumulated through joint efforts of husband and wife and owned by them in equal shares. The doctrine now exists in Arizona, California, Idaho, Louisiana, Nevada, New Mexico, Texas, and Washington.

COMPOUND INTEREST / Interest paid on the original principal and also on the unpaid interest that has accumulated. **Example:** $100 deposited in a 5 percent savings account earns $5 interest the first year. Its second-year earnings are 5 percent of $105, or $5.25.

CONDEMNATION / Taking private property for public use, with compensation to the owner, under *eminent domain*. Used by governments to acquire land for streets, parks, schools, etc., and by utilities to acquire necessary property. Also, declaring a structure unfit for use.

CONDITION(S) / Provision(s) in a contract that some or all terms of the contract will be altered or cease to exist upon a certain event. **Example:** If a house is destroyed by fire before closing, the buyer is not obligated to complete the purchase.

CONDITIONAL SALES CONTRACT / A contract for the sale of property stating that the seller retains title until the conditions of the contract have been fulfilled.

CONDOMINIUM / A system of ownership of individual units in a multi-unit structure, combined with joint ownership of commonly used property (sidewalks, hallways, stairs, etc.).

CONFORMITY PRINCIPLE / An appraisal principle that holds that property values tend to be maximized when the neighborhood is reasonably homogeneous in social and economic activity.

CONSIDERATION / Anything of value given to induce entering into a contract; it may be money, personal services, love and affection, etc.

CONSTANT PAYMENT LOAN / A loan on which equal payments are made periodically so as to pay off the debt when the last payment is made.

CONSTRUCTIVE NOTICE / The law presumes that everyone has knowledge of a fact when that fact is a matter of public record. **Example:** A buys land from B, believing that B is the owner. Since C's deed had been properly recorded, A had constructive notice of C's ownership and cannot claim ownership against C.

CONTIGUOUS / Actually touching; contiguous properties have a common boundary.

CONTINGENCY CLAUSE / See "Condition."

CONTRACT / An agreement between competent parties to do or not to do certain things for a consideration.

CONTRACT FOR DEED / See "Land Contract."

CONTRACT OF SALE / See "Agreement of Sale."

CONVENTIONAL LOAN / A mortgage loan other than one guaranteed by the Veterans Administration or insured by the Federal Housing Administration.

CONVEY / To deed or transfer title to another.

CONVEYANCE / The transfer of the title of real estate from one to another; the means or medium by which title of real estate is transferred.

COOPERATIVE / A type of corporate ownership of real property whereby stockholders of the corporation are entitled to use a certain dwelling unit or other units of space. Special income tax laws allow the tenant stockholders to deduct interest and property taxes paid by the corporation.

CORPOREAL / Visible or tangible. Corporeal rights in real estate include such things as the right of occupancy under a lease.

COST APPROACH / One of three appraisal methods of estimating value. The estimated current cost of reproducing the existing improvements, less the estimated depreciation, added to the value of the land, gives the appraised value. Same as "Appraisal by Summation."

COVENANTS / Promises written into deeds and other instruments agreeing to performance or nonperformance of certain acts, or requiring or preventing certain uses of the property.

CURABLE DEPRECIATION / Depreciation or deterioration that can be corrected at a cost less than the value that will be added.

CURTESY / The right of a husband to all or part of his deceased wife's realty regardless of the provisions of her will. Exists in only a few states.

DAMAGES / The amount recoverable by a person who has been injured in any manner, including physical harm, property damage, or violated rights, through the act or default of another.

DECREE / An order issued by one in authority; a court order or decision.

DEDICATION / The gift of land by its owner for a public use and the acceptance of it by a unit of government. **Example:** streets in a subdivision, land for a park, or a site for a school.

DEED / A written document, properly signed and delivered, that conveys title to real property. See "Bargain and Sale Deed," "General Warranty Deed," "Quitclaim Deed," "Special Warranty Deed."

DEED RESTRICTION / A clause in a deed that limits the use of land. **Example:** A deed might stipulate that alcoholic beverages are not to be sold on the land for twenty years.

DEFAULT / Failure to fulfill a duty or promise, or to discharge an obligation; omission or failure to perform any acts.

DEFEASANCE / A clause in a mortgage that gives the borrower the right to redeem his property after he has defaulted, usually by paying the full indebtedness and fees incurred.

DEFENDANT / The party sued in an action at law.

DEFERRED PAYMENTS / Money payments to be made at some future date.

DEFICIENCY JUDGMENT / A court order stating that the borrower still owes money when the security for a loan does not entirely satisfy a defaulted debt.

DELIVERY / Transfer of the possession of a thing from one person to another.

DEPRECIATION / In appraisal, a loss of value in real property due to age, physical deterioration, or functional or economic obsolescence. Also, in accounting, the allocation of the cost of an asset over its economic useful life.

DEVISE / A gift of real estate by will or last testament.

DEVISEE / One who inherits real estate through a will.

DIRECTIONAL GROWTH / The location or direction toward which a city is growing.

DISCHARGE IN BANKRUPTCY / The release of a bankrupt party from the obligation to repay debts that were, or might have been, proved in bankruptcy proceedings.

DISCOUNT POINTS / Amounts paid to the lender (usually by the seller) at the time of origination of a loan, to account for the difference between the market interest rate and the lower face rate of the note (often required when FHA or VA financing is used).

DISPOSSESS PROCEEDINGS / The legal process by a landlord to remove a tenant and regain possession of property.

DISTRIBUTEE / A person receiving or entitled to receive land as the representative of the former owner; heir.

DOCUMENTARY EVIDENCE / Evidence in the form of written or printed papers.

DOWER / Under common law, the legal right of a wife or child to part of a deceased husband's or father's property.

DURESS / Unlawful constraint exercised upon a person whereby he is forced to do some act against his will. **Example:** "Your signature or your brains will be on this contract."

EARNEST MONEY / A deposit made by a purchaser of real estate to evidence his good faith.

EASEMENT / The right, privilege, or interest that one party has in the land of another. **Example:** the right of public utility companies to lay their lines across others' property.

ECONOMIC DEPRECIATION / Loss of value from all causes outside the property itself. **Example:** An expensive private home may drop in value when an industrial plant is built nearby.

ECONOMIC LIFE / That remaining period for which real estate improvements are expected to generate more income than operating expenses cost.

ECONOMIC OBSOLESCENCE / See "Economic Depreciation."

EJECTMENT / Action to regain possession of real property, when there is no lease. **Example:** The holder of a conditional sales contract acts to regain possession when the buyer defaults.

EMINENT DOMAIN / The right of the government or a public utility to acquire property for necessary public use by condemnation; the owner must be fairly compensated.

ENCROACHMENT / A building, a part of a building, or an obstruction that physically intrudes upon, overlaps, or trespasses upon the property of another.

ENCUMBRANCE / Any right to or interest in land that diminishes its value. Includes outstanding mortgage loans, unpaid taxes, easements, deed restrictions.

ENDORSEMENT / The act of signing one's name on the back of a check or note, with or without further qualification; also, the signature itself.

EQUITY / The interest or value that the owner has in real estate over and above the liens against it.

EQUITY OF REDEMPTION / The right of a real estate owner to reclaim property before or shortly after it is sold through foreclosure proceedings, by the payment of the debt, interest, and costs.

EROSION / The gradual wearing away of land through processes of nature, as by streams and winds.

ESCHEAT / The reversion of property to the state in the event that the owner dies without leaving a will and has no legal heirs.

ESCROW / An agreement between two or more partie providing that certain instruments or property be placed with a third party for safekeeping, pending the fulfillment or performance of some act or condition.

ESCROW ACCOUNT / See "Trust Account."

ESCROW AGENT / Any person engaged in the business of receiving escrows for deposit or delivery.

ESTATE / The degree, quantity, nature, and extent of interest that a person has in real property.

ESTATE AT SUFFERANCE / The wrongful occupancy of property by a tenant after his lease has expired.

ESTATE AT WILL / The occupation of real estate by a tenant for an indefinite period, terminable by one or both parties at will.

ESTATE FOR LIFE / An interest in property that terminates upon the death of a specified person. See "Life Estate."

ESTATE FOR YEARS / An interest in land allowing possession for a definite and limited time.

ESTATE IN REVERSION / An estate left by the grantor for himself, to begin after the termination of some particular estate granted by him. **Example:** A landlord's estate in reversion becomes his to possess when the lease expires.

ESTOPPEL CERTIFICATE / A document by which the mortgagor (borrower) certifies that the mortgage debt is a lien for the amount stated. He is thereafter prevented from claiming that the balance due differed from the amount stated.

ET AL. / Abbreviation of *et alii,* "and others."

ET UX. / Abbreviation of *et uxor,* "and wife."

EVICTION / A legal proceeding by a lessor (landlord) to recover possession of property.

EVICTION, ACTUAL / Exists where one is removed from the property, either by force or by process of law.

EVICTION, CONSTRUCTIVE / Exists when physical conditions of the property render it unfit for the purpose for which it was leased, through the fault of the landlord.

EVICTION, PARTIAL / Exists where the possessor of the property is deprived of a portion thereof.

EXCLUSIVE AGENCY LISTING / Employment contract giving only one broker the right to sell the property for a specified time and also allowing the owner to sell the property himself without paying a commission.

EXCLUSIVE RIGHT TO SELL LISTING / Employment contract giving the broker the right to collect a commission if the property is sold by anyone, including the owner, during the term of the agreement.

EXECUTE / To make out a contract; to perform a contract fully.

EXECUTED CONTRACT / A contract all terms and conditions of which have been fulfilled.

EXECUTOR / A person designated in a will to carry out its provisions concerning the disposition of the estate.

EXECUTRIX / A woman who performs the duties of an executor.

FEDERAL DEPOSIT INSURANCE CORPORATION (FDIC) / Insures depositors' accounts in commercial banks.

FEDERAL HOUSING ADMINISTRATION (FHA) / An agency of the U. S. Government that insures to lenders the repayment of real estate loans.

FEE SIMPLE OR FEE ABSOLUTE / Absolute ownership of real property; owner is entitled to the entire property with unconditional power of disposition during his life, and it descends to his heirs and legal representatives upon his death intestate.

FHA LOAN / A mortgage loan insured by the FHA.

FHLB / Federal Home Loan Bank; a federally chartered bank that supplies credit to member banks.

FIDUCIARY / A person who, on behalf of or for the benefit of another, transacts business or handles money or property not his own.

FIRST MORTGAGE / A mortgage that has priority as a lien over all other mortgages. In cases of foreclosure the first mortgage will be satisfied before other mortgages.

FIXTURES / Personal property attached to the land or improvements so as to become part of the real estate.

FNMA / Federal National Mortgage Association, which buys and sells existing residential mortgages; known as "Fanny Mae."

FORECLOSURE / A legal procedure whereby property pledged as security for a debt is sold to pay the defaulted debt.

FORFEITURE / Loss of money or anything of value because of failure to perform under contract.

FRAUD / The intentional use of deception to purposely cheat or deceive another person, causing that person to suffer loss.

FREEHOLD / An interest in real estate without a predetermined time span. **Example:** a fee simple or a life estate.

FRONT FOOT / A standard measurement of land, applied at the frontage of its street line. Used for city lots of generally uniform depth.

FSLIC / Federal Savings and Loan Insurance Corporation, which insures deposits in savings institutions.

FUNCTIONAL DEPRECIATION / Loss of value from all causes within the property, except those due to physical deterioration. **Example:** poor floor plan or outdated plumbing fixtures.

FUNCTIONAL OBSOLESCENCE / See "Functional Depreciation."

GABLE ROOF / A pitched roof with sloping sides.

GAMBREL ROOF / A curb roof having a steep lower slope with a flatter upper slope above.

GENERAL WARRANTY DEED / A deed in which the grantor agrees to protect the grantee against any other claim to title of the property and provides other promises. See "Warranty Deed."

GIFT DEED / A deed for which the consideration is love and affection, and no material consideration is involved.

GI LOAN / Home loans guaranteed by the U.S. Veterans Administration (VA) under the Servicemen's Readjustment Act of 1944 and later. Also known as a VA loan. The VA guarantees restitution to the lender in the event of default.

GOVERNMENT RECTANGULAR SURVEY / A rectangular system of land survey that divides a district into 24-mile-square tracts from the meridian (north-south line) and the base line (east-west line); the tracts are divided into 6-mile-square parts called townships, which are in turn divided into 36 tracts, each one mile square, called sections.

GRACE PERIOD / Additional time allowed to perform an act or make a payment before a default occurs.

GRADE / Ground level at the foundation.

GRADED LEASE / See "Graduated Lease."

GRADIENT / The slope, or rate of increase or decrease in elevation, of a surface; usually expressed as a percentage.

GRADUATED LEASE / A lease that provides for graduated changes in the amount of rent at stated intervals; seldom used in short-term leases.

GRANT / A technical term used in deeds of conveyance of property to indicate a transfer.

GRANTEE / The party to whom the title to real property is conveyed; the buyer.

GRANTOR / The person who conveys real estate by deed; the seller or donor.

G. R. I. / Graduate of the REALTORS® Institute, which is affiliated with the National Association of REALTORS®.

GROSS INCOME / Total income from property before any expenses are deducted.

GROSS LEASE / A lease of property whereby the landlord (lessor) is responsible for paying all property expenses, such as taxes, insurance, utilities, and repairs.

GROSS RENT MULTIPLIER (GRM) / The gross rent multiplier is the sales price divided by the rental rate. Example: The sales price is $40,000; the gross monthly rent is $400; the GRM = $40,000/$400 = 100. It may also be expressed as an annual figure (8.333), i. e., the number of years of rent equalling the purchase price.

GROUND LEASE / An agreement for the rent of land only, often for a long term, at the expiration of which all of the real estate belongs to the landowner.

GROUND RENT / The rent earned by leased land.

GUARDIAN / One appointed by a court to administer the affairs of an individual who is not capable of administering his own affairs.

HABENDUM CLAUSE / The "to have and to hold" clause that defines or limits the quantity of the estate granted in the deed. Example: "To have and to hold for [one's] lifetime" creates a life estate.

HEIRS AND ASSIGNS / Terminology used in deeds and wills to provide that the recipient receive a "fee simple estate" in lands rather than a lesser interest.

HEREDITAMENTS / Any property that may be inherited, whether real or personal, tangible or intangible.

HIGHEST AND BEST USE / An appraisal term meaning that legally and physically possible use that, at the time of appraisal, is most likely to produce the greatest net return to the land and/or buildings over a given time period.

HIP ROOF / A pitched roof with sloping sides and ends.

HOLDER IN DUE COURSE / One who has taken a note, check, or similar asset (1) before it was overdue, (2) in good faith and for value, and (3) without knowledge that it had been previously dishonored and without notice of any defect at the time it was negotiated to him.

HOLDOVER TENANT / A tenant who remains in possession of leased property after the expiration of the lease term.

HOMESTEAD / Status provided to a homeowner's principal residence by some state statutes; protects home against judgments up to specified amounts.

HOMESTEAD EXEMPTION / In some jurisdictions, a reduction in the assessed value allowed for one's principal residence.

HYPOTHECATE / To pledge a thing as security without having to give up possession of it.

IMPROVEMENTS / Those additons to raw land tending to increase value, such as buildings, streets, sewers, etc.

INCHOATE / Recently or just begun; unfinished, begun but not completed. In real estate, this can apply to dower or curtesy rights prior to the death of a spouse.

INCOME / The money or other benefit coming from the use of something.

INCOME APPROACH / One of the three appraisal methods used in arriving at an estimate of the market value of property; the value of the property is the present worth of the income it is expected to produce during its remaining life.

INCOME PROPERTY / Property whose ownership appeal is that it produces income.

INCOMPETENT / A person who is unable to manage his own affairs by reason of insanity, imbecility, or feeblemindedness.

INCURABLE DEPRECIATION / A defect that cannot be cured or that it is not financially practical to cure; a defect in the "bone structure" of a building.

INDENTURE / A written agreement made between two or more persons having different interests.

INDEX LEASE / A lease where rentals are tied to an agreed-upon index of costs. **Example:** Rentals are to increase along with the Consumer Price Index.

INDUSTRIAL PROPERTY / Property used for industrial purposes, such as factories.

INJUNCTION / A writ or order issued under the seal of a court to restrain one or more parties to a suit or proceeding from performing an act that is deemed to be inequitable or unjust in regard to the rights of some other party or parties in the suit or proceeding.

IN REM / (Latin: "against the thing.") A proceeding against the realty directly, as distinguished from a proceeding against a person (used in taking land for nonpayment of taxes, etc.).

INSTALLMENTS / Parts of the same debt, payable at successive periods as agreed; payments made to reduce a mortgage.

INSTRUMENT / A written legal document, created to effect the rights and liabilities of the parties to it.

INSURABLE TITLE / A title that can be insured by a title insurance company.

INSURANCE COVERAGE / Total amount and type of insurance carried.

INTANGIBLE VALUE / Value that cannot be seen or touched. **Example:** the goodwill of an established business.

INTEREST / Rent for the use of money. Also, the type and extent of ownership.

INTEREST RATE / The percentage of a sum of money charged for its use. Also, the rate of return on an investment.

INTESTATE / A person who dies leaving no will or leaving one that is defective. His property goes to his legal heirs.

INVESTMENT PROPERTY / Property that is a business enterprise.

INVOLUNTARY LIEN / A lien imposed against property without consent of the owner (unpaid taxes, special assessments, etc.).

IRREVOCABLE / Incapable of being recalled or revoked; unchangeable, unalterable.

JEOPARDY / Peril, danger, risk. **Example:** Property pledged as security for a delinquent loan is in jeopardy of foreclosure.

JOINT TENANCY / Ownership of realty by two or more persons, each of whom has an undivided interest with the right of survivorship. **Example:** A and B own land in joint tenancy. Each owns half of the entire (undivided) property. Upon A's death, B will own the entire property, and vice versa.

JUDGMENT / A decree of a court stating that one individual is indebted to another and fixing the amount of the indebtedness.

JUDGMENT CREDITOR / One who has received a court decree or judgment for money due to him.

JUDGMENT DEBTOR / One against whom a judgment has been issued by a court for money owed.

JUDGMENT LIEN / The claim upon the property of a debtor resulting from a judgment. **Example:** A won't pay his debt to B. After establishing the debt in court, B may be allowed by the court to put a lien on A's real estate.

JUNIOR MORTGAGE / A mortgage whose claim against the property will be satisfied only after prior mortgages have been repaid.

LACHES / Delay or negligence in asserting one's legal rights.

LAND / The surface of the earth; any part of the surface of the earth. (NOTE: Legal definitions often distinguish land from water.)

LAND CONTRACT / A real estate installment selling arrangement whereby the buyer may use, occupy, and enjoy land, but no deed is given by the seller (so no title passes) until all or a specified part of the sale price has been paid.

LANDLORD / One who rents property to another; a lessor.

LANDMARK / A fixed object serving as a boundary mark for a tract of land.

LAND, TENEMENTS, AND HEREDITAMENTS / A phrase used in early English law to express all sorts of real estate.

LEASE / A contract in which, for a consideration called rent, one who is entitled to the possession of real property (lessor) transfers those rights to another (lessee) for a specified period of time.

LEASEHOLD / The interest or estate on which a lessee (tenant) of real estate has his lease.

LEASE WITH OPTION TO PURCHASE / A lease that gives the lessee (tenant) the right to purchase the property at an agreed-upon price under certain conditions.

LEGAL DESCRIPTION / Legally acceptable identification of real estate by (1) the rectangular survey, (2) metes and bounds, or (3) recorded plat (Lot and Block number).

LESSEE / A person to whom property is rented under a lease; a tenant.

LESSOR / One who rents property to another under a lease; a landlord.

LEVERAGE / Use of borrowed funds to increase purchasing power and, ideally, to increase the profitability of an investment.

LICENSE / Permission; also, a privilege or right granted by a state to an individual to operate as a real estate broker or salesperson.

LICENSEE / One who holds a real estate license.

LIEN / A charge against property making it security for the payment of a debt, judgment, mortgage, or taxes; it is a type of encumbrance.

LIEN, JUNIOR / A lien that will be paid after earlier liens have been paid.

LIFE ESTATE / A freehold interest in land that expires upon the death of the owner or some other specified person.

LIFE TENANT / One who is allowed to use property for his lifetime or the lifetime of another designated person.

LIS PENDENS / (Latin: "suit pending") Recorded notice that a suit has been filed the outcome of which may affect title to a certain land.

LISTING / A written employment contract between a principal and an agent authorizing the agent to perform services for the principal involving the latter's property; also, a record of property for sale by a broker who has been authorized by the owner to sell; also, the property so listed.

LITIGATION / The act of carrying on a lawsuit.

LITTORAL / Part of the shore zone of a large body of water.

LOT AND BLOCK NUMBER / A means of description of land that refers to a recorded plat. **Example:** Lot 6, Block F of the Sunnybrook Estates, District 2 of Rover County, Rhode Island.

LOT LINE / A line bounding a lot as described in a survey of the property.

MAI / A member of the American Institute of Real Estate Appraisers, which is affiliated with the National Association of REALTORS®.

MAJORITY / The age at which one is no longer a minor and is fully able to conduct one's own affairs; majority is 18 to 21 years, depending on the state.

MARGINAL PROPERTY / Property that is barely profitable to use. **Example:** The sale of cotton that has been efficiently raised yields $100; yet the cotton cost $99.99 to raise. The land is therefore considered marginal land.

MARKETABLE TITLE / A title that a court will consider so free from defect that it will enforce its acceptance by a purchaser.

MARKET APPROACH / See "Market Comparison Approach."

MARKET COMPARISON APPROACH / One of three appraisal approaches. Value is estimated by analyzing sales prices of similar properties (comparables) recently sold.

MARKET DATA APPROACH / See "Market Comparison Approach."

MARKET PRICE / The actual price paid in a market transaction. A historical fact.

MARKET VALUE / The highest price a buyer, willing but not compelled to buy, would pay, and the lowest price a seller, willing but not compelled to sell, would accept. Many conditions must be assumed to exist.

MATERIAL FACT / A fact that is germane to a particular situation; one that participants in the situation may reasonably be expected to consider.

MECHANIC'S LIEN / A lien given by law upon a building or other improvement upon land, and upon the land itself, as security for the payment for labor done upon, and materials furnished for, the improvement.

MEETING OF THE MINDS / Agreement by all parties to a contract to the exact terms thereof.

METES AND BOUNDS / A land description method that relates the boundary lines of land, setting forth all the boundary lines together with their terminal points and angles.

MILL / One tenth of a cent. Used in expressing tax rates on a per-dollar basis. **Example:** A tax rate of 60 mills means that taxes are 6 cents per dollar of assessed valuation.

MINOR / A person under an age specified by law (18 to 21 years, depending on the state).

MONUMENT / A fixed object and point established by surveyors to establish land locations.

MORTGAGE / A written instrument that creates a lien upon real estate as security for the payment of a specified debt.

MORTGAGE COMMITMENT / An agreement between a lender and a borrower to lend money at a future date, subject to the conditions described in the agreement.

MORTGAGEE / One who holds a lien on or title to property as security for a debt.

MORTGAGOR / One who pledges his property as security for a loan.

MULTIPLE LISTING / An arrangement among a group of real estate brokers; they agree in advance to provide information about some or all of their listings to the others and also agree that commissions on sales of such listings will be split between listing and selling brokers.

NAR / National Association of REALTORS®. An organization devoted to encouraging professionalism in real estate activities.

NET INCOME / Income from property or business after operating expenses have been deducted, but before deducting income taxes and financing expenses (interest and principal payments).

NET LEASE / A lease whereby, in addition to the rent stipulated, the lessee (tenant) pays such things as taxes, insurance, and maintenance. The landlord's rent receipt is thereby "net" of those expenses.

NET LISTING / A listing in which the broker's commission is the excess of the sale price over an agreed-upon (net) price to the seller; illegal in some states.

NET OPERATING INCOME / See "Net Income."

NONCONFORMING USE / A use that violates zoning regulations or codes but is allowed to continue because it began before the zoning restriction was enacted.

NOTARY PUBLIC / An officer who is authorized to take acknowledgments to certain types of documents, such as deeds, contracts, and mortgages, and before whom affidavits may be sworn.

NOTE / A written instrument that acknowledges a debt and promises to pay.

NOTICE TO QUIT / A notice to a tenant to vacate rented property.

OBLIGEE / The person in whose favor an obligation is entered into.

OBLIGOR / The person who binds himself to another; one who has engaged to perform some obligation; one who makes a bond.

OBSOLESCENCE / A loss in value due to reduced desirability and usefulness of a structure because its design and construction become obsolete; loss due to a structure's becoming old-fashioned, not in keeping with modern needs, with consequent loss of income.

OFFER AND ACCEPTANCE / See "Agreement of Sale."

OPEN-END MORTGAGE / A mortgage under which the mortgagor (borrower) may secure additional funds from the mortgagee (lender), usually stipulating a ceiling amount that can be borrowed.

OPEN LISTING / A listing given to any number of brokers without liability to compensate any except the one who first secures a buyer ready, willing, and able to meet the terms of the listing or secures the seller's acceptance of another offer. The sale of the property automatically terminates all open listings.

OPEN MORTGAGE / A mortgage that has matured or is overdue and is therefore "open" to foreclosure at any time.

OPERATING LEASE / A lease between the lessee and the sublessee who actually occupies and uses the property.

OPTION / The right to purchase or lease a property upon specified terms within a specified period. **Example:** the right to buy certain land within 90 days at $5000 per acre. The property becomes "reserved" for that time period.

ORAL CONTRACT / A verbal agreement. With few exceptions, verbal agreements for the sale or use of real estate are unenforceable.

OWNERSHIP RIGHTS TO REALTY / Possession, enjoyment, control, and disposition.

PACKAGE MORTGAGE / A mortgage arrangement whereby the principal amount loaned is increased to include personalty (e.g., appliances) as well as realty; both realty and personalty serve as collateral.

PARTITION / The division of real property between those who own it in undivided shares. **Example:** A and B own land as tenants in common until they partition it. Thereafter, each owns a particular tract of land.

PARTY WALL / A wall built along the line separating two properties, partly on each. Either owner has the right to use the wall and has an easement over that part of the adjoining owner's land covered by the wall.

PATENT / Conveyance of title to government land.

PERCENTAGE LEASE / A lease of property in which the rental is based on a percentage of the volume of sales made upon the leased premises. It usually provides for minimum rental and is regularly used for retailers who are tenants.

PERMANENT MORTGAGE / A mortgage for a long period of time (over ten years).

PERSONALTY / Personal property, i.e., all property that is not realty.

PHYSICAL DEPRECIATION or DETERIORATION / The loss of value from all causes of age and action of the elements. **Example:** broken window, hole in plaster, collapsed porch railing.

PLAT / A plan or map of a certain piece or certain pieces of land.

PLAT BOOK / A public record containing maps of land showing the division of the land into streets, blocks, and lots and indicating the measurements of the individual parcels.

PLOTTAGE / Increment in the value of a plot of land that has been enlarged by assembling smaller plots into one ownership.

POCKET CARD / Required for salespersons and brokers in most states. Issued by the state licensing agency, it identifies its holder as a licensee and must be carried at all times.

POLICE POWER / The right of any political body to enact laws and enforce them, for the order, safety, health, morals, and general welfare of the public.

POWER OF ATTORNEY / An instrument authorizing a person to act as the agent of the person granting it.

PREMISES / Land and tenements; an estate; the subject matter of a conveyance.

PREPAYMENT CLAUSE / A clause in a mortgage that gives a mortgagor (borrower) the privilege of paying the mortgage indebtedness before it becomes due. Sometimes a penalty must be paid if prepayment is made, but payment of the interest that is not yet due is waived.

PRIMARY LEASE / A lease between the owner and a tenant who, in turn, has sublet all or part of his interest.

PRINCIPAL / The employer of an agent or broker, the broker's or agent's client; also, the amount of money raised by a mortgage or other loan, as distinct from the interest paid on it.

PROBATE or PROVE / To establish the validity of the will of a deceased person.

PROPERTY / The rights that one individual has in lands or goods to the exclusion of all others; rights gained from the ownership of wealth.

PROPERTY LINE / The recorded boundary of a plot of land.

PROPERTY MANAGEMENT / The operation of property as a business, including rental, rent collection, maintenance, etc.

PRORATE / To allocate between seller and buyer their proportionate share of an obligation paid or due; for example, to prorate real property taxes or insurance.

PURCHASE MONEY MORTGAGE / A mortgage given by a grantee (buyer) to a grantor (seller) in part payment of the purchase price of real estate.

QUIET ENJOYMENT / The right of an owner or any other person legally entitled to possession to the use of property without interference.

QUIET TITLE SUIT / A suit in court to remove a defect, cloud, or suspicion regarding legal rights of an owner to a certain parcel of real property.

QUITCLAIM DEED / A deed that conveys only the grantor's rights or interest in real estate, without stating their nature and with no warranties of ownership. Often used to remove a possible cloud from the title.

RANGE LINES / Lines parallel to the principal meridian, marking off the land into 6-mile strips known as ranges; they are numbered east or west of the principal meridian in the Government Survey.

REAL ESTATE / Land and all attachments that are of a permanent nature.

REAL ESTATE INVESTMENT TRUST (REIT) / A "real estate mutual fund," allowed by income tax laws to avoid the corporate tax. It sells shares of ownership and must invest in real estate or mortgages.

REAL PROPERTY / The right to use real estate, as (1) fee simple estate, (2) life estate, or (3) leasehold estate. Sometimes also defined as real estate.

REALTOR® / A professional in real estate who subscribes to a strict Code of Ethics as a member of the local and state boards and of the National Association of REALTORS®.

REALTY / Real estate.

REAPPRAISAL LEASE / A lease where the rental level is periodically reviewed by independent appraisers.

RECORDING / The act of entering in a book of public record instruments affecting the title to real property. Recording in this manner gives notice to the world of the facts recorded.

REDUCTION CERTIFICATE / A document in which the mortgagee (lender) acknowledges the sum due on the mortgage loan. Used when mortgaged property is sold and the buyer assumes the debt.

RELEASE / The act by which some claim or interest is surrendered. Releases are frequently used when a mortgage covers more than one property (blanket mortgage), so that a particular parcel can be released upon some payment.

RELEASE CLAUSE / A clause, found in a mortgage, that gives the owner of the property the privilege of paying off a portion of the mortgage indebtedness, thus freeing a portion of the property from the mortgage.

RELICTION / Gradual subsidence of waters, leaving dry land.

REMAINDER / An estate that takes effect after the termination of a prior estate, such as a life estate.

REMAINDERMAN / The person who is to receive possession of the property after the death of a life tenant.

RENT / The compensation paid for the use of real estate.

REPLACEMENT COST / The cost of erecting a building to take the place of or serve the functions of a previous structure.

REPRODUCTION COST / The normal cost of exact duplication of a property as of a certain date. Reproduction differs from replacement in that replacement requires the same functional utility for a property, whereas reproduction is an exact duplication.

RESTRICTION / A limitation placed upon the use of property, contained in the deed or other written instrument in the chain of title.

RESTRICTION COVENANT / See "Restriction."

REVERSION / The right of a lessor to possess leased property upon the termination of a lease.

REVERSIONARY INTEREST / The interest a person has in property upon the termination of the preceding estate.

REVOCATION / An act of recalling a power of authority conferred, as a revocation of a power of attorney, a license, an agency, etc.

RIGHT OF SURVIVORSHIP / The right of a surviving joint tenant to acquire the interest of a deceased joint owner; the distinguishing feature of joint tenancy and tenancy by the entirety.

RIGHT-OF-WAY / The right to use a particular path for access or passage; a type of easement. Also, the areas of subdivisions dedicated to government for use for streets, roads, and other public access to lots.

RIPARIAN OWNER / One who owns land bounding upon a lake, river, or other body of water.

RIPARIAN RIGHTS / Rights pertaining to the use of water on, under, or adjacent to one's land.

SALES CONTRACT / A contract by which the buyer and seller agree to the terms of sale.

SALESPERSON / One who is licensed to deal in real estate or perform any other act enumerated by state real estate license law, while in the employ of a broker licensed by the state.

SALVAGE VALUE / The estimated value that an asset will have at the end of its useful life.

SANDWICH LEASE / Lease held by a lessee who sublets all or part of his interest, thereby becoming a lessor. Typically, the sandwich leaseholder is neither the owner of the fee estate nor the user of the property.

SATISFACTION PIECE / An instrument for recording and acknowledging final payment of a mortgage loan.

SECTION (of land) / One square mile in the Government Survey. There are 36 sections in a 6-mile-square township.

SEIZIN / The possession of realty by one who claims to own a fee simple estate or a life estate or other salable interest.

SEPARATE PROPERTY / Property acquired by either spouse prior to marriage or by gift or devise after marriage, as distinct from community property.

SETBACK / The distance from the curb or other established line within which no buildings may be erected.

SETTLEMENT STATEMENT / See "Closing Statement."

SEVERALTY / The ownership of real property by an individual as an individual.

SPECIAL ASSESSMENT / An assessment made against a property to pay for a public improvement by which the assessed property is supposed to be especially benefited.

SPECIAL WARRANTY DEED / A deed in which the grantor limits the title warranty given to the grantee to anyone claiming by, from, through, or under him, the grantor. The grantor does not warrant against title defects arising from conditions that existed before he owned the property.

SPECIFIC PERFORMANCE / A legal action in which the court requires a party to a contract to perform the terms of the contract when he has refused to fulfill his obligations. Used in real estate, since each parcel of land is unique.

S. R. A. / A person who is a Senior Residential Appraiser, a designation awarded by the Society of Real Estate Appraisers.

STATUTE / A law established by an act of a legislature.

STATUTE OF FRAUDS / A state law that provides that certain contracts must be in writing in order to be enforceable. Applies to deeds, mortgages, and other real estate contracts, with the exception of leases for periods shorter than one year.

STATUTE OF LIMITATIONS / A certain statutory period after which a claimant is barred from enforcing his claim by suit.

STEP-UP LEASE / See "Graduated Lease."

STIPULATIONS / The terms within a written contract.

STRAIGHT-LINE DEPRECIATION / Equal annual reductions in the book value of property. Used in accounting for replacement and tax purposes.

SUBDIVIDING / Dividing a tract of land into smaller tracts.

SUBDIVISION / A tract of land divided into lots or plots suitable for home-building purposes. Some states and localities require that a subdivision plat be recorded.

SUBJECT TO MORTGAGE / A buyer taking title to mortgaged real property but not personally responsible for the payment of any portion of the amount due. The buyer must make payments in order to keep the property; however, if he fails to do so, only his equity in that property is lost.

SUBLEASE / A lease from a lessee to another lessee. The new lessee is a sublessee or subtenant. See "Sandwich Lease."

SUBLET / See "Sublease."

SUBORDINATION CLAUSE / A clause or document that permits a mortgage recorded at a later date to take priority over an existing mortgage.

SURETY / One who guarantees the performance of another; a guarantor.

SURRENDER / The cancellation of a lease by mutual consent of the lessor and the lessee.

SURROGATE'S COURT (PROBATE COURT) / A court having jurisdiction over the proof of wills and the settling of estates and of citations.

SURVEY / The process by which a parcel of land is measured and its area ascertained; also, the blueprint showing the measurements, boundaries, and area.

TAX / A charge levied upon persons or things by a government.

TAX SALE / The sale of property after a period of nonpayment of taxes.

TEASER RATE / An unusually low interest rate offered for the first few months or year of a mortgage loan; used as an enticement to potential borrowers.

TENANCY AT SUFFERANCE / Tenancy established when a lawful tenant remains in possession of property after expiration of a lease.

TENANCY AT WILL / A license to use or occupy lands and tenements at the will of the owner.

TENANCY BY THE ENTIRETIES / An estate that exists only between husband and wife with equal right of possession and enjoyment during their joint lives and with the right of survivorship; i.e., when one dies, the property goes to the surviving tenant.

TENANCY IN COMMON / An ownership of realty by two or more persons, each of whom has an undivided interest, without the right of survivorship. Upon the death of one of the owners, his ownership share is inherited by the party or parties designated in his will.

TENANT / One who is given possession of real estate for a fixed period or at will.

TENEMENTS / Everything of a permanent nature; anything attached to the soil.

TENURE IN LAND / The mode or manner in which a man holds an estate in lands.

TERMITES / Insects that bore into wood and destroy it.

TERMS / Conditions and arrangements specified in a contract.

TESTAMENT / A will.

TESTATE / Having made a valid will.

TESTATOR / A man who makes a will.

TESTATRIX / A woman who makes a will.

"TIME IS OF THE ESSENCE" / A phrase that, when inserted in a contract, requires that all references to specific dates and times of day concerning performance be interpreted exactly.

TITLE / Evidence that the owner of land is in lawful possession thereof; evidence of ownership.

TITLE ABSTRACT / See "Abstract of Title."

TITLE INSURANCE / An insurance policy that protects the holder from any loss sustained by reason of defects in the title.

TITLE SEARCH / An examination of the public records to determine the ownership and encumbrances affecting real property.

TOPOGRAPHY / The state of the surface of the land; may be rolling, rough, flat, etc.

TORRENS SYSTEM / A title registration system used in some states; the condition of the title can easily be discovered without resorting to title search.

TORT / A wrongful act that is not a crime but that renders the perpetrator liable to the victim for damages.

TOWNSHIP / A six-mile-square tract delineated by Government Survey.

TRUST ACCOUNT / A bank account separate and apart and physically segregated from a broker's own funds, in which the broker is required by state law to deposit all moneys collected for clients. Called an "escrow account" in some states.

TRUST DEED / A conveyance of real estate to a third person to be held for the benefit of another. Commonly used in some states in place of mortgages that conditionally convey title to the lender.

TRUSTEE / One who holds property in trust for another to secure performance of an obligation; the neutral party in a trust deed transaction.

UNEARNED INCREMENT / An increase in the value of real estate due to no effort on the part of the owner; often due to an increase in population.

URBAN PROPERTY / City property; closely settled property.

USURY / Charging a rate of interest greater than that permitted by law.

VALID / Having force, or binding force; legally sufficient and authorized by law.

VA LOAN / See "GI Loan."

VALUATION / Estimated worth or price; also, valuing by appraisal.

VALUE / The worth of all the rights arising from ownership; the quantity of one thing that will be given in exchange for another.

VENDEE / A purchaser; buyer.

VENDEE'S LIEN / A lien against property under a contract of sale, to secure the deposit paid by a purchaser.

VENDOR / A seller.

VERIFICATION / Sworn statements before a duly qualified officer as to the correctness of the contents of an instrument.

VIOLATION / An act, a deed, or conditions contrary to law or permissible use of real property.

VOID / Having no force or effect; unenforceable.

VOIDABLE / Capable of being voided, but not void unless action is taken to void it. Contracts to real estate entered into by minors are voidable only by the minors.

WAIVER / The voluntary renunciation, abandonment, or surrender of some claim, right, or privilege.

WARRANTY / A promise or representation contained in a contract.

WARRANTY DEED / One that contains a covenant that the grantor will protect the grantee against any and all claims. Usually contains covenants assuring good title, freedom from encumbrances, and quiet enjoyment.

WATER TABLE / The distance from the surface of the ground to a depth at which natural ground water is found.

WILL / The disposition of one's property to take effect after death.

WITHOUT RECOURSE / Words used in endorsing a note or bill to denote that the future holder is not to look to the debtor personally in the event of nonpayment: the creditor has recourse only to the property. A form of exculpation.

ZONE / An area set off by the proper authorities for specific use, subject to certain restrictions or restraints.

ZONING ORDINANCE / Act of city or county or other authorities specifying the type of use to which property may be put in specific areas. **Example:** residential, commercial, industrial.

Chapter 3/*Fundamentals of Real Estate Law*

Introduction _____

This is the first chapter of subject matter material. Much of what is mentioned in this chapter will be discussed in greater detail in future chapters. But here we are going to summarize the whole of real estate law, with the exception of license and contract law.

The subject matter of this chapter is a very fertile source of license examination questions, particularly since it concerns things that the average layman knows little or nothing about. In this manner the examining authorities can make sure that successful licensing applicants have, indeed, studied the laws and customs of the real estate business and know enough about it for the public to trust them.

Property _____

Property refers to the legal rights to use and enjoy any thing. Strictly speaking, the term *property* does not refer to the things themselves, but to the legal rights that a society allows someone with regard to the use of and enjoyment of the things. In practice, however, we tend to use the word *property* to mean the things themselves, so we don't think it odd for someone to say, "That car is my property"; to be absolutely proper, he should be saying, "The *rights* to use and enjoy that car are my property."

That may sound like nitpicking, and perhaps it is, but when you are speaking of legal matters it is absolutely essential to be precise and clear, or you can land in serious trouble. If a contract is drawn up vaguely, or if the description of a piece of land is inexact, the preparer can be held responsible for problems presented by the ambiguity.

Property is divided into two kinds: *real property* and *personal property*. Respectively, these are also known as *realty* and *personalty*. Realty is the property rights to real estate; personalty is the property rights to everything else.

Real estate is defined as land and everything permanently attached to it. A "permanent attachment" is (a) anything that grows on the land, (b) anything that is built upon the land (including roads, fences, etc., as well as buildings), and (c) things that are called *fixtures*. Fixtures are those items that might appear to be personal property but are considered to be part of the land also. Fixtures might include window air conditioners, major appliances, draperies, and things of that nature. There is no cut-and-dried definition of a fixture, so much of the court disputes concerning real estate contracts are arguments over misunderstandings concerning what are and aren't fixtures.

Many objects can be either realty or personalty depending on how they are employed. A brick is personalty until it is mortared into place on the wall of a building, at which time it becomes realty. A tree is realty when it is growing, but when it is cut down it becomes personalty. Fixtures are the "gray area," where an argument could be made either way as to the nature of the item. Usually the courts decide such a problem based upon the answers to these questions: (1) How is the item attached to the property? The more "tightly" attached, the more likely it will be considered a fixture. (2) What was the intention of the person who attached it? If he intended it to be a permanent part of the real estate, then it probably will be a fixture. (3) What is the prevailing custom in that particular part of the world? Depending on where you are, some things may or may not be considered fixtures. For example, in some places, major appliances, air conditioners, draperies, and the like are considered part of the real estate, whereas elsewhere the seller would be considered perfectly within his rights to take them with him.

Both realty and personalty can be divided into the *tangible* and *intangible*. When we speak of realty, these are referred to as *corporeal* and *incorporeal*. Corporeal property is the right to use, own, enjoy real estate directly. The term *incorporeal* concerns the right to use property that actually belongs to another; examples would be easements, rights-of-way, or mere permission to use someone's property.

Estates in Land

The collection of rights that someone may have in real estate can be called an *estate* if it is large enough. Estates are divided into two groups: *freehold* and *nonfreehold*. The basic difference is that a freehold estate is of uncertain duration because it extends for at least one specified individual's lifetime, and we never know just how long that is going to be. The divisions of freehold estates are *inheritable* and *noninheritable*. Nonfreehold estates involve various kinds of leases. Leases are contracted for specific periods of time, so it is known exactly when these kinds of estates will cease to exist.

Inheritable estates are called *fee simple* estates. Basically these give their owners absolute rights to do whatever they want with the land involved, subject only to the general law, such as zoning and building codes, etc. Most important, as far as the law is concerned, is the right to *dispose* of the estate in any legal manner: by selling it, by giving it away, or by willing it to someone.

Noninheritable estates are called *life estates*. In a life estate arrangement the owner, called the *life tenant*, has the right to use, occupy, and enjoy the property so long as he lives, but upon his death the ownership of the property goes to someone who is predetermined. This someone is referred to as the *remainderman*. Since the life tenant has rights to the property only so long as he lives, he can transfer to others only those rights. Consequently he may sell his interest to someone, but that person would have to relinquish the property upon the original life tenant's death. The same would happen in the event that the life tenant leased the property to someone and died before the lease expired. Furthermore, the life tenant is considered to be the custodian of the property for the remainderman: he cannot allow the property to deteriorate beyond ordinary wear and tear, because he must protect the remainderman's interest in it.

Nonfreehold estates are leases for specific terms. The lessee, or tenant, has the right (unless he contracts to give it up) to assign or otherwise dispose of his leasehold rights if he has a *leasehold estate*. Furthermore, he has the right to use, occupy, and enjoy the real estate during the period of his lease.

An estate in land requires that its owner have the following rights: the right to *possess* the land, the right to *use* the land, and the right to *dispose* of his estate to someone else. Possession means, basically, just that: the right to occupy the land and make use of it, and to exclude everyone else from the land. If one has *some* rights to use land, but they do not include all possessory rights, then one is said to have an *interest* in land. An interest would occur when one has a month-to-month lease that either party could terminate at any time (tenancy at will) because no specific duration is mentioned. An interest also occurs when *license to use* is involved; here there is mere permission, and not even a contractual arrangement. This might occur when someone asks permission to come onto your land one afternoon to go fishing.

Creation of Estates in Land

Estates in land are created in the following ways: by *will, descent, voluntary alienation, involuntary alienation,* and *adverse possession*. One receives an estate *by will* if one inherits it by virtue of being *so designated in someone's will*. One receives an estate *by descent* if one is *designated by law* as the recipient of some property of a deceased person. This would occur if the person dies *intestate* (with no will); every state has laws governing the disposition of such property. Some states also have *dower* and/or *curtesy* laws, which have similar effects. Dower laws require that a man's wife and, sometimes, minor children are entitled to receive a certain interest in his property when he dies. Curtesy laws, which are much rarer, require that a man receive at least a certain portion of his deceased wife's property. Some states allow these heirs to gain fee simple estates, while others allow only life estates for dower and curtesy. Note that in many states which have dower laws, these laws have come under legal attack because of sex discrimination; they benefit women, but not men. Also, in those states which have curtesy laws as well, men's rights to their wives' estates usually are more limited than the dower rights given to wives. Many states have changed their laws (or are in the process of changing them) to give husbands and wives equal rights to one another's estates.

Voluntary alienation is the most common means whereby one receives estates in land. This term refers to voluntary exchanges, sales, and gifts, wherein the one who gives up the property does so willingly. *Involuntary alienation* occurs where the owner of an estate is forced, in a legal manner, to give up some or all of his rights by the action of law. This most commonly occurs in the case of bankruptcy or in having some other kind of legal judgment entered against one, such as a foreclosure or failure to pay property taxes.

Adverse possession is a special means of acquiring ownership. All states have statutes permitting adverse possession, which is the right of someone who has used another's land actually to receive a legal claim to that land, in fee simple. The ancient idea behind this is that if the true owner is so uninterested in his land that he does nothing during this period of time to prevent someone else from putting it to use, then the community is better off by letting this other person actually have the full rights to the land. Adverse possession cannot be acquired overnight; depending on the state, it takes from 6 to 40 years to establish these rights. The adverse possession must be *open, notorious, continuous*, and *hostile*. This means that the claimant, during the required time period, must have acted completely as if the property were his own, including defending his "rights" against encroachment by others and being perfectly open in his actions. The adverse possession must continue throughout the statutory period; you can't use someone's land for the summer of 1945 and later for the summer of 1975 and then claim that you've been using it for 30 years. Further, no tenant can claim against his landlord, because every time a tenant pays rent he legally acknowledges that the other is the true owner. Nor may one claim against the government, on the theory that one is already the nominal "owner" of public property.

Tenancies

Estates in land may be owned in a variety of ways, depending on the number of people involved and their relationship. These various forms of ownership are called *tenancies*. *Tenancy in severalty* is ownership by one person. *Tenancy in common* is a form of ownership by two or more persons. Each one owns an *undivided interest*, which means that he owns a fraction of each part of the realty. In this arrangement, each is entitled to his share of the profits and is responsible to the others for his share of the costs and expenses. No part of the land may be disposed of without the consent of all, unless they have a specific arrangement whereby less than unanimity can force a decision. Tenants in common need not own equal shares. They may dispose of their shares in any way they choose, unless they have specifically agreed upon some limitation; this means that A and B may buy real estate as tenants in common and later on B may sell his share to C, making A and C tenants in common. Further, a tenant in common may will his share to someone else or give it away.

Joint tenancy is similar to tenancy in common except for one important difference: joint tenants have the *right of survivorship*. This means that if a joint tenant dies his share is divided proportionally among the other surviving joint tenants. Consequently, a joint tenant cannot will his share to someone. However, he can sell or give his interest away; the new owners would then receive the status of tenants in common.

Tenancy by the entireties is a special form of joint ownership allowed only to married couples. In states where it is used, it protects the rights of the family to jointly owned property by providing the same basic rights and responsibilities of joint tenancy while also protecting the property against any foreclosure due to judgment or debt against one of the parties.

Community property is a system that exists in a few states (including the large ones of California and Texas*). Where community property laws exist, all property acquired by either husband or wife during a marriage is considered to belong half to each. These ownership rights transcend death and divorce; consequently, community property states do not have dower or curtesy laws.

All of the forms of tenancy just discussed have to do with freehold estates. There are two major types of tenancies that refer to nonfreehold estates:

Tenancy at will occurs when there is a lease arrangement, but no specific time period is agreed upon. Essentially, then, either party can terminate the arrangement whenever he wants (i.e., at will), so its duration is uncertain.

Tenancy at sufferance occurs when a tenant remains on the property after the expiration of a lease. It differs from tenancy at will in that many times some of the aspects of the original lease contract may be considered to be in force (such as those requiring notice before termination or prohibitions against certain kinds of uses or activities by the tenant). Many states have enacted laws that require that, even in the cases of tenancy at sufferance or at will, the parties give one another certain minimum notice before termination of the arrangement.

Homestead Laws

Many states have what are known as *homestead* laws. These have a number of effects, some of which are similar to those provided by dower and curtesy, and are referred to as probate homestead. In many states the homestead laws also protect one's home against certain kinds of judgments and claims. Usually this protection extends only to a specific dollar amount; the intent of these laws is to assure that even under the most difficult financial circumstances a homeowner may be assured that he will not lose his entire investment in his home.

Limitations on Estates and Interests

Very few estates or interests are completely free of all kinds of restrictions or encumbrances; usually one or more of the following will affect most of them: *easements, restrictive covenants,* or *liens.*

EASEMENTS

An easement is the right of one landowner to use the land belonging to another for a specific purpose. The most common kinds of easements are *access easements, utility easements,* and *drainage easements.* All of these allow someone who is *not* an owner of the affected property to make use of that property for some reason. An access easement allows someone to cross a property to get to (i.e., obtain access to) another property. These rights exist where one parcel of land is completely blocked by others from access to a public right-of-way. A utility easement is a right held by a utility company to put its utility lines on private property, usually for the purpose of providing service to that property. A drainage easement requires that a property owner not disturb a natural, or man-made, drainage pattern that crosses his land.

Easements are created in all the ways that estates are; most commonly, however, they are created by voluntary alienation or adverse possession. In some states, if one sells a part of one's land, so that the part sold does not have direct access to a public right-of-way, one is legally bound to provide the purchaser with an access easement.

---

*The others are Arizona, Idaho, Louisiana, Nevada, New Mexico, and Washington.

RESTRICTIVE COVENANTS

A restrictive covenant is a contract whereby a group of neighboring landowners agree to do (or *not* to do) a certain thing or things so as to mutually benefit all. Covenants most commonly occur in residential subdivisions and are created by the developer as a means of assuring prospective buyers that the neighborhood will be required to meet certain standards. Examples of covenants would be prohibitions against using one's lot for more than one single-family dwelling, limitations on minimum size of structures to be built, specification of architectural style, etc. In some states the entire collection of restrictions applying to a subdivision is called a *bill of assurance*.

LIENS

Liens are claims against the owner of a property, with that property being usable as security for the claim. Mortgages are liens, as are claims for unpaid property taxes. Also, anyone who has done work or provided materials so as to enhance the value of a property may, if he is not paid on time, secure a *mechanic's lien* against the property. If liens are not paid in the legal manner, the holder of the lien can foreclose against the property. *Foreclosure* is a legal process whereby someone holding a legal claim against a property may have the court order the property to be sold so as to provide funds to pay the claim.

Liens, restrictions, and easements are, legally speaking, *a part of the property* and cannot be separated from it without the consent of all parties involved. If one is considering buying property, he must be aware that all encumbrances on the property will remain with it after he acquires title, unless something is done to remove them.

Condominium

All states have passed laws that permit the establishment of *condominium* interests in land. Condominium is a legal term, describing a certain kind of ownership of land — it does *not* refer to any particular architectural style, and, in theory, any kind of property, serving any use, can be owned in condominium. In this form of ownership, one has title to a part of a larger piece of property, with the right to use one's part exclusively and the right to share some of the rest with the other owners. Typically, in a residential condominium one would have the right to use one's own dwelling unit, and no right to enter those owned by others; however, one would share the right, with the others, to use the "common property," which might include private drives within the project, recreational facilities, common hallways, elevators, etc. Most importantly, the law allows an owner of a condominium unit to mortgage and otherwise encumber his unit; if he defaults, a lienholder may force the sale of his unit, but the other owners in the condominium project cannot be held responsible for anything.

A residential condominium development usually has a "homeowner's association" or some similar group that is elected by the owners of the units in the project. The function of the association is to make sure that the common property in the development is taken care of and also to make and enforce whatever rules the owners as a group want to enforce within their private community. Many people who have bought condominium units have found later that the rules and regulations of the association might not permit them to do things that they like. For example, the association may have a rule limiting overnight guests to no more than two per unit, or requiring that only certain kinds of flowers be planted in the front yards. An owner who may wish to have more guests, or who might want to plant different flowers, can find himself up against the wishes of the association and will be required to conform to the rules.

Many condominium projects have quite a lot of common property: swimming pools, park areas, parking lots, bicycle paths, tennis courts, clubhouses, and gatehouses are examples. The owners of units in the project own these common elements together, as a group. Their association looks after the common property and assesses each unit owner a fee (called a condominium fee), usually monthly, to get the funds necessary to maintain it. Owners who do not pay these fees will find that the association usually has the legal power to file a lien on their unit in order to collect the necessary fees.

Title and Recordation

When one owns real estate, one is said to hold *title* to the land. There is no such thing as "title papers" to real estate, as there would be with automobiles and certain other chattels. Title refers to the validity of the available evidence that backs up one's claim to land. Normally, all deeds, liens, restrictions, and easements affecting land are *recorded*, usually in the courthouse of the county in which the land is located. Some leases, contracts of sale, and other documents may be recorded as well. The object of recordation is to provide a means whereby anyone may check the validity of any claim to land. In a legal sense, therefore, the ownership of all land and all rights to land should be a matter of record. These records are public, which means that anyone may examine them. It also means that anything that is recorded gives everyone *constructive notice* of the information recorded; this means that in a court of law one is assumed to be aware of all information in the public records.

The total of the evidence in the records will be the validity of the *title* an owner holds. *Good title is* title that cannot be impeached by the records. Title that appears to be good but is not is said to be *color of title*.

Eminent Domain and Escheat

There are two special ways in which the government may acquire title to real estate. The most important is *eminent domain;* this is the right of the government to acquire privately owned property to be put to a public use, even if the private owner is unwilling to dispose of it. This power of government is necessary in order that it may operate efficiently for the benefit of everyone; imagine the problems if, when the government decided to build a road, it had to look all over until it found willing sellers for land needed for the project — the road might wander all around, and it is quite possible that it couldn't be built at all.

In an eminent domain situation the government can't just seize the land; it must pay the owner of the land the "fair market value" of the land. However, once the government has established that it needs the land for a legitimate public use, there is no way to stop it. A landowner only can dispute the price being offered; if he thinks it is unfair, he may of course sue in court for a higher award and have the court make the final decision. Usually the government will approach the landowner to work out an amicable arrangement, and quite often the landowner agrees to the offered price and there is no dispute. If, however, the landowner is reluctant or refuses to negotiate, the government will *condemn* the affected land. Condemnation is a legal process whereby the owner is dispossessed of the property and must leave; he retains the right to dispute the price being offered, but once condemnation has begun a time will come when he must leave the land and it will be transferred to the government, whether or not the payment question has been settled. All levels of government have power of eminent domain; also, many states have granted limited eminent domain power to private firms such as railroads, utility companies, etc.

Escheat is a process whereby land for whom no legal owner exists reverts to government, which then can dispose of it or use it as it sees fit. It is most common when someone dies intestate and no legal heirs can be found.

Your State's Real Estate Law

The laws of the states vary considerably. Most state real estate licensing authorities make available literature that explains some of the special provisions of law that affect real estate in that state. To find the answers to the following questions, you should study the accompanying table (3-1) and the materials from your state. Then write your answers in the space provided.

Table 3-1.
OWNERSHIP AND INTERESTS IN REAL ESTATE:
The Fifty States and the District of Columbia*

STATE	Joint Tenancy	Tenancy by the Entirety	Community Property	Dower	Curtesy	Homestead	STATE	Joint Tenancy	Tenancy by the Entirety	Community Property	Dower	Curtesy	Homestead
Alabama	•			•	•	•	Missouri	•	•				•
Alaska		•				•	Montana	•			•		•
Arizona	•		•			•	Nebraska	•					•
Arkansas	•	•		•		•	Nevada	•		•			•
California	•		•			•	New Hampshire	•					•
Colorado	•					•	New Jersey	•	•		•	•	
Connecticut	•						New Mexico	•		•			•
Delaware	•	•		•	•		New York	•	•				•
District of Columbia	•	•		•			North Carolina	•	•		•		•
Florida	•	•		•		•	North Dakota	•					•
Georgia				•		•	Ohio		•		•		•
Hawaii	•	•		•	•	•	Oklahoma	•	•				•
Idaho	•		•			•	Oregon		•		•	•	•
Illinois	•					•	Pennsylvania	•	•				
Indiana	•	•					Rhode Island	•	•		•	•	
Iowa	•			•	•	•	South Carolina	•			•		•
Kansas	•			•		•	South Dakota	•					•
Kentucky	•	•		•	•	•	Tennessee	•	•		•		•
Louisiana	see below		•	see below		•	Texas	•		•			•
Maine	•					•	Utah	•	•				•
Maryland	•	•					Vermont	•	•		•	•	•
Massachusetts	•			•	•	•	Virginia	•	•		•	•	•
Michigan	•	•				•	Washington	•	•	•			•
Minnesota	•					•	West Virginia	•	•		•		•
Mississippi	•	•				•	Wisconsin	•			•		•
							Wyoming	•	•				•

---

*The States are arranged alphabetically; each column represents one of six estates or ownership interests. If there is a bullet (•) in that column it means that the State *permits* that feature. If there is no bullet, the State *does not permit* it.

Louisiana law comes from French civil law whereas the law in the other 49 States evolved from English common law. Therefore, the law in Louisiana is different, and Louisiana license applicants should study that State's law especially diligently. Among the other 49 States:

All permit fee simple estates.
All permit life estates.
All permit individual ownership (tenancy in severalty).
All permit tenancy in common.
All permit condominium.

yes

1. Does your state have *dower laws*?
   ☐ No   ☐ Yes; they apply to husbands *and* wives
   ☐ Yes, for wives only
   What are the dower rights of wives? _____

   _____

   _____

   What are the dower rights of children? _____

   _____

   _____

2. Does your state have *curtesy*?
   ☒ No
   ☐ Yes: What are the husband's rights? _____

   _____

   _____

3. Is your state a *community property* state?
   ☐ No
   ☐ Yes

4. Which tenancies does your state allow?
   Joint tenancy   ☒ Yes   ☐ No
   Tenancy by the entirety   ☐ Yes   ☐ No
   (All states allow tenancy in common, at sufferance, at will.)

5. Does your state have homestead laws?
   ☐ No
   ☒ Yes: What are the major provisions? _____

   _____

   _____

6. What is the statutory period for adverse possession in your state?
   For fee simple ownership   _____ years
   For easements   _____ years

   Are there any special situations that would shorten or lengthen the statutory period?
   ☐ No
   ☐ Yes: What are they? _____

   _____

   _____

   _____

Questions on Chapter 3 _____

1. Which of the following is most nearly described as personal property?
   (A) A fixture   (C) An improvement
   (B) A chattel   (D) Realty

2. Which of the following is not corporeal property?
   (A) A fee simple estate
   (B) A leasehold
   (C) An easement
   (D) A fixture

Questions 3, 4, and 5 concern the following situation:

Mr. Jones died; his will left to Mrs. Jones the right to use, occupy, and enjoy Mr. Jones's real estate until her death. At that time the real estate was to become the property of their son Willis.

3. Mrs. Jones is a
   (A) remainderman
   (B) life tenant
   (C) joint tenant
   (D) tenant in common

4. Willis is a
   (A) remainderman
   (B) life tenant
   (C) joint tenant
   (D) tenant in common

5. Mrs. Jones has a
   (A) fee simple estate in joint tenancy with Willis
   (B) fee simple estate as tenant in common with Willis
   (C) life estate
   (D) life estate in joint tenancy with Willis

6. Which of the following is not realty?
   (A) A fee simple estate
   (B) A leasehold for indefinite duration
   (C) Lumber
   (D) A life estate

7. Real estate is defined as
   (A) land and buildings
   (B) land and all permanent attachments
   (C) land and everything growing on it
   (D) land only

8. An item of personalty that is affixed to realty so as to be used as a part of it is
   (A) a fixture
   (B) a chattel
   (C) personal property
   (D) encumbered

9. A freehold estate is
   (A) one acquired without paying anything
   (B) any leasehold
   (C) any estate wherein one may use the property as one wishes
   (D) an estate of uncertain duration

10. Which is not considered a permanent attachment to land?
    (A) Anything growing on it
    (B) Fixtures
    (C) Chattels
    (D) Anything built upon the land

11. If one has some rights to use land, but not all possessory rights, one is said to have a(n)
    (A) interest in land
    (B) estate in land
    (C) life estate in land
    (D) tenancy in common

12. When one has permission to use land but has no other rights, one has
    (A) tenancy at sufferance
    (B) tenancy in common
    (C) license to use
    (D) a fee simple estate

13. One who receives title to land by virtue of having used and occupied it for a certain period of time, without actually paying the previous owner for it, receives title by
    (A) will
    (B) descent
    (C) alienation
    (D) adverse possession

14. One who dies leaving no will is said to have died
    (A) intestate
    (B) without heirs
    (C) unbequeathed
    (D) unwillingly

15. One who owns an undivided interest in land with at least one other, and having the right of survivorship, is said to be a
    (A) tenant in common
    (B) tenant at will
    (C) joint tenant
    (D) tenant at sufferance

16. Tenancy in severalty refers to
    (A) ownership by one person only
    (B) ownership by two persons only
    (C) ownership by at least three persons
    (D) a special form of joint ownership available only to married couples

17. Dower rights are rights that assure that
    (A) a husband receives a certain portion of his deceased wife's estate
    (B) wives and in some states children receive a certain portion of a deceased husband's (or father's) estate
    (C) a homeowner cannot lose his entire investment in his home
    (D) husbands and wives share equally in property acquired during marriage

18. An easement is
    (A) the right to use the property of another for any purpose
    (B) the right to use the property of another for a specific purpose
    (C) a private contract and does not permanently affect the realty
    (D) the right to keep another from using one's land illegally

19. The process whereby one holding a claim against property can have the property sold to pay the claim is
    (A) a lien
    (B) a covenant
    (C) a mechanic's lien
    (D) foreclosure

20. One who appears to own property, but does not, is said to have
    (A) good title
    (B) recorded evidence of title
    (C) constructive notice
    (D) color of title

21. When two people own undivided interests in the same realty, with right of survivorship, it is called
    I. tenancy in severalty
    II. tenancy in common
    (A) I only
    (B) II only
    (C) I and II
    (D) Neither I nor II

22. A fee simple estate is
    I. a freehold estate
    II. a life estate
    (A) I only
    (B) II only
    (C) I and II
    (D) Neither I nor II

23. Which of the following is considered a permanent attachment to land?
    I. Improvements to land
    II. Trees growing on the land
    (A) I only
    (B) II only
    (C) I and II
    (D) Neither I nor II

24. If one has some rights to land, but not all the possessory rights, one has
    I. a life estate
    II. an interest in land
    (A) I only   (C) I and II
    (B) II only   (D) Neither I nor II

25. One who has "color of title" to land has
    I. the appearance of title
    II. a right to one half the income from the land
    (A) I only   (C) I and II
    (B) II only   (D) Neither I nor II

TRUE — FALSE. Write *T* for true, *F* for false.

_F_ 26. An easement is the right to use the property of another upon the payment of rent.

_T_ 27. One who has permission to use land, but no lease, is said to have license.

_T_ 28. Tenancy in severalty refers to land ownership by one person.

_T_ 29. Tenancy at sufferance occurs when a tenant stays on after the expiration of a lease.

_F_ 30. All leases of six months or longer must be in writing to be enforceable.

FILL-INS. Fill in the blanks with the appropriate words or phrases.

31. _Dower_ laws in some states determine that a wife shall receive at least a certain portion of her deceased husband's real estate.

32. _Real Estate_ is defined as land and all attachments to it.

33. Ownership by more than one person, with each owner having an undivided interest that he may dispose of as he wishes, is called _Tenants in common_

34. A claim entered by one who has done work to improve real estate, but who has not been paid for it, is a _mechanic's lien_

ANSWERS

1.	B	10.	C	19.	D	27.	T
2.	C	11.	A	20.	D	28.	T
3.	B	12.	C	21.	D	29.	T
4.	A	13.	D	22.	A	30.	F
5.	C	14.	A	23.	C	31.	Dower
6.	C	15.	C	24.	B	32.	Real estate
7.	B	16.	A	25.	A	33.	tenancy in common
8.	A	17.	B	26.	F	34.	mechanic's lien
9.	D	18.	B				

PART II: REAL ESTATE BROKERAGE

Chapter 4 / *Agency Law*

A licensed real estate broker or salesperson is an *agent;* therefore his practice comes under the *laws of agency.* He is also affected by the Real Estate License Law of his state — this will be discussed in the next chapter.

An agency relationship involves two parties: the *principal* and the *agent.* The agency relationship is contractual, but it also is covered by the general precepts of agency law. In the real estate business, a broker acts as an agent for his *employer,* or principal, who is the owner of the property for which the broker is seeking a buyer or tenant. A licensed salesperson usually is treated as the agent of the *broker,* because license law does not permit salespersons to act without the supervision of a broker.

A real estate broker is a *special agent.* He is called this because his powers are limited, usually to finding someone with whom his principal can deal. A *general agent* is one whose powers are broader and may extend so far as to commit his employer to action. It should be noted that a real estate broker usually has little or no power actually to commit his principal to anything — that is, the principal may refuse to deal with anyone the broker brings to him, although he still may be liable to pay the broker a commission.

Duties of Parties

An agent is employed to deal with third parties on behalf of his principal. The agent is an employee of the principal and must follow his principal's instructions implicitly. Furthermore, he has a duty to act in his employer's best interests, even when doing so means that he cannot act in his own favor. More specifically, agency law requires that the agent abide by the following obligations to his principal:

- He must *obey* his principal's instructions (except, of course, when he is instructed to do something illegal).
- He must be *loyal* to his principal's interests.
- He must act in *good faith.*
- He is expected to use *professional judgment, skill,* and *ability* in his actions. This is particularly so in the case of licensed agents such as real estate brokers, because they are assumed to have met certain standards by virtue of having to be licensed.
- He must be able to *account* for all money belonging to others that comes into his possession. Real estate brokers often collect rents, earnest money payments, and other money on behalf of their principals.
- He must perform his duties *in person.* Normally, this would mean that he could not delegate his duties to anyone else unless the principal approved of the arrangement. Because of the nature of the real estate brokerage business and the establishment of the broker-salesperson relationship by all state licensing laws, a real estate broker has the implied right to delegate his function to duly licensed salespersons and brokers in his employ.
- He must keep his principal *fully informed* of developments affecting their relationship. In the case of a real estate broker, he should report all offers made on the principal's property, as well as all other information he acquires that may affect the principal's property, price, etc.

The principal has obligations to the agent as well. Most of these have to do with money: the principal is obliged to *compensate* the agent for his services, to *reimburse* the agent for expenses paid on behalf of the principal, and to *secure* the agent against any loss due to proper performance of his duties. The principal also has the implied duty to make the agent fully aware of his duties and to inform him fully about anything that will affect his performance.

Real Estate Agency Contracts

Agency contracts are *employment* contracts. Consequently, they do not come under the broad heading of real estate contracts and so are not necessarily required to be in writing by the Statute of Frauds. Of course, it is good practice to write them anyway. In real estate, an agency contract usually is called a *listing*. The details of drawing up these contracts will be discussed in Chapter 12. Here, however, we can briefly distinguish among the various kinds of listings. Among listings of property for *sale:*

An *open* listing is one in which the principal agrees to compensate the agent only if the agent actually finds the buyer with whom the principal finally deals. A single owner may have open listings with many brokers, since he is obliging himself to pay only upon performance, and the broker makes his effort at his own risk.

An *exclusive agency* listing is one in which the principal agrees to employ no other broker, and if the property is sold by any licensed agent a commission will be paid to the listing broker. State license law usually requires that any other agent must work *through* a broker having an exclusive listing; the participating brokers must then agree on a means by which they will share in the commission. However, the commission always will be paid to the listing broker, who then may pay a share to the other broker(s) who cooperated in the deal.

An *exclusive-right-to-sell* listing guarantees that the principal will pay the broker a commission regardless of who actually sells the property. This applies even if the principal finds the buyer himself, with no aid at all from the broker. Note that under the exclusive agency listing, the principal would not have to pay a commission if he found the buyer himself.

Usage of the term *exclusive listing* varies from one place to another. In some localities the term refers to an exclusive agency; in others it refers to the exclusive right to sell. And in still others it refers to both types interchangeably.

A *net* listing is one in which the principal agrees to receive a given net amount. The excess by which the sale price exceeds the net amount goes to the broker as his commission. In many states net listings are illegal; in many others they are not illegal but are "frowned upon" or otherwise disapproved of in some quasi-official manner. The big problem with net listings is that the agent is strongly tempted to act in his own interest rather than that of his employer. To illustrate, suppose a net listing contract with a proposed net to the seller of $30,000 is agreed upon. By law, anytime the broker solicits an offer he must report it to the principal. However, let us assume that an offer of exactly $30,000 is made; if the broker transmits it the seller probably will accept and the broker will receive no compensation. Clearly there is the temptation to illegally "hide" the offer, and any subsequent offers, until one yielding a "satisfactory" excess over the listed price is received; obviously such action flies in the face of the agent's legal responsibilities to his employer. A further source of trouble with net listings would arise when a knowledgeable agent deals with a naive seller; there may exist an opportunity for the agent to convince the seller to sign a net listing at a low price, thereby guaranteeing the agent a large commission when he finds a buyer who will pay true market value.

Earning the Commission

Under common law, a broker earns his commission when he produces a buyer (or tenant) with whom the principal is willing to deal. From then on, the risk that the deal actually will go through rests with the principal. However, many listing contracts today tend to spread that risk or give it back entirely to the broker by specifying that the commission is not payable until the sale closes.

As mentioned previously, the principal is not obliged to deal with anyone whom the broker brings; that is, the principal, by hiring the broker, incurs no legal responsibility to the *third party*. Consequently, one who is willing to pay the asking price and meet all the conditions set down by the principal in the listing agreement normally will have no legal recourse if the principal refuses to deal with him, unless the buyer's civil rights have been violated.

Nevertheless, the principal's obligations to the broker remain. In the listing agreement an acceptable price and terms of sale are specified. If the broker produces a *bona fide* offer that meets all these conditions, then the principal will be liable to pay the broker a commission even though he chooses not to accept the offer. This is required, because the broker has satisfied the terms of his employment contract, and there *is* a contract between him and the principal. There is *no* contract between the principal and third parties, so he is not liable to them.

If the broker's principal refuses to pay him a commission that the broker feels he has earned, he may sue in court to receive it. In order to be successful, he must prove three things:

(1) That he was *licensed* throughout the time, beginning with the solicitation of the listing until the closing of the deal and the passing of title (or the notification by the principal that he will not accept an offer that meets the terms of the listing agreement).

(2) That he had a contract of employment with the principal. The best evidence here is a written contract, and indeed some state licensing laws require that listings be written to be enforceable.

(3) That he was the "efficient and procuring cause" of the sale. In effect, this means that he actually brought about the sale within the terms of the listing contract. In an open listing it would mean that he actually found the eventual buyer. In an exclusive agency listing, he must have found the buyer or the buyer must have been found by a licensed agent. An exclusive-right-to-sell listing effectively defines the broker as having earned a commission when and if the property is sold.

Termination of an Agency Contract

Agency contracts can be terminated by a variety of events, though some of them are relatively uncommon. There are two divisions of these reasons: contracts can be terminated by the *actions of the parties* to them, or they may be terminated *by law* when certain events occur. Termination by the actions of the parties includes the following:

The contract is terminated by *performance* when both parties perform their duties as prescribed and the event for which the agency is created ends. In the real estate business, a listing agency contract would be terminated by performance when there is a "meeting of the minds" between the principal and the third party found by the agent. Sometimes, however, the contract will specify some other event (usually title closing, in the event of a listing for sale) as the actual termination of the contractual relationship.

The parties may *mutually agree* to terminate the relationship before it would have been terminated by performance.

The agent may *resign*. In this case, the agent may be liable to the principal for damages due to his breach of the contract, but he cannot be held to perform under the contract.

The principal may *discharge* the agent. Once again, the principal, too, can be liable for damages due to his breach of the contract, but he cannot be forced to continue the employment of the agent.

The agent may resign, or the principal may discharge the agent, without penalty if it can be proved that the other party was not properly discharging his duties under the contract. An agent would be justified in resigning if his principal, for example, did not provide him with enough information to do his job well or required that he perform some illegal act in the execution of his duties. An agent could be discharged justifiably if it could be shown that he was not faithful to his duties or was acting contrary to the interests of the principal.

Termination of the contractual relationship also occurs automatically, *by law*, with the occurrence of certain events, such as the following:

The *death of either party* terminates an agency relationship.

If either party becomes *legally incompetent*, the agency relationship ceases.

Bankruptcy of either party, so as to make continuation of the relationship impossible, terminates the relationship.

Destruction of the subject matter terminates any agency relationship. In real estate this would include such events as the burning down of a house or the discovery that there is another claim on the title that would make it impossible for the owner of the property to pass good and marketable title.

Questions on Chapter 4

1. A real estate broker is a
   - (A) general agent
   - (B) special agent
   - (C) secret agent
   - (D) travel agent

2. Which of the following is *not* required of an agent with respect to his principal?
   - (A) Loyalty
   - (B) To act in person
   - (C) To account for the agent's own personal finances
   - (D) To act in the principal's best interests

3. A listing contract that says that the broker will receive a commission no matter who sells the property is called a(n)
   - (A) open listing
   - (B) net listing
   - (C) exclusive agency listing
   - (D) exclusive-right-to-sell listing

4. Which of the following does not terminate an agency relationship?
   - (A) Making an offer
   - (B) The death of either party
   - (C) The resignation of the agent
   - (D) The destruction of the subject matter

5. To prove his right to a commission the broker must show
   - (A) that he was licensed throughout the transaction
   - (B) that he had a contract of employment
   - (C) that he was the "efficient and procuring cause" of the sale
   - (D) all of the above

6. A net listing is one
   - (A) that requires the broker to seek a net price for the property
   - (B) that is legal in all states
   - (C) that most ethical brokers would prefer to use
   - (D) in which the broker's commission is the amount by which the sale price exceeds the agreed-upon net price the seller desires

7. Among other things, the principal is obligated to
   - I. compensate the agent for his services
   - II. reimburse the agent for expenses incurred on behalf of the principal
   - (A) I only
   - (B) II only
   - (C) I and II
   - (D) Neither I nor II

8. A real estate broker must comply with
  I. agency law
  II. his state's real estate license law
  (A) I only
  (B) II only
  (C) I and II
  (D) Neither I nor II

9. A special agent is one
  I. whose powers are limited to some specific function
  II. who is required to report to a licensing agency
  (A) I only
  (B) II only
  (C) I and II
  (D) Neither I nor II

10. Among other things, the agent is obligated to
  I. act in the principal's best interests, unless they conflict with his own
  II. keep an accurate account of all money he receives on behalf of the principal
  (A) I only
  (B) II only
  (C) I and II
  (D) Neither I nor II

TRUE — FALSE. Mark *T* for true, *F* for false.

_____ 11. An agency relationship is one of employment.

_____ 12. A real estate broker may delegate his responsibilities to licensed salespersons in his employ.

_____ 13. If an agent brings an offer that exactly conforms to the requirements spelled out in the listing, the employer may reject it without incurring any liability to the third party who made the offer.

_____ 14. If a listed property is destroyed by fire, the listing contract is terminated.

_____ 15. Under common law, the broker earns his commission when the sale has been closed and title has been transferred to the buyer.

FILL-INS. Fill in the blank spaces with the appropriate words or phrases.

16. In an agency relationship, the employer is called the _____ .

17. When an agency expires because all parties have done what was agreed upon, it is said to have been terminated by _____ .

18. A listing in which the broker receives a commission only if he actually secures the buyer himself is called a(n) _____ listing.

ANSWERS

1.	B	6.	D	11.	T	15.	F
2.	C	7.	C	12.	T	16.	principal
3.	D	8.	C	13.	T	17.	performance
4.	A	9.	A	14.	T	18.	open
5.	D	10.	B				

Chapter 5/*Real Estate License Law*

Every state requires that real estate brokers and salespersons be licensed by the state before they can do business. Therefore, each state will have a set of laws referred to as the "Real Estate License Law," which describes the process of becoming licensed, the responsibilities of licensees, the administration of the license law, the means of removing licenses from those unfit to keep them, and miscellaneous items. The details of these laws will vary from state to state, but many of their general provisions will be the same.

Before you can study the material in this chapter effectively, you must get a copy of your state's law. No matter what else they may give you, all state licensing agencies will make available a copy of the state's licensing law to applicants for the licenses. Be sure to study this law carefully! Every state devotes a considerable portion (20 to 40 percent) of the licensing examination to a test of the applicant's knowledge of the license law; if you have not studied your state's law, you will have little or no chance to pass the examination.

This chapter will serve as a guide to study of your state's licensing laws. Since these laws differ in detail from state to state, it would be confusing to try to cover every state's variations in this chapter. A better way, then, is to provide this study guide, which you will supplement with a copy of your state's law. The second section of sample questions at the end of the chapter is designed to show you the *kinds* of questions you will encounter, as well as give you an opportunity to demonstrate your knowledge of your own state's law.

Licensing law can be subdivided into several general areas, such as those we use below. Of course, your state may not cover these areas in the same order we do here, but nearly everything in your state's law will be reviewed here. Do not be concerned if you have to skip around in your state's law to follow the study pattern in this book; the authorities don't care whether you know the sequence in which something appears — they want to make sure that you know the *content* of the law; if you follow the study pattern, you *will* know it.

In each section, plenty of blank space is provided for you to make note of the particular features of your state's law. Sometimes this can be accomplished by actually taping or pasting the relevant part of your state's law in the available space. Other times it will be easier just to make handwritten notes. Be sure to *cross out* items that *do not apply* to your state!

In any event, the following study pattern breaks down the license law into logical segments for the most effective studying:

I. Definitions
II. Exemptions to the License Law
III. Administration of the Law
IV. The Licensing Process
V. Fees
VI. How to Lose a Real Estate License
VII. Revocation Procedure
VIII. Handling of Trust Money
IX. Nonresident Licenses
X. Real Estate Recovery Fund
XI. Regulation of Real Estate Schools
XII. Penalties for Violating the License Law
XIII. Other Provisions

Before beginning the study pattern, you should *carefully read all the way through your state's law*. This will familiarize you with the basic provisions and will make it easier for you to look up items as they are discussed in the study pattern. As you read through the first time, note the following possible aids to study that may be included:

- Look for notes referring to specific legal cases in which a certain provision was upheld or interpreted.
- Check for explanatory notes providing examples that illustrate important points.
- Be particularly on the watch for portions of the law that have since been repealed or amended! Some states print only the law as it currently stands, but others will print all enacted laws relevant to licensing since the original one, even though they may have been repealed or amended later on. In such cases, there usually will be a notation to point out when the repeal or amendment took place. For study purposes, cross out any repealed or otherwise invalid parts of the printed license law you have.
- Look also for provisions that have been enacted but are not yet effective. Often a state law will allow a considerable time after it has passed until it takes effect. This is particularly evident in the case of laws that raise or tighten standards (especially educational) for licensure. Look also for laws containing schedules of provisions that take effect in the future. Many states have adopted schedules by which educational standards for licensure will be raised every so often until a particular goal is reached.
- Be sure to note the way in which the various provisions are numbered or otherwise identified. This will make it easier to understand parts of the law where reference is made to another part of the law.

Study Pattern for the License Law _____

I. DEFINITIONS

A. *Real Estate*. The definition of real estate usually includes most interests in land, buildings, and other improvements. Some states also require licensure for handling investment interests involving real estate, such as syndicates, the sale of businesses, etc.

_____

_____

_____

_____

B. *Broker*. Note the functions that are defined as those of a real estate broker. Usually there will be many of them.

_____

_____

_____

_____

C. *Salesperson*. Some states may use a different name for this job, such as associate, etc. Usually most of the functions will be the same as those for brokers, with the provision that the salesperson is an employee of a broker.

_____

_____

_____

_____

_____

D. *Broker employed by another broker.* Most states provide for this situation; the specific name given to it varies (i.e., associate broker, affiliate broker, employee broker, etc.).

_____

_____

_____

_____

E. *Corporate Broker.* Some states provide that a corporation may have a license if it satisfies certain requirements.

_____

_____

_____

_____

F. *Branch offices.* Under what conditions (if any) does your state allow a brokerage firm to have branch offices?

_____

_____

_____

_____

_____

II. EXEMPTIONS TO THE LICENSE LAW

List here all those who are exempt from your state's license law. This usually includes owners of property for sale or lease, those holding the owner's power of attorney, attorneys acting in the exercise of their duties, trustees, certain employees of owners, government, and some others.

_____

_____

_____

_____

III. ADMINISTRATION OF THE LAW

Most states have a Real Estate Commission that administers the license law. However, some states do not. In those states, the law is administered by a state agency such as the Department of State, or a State Licensing Board or Department. In either case, you will be asked how this administration is set up and what the organizational pattern is.

If your state has a Real Estate Commission, note the following information: How many commissioners are there? What are their required qualifications (i.e., residence in state, experience, licensed broker, etc.)? What is their compensation? How are they chosen and confirmed and by whom? Is there a required geographical distribution among them? How is the chairman chosen, and by whom? How are vacancies filled? How long do commissioners serve? Is there a date or time limit for the naming of new commissioners? How frequently does the commission meet? Where does it meet? How many constitute a quorum?

If your state does not have a real estate commission, look for these answers: Which state agency administers the Real Estate License Law? Where is it located? What, if any, representation is permitted to members of the real estate industry? How is such representation effected — who appoints whom? Are any qualifications required?

Regardless of whether or not your state has a commission, the following questions will be pertinent: What are the general powers of the agency or commission in the enforcement of the law? How is the *staff* of the agency or commission organized (i.e., is the head a Secretary, Executive Secretary, Commissioner, etc.? Are there limits on the size of the staff? Who hires them? Who determines their pay? etc.)? Does the commission or agency have a seal? Where are the offices located?

IV. THE LICENSING PROCESS

You must know *all* the steps to take to get *either* license; also, you must know the necessary qualifications to be met by anyone seeking a license. (Section V is devoted to cataloguing fees that licensees pay.)

A. Must an applicant for either license be sponsored by anyone (either by one who already has a license or by the future employing broker for a salesperson applicant)?

_____

_____

_____

_____

_____

B. What is the minimum age for

   1. salesperson: _____

   2. broker: _____

C. How much *general* education must applicants have (such as high school or the equivalent, etc.)?

   1. salesperson: _____

   2. broker: _____

D. What *special* education requirements must licensees meet? Distinguish between education required *before* getting a license and education needed *after* obtaining a license in order to retain the license. Also, are any substitutions (such as experience) permitted for any of these requirements?

   1. salesperson: _____

_____

_____

2. broker: _____
_____
_____

E. Will there be changes in educational requirements that the present law dictates to go into effect in the future? What are they, and when do they go into effect?

_____
_____
_____
_____
_____

F. Are there any specific *experience* requirements for either license? (Often a broker applicant is required to have been licensed as a salesperson for a certain minimum time.)

_____
_____
_____
_____
_____

G. Are licensees required to be bonded or to contribute to a "real estate recovery fund" or similar fund?

_____
_____
_____
_____
_____

H. Are there any other specific requirements that your state has?

_____
_____
_____
_____
_____

I. On what grounds can your state refuse to issue a real estate license to someone?

_____
_____
_____
_____
_____

V. FEES

Fill in the blank spaces in the following form to show the fees, and other pertinent information concerning them, that your state requires. The information should be broken down by broker/salesperson. There is a column for each. *Cross out* those fees that your state does not charge.

FEE	BROKER	SALESPERSON
APPLICATION FEE		
EXAMINATION FEE		
LICENSE FEE:		
(a) Amount of fee		
(b) How often payable?		
(c) When is it due?		
RENEWAL FEE:		
(a) Amount of fee if different from license fee		
(b) Penalty for late renewal?		
(c) When is license renewal due?		
TRANSFER FEES:		
(a) To new employing broker		
(b) Change of business address		
(c) Change to different branch of same firm		
(d) Any penalty for frequent transfers?		
DUPLICATE (REPLACEMENT) LICENSE FEE		
REAL ESTATE RECOVERY FUND:		
(a) Payment when becoming licensed		
(b) Later periodic payments		
(c) When are payments due?		
OTHER FEES:		
(a) Reactivating inactive license		
(b) License fee while inactive		
(c) _____		
(d) _____		

VI. HOW TO LOSE A REAL ESTATE LICENSE

Your license law will spell out a number of practices for which the authorities are allowed to revoke or suspend a licensee's license. These practices will be found in the license law itself, in a "code of ethics," or set of "rules and regulations," or in both places. We have grouped and listed the more common ones and have provided space for you to note any special provisions of your own law. *Cross out* the ones that your state's law does not mention, but *make sure* that your law does not specify the item in somewhat different wording! When in doubt, leave it in. All the practices listed below are poor business practice, at the very least, so even if you aren't sure your state law prohibits one of them, you ought to avoid it anyway. There is space for you to write in comments, if any.

The practices are grouped according to type.

A. MISHANDLING MONEY BELONGING TO OTHERS

1. Commingling trust (or escrow) money with one's own funds.

   _____
   _____
   _____

2. Not remitting funds quickly, once they are received.

   _____
   _____
   _____

3. Salesperson not remitting funds quickly to broker.

   _____
   _____
   _____

4. Accepting noncash payments on behalf of principal without principal's agreement. (Checks are considered to be cash.)

   _____
   _____
   _____

B. MISREPRESENTATION AND FRAUD

All of these practices are *misrepresentation or fraud*. Some state laws list a number of such practices; others simply say, ". . . for any misrepresentation or fraud . . . ," or some words to that effect.

1. False advertising.

   _____
   _____
   _____

2. Intentionally misleading someone.

   _____
   _____
   _____

3. Acting for more than one party to a transaction without the knowledge of all parties.

   _____

4. Using a trademark or other identifying insignia of a firm or organization (such as REALTORS®) of which one is not a member.

5. A salesperson pretending to be a broker or employed by a broker not his own.

6. Not identifying oneself as a licensee in any transaction in which one is also a party.

7. Taking kickbacks, referral fees, commissions, placement fees, etc., in association with one's duties from persons who are not one's principal, and without the principal's knowledge.

8. Guaranteeing future profits.

9. Offering property on terms other than those authorized by the principal.

10. Pretending to represent principals by whom one is not actually employed.

11. Failing to identify the broker in all advertising.

12. Others (specify):

C. IMPROPER BUSINESS PRACTICE

1. Failing to submit all offers to the principal.

_____
_____
_____

2. Attempting to thwart another broker's exclusive listing.

_____
_____
_____

3. Inducing someone to break a contract.

_____
_____
_____

4. Accepting a net listing.

_____
_____
_____

5. Failing to put an expiration date in a listing.

_____
_____
_____

6. Putting one's sign on a property without the owner's permission.

_____
_____
_____

7. Failing to post a required bond; failing to keep the bond up to date.

_____
_____
_____

8. Blockbusting.

_____
_____
_____

9. Discriminating.

_____
_____
_____

D. FAILURE TO IMPART REQUIRED INFORMATION

1. Failure to leave copies of contracts with all parties involved.

_____
_____
_____

2. Failure to deliver a closing statement to all parties entitled to one.

_____

_____
_____

3. Failure to inform some or all parties of closing costs.

_____
_____
_____

E. IMPROPER HANDLING OR PAYMENT OF COMMISSIONS

1. Paying a commission to an unlicensed person.

_____
_____
_____

2. Paying a commission to a licensee not in one's employ.

_____
_____
_____

3. A salesperson's receiving a commission from anyone other than his employing broker.

_____
_____
_____

F. OTHER

1. Being convicted of certain crimes (specify):

_____
_____
_____

2. Violating any part of the license law.

_____
_____
_____

3. Making false statements on the license application.

_____
_____
_____

4. Showing any evidence of "incompetence," "unworthiness," "poor character," etc. This is a "catch-all" provision usually found at the end of the list of specific offenses to drive home the point that *any* improper action can cost you your license. How does your state phrase this provision?

_____
_____
_____

5. Other provisions not covered above (specify):

_____
_____
_____

VII. REVOCATION PROCEDURE

Every state has a legal process whereby a license can be revoked or suspended. Your state law will spell this out very clearly. Look for the following:

A. Who can make a complaint against a licensee?

_____
_____
_____
_____
_____

B. What form must the complaint take?

_____
_____
_____
_____

C. To whom must it be submitted?

_____
_____
_____
_____

D. What discretion does the authority have with regard to acting on complaints?

_____
_____
_____
_____
_____

E. How are licensees notified of complaints against them?

_____
_____
_____
_____

F. Is there a time limit with regard to the time between the act and the complaint, or the receipt of the complaint and notification of licensee?

_____
_____
_____
_____

G. What rights does the licensee have?

_____
_____
_____
_____

H. How much time may elapse between a hearing and a decision?

_____
_____
_____
_____
_____

I. May any (or only some) parties to a hearing appeal to the courts? Which courts?

_____
_____
_____
_____
_____

J. How soon must an appeal be filed?

_____
_____
_____
_____
_____

K. Does a licensee retain his license if an appeal is filed?

_____
_____
_____
_____
_____

L. What are the penalties that the licensing authority may impose directly?

_____
_____
_____
_____
_____

M. What happens to licenses of salespersons whose broker loses his license?

_____
_____
_____
_____
_____

VIII. HANDLING OF TRUST MONEY

Brokers usually keep their principals' money in trust, in the form of rents, earnest money deposits, etc. The law usually contains provisions regulating such money and its handling. As a rule, it has to be put into a special account called a *trust account* or *escrow account*. Things to look for are: (1) How many different kinds of accounts must be maintained? (2) Can they be interest-bearing; if so, who gets the interest? (3) Must they be deposited in particular banks or with particular agents?

_____

_____

_____

_____

_____

IX. NONRESIDENT LICENSES

Every state has some regulation regarding out-of-state residents who desire to pursue the real estate business within the state. They handle it in one of three ways; find the one your state uses and make the appropriate notes in the space provided below. A state may choose to:

A. Issue nonresident licenses, by requiring nonresidents to take the state's licensing examination. What are the fees they must pay? Do they have to meet all the state's other qualifications? Must they maintain a license in their home state?

B. Prohibit out-of-state residents from operating within the state. The few states that have this provision usually allow the out-of-state licensee to operate within the state provided that all business is funneled through a *resident* licensee.

C. Allow some or all out-of-state licensees to operate on the basis of *reciprocity;* that is, the state will recognize the nonresident's qualification as having been determined by his home state and will issue him an in-state nonresident license on the basis of his being licensed in a reciprocating state. Most ETS examination states have reciprocity with one another, as do most of those using the California Multi-State examination.

_____

_____

_____

_____

_____

_____

_____

X. REAL ESTATE RECOVERY FUND

Not all states have Real Estate Recovery Funds or similar funds with different names. If yours does not, then cross out this section.

A Real Estate Recovery Fund is a fund set up and administered by an agency of the state for the purpose of providing redress for damages caused to members of the public by improper actions by real estate licensees. Usually the money comes from an "assessment" made upon licensees at the time the fund is set up and continuing periodically until the fund reaches a certain level. After that time, if the fund is depleted below a certain level, the assessments will begin again and continue until it is back to the desired level. Look for the following with regard to the Real Estate Recovery Fund:

How does one establish a claim? What process must be gone through before a claim can be paid? What happens to a licensee if a claim is paid because of an improper action of his? Are there any exceptions to the kinds of claims that may be paid? Are there any time limits within which claims must be made? Are there limits to the dollar amount of any single award?

_____

_____

_____

_____

_____

_____

_____

_____

XI. REGULATION OF REAL ESTATE SCHOOLS

More and more states are requiring some kind of real estate training of applicants and licensees. In order to assure that the training is proper and effective, some states have amended their licensing laws to give the state real estate licensing agency the power to regulate real estate schools that teach courses used to meet the educational requirements. Look for the following:

Does the law specify any particular curriculum that any or all of the courses must follow? Does the law permit the licensing agency to specify the curriculum? Does the law require that teachers have any particular qualifications? Is the licensing agency given the power to determine the qualifications of teachers?

_____

_____

_____

_____

_____

_____

_____

_____

_____

XII. PENALTIES FOR VIOLATING THE LICENSE LAW

Violation of the license law is a crime. Is it a misdemeanor, felony, etc.? What is the maximum penalty? Imprisonment, fine, or both? Is there any provision for repeat offenders? What happens to the license of a licensee who is convicted of violating the law? How does a conviction of violating the law affect a person's future right to get a real estate license?

_____

_____

_____

_____

_____

_____

_____

XIII. OTHER PROVISIONS

Use this space to note other important provisions of your state's license law that have not been covered so far.

_____

_____

_____

_____

_____

_____

_____

_____

_____

_____

_____

_____

_____

_____

_____

_____

_____

_____

_____

_____

_____

_____

_____

_____

_____

_____

_____

_____

Questions on Chapter 5

You will note that there are two sections of questions for this chapter. The first section is composed of 25 general questions, such as would apply in all states. The answers to these questions appear after them.

The second section is sort of a do-it-yourself question set. A great many questions are provided, but the answers to them depend upon the specifics of your state's laws. Therefore, no key to them is given; you must look up the answers in your copy of the law or your notes. More specific instructions appear with the questions in the second set.

GENERAL QUESTIONS

1. A licensee's license must be
   (A) carried in his (her) wallet at all times
   (B) posted in a public place in the broker's office
   (C) kept on the wall in the licensee's home
   (D) kept on the wall at the Real Estate Commission

2. A person must be licensed if he is to sell
   (A) his own home
   (B) property belonging to an estate for which he is executor
   (C) property belonging to other clients who pay him a commission
   (D) property he has inherited

3. A broker must place funds belonging to others in
   (A) his office safe, to which only he knows the combination
   (B) a safety deposit box
   (C) an account maintained by the Real Estate Commission
   (D) a trust, or escrow, account

4. License laws forbid
   I. collecting a commission from more than one party to a transaction
   II. soliciting for listings before one is licensed
   (A) I only   (C) I and II
   (B) II only   (D) Neither I nor II

5. A licensee's license can be revoked for
   (A) closing a deal
   (B) intentionally misleading someone into signing a contract that he ordinarily would not sign
   (C) submitting a ridiculous offer to a seller
   (D) all of the above

6. Real estate licenses, once received,
   (A) remain in effect indefinitely
   (B) are good for a limited period of time
   (C) must be filed in the county records
   (D) may be inherited by one's spouse

7. A broker's unlicensed secretary
   (A) may sell property providing she does it under the broker's direct supervision
   (B) may sell or negotiate deals so long as she does not leave the office
   (C) may refer interested clients to the broker or his employed licensees
   (D) all of the above

8. A broker may use escrow monies held on behalf of others
   (A) for collateral for business loans
   (B) for collateral for personal loans
   (C) to make salary advances to licensees in his employ
   (D) none of the above

9. In order to do business, a licensee must
   (A) make proper application for a license
   (B) pass a licensing examination
   (C) have a license issued by the appropriate state agency
   (D) all of the above

10. A licensee can lose his license for which of the following?
    I. Paying a commission to a nonlicensed person
    II. Using monies received as commissions to pay office help
    (A) I only   (C) I and II
    (B) II only   (D) Neither I nor II

11. A licensee can lose his license for
    I. selling properties quickly, at low prices
    II. buying property for his own use from his principal
    (A) I only   (C) I and II
    (B) II only   (D) Neither I nor II

12. Which of the following is not required to have a real estate license?
    (A) A resident manager of an apartment project
    (B) A resident manager of an apartment project who, for a fee, sells a house across the street
    (C) A student who sells houses as part of a research project
    (D) All of the above

13. A licensed salesperson (or whatever he may be called in your state)
    (A) must be under the supervision of a broker
    (B) can collect commission payments only from his broker
    (C) must have his license held by his employing broker
    (D) all of the above

14. In order to sell property belonging to a trust for which he is trustee, the trustee must have
    I. a broker's license
    II. a salesperson's license
    (A) I only   (C) I and II
    (B) II only   (D) Neither I nor II

15. One who is employed by a broker to rent property, but not to sell,
    I. must be licensed
    II. may be paid a salary or a commission
    (A) I only   (C) I and II
    (B) II only   (D) Neither I nor II

TRUE — FALSE.   Write *T* for true, *F* for false.

_____ 16. All states have real estate licensing laws.

_____ 17. It is against licensing law for a licensee to collect commissions from more than one party to a transaction.

_____ 18. No license is required for someone who sells no more than two properties per year for a commission.

_____ 19. Federal law prohibits the sale of real estate without a license.

_____ 20. License laws prohibit discrimination by licensees with regard to race.

_____ 21. A licensee who has had his license revoked for violating the license law may continue to operate his business if he has no other means of support.

_____ 22. Licensed real estate brokers must make full accounting for all trust monies which have come into their care, if requested to do so by the proper state authorities.

_____ 23. It is a violation of license law for a broker to charge consistently lower commissions than his competitors.

_____ 24. Salespersons who receive earnest money payments must turn them over to their brokers as soon as possible, so that they may be deposited in the broker's trust, or escrow, account.

_____ 25. A licensed salesperson may work for any licensed broker, so long as the one that holds his (or her) license approves.

ANSWERS

1. B	8. D	14. D	20. T
2. C	9. D	15. C	21. F
3. D	10. A	16. T	22. T
4. B	11. D	17. F	23. F
5. B	12. A	18. F	24. T
6. B	13. D	19. F	25. F
7. C			

Specific Questions Concerning Your State's License Law _____

No key is provided to the following questions because the answers can differ from one state to another. Go ahead and try to answer the questions; then check your answers by referring to your state's law and the notes you have made. A good practice would be to write your answers lightly in *pencil*. When you check them over after answering the questions, you will be able to erase the incorrect answers; at that point write in the correct answers in a dark pencil or pen. That way, the questions you missed will stand out, and in your future study you will be sure to take note of them as possible weak spots.

FILL-INS. Fill in the blank spaces with the proper word or phrase that reflects the license law of *your* state.

1. The examination fee for a salesperson's license is $_____ .

2. My state will reciprocally issue a real estate license to a licensee from any of the following states: _____

   _____

3. An applicant for a broker's license must be at least _____ years old.

4. A broker must deposit all earnest money payments in an account called a(n) _____

   _____ .

5. To get a salesperson's license, one must have the following general education achievement (high school, college, etc.) _____

6. The maximum imprisonment for violating license law is _____ .

7. Three kinds of people who are exempt from license law are _____ ,

   _____ , and _____ .

8. The license law is administered by _____ .

9. Before taking a licensing examination, a salesperson applicant must have at least _____ classroom hours of instruction in Real Estate Principles.

10. After passing his examination and becoming licensed, a salesperson has _____ months/years to take _____ classroom hours of (specify required subject matter) _____ in order to maintain his licensed status.

11. If a salesperson transfers his employment to a new broker, a transfer fee of $_____ must be paid.

12. The examination fee for the broker's license examination is $_____ .

13. Violation of license law is a (misdemeanor, felony, etc.) _____ .

14. A salesperson's license fee is $_____ every _____ year(s).

15. License renewal fees must be paid by (date due) _____ .

16. A salesperson may collect commission payments from _____ .

17. A broker may pay a "referral" fee of up to $_____ to unlicensed persons.

18. If a salesperson's license is renewed late, an additional fee of $_____ must be paid.

19. A broker's license fee is $_____ every _____ year(s).

20. A broker who is employed by another broker pays a license fee of $_____ .

21. To take the broker's license examination, one must have completed the following *real estate* education: _____
_____
_____

22. Nonresident license fees are _____ .

23. Only the following have the authority to revoke a real estate license: _____
_____

24. Earnest money deposits paid to brokers must be deposited in the appropriate account within (time limit) _____ .

25. A salesperson's license renewal fee is $_____ .

26. A broker's license renewal fee is $_____ .

27. In the case of a broker who transfers from employment by another broker to independent status, a fee of $_____ must be paid.

28. A salesperson whose license is inactive must reactivate it within _____ years or it will expire.

29. The fee for reactivating an inactive broker's license is $_____ .

30. A salesperson may not transfer his employment to a new broker more often than _____ times per year.

31. When a complaint is lodged against a licensee, he must be given at least _____ days' notice of any hearings that will be held.

32. The real estate salesperson's license examination is given _____ times per year.

33. The licensing examination is given in (city) _____ .

34. When a broker's license is renewed late, a late fee of $_____ is charged.

35. If a broker moves his place of business, a fee of $_____ is charged for reissuing new licenses showing the new address.

36. The fee for replacing a lost, stolen, or damaged license is $_____ .

37. Real estate licenses must be displayed (where?) _____ .

38. Before one may take the broker's license examination, one must have been a licensed salesperson at least _____ years.

39. The license fee for a broker's branch office is $_____ .

40. After a hearing of a complaint against a licensee, a decision must be rendered within _____ days/months.

TRUE — FALSE QUESTIONS.   Mark *T* for true, *F* for false.

_____ 41. Net listings are illegal in my state.

_____ 42. The Real Estate Commission has the power to specify the curriculum in the courses that licensees and prospective licensees must take to qualify for, or to keep, real estate licenses.

_____ 43. It is illegal to use sellers' powers-of-attorney in order to circumvent the license law.

_____ 44. My state has a Real Estate Recovery Fund.

_____ 45. Violation of license law is a misdemeanor.

_____ 46. One who has lost his real estate license as a result of a violation of license law may never be issued another license.

_____ 47. A convicted felon may not be issued a real estate license.

_____ 48. Brokers may deposit trust and escrow monies in interest-bearing accounts.

_____ 49. A nonresident of this state may not get any kind of license to do real estate business in this state.

_____ 50. There is no requirement for special real estate education for salespersons.

_____ 51. An out-of-state resident may be issued a license to do real estate business in my state provided that he passes the required examinations, meets educational and age requirements, and pays the specified fees.

_____ 52. When a hearing is held on a complaint against a licensee, the licensee may be represented at the hearing by an attorney.

_____ 53. Complaints against licensees must be submitted to the Real Estate Commission in writing.

_____ 54. Every time a complaint is filed against a licensee, a hearing must be held.

_____ 55. License fees must be paid every two years.

_____ 56. The license law requires that, at a specified date in the future, real estate education required of licensees will be greater than it is now.

_____ 57. In order to take the broker's license examination, one must satisfy a number of requirements, including the requirement that one have at least three years' experience as an actively licensed salesperson.

_____ 58. To hold a broker's license one must be at least 21 years of age.

_____ 59. All licensees must have a high school education or the equivalent.

_____ 60. An applicant for a salesperson's license must be sponsored by a licensed broker.

The following acts concern violations of license law. Mark *T* for those that your state's license law specifies as a violation. Mark *F* for those that are *not* specified.

_____ 61. Accepting a net listing

_____ 62. Making false statements on license applications

_____ 63. Specifying a closing to occur within 15 days of the signing of a contract of sale

_____ 64. Refusing to convey a ridiculous offer to a principal

_____ 65. A broker's paying a commission directly to another broker's licensed salesperson.

_____ 66. Paying a small referral fee to one who refers a prospect, but who takes no other action at all in the eventual transaction

_____ 67. Inducing a seller to break a listing contract with another broker

_____ 68. Advertising the broker's commission rates

_____ 69. Negotiating a commission rate on a sale

_____ 70. Failing to put an expiration date on a listing

_____ 71. Posting "for sale" signs in violation of local ordinances

_____ 72. Selling a home to a black family in a white neighborhood

_____ 73. Refusing to show a home in a white neighborhood to a black family

_____ 74. Failing to leave copies of contracts with all parties involved

_____ 75. Allowing someone other than a licensed real estate broker to prepare a closing statement

_____ 76. Failing to inform a homebuyer of all closing costs that he must pay

_____ 77. Refusing to negotiate a loan for a buyer

_____ 78. Putting one's sign on property without the owner's permission

_____ 79. Allowing a licensed salesperson to show property without the broker being present

_____ 80. Allowing a salesperson to handle a closing, even if the broker is present and supervising the salesperson

_____ 81. Accepting a placement fee from a loan company without the buyer's or seller's knowledge and consent

_____ 82. Guaranteeing to someone that he will be able to sell a property within two years at a profit of 50 percent or more

_____ 83. Intentionally lying in order to induce someone to enter into a contract

_____ 84. Buying property on which one collects a commission without identifying oneself as a licensee

_____ 85. Offering property at a lower price than the seller has authorized in the listing, or in later communication

_____ 86. Failing to identify the broker in all advertising

_____ 87. Placing a blind ad (one in which the fact that the property is being offered by an agent is not stated)

_____ 88. Collecting a commission from more than one party to a transaction

_____ 89. False advertising

_____ 90. Offering for sale property belonging to others upon which one has no listing

_____ 91. A salesperson's not remitting earnest money quickly to broker

_____ 92. Accepting a postdated check as earnest money after seller has agreed to do so

_____ 93. Commingling trust or escrow money with personal funds

_____ 94. Commingling trust or escrow money with the brokerage firm's general funds

_____ 95. Putting trust or escrow monies belonging to different people into the same trust or escrow account

_____ 96. Paying license fees for someone else

_____ 97. Doing business while one's license is inactive or is being held by the Real Estate Commission

_____ 98. Secretly collecting a commission from more than one party to a transaction

_____ 99. Attempting to deal directly with a seller who has signed an exclusive listing agreement with another licensee

_____ 100. Selling and renting property from the same office

MULTIPLE-CHOICE QUESTIONS. It is difficult to provide examples of such questions concerning specifics of state law. General examples were given in the previous section. For reference purposes, we include the following to give you an idea of the *kinds* of multiple-choice questions you might encounter. Note that one answer in some questions is left blank. If none of the other three answers is correct for your state, write the correct answer in the blank. Otherwise, ignore it.

101. License fees are paid
   (A) every year
   (B) every two years
   (C) _____
   (D) every three years

102. The license fees for brokers/salespersons are
   (A) $50/$20
   (B) the same for both
   (C) $40/$10
   (D) _____

103. In my state it is illegal to
   I. accept a net listing
   II. post "sold" signs on property for which a contract has been accepted
   (A) I only
   (B) II only
   (C) I and II
   (D) Neither I nor II

104. In my state
   I. brokers may not be employed by other brokers
   II. salespersons are called something else
   (A) I only
   (B) II only
   (C) I and II
   (D) Neither I nor II

105. The penalties for violating license law are a
   (A) fine of up to $500, imprisonment up to one year, or both
   (B) fine of up to $500, imprisonment up to six months, or both
   (C) fine of up to $1000, imprisonment up to one year, or both
   (D) _____

106. Licensees must pay fees for the following:
   (A) transferring employ to another broker
   (B) replacing a lost pocket card
   (C) reactivating an inactive license
   (D) A, B, and C
   (E) one or two of the above (specify which) _____
   (F) none of the above

107. When a complaint is made against a licensee and a hearing is scheduled, the licensee must be given the following notice of the hearing:
    (A) one week   (D) one month
    (B) ten days   (E) _____
    (C) two weeks

108. A licensee whose license is inactive or is being held by the Real Estate Commission must pay the following fees:
    (A) _____   (C) half those of active licenses
    (B) the same as active licensees (D) $40, broker; $20, salesperson

109. .A licensee may appeal a decision made at a hearing for a complaint against him directly to
    (A) Circuit Court   (C) Federal Court
    (B) State Supreme Court   (D) _____

110. A broker must keep all trust and escrow monies in
    I. a trust account or escrow account
    II. a checking account in a bank
    (A) I only   (C) I and II
    (B) II only   (D) Neither I nor II

If your state has a Real Estate Commission, answer the following (111 through 140):

FILL-INS. Fill in the blanks with the appropriate words or phrases.

111. The Real Estate Commission has _____ members.

112. They serve terms of _____ years.

113. They are appointed by _____.

114. Persons may be nominated for consideration for the post of Real Estate Commissioner by _____.

115. The Chairman of the Real Estate Commission is chosen by _____ _____.

116. The Real Estate Commission must meet (how often?) _____.

117. The Real Estate Commissioners are paid $_____.

118. The Real Estate Commission meets (where?) _____.

119. The geographical distribution of the homes of the Real Estate Commissioners must be _____.

120. A Real Estate Commissioner must have been a resident of this state for _____ years prior to assuming his post.

121. A Real Estate Commissioner must hold a _____ license and must have held it at least _____ years prior to assuming his post.

122. When a vacancy is created on the Commission, _____ appoints a new Commissioner to fill out the unexpired portion of the term.

123. The head of the *staff* of the Real Estate Commission is called _____ _____.

124. The offices of the Real Estate Commission are located at _____ _____.

125. For the Commission to transact any business, at least _____ members must be present.

TRUE — FALSE (on Real Estate Commissions). Mark *T* for true, *F* for false.

_____ 126. The Real Estate Commission sets the salaries of all people working for it.

_____ 127. The Real Estate Commission's budget is composed of all fees and charges it receives from licensees.

_____ 128. Real Estate Commission members cannot be reappointed to additional terms.

_____ 129. All Real Estate Commission members' terms expire at the same time.

_____ 130. Real Estate Commission members must be licensed brokers or salespersons.

_____ 131. The Real Estate Commission has no power to revoke or suspend licenses.

_____ 132. The Real Estate Commission may deny a license to anyone for any reason.

_____ 133. The Real Estate Commission has five members.

_____ 134. The Real Estate Commission cannot hold a hearing on a complaint against a licensee unless a quorum is present.

_____ 135. The Real Estate Commission has three members.

_____ 136. At least one member of the Real Estate Commission must be a member of the general public served by real estate licensees.

MULTIPLE-CHOICE EXAMPLES. Fill in blanks where necessary.

137. The members of the Real Estate Commission, when they assume their posts,
    I. must have been residents of the state at least five years
    II. must have held state real estate licenses at least five years
    (A) I only   (C) I and II
    (B) II only   (D) Neither I nor II

138. The members of the Real Estate Commission
    I. must be REALTORS®
    II. may not participate in the real estate business while holding their posts
    (A) I only   (C) I and II
    (B) II only   (D) Neither I nor II

139. The Real Estate Commission is responsible for
    (A) issuing real estate licenses
    (B) conducting hearings on complaints against licensees
    (C) setting fees for licenses
    (D) more than one of the above (specify which) _____

140. The term of a Real Estate Commissioner is
    (A) two years   (C) four years
    (B) three years   (D) _____

If your state has a Real Estate Recovery Fund (or similar fund), answer the following (141–160). The Real Estate Recovery Fund is referred to as the "Fund" in these questions, regardless of its specific name in your state.

FILL-INS. Fill in the blanks with the appropriate words or phrases.

141. When he first becomes licensed, a salesperson must pay $_____ into the Fund.

142. The maximum amount that can be paid on a single claim from the Fund is $_____ .

143. The Fund must be maintained at a minimum amount of $_____ .

144. When the Fund falls below $_____ , assessments will be made against all active licensees in the amounts of $_____ for brokers and $_____ for salespersons.

145. Claims must be made against the Fund within (time limit) _____ _____ of the time the alleged improper action took place.

146. No more than $_____ may be paid out of the Fund as a result of a single transaction.

147. In my state the name of the Fund is _____ .

148. If the Fund is too low to pay a claim in full, the claim, and _____% interest on the unpaid balance, will be paid when the Fund has risen.

149. A licensee on whose behalf a payment from the Fund has been made must pay it back, along with _____% interest.

150. When he first becomes licensed, a broker must pay $_____ into the Fund.

TRUE — FALSE. Mark *T* for true, *F* for false.

_____ 151. When a claim against the Fund has been paid on behalf of a licensee, his license is suspended or revoked and cannot be reissued until he has fully reimbursed the Fund.

_____ 152. A claim cannot be made against the Fund unless a court judgment has been issued against the affected licensee and it is obvious that he cannot pay it in full.

_____ 153. A discharge in bankruptcy does not relieve a licensee of any obligation he may have to the Fund.

_____ 154. A licensee may be exempted from Fund assessments if he posts a satisfactory bond with the Real Estate Commission.

_____ 155. Money in the Fund may be invested in state or federal obligations.

_____ 156. The Real Estate Commission has custody of the Fund.

_____ 157. If the Fund becomes dangerously depleted, the Real Estate Commission can levy a special assessment on all licensees for the purpose of augmenting the Fund.

_____ 158. Claims cannot be paid from the Fund unless they are due to fraudulent actions by licensees.

SAMPLE MULTIPLE-CHOICE. Fill in blanks where necessary.

159. To make a claim against the Fund, one must
    I. secure a court judgment against a licensee
    II. submit proof that the licensee cannot pay the judgment in full
    (A) I only   (C) I and II
    (B) II only   (D) Neither I nor II

160. The assessment to be paid into the Fund by new licensees is $_____ for new salespersons and $_____ for new brokers.
    (A) $20/$10   (C) $50/$50
    (B) $40/$20   (D) _____

If your state permits the Real Estate Licensing Authority to regulate real estate schools, answer questions 161–170.

FILL-INS.   Fill in the blanks with the appropriate words or phrases.

161. The curriculum required of applicants for a salesperson's license must include _____ hours, distributed as follows: _____

_____

162. The curriculum required of broker applicants must include _____ hours, distributed as follows: _____

_____

163. Teachers of authorized courses must have the following qualifications: _____

_____

164. Required courses cannot meet for more than _____ hours per day.

165. A real estate school must be given _____ days' notice of the licensing authority's intention to withdraw the school's approval.

TRUE — FALSE.   Mark *T* for true, *F* for false.

_____ 166. The licensing authority may determine the qualifications of teachers of approved courses.

_____ 167. A course cannot meet for more than three hours per day.

_____ 168. A broker's license applicant must have passed a course providing at least 30 hours of study in the area of valuation and appraisal.

_____ 169. The licensing authority must approve all real estate schools, even if their courses do not fulfill the educational requirement for licensure.

_____ 170. The licensing authority forbids the offering of courses designed specifically to get people through the licensing examination.

Chapter 6 / *Professionalism in the Real Estate Business*

Most licensed real estate business people think of themselves as professionals who provide valuable service to their communities. However, as in any business, there are those who do not devote themselves exclusively to ethical business practice, and there are some well-meaning persons who handle their business improperly out of ignorance.

As a licensed real estate agent, you will be responsible for your actions. If you are a broker, you will be responsible for the actions of the licensed salespeople who work for you. This means that if you do something in the course of your business that unjustifiably damages someone, you can be held liable in a court of law.

A concerned professional seeks to establish an ethical and reliable business for several reasons. First of all, by so doing he assures that his conduct is above reproach and that no one should have any complaint concerning his business activities. In addition, he helps to create for himself a reputation for reliability and fair dealing, which, in the long run, will contribute immeasurably to his business success. Finally, he adds to the image of his profession in the way he handles himself and his business.

Real estate licensees must abide by agency law and the license laws of their states, as well as the rules and regulations their state agencies set down for them. These matters were covered in the two previous chapters. However, it is still up to the individual businessperson to adopt his own standards of ethics because the laws permit a fairly broad range of practices.

Many successful and respected real estate licensees are REALTORS®. The term REALTOR® is a federally registered identifying term and may be used *only* to refer to a licensed real estate broker or salesperson who is a member of a local Board of REALTORS®, which is affiliated with the National Association of REALTORS®. It is absolutely improper to refer to anyone else as a REALTOR®. Local and national REALTORS® organizations are committed to the maintenance of high professional standards in the real estate industry. They, and associated real estate professional groups, provide educational seminars and instruction to their members as well as access to literature and materials designed to continually improve the capabilities, competence, and professional experience of their members. The success of the REALTORS® is noteworthy. In many communities people have learned to turn to REALTORS® for the best and most professional real estate service. Ironically, their success has been so pervasive that many people will use the very term REALTOR® to designate *any* real estate licensee, even though it is improper to do so. In fact, it is quite *illegal* for a non-REALTOR® to try to pass himself off as a REALTOR®.

Perhaps the most significant contribution which the REALTORS® make to the real estate industry is their dedication to and subscription to the REALTORS® CODE OF ETHICS. This code, which is reprinted on the following pages, illustrates the organization's concern with sound, ethical business practice and the importance of the real estate industry within a community. It is particularly concerned with the manner in which the real estate industry is uniquely endowed with the continuous opportunity to improve the community.

Note that the term REALTOR® is trademarked and should be written as it appears in this chapter (in capital letters, with the trademark [®] sign).

The NATIONAL ASSOCIATION OF REALTORS® reserves exclusively unto itself the right to comment on and interpret the code and particular provisions thereof. For the NATIONAL ASSOCIATION'S official interpretations of the code, see *Interpretations of the Code of Ethics: National Association of REALTORS®*.

REALTOR® *Code of Ethics**

PREAMBLE . . .

Under all is the land. Upon its wise utilization and widely allocated ownership depend the survival and growth of free institutions and of our civilization. The REALTOR® should recognize that the interests of the nation and its citizens require the highest and best use of the land and the widest distribution of land ownership. They require the creation of adequate housing, the building of functioning cities, the development of productive industries and farms, and the preservation of a healthful environment.

Such interests impose obligations beyond those of ordinary commerce. They impose grave social responsibility and a patriotic duty to which the REALTOR® should dedicate himself, and for which he should be diligent in preparing himself. The REALTOR®, therefore, is zealous to maintain and improve the standards of his calling and shares with his fellow-REALTORS® a common responsibility for its integrity and honor. The term REALTOR® has come to connote competency, fairness, and high integrity resulting from adherence to a lofty ideal of moral conduct in business relations. No inducement of profit and no instruction from clients ever can justify departure from this ideal.

In the interpretation of his obligation, a REALTOR® can take no safer guide than that which has been handed down through the centuries, embodied in the Golden Rule, "Whatsoever ye would that men should do to you, do ye even so to them."

Accepting this standard as his own, every REALTOR® pledges himself to observe its spirit in all of his activities and to conduct his business in accordance with the tenets set forth below.

ARTICLE 1

The REALTOR® should keep himself informed on matters affecting real estate in his community, the state, and nation so that he may be able to contribute responsibly to public thinking on such matters.

ARTICLE 2

In justice to those who place their interests in his care, the REALTOR® should endeavor always to be informed regarding laws, proposed legislation, governmental regulations, public policies, and current market conditions in order to be in a position to advise his clients properly.

ARTICLE 3

It is the duty of the REALTOR® to protect the public against fraud, misrepresentation, and unethical practices in real estate transactions. He should endeavor to eliminate in his community any practices which could be damaging to the public or bring discredit to the real estate profession. The REALTOR® should assist the governmental agency charged with regulating the practices of brokers and salesmen in his state.

---

*Published with the consent of the National Association of REALTORS®, author of and owner of all rights in the Code of Ethics of the National Association of REALTORS®, © National Association of REALTORS® 1974. All rights reserved. The National Association of REALTORS® reserves exclusively unto itself the right to comment on and interpret the Code and particular provisions thereof. For the National Association's official interpretation of the Code, see *Interpretations of the Code of Ethics: National Association of REALTORS®*.

ARTICLE 4

The REALTOR® should seek no unfair advantage over other REALTORS® and should conduct his business so as to avoid controversies with other REALTORS®.

ARTICLE 5

In the best interests of society, of his associates, and his own business, the REALTOR® should willingly share with other REALTORS® the lessons of his experience and study for the benefit of the public, and should be loyal to the Board of REALTORS® of his community and active in its work.

ARTICLE 6

To prevent dissension and misunderstanding and to assure better service to the owner, the REALTOR® should urge the exclusive listing of property unless contrary to the best interest of the owner.

ARTICLE 7

In accepting employment as an agent, the REALTOR® pledges himself to protect and promote the interests of the client. This obligation of absolute fidelity to the client's interests is primary, but it does not relieve the REALTOR® of the obligation to treat fairly all parties to the transaction.

ARTICLE 8

The REALTOR® shall not accept compensation from more than one party, even if permitted by law, without the full knowledge of all parties to the transaction.

ARTICLE 9

The REALTOR® shall avoid exaggeration, misrepresentation, or concealment of pertinent facts. He has an affirmative obligation to discover adverse factors that a reasonably competent and diligent investigation would disclose.

ARTICLE 10

The REALTOR® shall not deny equal professional services to any person for reasons of race, creed, sex, or country of national origin. The REALTOR® shall not be a party to any plan or agreement to discriminate against a person or persons on the basis of race, creed, sex, or country of national origin.

ARTICLE 11

A REALTOR® is expected to provide a level of competent service in keeping with the Standards of Practice in those fields in which the REALTOR® customarily engages.

The REALTOR® shall not undertake to provide specialized professional services concerning a type of property or service that is outside his field of competence unless he engages the assistance of one who is competent on such types of property or service, or unless the facts are fully disclosed to the client. Any person engaged to provide such assistance shall be so identified to the client and his contribution to the assignment should be set forth.

The REALTOR® shall refer to the Standards of Practice of the National Association as to the degree of competence that a client has a right to expect the REALTOR® to possess, taking into consideration the complexity of the problem, the availability of expert assistance, and the opportunities for experience available to the REALTOR®.

ARTICLE 12

The REALTOR® shall not undertake to provide professional services concerning a property or its value where he has a present or contemplated interest unless such interest is specifically disclosed to all affected parties.

ARTICLE 13

The REALTOR® shall not acquire an interest in or buy for himself, any member of his immediate family, his firm or any member thereof, or any entity in which he has a substantial ownership interest, property listed with him, without making the true position known to the listing owner. In selling property owned by himself, or in which he has any interest, the REALTOR® shall reveal the facts of his ownership or interest to the purchaser.

ARTICLE 14

In the event of a controversy between REALTORS® associated with different firms, arising out of their relationship as REALTORS®, the REALTORS® shall submit the dispute to arbitration in accordance with the regulations of their board or boards rather than litigate the matter.

ARTICLE 15

If a REALTOR® is charged with unethical practice or is asked to present evidence in any disciplinary proceeding or investigation, he shall place all pertinent facts before the proper tribunal of the member board or affiliated institute, society, or council of which he is a member.

ARTICLE 16

When acting as agent, the REALTOR® shall not accept any commission, rebate, or profit on expenditures made for his principal owner, without the principal's knowledge and consent.

ARTICLE 17

The REALTOR® shall not engage in activities that constitute the unauthorized practice of law and shall recommend that legal counsel be obtained when the interest of any party to the transaction requires it.

ARTICLE 18

The REALTOR® shall keep in a special account in an appropriate financial institution, separated from his own funds, monies coming into his possession in trust for other persons, such as escrows, trust funds, clients' monies, and other like terms.

ARTICLE 19

The REALTOR® shall be careful at all times to present a true picture in his advertising and representations to the public. He shall neither advertise without disclosing his name nor permit any person associated with him to use individual names or telephone numbers, unless such person's connection with the REALTOR® is obvious in the advertisement.

ARTICLE 20

The REALTOR®, for the protection of all parties, shall see that financial obligations and commitments regarding real estate transactions are in writing, expressing the exact agreement of the parties. A copy of each agreement shall be furnished to each party upon his signing such agreement.

ARTICLE 21

The REALTOR® shall not engage in any practice or take any action inconsistent with the agency of another REALTOR®.

ARTICLE 22

In the sale of property which is exclusively listed with a REALTOR®, the REALTOR® shall utilize the services of other brokers upon mutually agreed upon terms when it is in the best interests of the client.

Negotiations concerning property which is listed exclusively shall be carried on with the listing broker, not with the owner, except with the consent of the listing broker.

ARTICLE 23

The REALTOR® shall not publicly disparage the business practice of a competitor nor volunteer an opinion of a competitor's transaction. If his opinion is sought and if the REALTOR® deems it appropriate to respond, such opinion shall be rendered with strict professional integrity and courtesy.

ARTICLE 24

The REALTOR® shall not directly or indirectly solicit the services or affiliation of an employee or independent contractor in the organization of another REALTOR® without prior notice to said REALTOR®.

Where the word REALTOR® is used in this Code and Preamble, it shall be deemed to include REALTOR®-ASSOCIATE. Pronouns shall be considered to include REALTORS® and REALTOR®-ASSOCIATES of both genders.

The Code of Ethics was adopted in 1913. Amended at the Annual Convention in 1924, 1928, 1950, 1951, 1952, 1955, 1956, 1961, 1962, and 1974.

Questions on Chapter 6

1. The term REALTOR® is
   I.   a registered trademark
   II. one which can be used by any licensed broker
   (A) I only
   (B) II only
   (C) I and II
   (D) Neither I nor II

2. A truly professional real estate practitioner should not
   (A) engage in racial discrimination
   (B) sell property he knows is not a good buy because of hidden defects
   (C) convince a seller to sell at a low price because the buyer is a friend
   (D) all of the above

3. A REALTOR® is
   (A) anyone who is a real estate broker
   (B) anyone who deals in real estate in a professional and competent manner
   (C) a member of a local Board of REALTORS®, which is affiliated with the National Association of Real Estate Brokers
   (D) none of the above

4. A REALTOR® may
   (A) offer legal advice in matters in which he is knowledgeable
   (B) use the name REALTOR® in his advertising
   (C) not sell property listed by non-REALTORS®
   (D) all of the above

5. In order to sell property, one must
   (A) have a REALTOR's® license
   (B) belong to a REALTORS® association
   (C) hire only REALTORS®
   (D) none of the above

ANSWERS

| 1. A | 2. D | 3. D | 4. B | 5. D |

PART III: REAL ESTATE CONTRACTS

Chapter 7/*Introduction to Contracts*

Most people have a little familiarity with contracts, though contracts may appear more awesome than anything else. A popular misconception is that a contract must be filled with obscure, legalistic language and lots of nearly invisible fine print. Many contracts do appear this way, but often it is an unnecessary elaboration. While it is true, as we shall see, that contracts must conform to certain standards, usually the only requirement of the *language* in them is that it *clearly say what it is supposed to say*. These days there is an admirable trend to simplify and clarify the language of most contracts, eliminating elaborate language that serves no useful purpose. We can approach the study of contracts with confidence; a little familiarity with them will reveal the basic logic and sensibility behind the laws and customs that surround them and will eliminate the mystery that usually clouds the layman's view of contracts.

Contracts and Real Estate

The real estate business is dominated by contracts. Buying, selling, mortgaging, leasing, and listing real estate all involve particular kinds of contracts that we must study. So, to become familiar with the real estate business, we must devote a considerable part of our study to contracts *in general*, as well as to the *specific kinds* that concern real estate.

For convenience we divide real estate contracts into two rather loosely defined groups. Our *major* contracts are associated with the kinds of real estate dealings that most frequently occur: these are *listings, contracts of sale, deeds, mortgages,* and *leases*. Other contractual arrangements, which involve particular kinds of circumstances and so are less frequently encountered, constitute our group of *minor* contracts. Note that this division into major and minor is a grouping we are making for our own convenience. The law and the courts do not make this distinction: to them a contract is a contract, and the parties to all contracts have the same rights of access to the courts and to legal enforcement of their contractual promises.

REAL ESTATE CONTRACTS

Figure 7–1 arranges the major contracts in an example of the order in which they might be encountered in a typical series of transactions. First an owner enters into a *listing contract* with a broker; in this contract the seller agrees to pay a commission when the broker has found an acceptable buyer for the listed property. Then the buyer and seller will sign a *contract of sale*, in which they agree that at some time in the future the seller will convey the property to the buyer; this occurs when the *deed* is executed by the seller and delivered to the buyer. The buyer may then seek to borrow part of the cost of the property, so he offers a lender a *mortgage* as collateral for the *note*, which evidences the debt he owes. Also, he decides to rent part of the premises to someone else, with whom he enters into a *lease* contract.

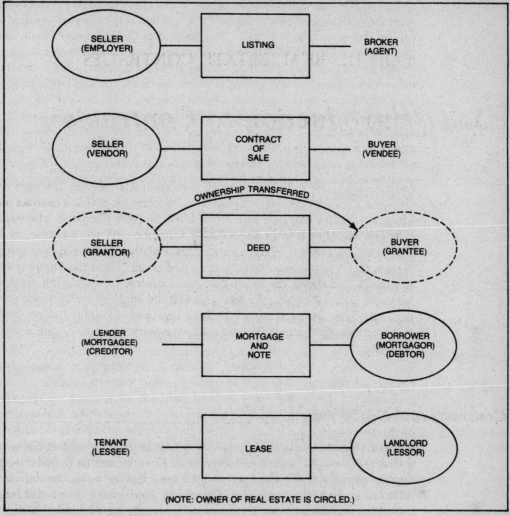

Fig. 7-1.   Major Contracts

PARTIES TO CONTRACTS

In each of these contracts, the parties have specific names. In a listing contract, the seller is the *employer* and the broker is the *agent*. In the contract of sale, the seller becomes the *vendor* and the buyer is the *vendee*. The parties to the deed are the *grantor* and the *grantee*; the mortgage contract is between the *mortgagor* (owner) and *mortgagee* (lender). The *lessor's* real estate is made available to the *lessee* in a lease contract. Generally, the suffix *-or* refers to one who conveys rights, privileges, or something else of value, to the one whose title has the suffix *-ee*. In subsequent chapters each of these contracts will be discussed in detail, but first we examine the basic principles that apply to all contracts.

WHAT IS A CONTRACT?

A contract is an agreement between two or more *parties*, in which each of the parties pledges to do, or is shown to have done, *something* that will benefit the others. This "something" can take a multitude of forms. A common one is a payment of money, though contracts involving no money payment can be perfectly valid. Each of the parties must be shown to benefit, so contracts must involve *exchanges* of benefits. A gives up something to B, in return for which B gives up something to A. A common example would be a purchase: I give up money to you and you give up the thing I am buying from you. However, we can create a valid contract without involving money. I can swap my automobile for your lawn mower. Or we can agree that neither of us will build ugly structures on our land where they will be in the line of sight of the other. While there are other requirements that must be met, the critical test of the validity of the contract is the issue of whether or not the parties can be shown to benefit from it. The amount of benefit doesn't really matter, but if it is totally lacking then usually there is no contract, for it is an ancient precept of law that no one should give something for nothing. If *any* measurable or identifiable benefit is mentioned in the contract, then that will suffice. This means that if you and I sign an agreement that says simply I will give you my automobile next Tuesday, then no court will require me actually to live up to this promise, because no mentioned benefit *to me* appears in it. However, if our agreement says that I will give you my car next Tuesday in return for one dollar paid by you to me, then the courts *will* enforce the agreement against me: it will be a contract because I am receiving some benefit. The fact that my car may be worth much more than one dollar is immaterial here; all that matters is that we *both* receive *some* benefit: you get my car and I get your dollar.

ENFORCEMENT OF CONTRACTS

A valid contract has the "force of law" among the parties to it. It is as if they had agreed to "pass" a law among themselves and promised to abide by it. However, when someone violates the provisions of a contract, the police, or a flock of judges and bailiffs, do not descend upon him and demand that he keep his bargain. In fact, the law will do nothing about private contractual disputes unless one of the injured parties petitions the court to intervene. At that point, the law requires the affected parties to appear and to present their arguments. Then the court (i.e., a judge or a jury) makes a decision as to what is to be done, and by whom. (This description, of course, is somewhat oversimplified; resolving a contractual dispute — or any other — in court often consumes considerable time and expense.) It is likely that many violated contracts never reach court because the offended parties do not want the bother of a court case. Even so there is always that possibility; all parties to a contract have the inherent right to request the court to render judgment if they feel that other parties to the agreement are not living up to it. Generally, one who brings a contract to court has two remedies available. First, he can ask that the court require *specific performance* of the offending party; this means that he wants the court to order the other party to live up to the agreement. Often, however, by the time a contract dispute reaches court it is too late for mere performance to do any (or enough) good. In such a case, the injured party may seek *damages*. Here he would claim that he had suffered some loss due to the other party's violation of the contract and would ask that the court order the violator to make the loss good. Note the use of the words *court order* here. Once the court has reached a decision, the parties to the dispute are *required by law* to abide by it.* If they do not, they are in contempt of court and can be jailed or fined if need be. In this manner, behind every contractual arrangement there lies the threat of court action, which can be backed up by potentially severe penalties.

Most contract cases that come to court are not cut-and-dried. Rarely does someone enter into a contract with the intention to violate it; furthermore, one who *knows* that he is in violation of a contract rarely has the stubbornness (or foolishness) to go ahead with a court showdown he knows he will lose. What usually happens is that *all* parties to a dispute think they are right and the other(s) wrong. The parties *interpret* their agreement differently and are unable to resolve their differences. By taking the matter to court, they ask the court to render a judgment as to who is right and what is to be done.

Requirements of Valid Contracts

A contract cannot be considered by a court unless it is valid. While certain kinds of contracts may have additional requirements for validity, *all* contracts must have the following

---

*This assumes that the decision is not appealed. But even if it is appealed, this only delays an eventual unappealed, or unappealable, decision, which must be respected.

attributes:
1. Mutual agreement
2. Consideration
3. Legally competent parties
4. Lawful purpose
5. Legal form

1. MUTUAL AGREEMENT

Mutual agreement (often referred to as *offer and acceptance, reality of consent, mutual assent, meeting of the minds*, and similar phrases) means that all parties recognize that an offer has been made and has been accepted by the other parties. All are agreed as to what each party has done, with respect to the contract, as well as to what each party is still required to do in the future. Generally, the parties will agree to do, or not to do, some thing or things, in return for some kind of obligation from the others.

Provided that the other essentials of a contract are present, once an offer has been accepted, a contract exists. The one making the offer is the offeror, and the one to whom it is made is the *offeree*. The actions of both of them in creating the contract must be shown to be intentional and deliberate: generally their signatures to a written contract are evidence of this, provided that no fraud, misrepresentation, duress, or mistake is present. However, many binding contracts need not be written; in such cases it is the testimony of the affected parties that provides the evidence that an agreement exists. (Fraud, misrepresentation, etc., are discussed later in this chapter.)

2. CONSIDERATION

Legal consideration refers to the "benefit" received by the parties. Each party must be shown to be obligated to do (or not to do) something, in return for some action or nonaction by the other parties to the contract. The benefit can take many forms; all that must be shown is that the party receiving the benefit agreed that it was of use to him and that he was willing to obligate himself in some way in order to get it. Payment of money is always consideration, as is the transfer of ownership of anything that can be shown to have a market value. In addition, the transfer of many *rights* is consideration also; as an example, a lease transfers rights to use property, but not ownership of the property.

Examples. Here are some examples of consideration in a contractual relationship:
1. A pays $50,000 to B. B transfers ownership of the house to A.
2. A pays B $200 per month. B give A the right to use an apartment for each month for which A pays.
3. A pays B $2.50. B lets A watch a movie in B's theater.
4. A agrees not to hang his laundry outside where B and C can see it. B agrees not to hang his laundry where A and C can see it. C agrees not to hang his laundry where A and B can see it.
5. A agrees to use his best efforts to try to find a buyer for B's house. B agrees to pay A a commission of 6 percent of the sale price if A finds a suitable buyer.
6. A agrees to pay B $50,000 in 60 days, at which time B will transfer to A ownership of a particular house.
7. A pays B $1000. B gives A the right to purchase B's land for $25,000 at any time of A's choosing during the next six months.
8. A transfers ownership of his house to B. B transfers to A the ownership of his parking lot, four albums of rare stamps, two sets of dishes, and a mongrel dog.
9. A pays B $10,000. B transfers to A the ownership of a producing diamond mine in South Africa.
10. A transfers to his son, A, Jr., the ownership of the family estate in return for the "love and affection" which A, Jr. has given to A in the past.
11. A pays B $10,000. B agrees to pay A $126.70 per month for the next ten years.
12. A pays B $10,000. B gives A the right to have B's house sold if B defaults on his debt to A.

In all of these instances there exists legal consideration; these examples show but a few of the many forms it can take. In many cases it includes the payment of money; in (4), (8), and (10), however, no money changes hands. In most, the consideration involves the parties doing something or performing some act; in (4), however, the parties agree *not* to do something. Examples (2), (3), (4), (7), and (12) include the exchange of rights; (5) includes the exchange of services; and the others involve the exchange of ownership of things.

These are examples of real estate contracts we will examine in more detail later. Example (2) is a *lease;* (4) is a *restrictive covenant;* (5) is a *listing;* (6) is a *contract of sale;* (7) is an *option;* (12) is a *mortgage;* and (1), (8), (9), and (10) are *deeds.* Many of these contracts are purchases of one kind or another; examine (11) closely and you will discover that it is a *loan* or a *note:* A lends B $10,000, which B agrees to repay (at a 9 percent interest rate) in equal monthly installments of $126.70 for the next ten years. Example (5) is a *listing;* it is also an *employment contract,* wherein the services of one of the parties are purchased by the other party.

Good and Valuable Consideration. In all except (10) we have *"valuable" consideration.* Valuable consideration is anything that would be of value to practically everyone and, thus, could be sold for money. Money, of course is "valuable," as is ownership of things, the receipt of someone's services, receipt of various kinds of rights, and the like. However, things such as friendship, love, affection, and the like are not valuable consideration, because their value is entirely subjective. You may set a very high value upon the attention and friendship you receive from your best friend, but to most of the rest of us the attention is valueless, since we don't even know him. Furthermore, someone's affection is not a transferable benefit. Rights, ownership, money, services, and such things can be passed on (or sold) to practically anyone. But you can't sell your best friend's affection to someone else. Consequently, such things as friendship and love are called *"good" consideration.* They are of value to the one who receives them, and if he agrees to transfer benefit in return for them he can be held to his bargain.

The law does *not* require that *equal* consideration accrue to all parties. So long as consideration is there, the law is satisfied, provided of course there is no fraud or duress involved. There is only one exception to this: the courts will not enforce a contract requiring the simultaneous exchange of different sums of money.

3. LEGALLY COMPETENT PARTIES

Competent parties are persons who have the legal right to enter into contractual arrangements. Not all legal persons are human beings: corporations, partnerships, trusts, and some other organizations can be parties to a contract too. You can contract to purchase an automobile from ABZ Auto Sales, Inc., even though this company is not a living, breathing being. Furthermore, not all humans are competent to contract; many are legally unable to do so and many more may contract only under carefully defined circumstances.

Nonhuman Parties. Usually each party to a contract must assure himself of the other's legal competence. Dealing with nonhuman parties, we should note that while the law places few restrictions upon the possible contracting ability of these organizations, often they will operate under self-imposed restrictions. A corporation's charter, for example, can permit or prevent certain kinds of contractual agreements on the part of the organization; in addition, it can provide that some or all of the permitted functions be carried out in certain ways. So when one contracts with an organization he must assure himself, first, that the outfit is permitted to engage in such a contract, and, second, that the contract is executed and carried out consistent with the organization's permitted limitations and prescribed methods.

People. Among people, there are two major categories of incompetent parties and several minor ones. These are:
a. Infants
b. Insane persons
c. Drunkards, convicts, and others

a. *Infants* (or minors) are people who have not yet attained the age of majority, which is 18 to 21 in various states. While you may not think that a hulking 17-year-old football star could be incompetent at *anything*, the law says he is. Furthermore, one who may be immature, ignorant, or naive in business judgment still may be considered by the law to be perfectly competent to take responsibility for his actions provided he has attained the age of majority. Minors are not prohibited from contracting, so no law is broken if a minor signs a contract. However, the contract is viewed in a special way by the law: the minor can *void* the contract later on, if he wishes, but adult parties to the contract do *not* have that privilege. The minor may not, however, void (or *disaffirm*) only *part* of the contract; he must abandon it entirely. If he contracts to buy property from an adult, he will have the right to declare the contract void, if he wishes, any time before it is carried out. The adult, however, must honor the contract unless and until the minor actually disaffirms it. So if the adult does not keep his bargain, the minor can sue. The adult will receive no help from the courts if the minor disaffirms. However, the minor cannot, say, disaffirm the part of the contract that specifies he must pay for the property, while at the same time requiring the adult to transfer it to him anyway; he must abandon the *entire* contract. Furthermore, if he disaffirms it after the adult party has provided him some benefit under it, he may have to pay for that which he had already received by the time he decided to void the contract.

The whole idea behind the legal specification of some people as incompetent is a matter of protection. An *infant* is considered too young to bind himself to agreements; the law gives him protection by allowing him to void most agreements that he gets himself into. Once an infant attains the age of majority he becomes an adult and loses this protection, but he *is* given a "reasonable" time beyond the attainment of majority to decide if he will disaffirm any contracts that he had entered into as a minor.

b. *Insane Persons.* The law also extends this "protection" to other categories of people, the largest being *insane persons.* Unlike infancy, however, insanity is a state that can come and go. One who is sane can become insane, and one who is insane can become cured and so become sane again. Also, it is possible for one who is under severe stress or suffering from some other transitory disturbance to become so disoriented that the law may extend the protection of incompetence to him during that episode.

Legal protection of an insane person takes two forms. First, if he has had a guardian appointed by the court, then all contracts he enters into are *void*, and he has no capacity to contract at all. Notice that the infant's contracts are *voidable*, whereas the contracts of an insane person under guardianship are *void*. If the insane person has no guardian, his contracts, too, are voidable rather than void. He has the choice to require that his bargains with others be carried out or to disaffirm the contracts.

Neither the infant nor the insane person may disaffirm *all* kinds of contracts; generally, courts will enforce against them contracts for *necessaries*. Necessaries are such things as food, clothing, shelter, and, sometimes, other things as well. For example, in some cases contracts for employment or for education may be considered necessaries. Once again, the law is extending another form of protection: an adult usually will not care to contract with an infant or someone else he knows may later plead incompetence and void the contract. Consequently, a truthful incompetent may be at a serious disadvantage if his personal circumstances *require* him to contract. Therefore, the law allows some incompetents what amounts to a limited competency. For those things that are "necessary" to them they are allowed to create binding contracts, which they cannot disaffirm and which a court can enforce against them. This will give other competent parties the protection *they* seek in any contractual arrangement and removes any reluctance they may have to deal with an incompetent.

c. *Other Incompetency.* Certain other forms of incapacity "earn" one the legal protection of incompetency. One who is severely intoxicated with alcohol or under the dominating influence of drugs known to affect judgment may have his contracts made at such times later considered voidable. Many states consider felon prisoners to be without the right to contract; this situation is described by the rather grim term of *civilly dead.* Usually when the sentence has been served, and sometimes at the time parole is secured, most rights will be restored.

4. LAWFUL PURPOSE

A contract that requires any of its parties to violate the law usually is void. However, if it is possible to do so without impairing the contract's basic purpose, a court will uphold the contract but strike out that part requiring an illegal act. A very good example concerns the Federal Fair Housing Act of 1968. Among other things, this law declared illegal certain restrictive deed covenants that required buyers of some real estate to agree they would resell only to people of certain racial or cultural backgrounds. At the time the law was enacted vast numbers of deeds to homes contained such clauses, but that did not void all of those deeds. The outlawing of these clauses had no great effect upon the main purpose of the deeds, which was to transfer title to realty in return for consideration. However, if someone had created a special agreement only for the purpose of restricting the racial or cultural background of purchasers of certain real estate, then that entire contract would have been voided by the enactment of the law. If this kind of agreement came into being after the law was passed, then it would be void from the beginning and would *never* be a contract.

The essential rule of lawful purpose, then, is that a contract that exists substantially for the purpose of requiring an illegal act is void. So, also, is one in which an illegal act is required, the elimination of which would materially alter the purpose or effect of the contract. Where an illegal act is included in a contract but is not essential to the basic intent or purpose of the agreement, a court often will void only the illegal part while letting the remainder stand.

5. LEGAL FORM

Some contracts are required to follow a certain form or to be drawn in a certain manner. For example, deeds and contracts of sale require that "legal" descriptions of the property be included; if they are missing or are defective then the entire contract may be invalid. It should be pointed out, though, that much of the wordy, archaic language that frequently appears in contracts is *not* required by any law and appears only as a result of tradition.

Statute of Frauds: Real Estate Contracts Must Be Written. For most real estate contracts, however, there is one critical requirement with respect to form: generally, all real estate contracts, except (1) listings and (2) leases of one year or less, *must be written*. This grows out of the fact that each state has enacted a law called the Statute of Frauds, which requires that all contracts of certain types be written if legal means are to be used to enforce them. Included in these categories are all contracts in which land or an interest in land is sold and contracts that cannot be performed within one year. This latter category, then, would include lease contracts extending more than one year.

A listing contract, however, does not require the sale of land or an interest in land among its parties (although it often is tied into such a sale to a third party). It is a contract of *employment*, which is a category not covered by the Statute of Frauds. However, many states, in their real estate licensing laws, require that listings, also, be in writing; you will have to consult the laws of your state to see what its requirement is.

The definition of "land or an interest in land" is very specific and also quite broad. It includes future interests, so, in addition to deeds, contracts of sale must be written. It includes partial interests, so mortgages must be written. It includes improvements to land and attachments to it, so contracts involving purchase of buildings or growing plants must be written, even if the actual land beneath them is not part of the transaction. However, once an attachment to land is severed from it (such as trees being cut down or crops being reaped) it becomes personal property and is no longer subject to that part of the Statute of Frauds covering realty. This law, however, usually covers much more than just realty contracts, so it is quite possible that many other nonrealty contracts can also be required by law to be written.

Duress, Misrepresentation, and Fraud _____

All parties to a valid contract must have entered into it willingly and without having been misled as to pertinent facts concerning the arrangement. Consequently, you cannot expect a court to enforce a contract against someone if you have pointed a gun at his head to force him to sign, or if you have deliberately or unintentionally misled him so that he agreed, based on this false information. The former kind of situation is described as one of *duress;* the latter is either *misrepresentation* or *fraud.*

DURESS

Duress can take any number of forms. When circumstances force someone to do something against his will, one could say that duress exists, but the law does not always see it that way. If the duress is caused by a party who benefits under the contract, then a court usually will recognize it as such; this would cover situations such as forcing someone's assent by threatening him illegally. But other circumstance can create duress: Jones discovers that he has a rare, expensive disease and must sell his home in order to raise money for payment for the cure. One who buys from him at this time might make an advantageous deal legally, if Jones is in a hurry to sell. If the duress is caused by one's own action the court is reluctant to recognize it. If you buy a new house and thereby create a situation where you are desperate to sell your old home, then that is pretty much your own fault. If you create your own duress, you usually have to suffer with it.

MISREPRESENTATION AND FRAUD

Misrepresentation and fraud go a few steps further: here someone is led into a bad bargain on the basis of false information. Misrepresentation is loosely defined as *unintentional* giving of false information, whereas fraud is *deliberate*. There is another difference, too: fraud is a *crime* as well as a civil wrong. This means that whereas a victim of either fraud or misrepresentation is entitled to compensation for what he was misled into losing, a victim of fraud also may sue for punitive damages, which is a form of extra payment required of the culprit as a kind of punishment. Finally, the perpetrator of a fraud may also be prosecuted in criminal court and may end up being convicted and imprisoned.

Proving Misrepresentation or Fraud. A victim must prove three things to show that misrepresentation or fraud exists: (1) He must show that the incorrect information was relevant to the contract he is disputing — that is, it was *material*. (2) He must show that it was reasonable for him to rely upon this false information. (3) He must show that this reliance led him to suffer some loss as a result.

Let's consider an example. Brown considers buying Green's house. Brown asks Green if the house is free of termites and Green says that it is. Actually the house is infested. If Brown later buys the house based, in part, upon this information and subsequently discovers termite infestation, he may have a case. The point at issue is material: it is reasonable for him to base his decision to buy at least partly upon the assurance that no termites inhabit the premises. When he finds them, it is obvious that he has suffered a loss; therefore the first and third conditions are met. Now he must show that it was reasonable to rely upon Green (the owner at the time) to give him accurate information on this matter. If the court agrees with him he has proven his case. If Green knew about the termites and deliberately lied, then he has committed fraud. If he truly thought there were no termites, then he has misrepresented.

If one or more of the three conditions are missing, fraud or misrepresentation cannot be claimed successfully. So if Brown had not bought Green's house, he could not claim relief, since he suffered no loss due to the falsehood. If he had asked a neighbor a few houses away about the termite problem in Green's house and had depended upon the neighbor's incorrect information, it is unlikely that he could get help from the court, because he would have great difficulty showing that it was reasonable to rely upon a neighbor for this kind of information.

Some Information Must Be Divulged. For some kinds of contracts, the law requires that certain information be divulged by at least some of the parties. If it is not, then misrepresentation or fraud may exist. For example, most licensing laws require that brokers inform other parties if they (the brokers) are acting as principals in the contract, as well as agent. Also, most states require a broker to disclose which party he is acting for, especially if more than one party to a transaction is paying him a commission.

Discharge and Breach of Contracts

Contractual arrangements can be terminated in two general ways. *Discharge* of a contract occurs when no one is required to perform under it anymore. *Breach of contract* occurs when one party makes performance impossible, even when other parties are willing, by refusing to do his part or by otherwise preventing discharge of the contract.

DISCHARGE

Discharge can be considered the "amicable" situation in which the parties to a contract agree that the arrangement is terminated. Most often, discharge occurs by *performance:* this means that everyone has done what he has promised to do and nothing more is required of anyone. Other forms of discharge include agreement to terminate a contract, for one reason or another, before it would have been discharged by performance. Such a reason might be the substitution of a new party for one of the original parties; this original party, then, would have had his duties discharged. Sometimes the parties may decide to terminate one agreement by substituting another one for it. Discharge can also occur when the parties simply agree to abandon the contract without substituting anyone or any other for it.

Statute of Limitations. The law limits the time available to contracting parties during which they can take a dispute concerning a contract to court; this is the Statute of Limitations and in the various states it sets different kinds of limits upon different kinds of contracts. But once the limit has passed, a dispute will not be heard in court, so, in that sense, the contract may be said to be discharged, because it can no longer be enforced. It is greatly advisable that any agreement discharging a contract for reasons other than performance or limitation be in writing. Under some situations (particularly when some, but not all, parties have performed or begun to perform under the contract) an agreement discharging an existing contract *must* be in writing.

BREACH

Breach is a situation where a party violates the provisions of a contract; often this action can be serious enough to terminate the contract by making it impossible to continue the arrangement. The injured parties must seek remedy from the court; usually it takes the form of a judgment for *damages* against the party causing the breach. Sometimes, however, it may be feasible to secure a judgment for *specific performance*, which requires the breaching party to perform as he had agreed. In order to be successful in court, the injured parties must be able to show that a breach has indeed occurred. A failure by a party to perform entirely as specified in the contract constitutes a breach. So does a declaration that he does not intend to perform. Finally there is a breach if a party creates a situation wherein it is impossible for every party to a contract to perform as specified. Once any of these events has occurred there is a breach, and one attribute of a breaching of a contract is that it terminates the obligations of the other parties as well. One who has breached a contract cannot have that agreement held good against any of the other parties.

INJUSTICE

The court will not enforce a contract if doing so will carry out an obvious injustice. While the law is precise, its enforcement is allowed to be compassionate. Consider a case where Smith and Jones come to an *oral* agreement, wherein Smith pays money to Jones, and Jones transfers title to a piece of land to Smith. Smith then builds a house upon the land, whereupon Jones claims title to the land (and to the attachments, including the house) on the grounds that the contract transferring title was oral and therefore invalid. In a case as cut-and-dried as this the court would award title to Smith in spite of the fact that there is no written contract. There would be two reasons for this. First, there is a principle of law that will recognize an oral contract of this nature provided that the purchaser has "substantially" improved the property; otherwise he clearly would suffer unjustly. Second, if Jones had engineered the entire scheme specifically in order to take advantage of Smith, then Jones's case would be dismissed; you can't make use of the law to give you an unfair advantage over someone who is acting in good faith.

OUTSIDE CIRCUMSTANCES

Finally, a contract can be terminated due to some outside circumstance. For example, new legislation may invalidate some kinds of contracts. If one of the parties dies, that usually will void a contract; if a party becomes ill or injured to the point where he cannot perform, he often can void a contract without penalty. If it turns out that the parties have made a mistake as to what their agreement constitutes, then the contract can be nullified. As an example: Emmett thinks a contract of sale involves his purchase of Ted's property on *First* Street and Ted thinks he has agreed to sell Emmett the property he owns on *Twenty-first* Street. In such a case there is no contract, because there hasn't been a meeting of the minds. Finally, if the subject matter of the contract is destroyed, the contract ceases to exist.

Questions on Chapter 7

1. A contract in which an owner of real estate employs a real estate broker for the purpose of finding a buyer for the real estate is a
   (A) deed
   (B) contract of sale
   (C) listing
   (D) lease

2. A contract in which property is transferred from one person to another is a
   (A) deed
   (B) contract of sale
   (C) listing
   (D) lease

3. The two parties to a lease contract are the
   (A) landlord and the serf
   (B) rentor and the rentee
   (C) lessor and the lessee
   (D) grantor and the grantee

4. The requirement that all parties to the contract have an understanding of the conditions and stipulations of the agreement is
   I. reality of consent
   II. meeting of the minds
   (A) I only
   (B) II only
   (C) I and II
   (D) Neither I nor II

5. Consideration that has value only to the person receiving it is
   I. good consideration
   II. valuable consideration
   (A) I only
   (B) II only
   (C) I and II
   (D) Neither I nor II

6. One who is too young to be held to a contractual arrangement is called
   I. youthful
   II. incompetent
   (A) I only
   (B) II only
   (C) I and II
   (D) Neither I nor II

7. One who is otherwise incompetent to contract may be bound to contracts for
   (A) anything but real estate
   (B) real estate only
   (C) necessaries
   (D) food, clothing, and shelter not to exceed $100 per week

8. Which of the following contractual arrangements would be unenforceable?
   (A) A agrees to buy B's house.
   (B) A agrees with B that B shall steal money from C.
   (C) A agrees to find a buyer for B's car.
   (D) A agrees with B that B shall make restitution to C for money stolen by B.

9. The law that requires that most real estate contracts be written to be enforceable is the
   (A) Statute of Limitations
   (B) Statute of Frauds
   (C) Statute of Written Real Estate Agreements
   (D) Statute of Liberty

10. A contract in which A agrees to allow B to use A's real estate in return for periodic payments of money by B is a
    (A) deed
    (B) contract of sale
    (C) lease
    (D) mortgage

11. When one deliberately lies in order to mislead a fellow party to a contract, it is
    (A) fraud
    (B) misrepresentation
    (C) legal, if no third parties are hurt
    (D) all right, if it is not written into the contract

12. Holding a gun to someone's head to force him to sign a contract is
    (A) attempted murder
    (B) permissible only in exceptional circumstances
    (C) duress
    (D) rude and inconsiderate but not illegal so long as the gun doesn't go off

13. When a party to a contract makes performance under it impossible it is
    (A) breach of contract
    (B) discharge of contract
    (C) performance of contract
    (D) abandonment of contract

14. A contract in which A agrees to purchase B's real estate at a later date is a(n)
    (A) deed
    (B) option
    (C) contract of sale
    (D) lease

15. Contracts made by a minor are
    (A) enforceable at all times
    (B) void
    (C) voidable by either party
    (D) voidable only by the minor

16. Most incompetent parties are
    I. minors
    II. insane persons
    (A) I only
    (B) II only
    (C) Both I and II
    (D) Neither I nor II

17. The parties to a deed are the
    (A) vendor and vendee
    (B) grantor and grantee
    (C) offeror and offeree
    (D) acceptor and acceptee

18. If A and B have a contractual arrangement and B violates the contract, A may
    (A) do nothing but suffer the consequences
    (B) sue in court for damages and/or specific performance
    (C) call the police and have B arrested unless he agrees to cooperate
    (D) damage B to the extent that he has damaged A

19. A agrees to sell his brand new limousine to B in return for one dollar. Later A wishes to back out of the deal.
    (A) He may not do so.
    (B) He may do so because he is not getting the true value of the limousine.
    (C) He may only require that B pay a fair price for the limousine.
    (D) Both actions are clear evidence of insanity, so the contract is void.

20. A agrees to trade his car to B in exchange for a vacant lot that B owns.
    (A) This is a valid contractual arrangement.
    (B) This is not a contract, because no money changes hands.
    (C) This is not a contract, because you can't trade unlike items.
    (D) This is not a valid contract, because the car is titled in A's name.

TRUE — FALSE. Mark *T* for true, *F* for false.

_____ 21. A contract has the "force of law" among the parties to it.

_____ 22. A suit in court that asks that a party to a contract be required to do what he agreed upon is not valid.

_____ 23. A restrictive covenant is usually a clause in a lease that prevents the tenant from doing certain things with or on the leased premises.

_____ 24. A corporation may be a party to a contract.

_____ 25. One who discovers that he has entered into a contract with a minor may void the contract.

_____ 26. All real estate contracts must be written on preprinted forms such as those used as examples in this book.

_____ 27. In a contractual arrangement it is not required that equal consideration accrue to all the parties.

_____ 28. Things such as friendship, love, etc., are called "good consideration" if they are used as the consideration in a contract.

_____ 29. A minor can disaffirm all of his contracts and incur no penalty at all for doing so regardless of the damage it may cause other parties.

_____ 30. A lease of one year or less need not be written.

FILL-INS. Fill in the blanks with the appropriate words or phrases.

31. A contract in which A agrees to give B the right to buy A's property at a specific price, during a specific time, is _____.

32. The contract whose parties are the grantor and grantee is the _____.

33. The law that requires that most real estate contracts be written is the _____ _____.

34. The parties to a contract of sale are called the _____.

35. The five essential parts to a contract are _____, _____ _____, _____, _____ and _____.

ANSWERS

1.	C	11.	A	21.	T	31.	an option
2.	A	12.	C	22.	F	32.	deed
3.	C	13.	A	23.	F	33.	Statute of Frauds
4.	C	14.	C	24.	T	34.	vendor and vendee
5.	A	15.	D	25.	F	35.	(1) mutual agreement *or* reality of
6.	B	16.	C	26.	F		consent *or* meeting of the minds;
7.	C	17.	B	27.	T		(2) consideration; (3) competent
8.	B	18.	B	28.	T		parties; (4) legal purpose;
9.	B	19.	A	29.	F		(5) legal form
10.	C	20.	A	30.	T		

Chapter 8/*Description of Land*

Recognized, uniform methods of land description are absolutely essential to proper contractual transactions involving land. If the land in a transaction cannot be identified, then our legal system will not recognize the transaction as binding. Therefore, proper description of the land involved is an essential part of contracts of sale, deeds, leases, options, mortgages, listings, and virtually all other kinds of real estate contracts.

There are four generally accepted methods of land description in the United States. These are:

1. Rectangular survey
2. Metes and bounds descriptions
3. Lot and block number descriptions
4. Monument or occupancy descriptions

The purpose of all of these is to *identify* real estate. Often, in the terminology of the real estate business, descriptions are called "legal descriptions," giving the impression that there is some particular formula that must be followed. Actually, the only legal point of any importance is that the description is *sufficient to identify the property*. If the property can be identified from the description given, then the description is good. Otherwise, no matter how elaborate it may appear, it is faulty.

Most description methods are designed to demonstrate to a surveyor a means of marking the outline of the land on the ground. Note that most descriptions do not include buildings; remember that real estate is land *and all attachments to it*, so a description of the land automatically includes all improvements, unless they are *specifically* excluded.

Rectangular Survey Descriptions

The U.S. Government Rectangular Survey is used in the states indicated in Figure 8–1. If your state is *not* one of them, then you do not have to read this section and can skip to the next section on metes and bounds.

The Government Rectangular Survey divides the land into squares six miles on a side; these are called *townships*. The townships are identified with respect to their distance from the *base line* and *principal meridan*. There are several sets of principal meridians and base lines throughout the country, so each principal meridian carries a name or number to distinguish it from all the others; each one has a single base line paired with it.

Principal meridians are imaginary lines that run north-south. Base lines are imaginary lines that run east-west. Parallel to the principal meridians are other *meridians*, each six miles apart. Parallel to the base line are other lines called *parallels;* each of these is also six miles apart. Altogether, this system of north-south meridians and east-west parallels cuts the map up into a grid of six-mile squares, as in Figure 8–2.

The vertical (north-south) rows of townships are called *ranges*, and the horizontal (east-west) rows of townships are called *tiers*. Each township can be identified by labeling the range and tier in which it is found. The ranges and tiers are numbered depending upon their distance and direction from the principal meridian, or base line. For example, the principal meridian will have a row of townships on each side of it. The one to the east is

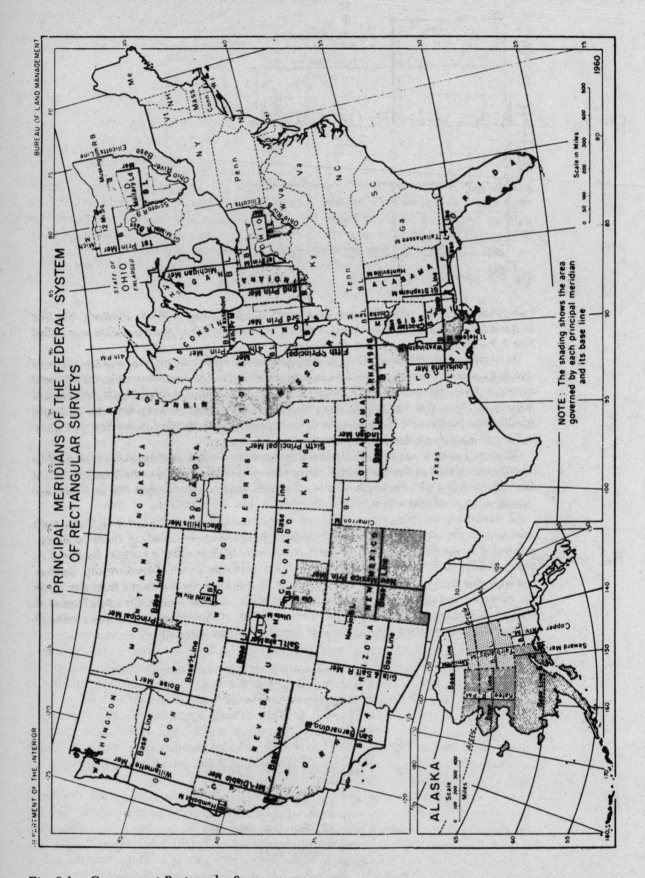

Fig. 8-1. Government Rectangular Survey

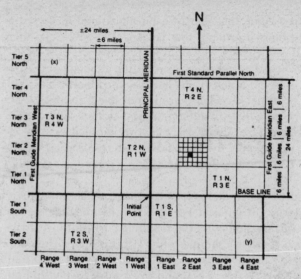

Fig. 8-2.   Six-Mile Square Grid

called *Range 1 East*, while the one to the west is called *Range 1 West*. Similarly, the tier immediately north of the base line is called *Tier 1 North*, while the one below it is called *Tier 1 South*.

To specify a particular township, a description must state both the tier and the range in which it appears. These specifications usually are given in abbreviations such as T3N ((Tier 3 North) or R4W (Range 4 West). Figure 8–2 identifies a number of townships by this kind of description; note that you simply count the number of ranges (or tiers) from the principal meridian (or base line) to the particular township, and specify the direction taken. In Figure 8–2 try to identify all the unmarked townships for practice.

Of course, most tracts of land are less than six square miles, so it becomes necessary to identify which *part* of the township is the specific piece of land under consideration. This is done by dividing the township into smaller and smaller parcels until the one you are interested in is all that is left.

All townships are divided into one-mile squares, as shown in Figure 8–3. Since each township is six miles square, it will contain 36 square miles. Each of these is always numbered as shown in Figure 8–3. Each square-mile tract is called a *Section*. Section 1 in any township, then, is the square mile at the very northeast corner of the township; Section 2 is immediately west of Section 1, etc. Section 21 will be in the fourth row from the top of the township and in the third column from the west. In other words, the north border of Section 21 is three miles south of the north boundary of the township; the east border of Section 21 is three miles west of the east boundary of the township.

6	5	4	3	2	1
7	8	9	10	11	12
18	17	16	15	14	13
19	20	21	22	23	24
30	29	28	27	26	25
31	32	33	34	35	36

T2N, R2E

Fig. 8-3.   Numbering for Township Grids

As an example, let us assume that the township illustrated in Figure 8–3 is the one in Figure 8–2 with the sections drawn in; that is, it is T2N, R2E. If, then, we wanted to describe Section 21 of this township, we would write, "Sec. 21, T2N, R2E." We also would have to specify which principal meridian we were using, although in those states where only one principal meridian is used it is not strictly necessary to identify it in a valid description.

Notice that for each principal meridan there is only *one* T2N, R2E. All other townships using that principal meridian will be in different ranges or tiers, or both. Furthermore, each township has only *one* Section 21. Therefore, a description such as "Sec. 21, T2N, R2E, 5th PM" describes a single square-mile tract of land in eastern Arkansas, on the Fifth Principal Meridian. "Sec. 21, T2N, R2E, Boise Meridian" describes a square-mile tract in southwestern Idaho.

If the tract of land under consideration is smaller than a square mile, then we must further subdivide the section in which it appears. We do this by dividing the section into quarters or halves; if necessary we further subdivide the resulting parts until we arrive at the tract we are considering. Figure 8–4 shows examples of how this is done. The entire section can be divided into four quarters: the northeast, northwest, southeast, and southwest quarters. These would be written NE¼, NW¼, SE¼, and SW¼ respectively. In Figure 8–4 the SE¼ is shown; the others have been further subdivided. The NW¼ has been divided into two halves, E½ and W½. The proper descriptions of these, then, would be E½, NW¼, Sec. 21, T2N, R2E and W½, NW¼, Sec. 21, T2N, R2E.

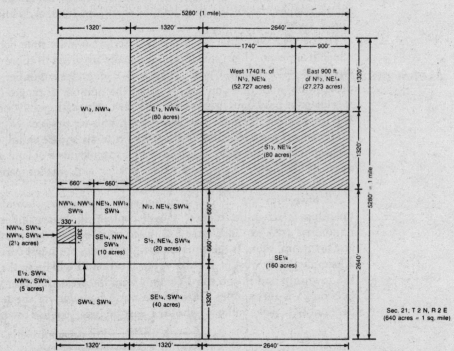

Fig. 8-4.   Subdivision of a Small Section

The SW¼ of this section has been divided into a number of smaller parcels; the proper description of each is given. The smallest is the shaded tract NW¼, SW¼, NW¼, SW¼, Sec. 21, T2N, R2E. The NE¼ of the section has been divided slightly differently: the N½ is divided by the distance from the boundary of N½, NE¼.

Each square mile contains 640 acres. The quarters, then, contain 160 acres each. Further subdivision yields smaller tracts that can be easily measured in terms of acreage; all the tracts subdivided in Figure 8–4 have the acreage indicated. In any case, it is a simple matter to determine acreage from most rectangular survey descriptions. Very simply, multiply the series of fractions given in the description; then multiply the result by the 640 acres contained in the section. For example, the NW¼ contains 160 acres, because ¼ × 640 = 160. The very small tract cited in the previous paragraph is NW¼, SW¼, NW¼, SW¼, so its acreage would be ¼ × ¼ × ¼ × ¼ × 640 = 2½ acres.

Tracts described such as those in the N½, NE¼ aren't quite so easy to determine, since they aren't given entirely in fractions of the full section. For these, however, it is a relatively simple matter to determine the lengths of the sides in feet; from there the total number of square feet can be determined. An acre contains 43,560 square feet; therefore by dividing the square footage of the entire tract by 43,560 we can obtain the acreage of the tract.

It is sometimes impossible to describe a specific tract using one single rectangular survey description; in those cases it is perfectly all right to use several descriptions, each of which describes part of the tract, making sure that all the descriptions together will describe the entire tract. For example, the large L-shaped shaded tract would be described as "E½, NW¼ and S½, NE¼; Sec. 21, T2N, R2E." Note, however, that it is almost always necessary that rectangular survey descriptions be of fairly regular tracts with straight sides. The boundaries almost always must run north-south or east-west. Usually the survey is not a good system for describing irregular tracts, tracts with curved or wandering boundaries, and very small tracts; these are better described using other methods.

One final feature of this description system must be noted: north-south lines on our planet are not parallel because they all meet at the poles. Therefore, the meridians must be adjusted every so often to keep them from getting too close together. This is done by shifting every *fourth* meridian, each 24 miles away from the base line. These meridians are called *guide meridians* and are shown in Figure 8–2. The parallels at which the adjustments take place are called *standard parallels;* they are every fourth parallel. Standard parallels and guide meridians are named to indicate their number and direction from the respective base line or principal meridian.

Metes and Bounds Descriptions

Metes and bounds descriptions describe to the surveyor how to locate the corners of a tract. By locating the corners, one also locates the sides, since they run from corner to corner. Following is a metes and bounds description of Lot #15 in Figure 8–5. This lot also is shown enlarged in Figure 8–6.

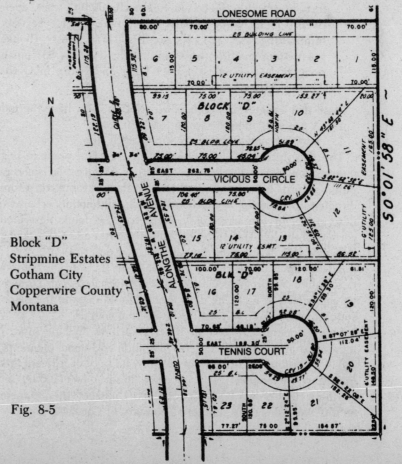

Block "D"
Stripmine Estates
Gotham City
Copperwire County
Montana

Fig. 8-5

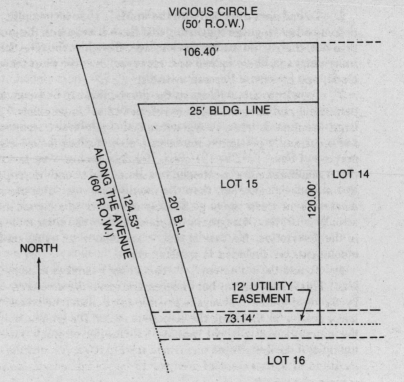

Fig. 8-6. Lot 15, Block "D," Stripmine Estates

"BEGINNING at a point being the southeast corner of the intersection of Vicious Circle and Alongthe Avenue, thence one hundred and six and forty-hundredths feet (106.40') north 90°0'0" east, thence one hundred and twenty feet (120.00') south 0°0'0" east, thence seventy-three and fourteen-hundredths feet (73.14') south 90°0'0" west, thence one hundred and twenty-four and fifty-three hundredths feet (124.53') north 15°29'26" west to the point of beginning; said tract lying and being in Gotham City, Copperwire County, Montana."

Note that a metes and bounds description must have the following components:
1. A properly identified *point of beginning*.
2. *Distance* and *direction* given for each side.

The description above contains all these. The point of beginning is identified as the intersection of two public streets; this is permissible, since one may always consult the public records to find out exactly where these streets are. From that point, the surveyor is directed to proceed a certain distance, and in a certain direction. By following this description, he can arrive *only* at the specific points described, and these points are the corners of the lot. Therefore, he will have outlined the particular plot of land in question by following this description; thus it is a good description.

The accuracy of the description is the only point of any consequence in a court of law. The description can progress clockwise or counterclockwise. Directions (north, south, etc.) may be capitalized or not. The description should include the name of the city (or county) and state in which the real estate is located, of course.

Often a metes and bounds description may include more language than in the fairly minimal example provided here. Common additional elements are:
1. To define the street rights-of-way, lot lines of adjacent lots, etc., along which directed lines travel. **Example:** ". . . thence one hundred feet (100.00') north 63°30'0" west along the southern right-of-way boundary of Thirtieth Street, thence one hundred feet (100.00') north 88°0'0" west along the southern boundary of Lot #44, . . ."

2.   To end each direction with the words ". . . to an iron pin . . ." or ". . . to a point . . ." or some other language suggesting that there is a mark on the ground to refer to. More often than not, there is no marker in existence, though at the time the lot originally was laid out, many years ago, there indeed was. However, over the years these things get lost, disappear, erode, and otherwise become invisible.

3.   To refer to actual things on the ground that can be found. If these things are relatively permanent and obvious, they are referred to as "monuments." These would be things like large, identifiable trees, visible streambeds, milestones, stone walls or other constructions, and occasionally genuine monuments placed at a location by original surveyors for the very purpose of being used as a reference for descriptions. One serious point to keep in mind is that if monuments are mentioned in a metes and bounds description, and the directed lines and monuments conflict, then the monuments rule. This means that if the distance and measurement given say to go 200 feet due north to a certain milestone and the milestone actually is 193 feet, 6 degrees west of north, then the latter is the measurement that will rule in the description. Because of this, it sometimes can cause confusion or error if too many monuments are included in a description.

4.   To add the statement ". . . containing x number of acres (square feet, etc.), more or less." This is convenient, but unnecessary; given the measurements and directions supplied by the description, it always is possible to calculate the area of the parcel if need be. The major reason for including the acreage is so that the grantor is protected against an error in the description that might indicate the transfer of much more (or much less) land. For example, if the description mentions a tract of 100 acres, and the tract actually is only 10, the inclusion of a statement of area would be an immediate indication that the description contained a mistake.

The point of beginning of a metes and bounds description must use a point of reference outside the description of the property itself. In urbanized areas, it is very common to use the nearest intersection of public roads or streets, as in the sample description given. (If that description had been of Lot #14, which is not at the corner, it would have begun as follows: "BEGINNING at a point on the south boundary line of the right-of-way of Vicious Circle, one-hundred-and-six and forty-hundredths feet (106.40') east of the southeast corner of the intersection of the rights-of-way of Vicious Circle and Alongthe Avenue. . . ." In Government Survey states, a point of reference can be a survey location. Many states also have had their own surveys made in all or part of the state, and reference points from these may be used. Indeed, one may refer to any point on earth that can be located using instructions from any publicly recorded document. Once the reference point has been defined, the actual beginning point of the parcel in question is identified by distance and direction from the reference point.

Distance may be expressed in any known unit of measurement, although the most common by far is feet. Directions are given according to the compass. However, in most parts of the U.S. there are two "sets" of compass directions: magnetic bearings and true bearings. Magnetic bearings refer to the magnetic poles, and true bearings refer to the geographic poles. If magnetic bearings are used, then in order to achieve true bearings they must be corrected for the location and the date at which the survey was made. This results from the fact that the magnetic pole is not at the same location as the true pole; furthermore, the magnetic pole "drifts" and so is located slightly differently at different times.

By convention, compass bearings are described as so many degrees east or west (or south). There are 360 degrees in a full circle, 90 degrees in a right (square) angle. The symbol for *degree* is °, so 90° means 90 degrees. Each degree is divided into 60 "minutes" (symbol ') and each minute is composed of 60 "seconds" (symbol "). The statement N 44°31'56" E is read, "North 44 degrees, 31 minutes, 56 seconds east."

Due east is exactly 90° away from north, toward the east; it is written as N 90° E. "Due" northeast would be half that distance from true north, so it would be written N 45° E. If directions are south of due east or west, they are measured by their deviation from true south. A direction slightly north of due west would be N 89° W; if it were slightly *south* of due west, it would be S 89° W. These and several other examples of various directions are shown in Figure 8–7.

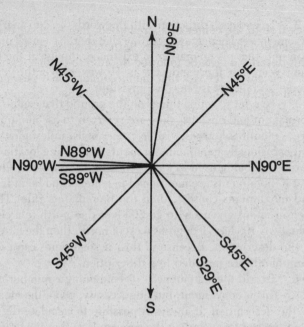

Fig. 8-7. Compass Bearings

Lot and Block Number

Lot and block number descriptions are common in urban areas where *plats* of subdivisions have to be recorded. A plat is a map of the manner in which land is divided into lots; Figure 8–5 is an example of a plat. If the plat is a matter of public record (i.e., has been recorded), then it is quite sufficient to refer to it for the legal description of property it illustrates. For example, it would be enough to describe Lot #15 on that plat as "Lot #15, Block D, Stripmine Estates, Gotham City, Copperwire County, Montana." Given this description, a surveyor can look up this subdivision in the records, find the plat of Block D, and from that get all the information he needs to do an accurate survey of the lot.

These descriptions are very simple to do and take little space. Therefore, in areas where the records are such that they can be used, they are very popular. It should be pointed out, also, that it is permissible to make reference to *any* recorded document in the preparation of a description. Thus, if lot and block descriptions are impossible, it may be possible simply to refer to a previous deed or other recorded instrument in which a description of the property appears. This should be done only if the previous description is exactly the same as the one to be used at present; even so, it is potentially inconvenient in that while copies of plats are easily obtained, and often can be received directly from developers and dealers, old deeds and other documents have to be dug out of the records.

Monument and Occupancy Descriptions

Monument descriptions are similar superficially to metes and bounds descriptions. The difference is that monument descriptions rely entirely upon monuments and specify no distance or direction, except from the monuments themselves to important points of the survey. A monument description might read: "Beginning at the intersection of Highway 9 and County Road 445, thence along the right-of-way of County Road 445 to the end of a stone wall; thence from the end of the stone wall through the center of a large, freestanding oak tree to the center of a streambed; thence along the streambed to the point where the streambed intersects Highway 9; thence along Highway 9 to the point of beginning." Since this description can be followed in order to outline the property, it is a valid description but there is always the risk that the monuments may move or disappear. These descriptions are used mainly for large rural tracts of relatively inexpensive land, where a full survey may entail much greater expense than is warranted by the usefulness of the land.

Occupancy descriptions are very vague: "All that land known as the Miller Farm"; "All that land bordered by the Grant Farm, Happy Acres Home for the Elderly, the Ellis Farm, and State Highway 42." With this kind of description one must rely on the community's general impression of what constitutes the Miller Farm, the Grant Farm, etc. As such, these are very weak descriptions, because they indicate no specific boundaries at all. A similar situation arises out of the use of street addresses as descriptions. While houses and buildings usually do have the address numbers visibly displayed on them, these give no indication at all of the actual extent of the property.

Limits of Descriptions

It is important that you understand that descriptions, while they may accurately describe land, do not provide any guarantee of *title* to that land. A deed that contains a perfectly usable description of a tract of land may be worthless if the grantor has little or no right to convey title to that particular tract. Just because a deed or contract of sale contains a particular description does not guarantee the buyer that his claim to the described land will hold up in court. It can only do so if the seller actually had the legal right to transfer the land he described. One cannot sell, give, or otherwise bargain away what one does not own.

Questions on Chapter 8

Answer questions 1–20 only if your state uses the Rectangular Survey. If it does not, skip to question 21 and begin there.

1. What is the proper description of the township whose *northeast* corner is 36 miles west of the principal meridian and 6 miles south of the base line?
   (A) T2S, R7W (C) T1S, R6W
   (B) T1S, R7W (D) T2S, R6W

2. What is the proper description of the section whose *northwest* corner is 5 miles east of the principal meridian and 2 miles north of the base line?
   (A) Sec. 23, T1N, R1E (C) Sec. 29, T1N, R1E
   (B) Sec. 24, T1N, R1E (D) Sec. 25, T1N, R1E

3. The guide meridians are _____ miles apart.
   (A) 12 (C) 24
   (B) 4 (D) 18

4. The east-west lines at which guide meridians are adjusted are
   (A) adjustment lines (C) parallels of adjustment
   (B) base line extensions (D) standard parallels

5. A square mile contains _____ acres.
   (A) 640 (C) 1000
   (B) 5280 (D) 160

Questions 6–13 concern the figure shown at right.

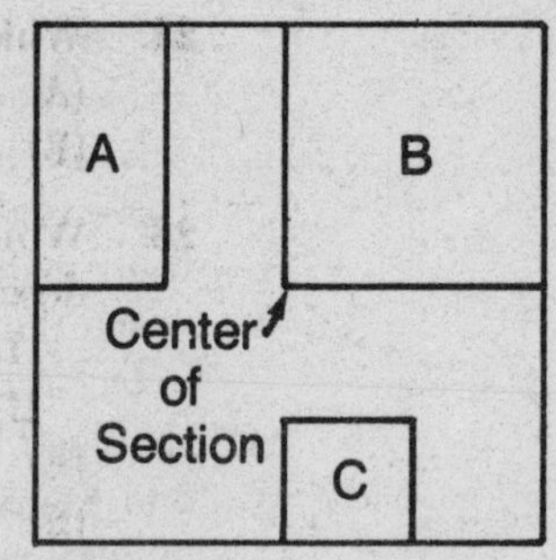

Fig. A

6. The tract marked A contains _____ acres.
   (A) 640
   (B) 160
   (C) 80
   (D) 40

7. The tract marked B contains _____ acres.
   (A) 640
   (B) 160
   (C) 80
   (D) 40

8. The tract marked C contains _____ acres.
   (A) 640
   (B) 160
   (C) 80
   (D) 40

9. The description of Tract A is
   (A) NW¼, NW¼
   (B) N½, NE¼
   (C) W½, NW¼
   (D) W½, N½

10. The description of Tract B is
    (A) NE¼
    (B) NE½
    (C) NE¼, NE¼
    (D) NE¼, NE¼, N½

11. The description of Tract C is
    (A) SE¼, SE¼
    (B) SW¼, SW¼
    (C) SE¼, SW¼
    (D) SW¼, SE¼

12. Assume that the illustrated section is Section 8 of a particular township. What section would you be in if you traveled exactly 2¾ miles due *south* from the *center* of Section 8?
    (A) Sec. 11
    (B) Sec. 12
    (C) Sec. 20
    (D) Sec. 29

13. Assume that the southeast corner of the section is exactly 28 miles south of the base line and 11 miles west of the principal meridian. In what township is it located?
    (A) T2W, R5S
    (B) T5S, R2W
    (C) T6S, R2W
    (D) T6S, R3W

TRUE — FALSE. Mark *T* for true, *F* for false.

_____ 14. A township contains 36 sections of ½ acre each.

_____ 15. The NW¼ of the NE¼ of the SE¼ contains 10 acres.

_____ 16. The guide meridians are corrected every 24 miles to account for the curvature of the earth.

_____ 17. The base line runs east and west and all sections are defined by the number of miles they are from the base line.

FILL-INS. Fill in the blanks with the word or phrase that best completes the sentence.

18. The N½ of the SW¼ of the SE¼ contains _____ acres.

19. The north-south line from which ranges are measured is the _____.

20. The section in the southwestern corner of a township is numbered _____.

The remaining questions concern description techniques used in *all* states.

21. The line behind which all buildings on a lot must be placed is called the
    (A) set line
    (B) setback, or building line
    (C) construction limit
    (D) backup, or setdown line

22. Which of the following is most nearly due west?
(A) N 88° W
(C) S 89°58'3" W
(B) N 79°66'43" W
(D) W 0°4' N

23. Which of the following would not be a proper way to set a beginning point for the description of Lot #10?
    I. BEGINNING at the southwest corner of Lot #10 . . .
    II. BEGINNING at the street intersection nearest Lot #10 . . .
(A) I only
(C) I and II
(B) II only
(D) Neither I nor II

24. "All that land known as the Jones Farm" is which kind of description?
(A) Invalid
(C) Metes only
(B) Occupancy
(D) Rural

Questions 25–30 refer to the following plat.

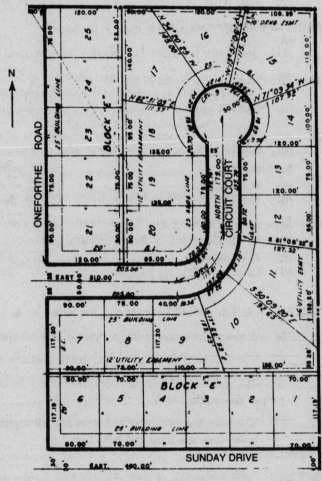

BLOCK "E"
QUAGMIRE VILLAGE
METROPOLIS
ELKO COUNTY
NEVADA

Fig. B

25. Which lot has the most footage on Circuit Court?
(A) Lot 10
(C) Lot 20
(B) Lot 18
(D) Lot 21

26. Which lot has the most street footage?
(A) Lot 7
(C) Lot 20
(B) Lot 18
(D) Lot 21

27. How many lots border on Circuit Court?
    (A) 9   (C) 16
    (B) 15   (D) 21

28. How many lots have sides that are *not* straight?
    (A) 8   (C) 10
    (B) 9   (D) 11

29. How many lots front on more than one street?
    (A) 1   (C) 3
    (B) 2   (D) 4

30. Which lots have the *fewest* straight sides?
    (A) Lots 10, 11, 14, 15, 16, 17, 20
    (B) Lots 10, 11, 14, 16
    (C) Lots 11, 14, 16
    (D) Lots 11, 16

TRUE — FALSE. Mark *T* for true, *F* for false.

_____ 31. In Figure B, no lot exceeds one acre in size.

_____ 32. In Figure B, a metes and bounds description of Lot #8 could begin: "BEGINNING at a point on the south right-of-way line of Circuit Court, ninety feet (90′) east of the southeast corner of the intersection of the rights-of-way of Circuit Court and Oneforthe Road . . ."

_____ 33. Lot 10 is the only lot with five sides in Figure B.

_____ 34. There are no easements drawn on this plat (Figure B).

_____ 35. The smallest lots in Figure B are lots 1, 2, 3, 4, and 5.

_____ 36. A metes and bounds description may not be used if a rectangular survey description of the property is available.

_____ 37. A metes and bounds description may not refer to points that have been located by the rectangular survey.

FILL-INS. Fill in the blanks with the proper words or phrases.

38. The two specific requirements of a metes and bounds description are _____ _____ and _____ .

39. A description that refers only to landmarks on the ground is a _____ .

40. A proper description for Lot 15 in Figure B is _____ _____

ANSWERS

1.	A	12.	D	22.	C	33.	F
2.	D	13.	B	23.	C	34.	F
3.	C	14.	F	24.	B	35.	T
4.	D	15.	T	25.	C	36.	F
5.	A	16.	T	26.	D	37.	F
6.	C	17.	F	27.	B	38.	point of beginning, distance and
7.	B	18.	20	28.	C		direction
8.	D	19.	principal	29.	C	39.	monument description
9.	C		meridian	30.	D	40.	Lot 15, Block E, Quagmire
10.	A	20.	31	31.	T		Village, Metropolis, Elko
11.	D	21.	B	32.	T		County, Nevada

Chapter 9/*Contracts of Sale*

A contract for the sale of real estate is a document that sets forth the rights and obligations of the purchaser(s) and seller(s). Days, weeks, or months later, at a ceremony called a *closing*, the seller(s) will deliver a deed that transfers legal title to the property; the purchaser(s) will surrender payment for the property as set forth in the contract of sale.

It is possible to sell property merely by delivery of a deed in exchange for payment and thus obviate the contract of sale. However, the parties, especially the buyer, would incur substantial risk. A title search must be performed to satisfy the buyer that the seller can give ownership. Time is required to arrange such a search. The buyer may also need time to arrange financing. Most lenders will consider real estate loans only after they have studied the contract of sale. It is indeed rare for a transfer of real estate to be completed without a contract of sale. Furthermore, it is of paramount importance that all parties involved in a transaction understand their contractual obligations and privileges.

Upon completion of the contract of sale, the purchaser (vendee) receives an "equitable" title. Equity, in law, attempts to treat things as they should be to be fair and considers the purchaser to have "equitable title" although legal title remains with the seller (vendor) until closing. So if there is a casualty loss — a fire, for example — before closing, the risk may be upon the purchaser. However, considering that equity is intended to be fair, the risk of loss before closing should not pass automatically to the purchaser in all instances. There are situations in which the seller should be responsible and courts will hold him to be so. In order to avoid potential problems concerning risk of loss, it is best to specify in the contract of sale who has the burden of loss prior to closing and which party is obligated to complete the transaction and to receive the proceeds from insurance.

The Statute of Frauds requires contracts for the sale of real estate to be in writing to be enforceable. The *parol evidence* rule prevents oral testimony from being introduced when it conflicts with better (written) evidence. Consequently, care should be exercised in the preparation of a contract of sale.

Requirements of a Valid Contract of Sale

There are six essentials of a valid contract of the sale of real estate:
1. Competent parties
2. Offer and acceptance
3. Adequate description of the property
4. Consideration
5. Lawful Purpose
6. Written and signed

1. COMPETENT PARTIES

Parties must be considered legally competent. Insane persons, drunkards, those who are sick, or under great duress or other mental handicaps may be incompetent. Those who have been declared incompetent by courts may sell property through their legal guardian. Corporation officers may contract for their corporation when they have such authority. A cautious party should request to see such authority in the corporation's bylaws and the minutes of directors' meetings.

Minors may buy and sell property, and they also have the right to disaffirm (repudiate) their transactions. Shortly after reaching adult age, minors can disaffirm sales and purchases, including unprofitable ones, whereas adults, even those who deal with minors, do not have this powerful right.

2. OFFER AND ACCEPTANCE

For a contract to be valid, the parties involved must be identified. Furthermore, one party must offer something and the other accept. When they reach an agreement, there is said to be a "meeting of the minds." A mutual mistake, misrepresentation, fraud, undue influence, or duress are possible reasons for a contract to be declared void.

One party who offers a contract to another may be presented with a counter-offer. At that point he is relieved of his original offer. He may accept or reject the counter-offer as he pleases and is no longer bound by the original offer. There is not a meeting of the minds until both parties agree to a contract.

3. ADEQUATE DESCRIPTION OF THE PROPERTY

For a description to be adequate, it need not be a fully accurate legal description but it must point out a specific piece of real estate in such a way that only one tract is identified. A house identified only by street number is generally adequate provided that the city, county, and state are noted. Property described as "my frame house" may be adequate provided the seller (vendor) owns only one such house.

4. CONSIDERATION

Each party must promise to surrender something, for a valid contract to exist. The amount of money, other property, or services to be surrendered in exchange for the deed at closing should be clearly stated in the contract of sale.

5. LAWFUL PURPOSE

To be enforceable, an agreement must have a purpose that is not forbidden by law or is not contrary to public policy. If A writes, "I will deed my house to you provided that you promise to use it for an illegal purpose," there is not a legal object. The contract will be void.

6. WRITTEN AND SIGNED

To prevent fraudulent proof of a fictitious oral contract, the Statute of Frauds requires that contracts of sale for real estate be written. To be enforced by a principal, it must be signed by the other principal or by someone acting for him under a power of attorney. A person with a power of attorney is called an attorney-in-fact. That person need not be an attorney-at-law.

Parts of a Real Estate Contract of Sale

A contract of sale for real estate will normally contain certain parts. These parts and their purpose are as follows:

Part	*Purpose*
Parties:	States the names of the seller (vendor) and buyer (vendee).
Property description:	Provides a legal or an adequate description of the subject property and fixtures included.
Sales price:	States the amount to be paid in cash at closing and from the proceeds of financing.

Part	Purpose
Financing conditions:	Purchaser stipulates acceptable conditions of financing, including the type of loan, loan-to-value ratio, interest rate, monthly payments.
Earnest money:	Notes the amount of the good faith deposit presented to the seller or his agent. Also called hand money or escrow money.
Type of deed:	Describes the type of deed to be given at closing.
Title evidence:	Describes the type of evidence to be considered satisfactory assurance that the seller can give title.
Title approval:	Describes rights of purchaser and seller in the event that purchaser objects to a flaw in the title.
Property condition:	States whatever changes (if any) are required to be made to the property.
Prorations:	Calls for the proration of prepaid or unpaid taxes, insurance, rents, etc., between buyer and seller.
Loss:	Affixes responsibility for casualty losses until closing.
Possession:	Establishes a date for possession.
Closing:	Establishes a date for closing.
Broker:	Acknowledges the existence of a real estate broker, the commission rate, and which principal is to pay the commission.
Default:	Describes the obligations of parties in the event one fails to perform.
Miscellaneous provisions:	States whatever other provisions buyer and seller agree upon.
Signatures:	Principals, brokers, escrow agents.

Questions on Chapter 9

1. Whenever all principals agree to the terms of a real estate contract, there has been
   (A) legality of object
   (B) meeting of the minds
   (C) reality of consent
   (D) bilateral consideration

2. The law that requires contracts for the sale of real estate to be in writing to be enforceable is the
   (A) Statute of Frauds
   (B) Statute of Limitations
   (C) Statute of Liberty
   (D) parol evidence rule

3. One who has the power to sign the name of his principal to a contract of sale is a(n)
   (A) special agent
   (B) optionee
   (C) tenant in common
   (D) attorney-in-fact

4. A valid contract of purchase or sale of real property must be signed by the
   (A) broker
   (B) agent and seller
   (C) seller only
   (D) buyer and seller

5. Hand money paid upon the signing of an agreement of sale is called
   (A) an option
   (B) a recognizance
   (C) earnest money
   (D) a freehold estate

6. What is *not* an essential element of valid contract?
   (A) Offer and acceptance
   (B) Capacity of participants
   (C) Without ambiguity
   (D) Lawful purpose

7. A seller of real estate is also known as the
   (A) vendee
   (B) grantor
   (C) vendor
   (D) grantee

8. To each sales agreement there must be
   I. an offer and an acceptance
   II. a mortgage loan
   (A) I only
   (B) II only
   (C) I and II
   (D) Neither I nor II

9. If, upon receipt of an offer to purchase under certain terms, the seller makes a counter-offer, the prospective purchaser is
   (A) bound by his original offer
   (B) bound to accept the counter-offer
   (C) bound by the agent's decision
   (D) relieved of his original offer

10. A contract that has no force or effect is said to be
    I. voidable
    II. void
    (A) I only
    (B) II only
    (C) I and II
    (D) Neither I nor II

11. A sales agreement to be enforceable must have
    (A) the signature of the wife of a married seller
    (B) an earnest money deposit
    (C) competent parties
    (D) witnesses

12. Generally, if a minor has signed a contract, the contract is
    I. voidable by the adult
    II. voidable by the minor
    (A) I only
    (B) II only
    (C) I and II
    (D) Neither I nor II

TRUE — FALSE. Mark *T* for true, *F* for false.

_____ 13. A contract of sale is invalid if it is not signed by a licensed real estate broker.

_____ 14. After a contract of sale is entered into, it is possible that, if the building burns down, the loss will be the buyer's.

_____ 15. A contract of sale need not be written if it is closed within one year.

_____ 16. If an adult discovers that he has signed a contract of sale with a minor, he can refuse to grant title until the minor reaches the age of majority.

_____ 17. The sale price and conditions of the sale should be clearly stated in a contract of sale.

_____ 18. One who is an attorney-in-fact must also be an attorney-at-law.

_____ 19. A contract of sale should relate the type of deed to be given at closing.

_____ 20. A contract of sale usually should stipulate that the closing will occur within one or two days of the date of the contract of sale.

FILL-INS. Fill in the blanks with the proper words or phrases.

21. At the time a contract of sale is created, _____ title passes to the buyer.

22. The parties to a contract of sale are called the _____ and _____ .

23. The _____ rule prevents oral testimony from being introduced when it conflicts with written evidence.

24. Minors have the right to _____ their transactions.

ANSWERS

1.	B	7.	C	13.	F	19.	T
2.	A	8.	A	14.	T	20.	F
3.	D	9.	D	15.	F	21.	equitable
4.	D	10.	B	16.	F	22.	vendor, vendee
5.	C	11.	C	17.	T	23.	parol evidence
6.	C	12.	B	18.	F	24.	disaffirm

Chapter 10/ Deeds

To transfer an interest in real estate during one's lifetime, the owner (grantor) surrenders a *deed of conveyance* to another (grantee). The deed of conveyance, also simply called a *deed*, is covered by the Statute of Frauds; consequently, it must be in writing to be enforceable. A deed may and should be recorded in the county courthouse to give constructive notice of its existence.

Types of Deeds

There are two basic types of deeds — *warranty* (also known as general warranty) and *quitclaim.* Either type is adequate to convey the interest that the grantor has in property (if any).

The warranty deed contains assurances by the grantor
1. that he has title to the property and the power to convey it (covenant of seizin)
2. that his title is good against claims by others (covenant of quiet enjoyment)
3. that the property is free of encumbrances except as specified (covenant against encumbrances)
4. that he will perform whatever else is necessary to make the title good (covenant of further assurances)
5. that he will forever defend the rights of the grantee (covenant of warranty forever)

The warranty deed is the best type of deed for a grantee to receive.

In contrast, the quitclaim deed carries no warranties whatsoever. The grantor gives up all of his rights to the property without even implying that he has or has ever had any rights to the property. Should the grantor be possessed of the property in fee simple absolute, then a quitclaim deed serves to transfer complete ownership. However, if a grantor owns nothing, that is exactly what a grantee will receive from the quitclaim deed. The quitclaim deed is usually used to clear up an imperfection in the title, which is called a *cloud on title.*

A deed that contains some but not all of the covenants of a warranty deed is a *special* or *limited warranty* deed. Special warranty deeds typically contain assurances only against claims that may have originated while that grantor held title. It does not protect against claims that originated previously to that.

Bargain and sale deeds contain no warranties, but only an assurance that the grantor has an interest in the property. A grantor need not state precisely what his interest is or whether the property is unencumbered. It is up to the grantee to ascertain, prior to closing, the grantor's interest in the property.

There are many other types of deeds, including a *trustee's deed* (used to transfer property from a trust); a *referee's deed* in foreclosure; a *sheriff's deed*; an *administrator's deed*, etc. Most of these are used by persons who must transfer the title of another's property. In these situations, the authorized transferor does not wish to personally warranty title from all claims, so the deed given contains a limited warranty.

Deed Requirements

The following elements must be present in a deed for it to be considered valid:
1. A legally competent grantor

2. A designated grantee
3. Consideration — even though only a token amount is shown
4. Words of conveyance
5. The interest being conveyed
6. A description of the property
7. Grantor's proper signature
8. Delivery of the deed and acceptance

The traditional deed has the following five parts:

Part of Deed	Purpose
1. Premises	Names of parties, exploratory facts, words of conveyance, consideration, legal description of the property
2. Habendum	The "to have and to hold" clause, which may describe a limit to the quantity of the estate being granted, such as, "to have and to hold forever" or "to have and to hold for life"
3. Testimonium	The part of the deed that contains warranties (if any)
4. Execution	Date, signatures, and seal if applicable
5. Acknowledgment	Attestation by a public officer, usually a notary public, as to the genuineness of grantor's signature. (Although acknowledgment is not required to transfer title, it is usually required for the deed to be recorded.)

Execution of the Deed

For it to be considered complete, a deed must be signed by the grantor and delivered to the grantee or delivered in escrow. Occasionally, problems arise when an undelivered deed is found in the grantor's home after his death. The grantee named may claim ownership, but since the grantor never delivered the deed, courts will not agree that transfer was intended.

The requirement for delivery of the deed generally is considered very literally; that is, the grantee actually must have come into physical possession of the document in order for title to be considered transferred to him. The grantee may arrange for his agent to accept delivery for him. A common form of such delivery is *delivery in escrow*. In this situation, the grantor delivers the deed to a trustee or escrow agent, who holds it pending completion of some required action by the grantee (such as payment in full of a note given in payment for all or part of the price). In this case delivery is considered to have occurred as soon as the escrow agent or trustee receives the deed, so title is transferred. However, since he has no deed in his possession, the grantee will have difficulty disposing of the title himself until he fulfills the necessary requirements to get the deed released to him by the agent.

Figures 10–1 and 10–2 identify the relevant parts of a warranty deed and a quitclaim deed. Note that the quitclaim has nothing in it that could technically be called a testimonium. This is because the quitclaim contains no warranty; the grantee receives whatever interest the grantor may have in the property, but the nature of that interest usually is not stated, and since the grantor will defend against no claim but his own, the document itself is adequate evidence against him. Consequently, no warranty is included.

Questions on Chapter 10

1. X hands Y a deed with the intent to pass title and orally requests Y not to record the deed until X dies. When is the deed valid?
   (A) Immediately
   (B) When Y records the deed
   (C) When X dies
   (D) Never

2. A quitclaim deed conveys only the interest of the
   (A) guaranteed
   (B) property
   (C) claimant
   (D) grantor

WARRANTY DEED

STATE OF GEORGIA,

_____ County.

THIS INDENTURE, made this_____ day of_____

in the year of our Lord One Thousand Nine Hundred and_____

Between_____

of the State of_____ and County of_____ of the first part

and_____

of the State of_____ and County of_____ of the second part.

WITNESSETH: That the said part_____ of the first part, for and in consideration of the sum of

_____ DOLLARS

in hand paid at and before the sealing and delivery of these presents, the receipt whereof is hereby acknowledged, ha_____

granted, bargained, sold and conveyed and by these presents do_____ grant, bargain, sell and convey unto the said

part_____ of the second part, _____ heirs and assigns, all that tract and parcel of land

lying and being in_____

PREMISES

TO HAVE AND TO HOLD the said bargained premises, together with all and singular the rights, members and appurtenances thereof, to the same being, belonging or in any wise appertaining, to the only proper use, benefit and behoof
of_____ the said part_____ of the second part, _____ heirs and assigns forever, IN FEE SIMPLE.

HABENDUM

And the said part_____ of the first part, for _____ heirs, executors and administrators
will warrant and forever defend the right and title to the above described property unto the said part_____ of the
second part, _____ heirs and assigns, against the lawful claims of all persons whomsoever.

TESTIMONIUM

IN WITNESS WHEREOF, That the said part_____ of the first part ha_____ hereunto set_____ hand_____
and affixed_____ seal_____, the day and year above written.

Signed, sealed and delivered in the presence of:

_____ (Seal)

_____ (Seal)

_____ (Seal)

_____ (Seal)

_____ (Seal)

EXECUTION

**ACKNOWL-
EDGEMENT**

Fig. 10-1.   Warranty Deed

QUIT-CLAIM DEED

STATE OF GEORGIA,_____County.

THIS INDENTURE, made this_____day of_____in the year of our Lord One Thousand Nine Hundred and_____

between_____of the first part,

and_____of the second part.

WITNESSETH: That the said part_____of the first part for and in consideration of the sum

of_____Dollars,

cash in hand paid, the receipt of which is hereby acknowledged,_____bargained, sold and do_____

by these presents bargain, sell, remise, release, and forever quit-claim to the said part_____of the

second part,_____heirs and assigns, all the right, title, interest, claim or demand which the said

part_____of the first part ha_____or may have had in and to_____

with all the rights, members and appurtenances to the said described premises in anywise appertaining or belonging.

TO HAVE AND TO HOLD the said described premises unto the said part_____of the second

part_____heirs and assigns, so that neither the said part_____of the first part nor_____

heirs, nor any other person or persons claiming under_____shall at any time, claim or demand

any right, title or interest to the aforesaid described premises or its appurtenances.

IN WITNESS WHEREOF, the said part_____of the first part ha_____hereunto set

hand_____and affixed_____seal_____the day and year above written.

Signed, sealed and delivered in presence of

_____(Seal)

_____(Seal)

_____(Seal)

_____(Seal)

PREMISES

HABENDUM

(NO TESTI-MONIUM)

EXECUTION

ACKNOWL-EDGEMENT

Fig. 10-2. Quitclaim Deed

3. Which of the following forms of deeds have one or more guarantees of title?
   (A) Quitclaim deed
   (B) Executor's deed
   (C) Warranty deed
   (D) Special form deed

4. The part of conveyance that defines or limits the quantity of the estate granted is
   (A) habendum
   (B) premises
   (C) equity
   (D) consideration

5. The Statute of Frauds Law
   (A) requires certain contracts to be in writing to be enforceable
   (B) requires a license to operate as a broker or a salesperson
   (C) regulates escrow accounts
   (D) regulates fraud conveyance

6. For a deed to be recorded, it must be in writing and must
   (A) be signed by grantee
   (B) recite the actual purchase price
   (C) be acknowledged
   (D) be free of all liens

7. The most comprehensive ownership of land at law is known as
   (A) estate for years
   (B) life estate
   (C) fee simple
   (D) defeasible title

8. From the standpoint of the grantor, which of the following types of deeds creates the least liability?
   (A) Special warranty
   (B) General warranty
   (C) Bargain and sale
   (D) Quitclaim

9. The recording of a deed
   (A) passes the title
   (B) insures the title
   (C) guarantees the title
   (D) gives constructive notice of ownership

10. Title to real property may pass by
    (A) deed
    (B) bill of sale
    (C) both A and B
    (D) neither A nor B

11. Real property title may be conveyed by
    (A) adverse possession
    (B) inheritance
    (C) deed
    (D) all of the above

12. A warranty deed protects the grantee against a loss by
    (A) casualty
    (B) defective title
    (C) both A and B
    (D) neither A nor B

13. Recordation of a deed is the responsibility of the
    (A) grantor
    (B) grantee
    (C) both A and B
    (D) neither A nor B

14. Deeds should be recorded
    (A) as soon as possible after delivery
    (B) within thirty days of delivery
    (C) both A and B
    (D) neither A nor B

15. A deed of conveyance must be signed by
    (A) grantee and grantor
    (B) only the grantor
    (C) both A and B
    (D) neither A nor B

16. A deed to be valid need not necessarily be
   (A) signed
   (B) written
   (C) sealed
   (D) delivered

17. The party to whom a deed conveys real estate is the
   (A) grantee
   (B) grantor
   (C) beneficiary
   (D) recipient

18. Deeds are recorded in the
   (A) county courthouse
   (B) city hall
   (C) Federal Land Book
   (D) state capital

19. A deed must
   (A) contain the street address
   (B) state the nature of the improvement on the land (dwelling)
   (C) contain adequate description to identify the property sold
   (D) state total area in the tract, more or less

20. What is the maximum number of grantees that can be named in a deed?
   (A) Two
   (B) No limit
   (C) Four
   (D) Ten

21. Property is identified in a deed by the
   (A) habendum
   (B) consideration
   (C) description
   (D) acknowledgment

22. When a notary public or other qualified official attests to the signature on a deed or mortgage, it is called an
   (A) authorization
   (B) acknowledgment
   (C) execution
   (D) authentication

23. For which reason or reasons is a deed recorded?
   (A) To insure certain title
   (B) To give notice to the world
   (C) Because it is required by the state
   (D) To save title insurance cost

24. Ownership of property is transferred when
   (A) grantor signs the deed
   (B) the grantor's signature has been notarized
   (C) delivery of the deed is made
   (D) the correct documentary stamps are put on the deed and canceled

25. From the point of view of the grantee, the safest kind of deed that can be received is a
   (A) general warranty deed
   (B) special warranty deed
   (C) quitclaim or release deed
   (D) trustee's deed

26. Which of the following statement(s) is (are) true?
   (A) A quitclaim deed transfers whatever interest a grantee has in property.
   (B) A quitclaim deed carries a warranty of good title.
   (C) Both A and B
   (D) Neither A nor B

TRUE — FALSE. Mark *T* for true, *F* for false.

_____ 27. The warranty in a deed guarantees that the real estate will be in good condition for a certain length of time.

_____ 28. A warranty deed is the best kind of deed for a grantee to receive.

_____ 29. A quitclaim normally does not include a description of the specific rights granted to the grantee.

_____ 30. A deed must be in writing, and if it is to be recorded it must be acknowledged as well.

_____ 31. An executor's deed would contain a full and general warranty.

_____ 32. A deed must show consideration, though it is usually permissible to state a "nominal" amount, i.e., less than the true amount.

FILL-INS. Fill in the spaces with the appropriate words or phrases.

33. A deed that conveys only the interest of the grantor is a _____ .

34. The part of the deed that contains the warranties, if any, is called the _____
_____ .

35. The part of the warranty that guarantees that the property is free from encumbrances is the _____ .

ANSWERS

1.	A	10.	A	19.	C	28.	T
2.	D	11.	D	20.	B	29.	T
3.	C	12.	B	21.	C	30.	T
4.	A	13.	B	22.	B	31.	F
5.	A	14.	A	23.	B	32.	T
6.	C	15.	B	24.	C	33.	quitclaim
7.	C	16.	C	25.	A	34.	testimonium
8.	D	17.	A	26.	D	35.	covenant against
9.	D	18.	A	27.	F		encumbrances

Chapter 11 / *Leases and Property Management*

A lease is a contract that transfers possession of property in exchange for rent.

The real estate owner is known as the *landlord* or *lessor*; the user is the *tenant* or *lessee*. The landlord retains a *reversionary right*; that means that he retains the right to use the property upon expiration of the lease. The tenant holds a *leasehold estate*, that is, a personal property interest that gives the tenant the right to use the property for the lease term and under the conditions stipulated in the lease.

Types of Leasehold Estates

1. Estate for years
2. Estate from year to year
3. Tenancy at will
4. Tenancy at sufferance

An *estate for years* has a stated expiration date. The period included may be only one day or over fifty years. When the lease term ends, the tenant is to vacate the property.

An *estate from year to year* does not have a fixed expiration date. It is automatically renewed for another period (week, month, year) unless adequate notice for termination is given. One period of notice is generally adequate, though less than one year is acceptable in the case of a year-to-year lease.

A *tenancy at will* allows the tenant to remain with the consent of the landlord. At any time, either the tenant or the landlord may terminate the agreement. "Emblements" arise by operation of law to give tenants-at-will the right to harvest growing crops.

When a tenant holds property beyond the lease term and without the landlord's consent, he is a "holdover tenant." The form of estate is called *tenancy at sufferance*. A holdover tenancy has the fewest rights of any leasehold estate.

Requirements of a Valid Real Estate Contract

Since a lease is a contract for the use of real estate, it must meet all the requirements for a valid real estate contract. These requirements include:

1. Offer and acceptance
2. Competent parties
3. Consideration
4. Adequate description of the property
5. Written form

In most states, an oral lease for less than one year will be binding. Any provision that is legal can be included in a lease. Some common lease provisions are discussed.

SOME COMMON LEASE PROVISIONS

Rent. Rent may be payable in any form that the parties agree upon. Typically, rent is payable in money, but it may also be payable in crops, labor, etc. — whatever the landlord and tenant agree upon. *Straight* or *flat* leases are those calling for level amounts of rent. *Step-up* or *step-down, graduated,* or *reappraisal* leases are leases that provide for fluctuating rental amounts.

Percentage leases require the tenant to pay, as rent, a percentage of sales. Usually a basic rent is stipulated to guarantee a minimum amount. As an example, a lease may require that a retailer-tenant pay $10,000 rent annually, plus 2 percent of gross sales in excess of $500,000. Should sales be under $500,000, the rent is $10,000; for sales of $600,000, the rent would be $12,000; that is, $10,000 basic plus 2 percent of the $100,000 excess sales.

Operating Expenses. A lease that requires the landlord to pay operating expenses, such as utilities, repairs, insurance, and property taxes, is called a *gross lease*. The lessor considers the rent to be gross income and receives net operating income after he pays operating expenses out of his own pocket. A *net lease* is one that requires the tenant to pay operating expenses. The landlord receives the rent as a net return.

The terms *net* and *gross*, though often used, may be inadequate to describe a lease. *Hybrid, semi-net,* and *net-net* are terms used to describe the degree to which a party may be responsible for operating expenses. Careful reading of a lease by interested parties is necessary to avoid misunderstandings.

Escalation. *Escalation* or *step* provisions are found in long-term gross leases. Should certain operating expenses exceed a designated amount, the increase is passed on to the tenant.

Assignment and Subletting. Unless specifically prohibited in a lease, a tenant has the right to assign or sublet. In either case, the original lessee remains liable to fulfill the lease contract.

An *assignment* occurs when the tenant transfers all rights and obligations of the lease to a third party. The assignee (third party) receives all the rights and obligations that are stipulated in the lease.

Should the original tenant wish to keep a portion of the property for his own use or to rent the premises to a third party for a term shorter than his lease, he may sublet. Subletting involves a second lease; the original tenant becomes a lessor for part of the property or for the entire property for part of the lease term.

Sale of the Property. When leased property is sold, the lease survives the sale. The tenant is allowed to continue use under the lease terms.

Termination of a Lease. The normal termination of a lease is the result of *performance*. When landlord and tenant have both fulfilled their lease obligations, there is said to be performance.

Another method of terminating a lease is by *agreement*. Landlord and tenant may agree to terminate the lease before its stated expiration date. Compensation may be included in such an agreement.

A *breach* may also cause termination. When either party fails to perform under a lease, there is said to be a breach. While a breach can terminate a lease, it does not cancel all provisions. The violating party may be held liable for damages. When a tenant has breached a lease, the landlord's remedy is in court. Using a court order, a landlord may eject or *evict* a tenant.

A tenant who vacates property before the fixed expiration date of a lease is responsible for the remaining rent. If the property is eventually leased, the tenant owes only the difference in rent, plus expenses incurred in obtaining a substitute tenant. But vacating property fails to terminate a lease.

Lease provisions frequently encountered are described below. (Not all of the provisions will be found in every lease.)

Provision	*Purpose*
Premises	Describes the property being leased
Term	States the term of the lease

Provision	Purpose
Rent	Describes rental amount, date, and place payable
Construction of Building and Improvements	Describes improvements for proposed property or property to be renovated to suit tenant
Common Area	Describes maintenance of commonly used areas, such as those in shopping centers
Taxes	States who will pay ad valorem taxes and escalation amounts
Repairs	States which party is responsible for repairs and maintenance
Alterations	States responsibilities and rights of tenant to alter improvements
Liability Insurance	Designates party who is responsible to carry liability insurance and the extent
Other Insurance	Designates party who is responsible to carry hazard insurance and the extent
Damage by Fire and Casualty	Describes operation of lease in the event of a fire or other casualty
Payment for Utilities	States which party must pay charges for water, heat, gas, electricity, sewage disposal, and other utilities
Subordination	Describes rights between landlord and tenant in the event of mortgage foreclosure
Certificate of Lease Status	Obligates tenant to inform mortgage lender of occupancy and rent status
Condemnation and Eminent Domain	Describes operation of lease in the event of a taking or partial taking of the property
Compliance of Law	Requires landlord and tenant to comply with laws and ordinances
Access to Landlord	Allows landlord to inspect property
Mechanic's Liens	Describes the discharge of mechanic's liens
Assignment and Subletting	Limits the tenant's rights to assign or sublet
Nonliability of Landlord	Frees landlord from liability due to injury or damage within premises
Right to Cure Defaults	Allows landlord to cure tenant defaults and require reimbursement
Use	Permits tenant the use of property for specific purposes
Notices	Describes method to serve notice to a party
Definitions	Defines terms used in the lease
Partial Invalidity	Describes operation of lease when parts of lease are held to be invalid
Waiver of Redemption	Permits tenant to waive all rights upon lease expiration
Bankruptcy or Insolvency	Describes required notice and operation of lease in the event of bankruptcy
Default	Defines lease default
Surrender	Describes how tenant is to leave property upon expiration of the lease
Arbitration	Provides a method to settle disputes
Brokers	Notes whether a broker was involved in lease negotiation
Encumbrances	Describes rights and obligations of parties to deliver and return property (with respect to liens, easements, etc.)
Quiet Enjoyment	Agreement by landlord that tenant, while he performs, may have, hold, and enjoy property without interferences
Other Restrictions	May limit the leasing of space in a shopping center to a competitor

Provision	*Purpose*
Entire Agreement	States that the written lease is the entire agreement
Percentage Clause	Stipulates conditions affecting a percentage lease
Recapture Clause	Stipulates that in a percentage lease a lessor may terminate lease if lessee's revenues do not attain a specified level within a certain length of time

Property Management

Property Management is the business of seeking and negotiating with tenants for other people's real estate. It is a real estate brokerage function, and property managers in all states are required to hold real estate sales or brokerage licenses. (*Resident managers* of apartment buildings or projects are allowed by most states to function without a license, provided that they do not manage any other properties and are employed either by the property owner or a properly licensed property manager.)

Some brokers who claim to be "property managers" may do little more than find tenants for vacant properties, and collect payment for doing so. Actually, a *professional* property manager does a lot more. In fact, he is able to do everything associated with the proper management of a property and, thus, require the owner to do nothing at all. Property management functions include leasing, negotiating with potential tenants, advertising, developing leasing plans, arranging maintenance and repairs, paying all bills (out of rent receipts), etc. Of course, property managers are paid for their service. Normally, their payment is a commission on rent payments collected; however, they may instead (or also) receive a flat fee for their services.

Certain special kinds of lease arrangements often are found in managed properties. Retail property (shopping centers, etc.) often features *percentage leases*. In this type of lease, all or part of the tenant's rent is a percentage of the tenant's gross business revenues. The theory here is that a well-managed and popular shopping center will generate good business for tenants and, so, they are willing to pay part of it as rent. Also, the property manager is encouraged to promote and advertise the shopping center because by doing so he gets more people to come to it, spend more money and, thus, generate more rent.

Many percentage leases contain *recapture clauses*. These allow the property manager to void the lease if the tenant's business does not do at least a certain volume of business within a certain time. This guards against the management getting stuck with a poor tenant or one which does not do or draw much business.

Questions on Chapter 11

1. Which of the following statements is correct?
   (A) The tenant is known as the lessor.
   (B) The owner leasing property is the lessee.
   (C) The tenant is the lessee.
   (D) None of the above.

2. Under a net lease, who is liable for payment of insurance and repairs?
   (A) Lessor
   (B) Lessee
   (C) Sublessee
   (D) Both lessor and lessee

3. A gross lease requires the tenant to pay rent based on
   (A) gross sales
   (B) net sales
   (C) gross profit
   (D) none of the above

4. A percentage lease requires the tenant to pay
   (A) a percentage of taxes and insurance
   (B) a percentage of net income as rent
   (C) a percentage of sales as rent
   (D) none of the above

5. A tenant is delinquent in paying rent. The landlord should
   (A) call the sheriff to evict him
   (B) bring a court action
   (C) give thirty days' notice
   (D) turn off water, lights, etc.

6. A lease that requires the landlord to pay operating expenses of the property is called a(n)
   (A) gross lease
   (B) assigned lease
   (C) percentage lease
   (D) net lease

7. A lease for less than one year
   (A) may be oral
   (B) must be in writing
   (C) may be oral but must be reduced to writing within one year
   (D) is always invalid

8. When a tenant transfers the rights and obligations of an existing lease to another tenant, it is called
   (A) assignment of lease
   (B) a release
   (C) subletting
   (D) an eviction

9. A contract that transfers possession but not ownership of property is a(n)
   (A) special warranty deed
   (B) option
   (C) easement
   (D) lease

10. When an individual holds property past the expiration of a lease without the landlord's consent, the leasehold estate he has is a
   (A) tenancy at sufferance
   (B) freehold estate
   (C) common of pasturage
   (D) holdover tenant

11. A sublease is a
   (A) lease made by a lessor
   (B) lease made by a lessee and a third party
   (C) lease for basement space
   (D) condition of property

12. A landlord rents a store to a furniture retailer on a "percentage lease." On which of the following is the percentage usually based?
   (A) Market value
   (B) Sales price
   (C) Tenant's gross sales
   (D) Tenant's net income

13. Which of the following will not terminate a lease?
   (A) Performance
   (B) Breach
   (C) Surrender
   (D) Vacancy

14. When a leased property is sold, what effect does the sale have upon the tenant?
   (A) Tenant must record lease in recorder's office.
   (B) Tenant must obtain an assignment from the purchaser.
   (C) No effect.
   (D) Tenant must move out after reasonable notice.

15. A lease for more than one year *must* be in writing to be enforceable because
   (A) the landlord or tenant might forget the terms
   (B) the tenant must sign the agreement to pay rent
   (C) the Statute of Frauds requires it
   (D) the lease can then be assigned to another person

16. A lease can state the rent to be paid in
   (A) labor
   (B) crops
   (C) cash
   (D) any of the above

17. An estate at will is a(n)
   (A) limited partnership
   (B) tenancy of uncertain duration
   (C) inheritance by will
   (D) life tenancy

18. A reversionary interest
    (A) expires when a lease is signed
    (B) allows land to escheat at the termination of a lease
    (C) is a landlord's right to use of property upon expiration of a lease
    (D) constitutes a breach of a lease

19. A leasehold estate is
    (A) a large home built on leased land
    (B) a personal property interest in real estate
    (C) a landlord's interest in realty
    (D) none of the above

20. Escalation clauses in a lease provide for
    (A) term extensions
    (B) elevator and escalator maintenance
    (C) increased rentals because of higher operating expenses
    (D) purchase options

21. Which of the following statements is true?
    (A) Property managers are required to be licensed in all states.
    (B) Percentage leases are illegal in many states.
    (C) An unlicensed person may solicit tenants for several properties provided that he/she works for a licensed property manager.
    (D) Property managers do not negotiate leases.

22. Which of the following statements is true?
        I. Property management is a real estate brokerage function.
        II. Resident managers sometimes do not have to be licensed.
    (A) I only   (C) Both I and II
    (B) II only   (D) Neither I nor II

23. One who remains on leased property, without the landlord's consent after the expiration of a lease is
    (A) a tenant at will.   (C) a tenant in common.
    (B) a tenant *par duration*.   (D) a tenant at suffrance.

24. A lease which requires that all or part of the tenant's rent be based upon the tenant's revenues is
    (A) a lease at will.   (C) a percentage lease.
    (B) a flat lease.   (D) a gross lease.

TRUE — FALSE. Mark *T* for true, *F* for false.

_____ 25. The parties to a lease are the leasor and the leasee.

_____ 26. A tenancy at will may be terminated at any time by either tenant or landlord.

_____ 27. A lease that calls for a level amount of rent throughout the lease period is called a "straight" or "flat" lease.

_____ 28. A "net lease" is one that requires the tenant to pay operating expenses.

_____ 29. A lease of more than one year must be in writing to be enforceable.

_____ 30. Property managers normally do not handle repairs and maintenance of the properties that they manage.

_____ 31. Property management is a brokerage function, so property managers are required to hold real estate licenses.

FILL-INS. Fill in the blanks with the appropriate words or phrases.

32. A lease that requires the tenant to pay part of his business revenue taken in on the leased property as all or part of his rent is a _____ .

33. When a tenant leases all or part of his rented premises to a third party, this new lease is called a _____ .

34. A lease that requires the landlord to pay all operating expenses of the property is a _____ .

35. A lease in which the rent is automatically raised periodically during the lease period is a _____ .

36. A lease that has no fixed expiration date (is automatically renewed at the end of each lease period unless notice is given) is an estate _____ .

37. A _____ is one who solicits tenants, negotiates leases, arranges maintenance and repair, etc. of other peoples' real estate.

ANSWERS

1.	C	11.	B	20.	C	29.	T
2.	B	12.	C	21.	A	30.	F
3.	D	13.	D	22.	C	31.	T
4.	C	14.	C	23.	D	32.	percentage lease
5.	B	15.	C	24.	C	33.	sublease
6.	A	16.	D	25.	F	34.	gross lease
7.	A	17.	B	26.	T	35.	step or graduated lease
8.	A	18.	C	27.	T	36.	from year to year
9.	D	19.	B	28.	T	37.	property manager
10.	A						

Chapter 12/*Listings*

A *listing* is a contract of employment between a principal (property owner) and an agent (broker) to sell or lease real estate. Under the terms of the listing contract, the principal agrees to pay the broker a commission when he locates a party who is ready, willing, and able to buy or lease the listed property at its list price. Should an offer be tendered for less than the list price, the broker is entitled to a commission only if the transaction is consummated.

Normally, the seller pays the commission at closing. It is possible for a buyer to agree to pay a commission in lieu of the seller or in addition to the seller, so long as all parties are aware of the circumstances.

Types of Listings

Listings can be categorized into five broad types as follows:
1. Open listings
2. Exclusive agency listings
3. Exclusive right to sell listings
4. Net listings
5. Multiple listings

Each type is described.

1. OPEN LISTINGS

Using an open listing, the principal offers the broker a commission provided that he secures a purchaser. The owner reserves the right to list the property with other brokers or to sell the property himself. Thus, the open listing is open to other real estate brokers. All open listings are automatically canceled upon a sale of the property, so that the seller pays no more than one commission.

2. EXCLUSIVE AGENCY LISTINGS

An exclusive agency listing is one whereby a broker is employed to the exclusion of all other brokers. The owner retains the right to sell the property himself without paying a commission. However, if the property is sold by a broker other than the listing broker, the listing broker is still entitled to a commission.

3. EXCLUSIVE RIGHT TO SELL LISTINGS

The exclusive right to sell listing allows the employed broker to collect a commission upon the sale, no matter who sells the property. Whether the employed broker, another broker, or the owner procures a purchaser, a broker with an exclusive right to sell gains his fee upon the sale.

At first, such a contract may seem to be to a seller's disadvantage. Even if the seller procures a buyer on his own, or another broker finds one, the listing broker earns a commission. But this rigid arrangement gives the listing broker comfort that the property is available for sale by him only. Brokers employed by other types of listings may be dismayed to learn that property has been sold by the owner or another broker. This will not occur under an exclusive right to sell, so the employed broker has more incentive to devote his efforts and spend money to promote the sale of the listed property. In recognition of this, most real estate boards emphasize the exclusive right to sell listing, particularly for single-family dwellings.

4. NET LISTINGS

A net listing is one in which the property owner fixes the amount that he wishes to receive from a sale. He informs the broker, for example, that he wants a $40,000 check from the sale. The broker may keep any amount as a commission so long as the seller "nets" $40,000. Thus, if the sale price is $40,001, the commission is $1; a sale at $43,726 yields a $3726 commission.

Many organizations frown on net listings and suggest that, when offered a net listing, the broker add his customary charge to the net amount and then inform the seller of the resulting list price. For example, a 6 percent commission rate added to a $40,000 net figure results in a $42,553.19 offering price. Six percent of $42,553.19 is $2,553.19, leaving $40,000 for the seller. The arithmetic works as follows:

$$\frac{\text{Net amount to seller}}{\text{Fraction of sales price to seller*}} = \text{List price with commission}$$
$$(\text{*100\% less commission})$$

Using the $40,000 net figure and the 6 percent rate of commission, the list price becomes:
$$\frac{\$40,000}{.94} = \$42,553.19$$

5. MULTIPLE LISTINGS

Some brokers, in a given geographical area, may agree to pool all of their listings. They form a Multiple Listing Association to coordinate activities. Through that association, brokers agree to share their exclusive right to sell listings. Then, any cooperating broker may sell property that another has listed. Upon the sale of multiple-listed property, the commission is split between the listing and the selling broker in accordance with the agreement established by the multiple listing association, and a small fraction of the commission is paid to the association to cover their expenses of operation. Expenses include the periodic publication, in writing and/or by computer, of the features of all listed property of those belonging to that multiple listing association.

Selecting a Form

No special form is required for a listing. However, it is important to read the form used, to gain an understanding of the type of listing. An example of a listing contract form is shown at the end of this chapter.

Agency Law

A broker is an agent for his principal. The broker's duties, obligations, and responsibilities to his principal are covered by the Law of Agency. Chapter 4 of this book adequately describes this body of law as it pertains to real estate brokerage.

Rate of Commission

As a matter of law, commission rates for the sale of real estate are negotiable between the principal and his broker. The rate or amount should be specified in the listing contract to avoid misunderstandings.

Listing Period

Contracts for the listing of real estate should have a fixed expiration date. Most provide 60 to 120 days for the sale of single-family homes and up to six months for commercial property and apartment complexes. The law does not establish limits, so the actual period agreed upon is a matter of negotiation.

Occasionally, after having been shown a particular piece of property through a broker, a prospect and the property owner may arrange a sale "behind the broker's back." Together they wait for the listing to expire, then contract for the sale without advising the broker, in an attempt to elude the payment of a commission. Despite the fact that the listing has expired, courts are likely to require payment to a licensed broker whose listing expired, if he can show that he was the procuring cause of the sale.

Termination of Listings

Listing agreements may be terminated either by the parties or by operation of law. Methods to terminate a listing are —

Termination by the parties:

1. *Performance.* The broker procures a purchaser; the listing contract is terminated when the sale is completed.
2. *Mutual consent.* Both parties agree to terminate the listing.
3. *Expiration of agreed time.* Listings generally have a definite expiration date. If they don't, the listing ends after a reasonable period. In many states listings must have a fixed expiration date.
4. *Revocation by the principal.* At any time, the principal may revoke authority given to the broker. However, he may be liable for damages resulting from the breach of contract, but not if he can show the agent to have been negligent in his duties, as by disloyalty, dishonesty, or incompetence.
5. *Revocation by the broker.* An agent may terminate the listing contract or abandon it. However, he may be held liable for damages to the principal because of failure to complete the object of the listing contract.

Termination by law:

1. *Death of either party.* The death of either the principal or the broker generally causes termination of a listing contract.
2. *Bankruptcy of either party.* Bankruptcy of a principal or an agent would normally terminate an agency.
3. *Insanity of either party.* If either party were judged to be insane, he is considered incapable of completing the contract; therefore, the listing contract would terminate.
4. *Destruction of the property.* If the property upon which the agency had been created was destroyed, the agency is terminated.

Questions on Chapter 12

1. When more than one broker is employed by an owner to sell real estate, there exists a(n)
   (A) exclusive agency listing
   (B) open listing
   (C) exclusive right to sell
   (D) unilateral listing

2. To collect a commission in court, a broker must
   (A) show he is licensed
   (B) show he had a contract of employment
   (C) show he is the cause of the sale
   (D) all of the above

3. The broker's responsibility to the owner of realty is regulated by
   (A) the law of agency
   (B) the law of equity
   (C) rendition superior
   (D) investiture

4. What is a real estate listing?
   (A) A list of brokers and salespersons
   (B) A list of property held by an owner
   (C) The employment of a broker by an owner to sell or lease
   (D) A written list of improvements on land

5. Under an open listing
   (A) the seller is not legally required to notify other agents in the case of sale by one of the listing brokers
   (B) the owner may sell the property without paying a commission
   (C) both A and B
   (D) neither A nor B

6. If the listing owner sells his property when the listing agreement is valid, he is liable for a commission under a(n) _____ listing agreement.
   (A) net
   (B) exclusive right to sell
   (C) exclusive agency listing
   (D) open

7. Under an exclusive agency listing,
   (A) the seller may sell of his own efforts without obligation for a commission
   (B) the broker receives a commission regardless of whether the property is sold
   (C) both A and B
   (D) neither A nor B

8. The listing agreement may not be terminated
   (A) without compensation if the broker has found a prospect ready, able, and willing to buy on the seller's terms
   (B) because of incompetence of the prospect
   (C) if the seller files for bankruptcy
   (D) if the listing agreement is for a definite time

9. The multiple listing
   (A) is illegal in certain states
   (B) is a service organized by a group of brokers
   (C) requires that members turn over eligible listings within 12 days
   (D) causes lost commission

10. Under _____, brokers are reluctant actively to pursue a sale, because of the risk of losing a sale to competing brokers.
    (A) an exclusive right to sell listing
    (B) a net listing
    (C) an open listing
    (D) a multiple listing

11. Principals may sell their property without paying a commission under
    (A) an open listing
    (B) an exclusive agency listing
    (C) both A and B
    (D) neither A nor B

12. The rate of commission is normally fixed under
    (A) a net listing
    (B) an open listing
    (C) both A and B
    (D) neither A nor B

13. Buyer and seller both may pay a commission so long as
    (A) all parties are aware of the situation
    (B) payments are to the same broker
    (C) both A and B
    (D) neither A nor B

14. It is possible to terminate a listing by
    (A) revocation by the principal   (C) both A and B
    (B) revocation by the agent   (D) neither A nor B

15. An exclusive right to sell listing enables
    (A) the seller to sell the property himself without paying a commission
    (B) cooperating brokers to sell and earn a commission
    (C) both A and B
    (D) neither A nor B

TRUE — FALSE.   Mark *T* for true, *F* for false.

_____ 16. Real estate associations strongly suggest that members secure net listings.

_____ 17. A listing agreement may be terminated by agreement of the parties.

_____ 18. A listing agreement is terminated when the subject property is destroyed by fire.

_____ 19. The rate of commission is set by the National Association of REALTORS®.

_____ 20. If no expiration date is written in a listing contract, then the contract is forever binding.

FILL-INS.   Fill in the blanks with the appropriate words or phrases.

21. A listing whereby the owner reserves the right to give other brokers the same listing is a(n) _____ listing.

22. When brokers in a given area form an organization for the purpose of cooperating and sharing listings there is a(n) _____ listing organization.

23. How much is the commission on a $35,000 sale at a 6% commission rate? _____

24. Listings may be terminated by operation of law and by _____ .

25. The listed price is $40,000. The broker presents a bona fide offer for $39,500. The broker is/is not (choose one) entitled to a commission even if the seller refuses to accept.

ANSWERS

1.	B	8.	A	14.	C	20.	F
2.	D	9.	B	15.	D	21.	open
3.	A	10.	C	16.	F	22.	multiple
4.	C	11.	C	17.	T	23.	$2100
5.	C	12.	B	18.	T	24.	the parties
6.	B	13.	A	19.	F	25.	is not
7.	A						

Completing Listing Contracts

In some states, salespersons and/or broker examinees are required to complete a listing contract from information that is provided in narrative form. Then, examinees must answer questions using the listing that they have completed as the only source of information.

The listing form used for examinations is self-explanatory. In filling out the blank listing, an examinee should make certain that all of the relevant information is used. The examinee must not add anything that is not given as information. From the narrative description below, fill out the listing form given; then answer the questions that follow it.

LISTING CONTRACT NARRATIVE

You are a sales person for Able Realty. On May 10, 1988, you list a ten-year-old house owned by Mr. & Mrs. Nebulous under an exclusive right to sell listing for three months. The property is a one-story brick house with four bedrooms and two baths. It has a full basement, which measures 35 ft. × 40 ft. The lot measures 120 ft. × 70 ft.; it is fenced. It is described as Lot 9, Block F, of the Lake Alpine Subdivision, Banks County, Maryland. It is also known as 1314 Geneva Drive, Hometown, Maryland.

The house has central air conditioning and an entrance foyer. The living room measures 15 ft. × 12 ft. Bedrooms are about average size for this type of house, in your opinion. It has an eat-in kitchen with a built-in oven and range. The owners state that the dishwasher and refrigerator will remain, but they plan to take the clothes washer and dryer.

The house is heated by natural gas. Water is heated the same way. Water is supplied by the county. The house is on a sewer line.

Bunn is the elementary school; Gunter, the junior high; Washington, the high school.

The tax rate is 60 mills; the latest tax appraisal is $35,000; the assessment ratio is 40 percent.

You list the house for $39,500. The commission rate is 6 percent. There is an existing, assumable 7¾% mortgage on the property. The current balance is $29,700, with equal monthly payments of $230.87. The owners will accept a second mortgage for up to $2500 at an 8 percent interest rate for seven years.

Prepare the listing contract. Then, put aside the narrative and, using the listing contract you have prepared, answer the questions that follow.

Questions on Listing Contract Narrative

1. Which of the following is correct?
   (A) The washer and dryer remain.
   (B) The refrigerator remains.
   (C) Both A and B
   (D) Neither A nor B

2. The listing expires on
   (A) May 10, 1983
   (B) July 10, 1983
   (C) July 9, 1983
   (D) none of the above

3. Which of the following is correct?
   (A) Natural gas heats the house.
   (B) The house is on a sewer line.
   (C) Both A and B
   (D) Neither A nor B

4. Taxes for the year are
   (A) $210
   (B) $840
   (C) $2100
   (D) none of the above

5. If sold at the listed price, the commission would be
   (A) $1782
   (B) $2160
   (C) $2370
   (D) none of the above

EXCLUSIVE AUTHORIZATION TO SELL

SALES PRICE: _____ TYPE HOME _____ TOTAL BEDROOMS _____ TOTAL BATHS _____

ADDRESS: _____ JURISDICTION OF _____

AMT. OF LOAN TO BE ASSUMED $ _____ AS OF WHAT DATE: _____ TAXES & INS. INCLUDED: _____ YEARS TO GO _____ AMOUNT PAYABLE MONTHLY $ _____ @ ___ % TYPE LOAN _____

MORTGAGE COMPANY _____ 2nd TRUST $ _____

ESTIMATED EXPECTED RENT MONTHLY $ _____ TYPE OF APPRAISAL REQUESTED: _____

OWNER'S NAME _____ PHONES: (HOME) _____ (BUSINESS) _____

TENANTS NAME _____ PHONES: (HOME) _____ (BUSINESS) _____

POSSESSION _____ DATE LISTED: _____ EXCLUSIVE FOR _____ DATE OF EXPIRATION _____

LISTING BROKER _____ PHONE _____ KEY AVAILABLE AT _____

LISTING SALESMAN _____ HOME PHONE: _____ HOW TO BE SHOWN: _____

(1) ENTRANCE FOYER ☐ CENTER HALL ☐	(18) AGE	AIR CONDITIONING ☐	(32) TYPE KITCHEN CABINETS
(2) LIVING ROOM SIZE FIREPLACE ☐	(19) ROOFING	TOOL HOUSE ☐	(33) TYPE COUNTER TOPS
(3) DINING ROOM SIZE	(20) GARAGE SIZE	PATIO ☐	(34) EAT-IN SIZE KITCHEN ☐
(4) BEDROOM TOTAL: DOWN UP	(21) SIDE DRIVE ☐	CIRCULAR DRIVE ☐	(35) BREAKFAST ROOM ☐
(5) BATHS TOTAL: DOWN UP	(22) PORCH ☐ SIDE ☐ REAR ☐	SCREENED ☐	(36) BUILT-IN OVEN & RANGE ☐
(6) DEN SIZE FIREPLACE ☐	(23) FENCED YARD	OUTDOOR GRILL ☐	(37) SEPARATE STOVE INCLUDED ☐
(7) FAMILY ROOM SIZE FIREPLACE ☐	(24) STORM WINDOWS ☐	STORM DOORS ☐	(38) REFRIGERATOR INCLUDED ☐
(8) RECREATION ROOM SIZE FIREPLACE ☐	(25) CURBS & GUTTERS ☐	SIDEWALKS ☐	(39) DISHWASHER INCLUDED
(9) BASEMENT SIZE	(26) STORM SEWERS ☐	ALLEY ☐	(40) DISPOSAL INCLUDED ☐
NONE ☐ 1/4 ☐ 1/3 ☐ 1/2 ☐ 3/4 ☐ FULL ☐	(27) WATER SUPPLY		(41) DOUBLE SINK ☐ SINGLE SINK ☐
(10) UTILITY ROOM SIZE	(28) SEWER ☐	SEPTIC ☐	STAINLESS STEEL ☐ PORCELAIN ☐
TYPE HOT WATER SYSTEM:	(29) TYPE GAS: NATURAL ☐	BOTTLED ☐	(42) WASHER INCLUDED ☐ DRYER INCLUDED ☐
(11) TYPE HEAT	(30) WHY SELLING		(43) PANTRY ☐ EXHAUST FAN ☐
(12) EST. FUEL COST			(44) LAND ASSESSMENT $
(13) ATTIC ☐	(31) DIRECTIONS TO PROPERTY		(45) IMPROVEMENTS $
PULL DOWN STAIRWAY ☐ REGULAR STAIRWAY ☐ TRAP DOOR ☐			(46) TOTAL ASSESSMENT $
(14) MAIDS ROOM ☐ TYPE BATH			(47) TAX RATE
LOCATION			(48) TOTAL ANNUAL TAXES $
(15) NAME OF BUILDER			(49) LOT SIZE
(16) SQUARE FOOTAGE			(50) LOT NO. BLOCK SECTION
(17) EXTERIOR OF HOUSE			

NAME OF SCHOOLS: ELEMENTARY: _____ JR. HIGH: _____

HIGH _____ PAROCHIAL: _____

PUBLIC TRANSPORTATION: _____

NEAREST SHOPPING AREA: _____

REMARKS: _____

Date: _____

In consideration of the services of _____ (herein called "Broker") to be rendered to the undersigned (herein called "Owner"), and of the promise of Broker to make reasonable efforts to obtain a Purchaser therefor, Owner hereby lists with Broker the real estate and all improvements thereon which are described above (all herein called "the property"), and Owner hereby grants to Broker the exclusive and irrevocable right to sell such property from 12:00 Noon on _____ , 19_____ until 12:00 Midnight on _____ , 19____ (herein called "period of time"), for the price of _____ Dollars ($ _____) or for such other price and upon such other terms (including exchange) as Owner may subsequently authorize during the period of time.

It is understood by Owner that the above sum or any other price subsequently authorized by Owner shall include a cash fee of _____ per cent of such price or other price which shall be payable by Owner to Broker upon consummation by any Purchaser or Purchasers of a valid contract of sale of the property during the period of time and whether or not Broker was a procuring cause of any such contract of sale.

If the property is sold or exchanged by Owner, or by Broker or by any other person to any Purchaser to whom the property was shown by Broker or any representative of Broker within sixty (60) days after the expiration of the period of time mentioned above, Owner agrees to pay to Broker a cash fee which shall be the same percentage of the purchase price as the percentage mentioned above.

Broker is hereby authorized by Owner to place a "For Sale" sign on the property and to remove all signs of other brokers or salesmen during the period of time, and Owner hereby agrees to make the property available to Broker at all reasonable hours for the purpose of showing it to prospective Purchasers.

Owner agrees to convey the property to the Purchaser by warranty deed with the usual covenants of title and free and clear from all encumbrances, tenancies, liens (for taxes or otherwise), but subject to applicable restrictive covenants of record. Owner acknowledges receipt of a copy of this agreement.

WITNESS the following signature(s) and seal(s):

Date Signed: _____ _____ (SEAL)
(Owner)

Listing Broker _____

Address _____ Telephone _____ _____ (SEAL)
(Owner)

_____

6. The balance on the existing mortgage is
   (A) $29,700
   (B) $35,000
   (C) $2500
   (D) $39,500

7. Which of the following is correct concerning schools?
   (A) Gunter — junior high
   (B) Bunn — high
   (C) Washington — elementary
   (D) None of the above

8. Which features does the house have?
   (A) Central air conditioning
   (B) A fireplace
   (C) Both A and B
   (D) Neither A nor B

9. The basement measurements are
   (A) 30 ft. × 40 ft.
   (B) 40 ft. × 40 ft.
   (C) 35 ft. × 40 ft.
   (D) none of the above

10. The lot is in Block _____ of the Lake Alpine Subdivision.
    (A) A
    (B) B
    (C) C
    (D) None of the above

11. Which of the following is correct?
    (A) There is an eat-in kitchen.
    (B) The dining room is 15 ft. × 12 ft.
    (C) Both A and B
    (D) Neither A nor B

12. The listing is for a period of
    (A) 90 days
    (B) three months
    (C) both A and B
    (D) neither A nor B

13. The house has
    (A) four bedrooms
    (B) a wood exterior
    (C) both A and B
    (D) neither A nor B

ANSWERS

1. B	5. C	8. A	11. A
2. D	6. A	9. C	12. B
3. C	7. A	10. D	13. A
4. B			

The properly filled-out contract follows:

EXCLUSIVE AUTHORIZATION TO SELL

SALES PRICE: $39,500   TYPE HOME One-story   TOTAL BEDROOMS 4   TOTAL BATHS 2

ADDRESS: 1314 Geneva Drive   JURISDICTION OF: Hometown, Banks County, Md.

AMT. OF LOAN TO BE ASSUMED $ 29,700   AS OF WHAT DATE: 5/10/83   TAXES & INS. INCLUDED: no   YEARS TO GO   AMOUNT PAYABLE MONTHLY $ 230.87 @ 7¼ %   TYPE LOAN

MORTGAGE COMPANY

ESTIMATED EXPECTED RENT MONTHLY $ 2nd TRUST $ TYPE OF APPRAISAL REQUESTED

OWNER'S NAME Mr. & Mrs. Nebulous   PHONES: (HOME)   (BUSINESS)

TENANTS NAME   PHONES: (HOME)   (BUSINESS)

POSSESSION   DATE LISTED: 5/10/83   EXCLUSIVE FOR 3 months   DATE OF EXPIRATION 8/10/83

LISTING BROKER Able Realty   PHONE   KEY AVAILABLE AT

LISTING SALESMAN You   HOME PHONE: HOW TO BE SHOWN

(1) ENTRANCE FOYER X CENTER HALL ☐	(18) AGE 6 Cent. AIR CONDITIONING X	(32) TYPE KITCHEN CABINETS
(2) LIVING ROOM SIZE 15'x12' FIREPLACE ☐	(19) ROOFING TOOL HOUSE ☐	(33) TYPE COUNTER TOPS
(3) DINING ROOM SIZE	(20) GARAGE SIZE PATIO ☐	(34) EAT-IN SIZE KITCHEN X
(4) BEDROOM TOTAL: 4 DOWN UP	(21) SIDE DRIVE ☐ CIRCULAR DRIVE ☐	(35) BREAKFAST ROOM ☐
(5) BATHS TOTAL: 2 DOWN UP	(22) PORCH ☐ SIDE ☐ REAR ☐ SCREENED ☐	(36) BUILT-IN OVEN & RANGE X
(6) DEN SIZE FIREPLACE ☐	(23) FENCED YARD yes OUTDOOR GRILL ☐	(37) SEPARATE STOVE INCLUDED ☐
(7) FAMILY ROOM SIZE FIREPLACE ☐	(24) STORM WINDOWS ☐ STORM DOORS ☐	(38) REFRIGERATOR INCLUDED X
(8) RECREATION ROOM SIZE FIREPLACE ☐	(25) CURBS & GUTTERS ☐ SIDEWALKS ☐	(39) DISHWASHER INCLUDED X
(9) BASEMENT SIZE 35'x40'	(26) STORM SEWERS ☐ ALLEY ☐	(40) DISPOSAL INCLUDED ☐
NONE ☐ 1/4 ☐ 1/3 ☐ 1/2 ☐ 3/4 ☐ FULL X	(27) WATER SUPPLY County	(41) DOUBLE SINK ☐ SINGLE SINK ☐
(10) UTILITY ROOM SIZE	(28) SEWER X SEPTIC ☐	STAINLESS STEEL ☐ PORCELAIN ☐
TYPE HOT WATER SYSTEM: Nat'l. Gas	(29) TYPE GAS: NATURAL X BOTTLED ☐	(42) WASHER INCLUDED no DRYER INCLUDED no
(11) TYPE HEAT Natural Gas	(30) WHY SELLING	(43) PANTRY ☐ EXHAUST FAN ☐
(12) EST. FUEL COST		(44) LAND ASSESSMENT $
(13) ATTIC ☐	(31) DIRECTIONS TO PROPERTY	(45) IMPROVEMENTS $
PULL DOWN STAIRWAY ☐ REGULAR STAIRWAY ☐ TRAP DOOR ☐		(46) TOTAL ASSESSMENT $ 35,000x40%
(14) MAIDS ROOM ☐ TYPE BATH		(47) TAX RATE 60 mills
LOCATION		(48) TOTAL ANNUAL TAXES $
(15) NAME OF BUILDER		(49) LOT SIZE 120'x70'
(16) SQUARE FOOTAGE		(50) LOT NO. 9 BLOCK F SECTION
(17) EXTERIOR OF HOUSE Brick		Lake Alpine Subdivision

NAME OF SCHOOLS: ELEMENTARY: Bunn   JR. HIGH Gunter

HIGH Washington   PAROCHIAL

PUBLIC TRANSPORTATION:

NEAREST SHOPPING AREA:

REMARKS: Seller will accept 2nd Mtg. for up to $2500 at 8% interest rate for 7 years.

Date: May 10, 1983

In consideration of the services of Able Realty (herein called "Broker") to be rendered to the undersigned (herein called "Owner"), and of the promise of Broker to make reasonable efforts to obtain a Purchaser therefor, Owner hereby lists with Broker the real estate and all improvements thereon which are described above (all herein called "the property"), and Owner hereby grants to Broker the exclusive and irrevocable right to sell such property from 12:00 Noon on May 10, 19 83 until 12:00 Midnight on Aug. 9, 19 83 (herein called "period of time"), for the price of Thirty-nine Thousand Five Hundred———— Dollars ($ 39,500.———) or for such other price and upon such other terms (including exchange) as Owner may subsequently authorize during the period of time.

It is understood by Owner that the above sum or any other price subsequently authorized by Owner shall include a cash fee of 6% per cent of such price or other price which shall be payable by Owner to Broker upon consummation by any Purchaser or Purchasers of a valid contract of sale of the property during the period of time and whether or not Broker was a procuring cause of any such contract of sale.

If the property is sold or exchanged by Owner, or by Broker or by any other person to any Purchaser to whom the property was shown by Broker or any representative of Broker within sixty (60) days after the expiration of the period of time mentioned above, Owner agrees to pay to Broker a cash fee which shall be the same percentage of the purchase price as the percentage mentioned above.

Broker is hereby authorized by Owner to place a "For Sale" sign on the property and to remove all signs of other brokers or salesmen during the period of time, and Owner hereby agrees to make the property available to Broker at all reasonable hours for the purpose of showing it to prospective Purchasers.

Owner agrees to convey the property to the Purchaser by warranty deed with the usual covenants of title and free and clear from all encumbrances, tenancies, liens (for taxes or otherwise), but subject to applicable restrictive covenants of record. Owner acknowledges receipt of a copy of this agreement.

WITNESS the following signature(s) and seal(s):

Date Signed: _____   _____ (SEAL) (Owner)

Listing Broker _____

Address _____ Telephone _____   _____ (SEAL) (Owner)

Chapter 13/*Other Real Estate Contracts*

People dealing in real estate may want to accomplish transactions that do not fall within the categories of contracts discussed in chapters 9 through 12. Contracts not included in those categories are:

1. Contracts for the exchange of real estate
2. Contracts for deed
3. Options
4. Assignments
5. Novations

Each of these contracts is discussed below.

Contracts for Exchange

This type of contract is used when principals are to exchange property. If both properties are of equal value and both unencumbered, they may be swapped without additional consideration. This may be beneficial to the principals. For example: one person may own land and want income-producing property, whereas the other party may have reverse holdings and needs. A swap accomplishes the objectives of both parties. Further, if it is an even swap of real estate used in trade or business or held as an investment, and no additional consideration is given, the transaction might be tax-free for both parties, even though the properties exchanged for are worth much more than the original cost of the property traded away.

More often than not, properties exchanged are of different values. The party who gives up the lower-valued property must also give other consideration so that the trade becomes a fair one, thus acceptable to both parties. Personal property (cash, autos, diamonds, etc.) put into an exchange to equalize the value of all property exchanged is called "boot." The party who receives "boot" may be taxed to the extent of the unlike property received, or, if less, to the gain realized.

Mortgaged property can be exchanged. For example: suppose Mr. Jones owns a $10,000 vacant lot free and clear; Mr. Smith owns a $50,000 building with a $40,000 mortgage against it. Since the equity of both is $10,000, the exchange would be a fair trade. Smith's "boot" received is relief from a $40,000 debt.

Two-way exchanges may be more or less difficult to accomplish than three-way trades, or trades involving four parties. There is no limit to the number of parties involved in an exchange.

Contracts for Deed

A contract for deed is one in which the property seller finances the sale but does not surrender the deed until all payments have been made. This type of contract typically allows the purchaser to gain possession, but not ownership, of the land while paying for it. Since the seller does not give up a deed until the final payment, he is well protected in the event of default. He does not have to go through foreclosure because the land is still legally his.

A contract for deed is also known as a "land contract" and "installment land sale contract." It is frequently used for the sale of subdivided land, especially in resort communities.

Options

An option gives its holder the right, but *not* the obligation, to buy specific property within a certain time at a specified price. The option need not be exercised. An *optionee* can elect not to purchase the property, in which case amounts paid to acquire the option belong to the property owner, who is the *optionor*.

Consideration must be paid with an option. Upon exercise of the option, the amount paid for the option may or may not apply to the sales price, depending upon the agreement.

An option may be used by a speculator who is uncertain whether a significant increase in the value of the property is forthcoming. Through purchasing an option, he can be assured of a fixed price for the property in a set time span. If the value increase materializes, he exercises the option. Otherwise, he lets it lapse and loses only the cost of the option. The holder of an option may sell the option itself (at a gain or a loss) if he wishes to do so.

Assignments

Assignments refer to the transfer of contracts. Through an assignment, one may convey to someone else one's rights under a contract. A lease may be assigned, as may a contract of sale, a deed, an option, etc. The one who gives or assigns the contract is the assignor; the receiver, the assignee. It should be noted that the assignor is not automatically relieved of his duties to other parties under the earlier contract. If a lease contract exists and is assigned, for example, the original lessee is still bound to pay rent if the assignee fails to do so.

Novations

A novation is a contract used to substitute a new contract for an existing contract between the same parties. It may also be used to substitute or replace one party to a contract with a different party. Thus, a novation is used to amend an agreement or substitute parties involved.

It should be remembered that a novation must be bilateral: both parties must agree to it. For example, suppose a home is to be sold, with the buyer assuming the seller's mortgage. Since the seller made a contract to repay the debt, he cannot automatically substitute the new buyer for himself on the debt. Acceptance of the substitution must come from the lender. The process used for this substitution is called a novation. In such a case, the original contract has been assigned, while at the same time the assignor has been relieved of his obligations to other parties to the contract.

Questions on Chapter 13

1. Property that is unlike real estate used to equalize the value of all property exchanged is called
   (A) listing
   (B) gain
   (C) boot
   (D) equalizers

2. Mr. Hill has a six-month option on ten acres at $1000 per acre. Mr. Hill may
   (A) buy the property for $10,000
   (B) sell the option to another
   (C) not buy the land
   (D) all of the above

3. A contract that gives someone the right but not the obligation to buy at a specified price within a specified time is a(n)
   (A) contract for sale
   (B) option
   (C) agreement of sale
   (D) none of the above

4. A contract for deed is also known as a(n)
   I. installment land sales contract
   II. land contract
   (A) I only
   (B) II only
   (C) I and II
   (D) Neither I nor II

5. Which of the following best describes an installment or land contract?
   (A) A contract to buy land only
   (B) A mortgage on land
   (C) A means of conveying title immediately, while the purchaser pays for the property
   (D) A method of selling real estate whereby the purchaser pays for the property in regular installments, while the seller retains title to the property

6. Mr. Beans owns land worth $5000; Mr. Pork owns a house worth $30,000, subject to a $20,000 mortgage that Beans will assume. For a fair trade,
   (A) Pork should pay $5000 cash in addition
   (B) Beans should pay $5000 cash in addition
   (C) they may trade properties evenly
   (D) none of the above

7. A method used by a speculator to tie up land awaiting value enhancement but without obligating himself is through
   (A) installment land contract
   (B) option
   (C) contract for deed
   (D) A and C only

8. Mr. Smith wants to buy Jones's house and assume the 6 percent mortgage. Jones should
   (A) assign the debt
   (B) grant an option on the debt
   (C) ask the lender for a novation to substitute Smith
   (D) none of the above

9. Larry assigned his rights to use leased property to Allen. Allen stopped paying rent. Larry may
   (A) sue Allen for the rent
   (B) not pay the property owner since he hasn't received payment from Allen
   (C) both A and B
   (D) neither A nor B

10. Treasure Homes sold a lot to Mr. Kay under an installment land sales contract. Upon making the down payment, Mr. Kay is entitled to
    I. a warranty deed
    II. use the property
    (A) I only
    (B) II only
    (C) I and II
    (D) Neither I nor II

TRUE — FALSE. Mark *T* for true, *F* for false.

_____ 11. A contract for the exchange of real estate may have no more than two parties.

_____ 12. Every option must have consideration.

_____ 13. To completely free yourself of a debt, merely assign that debt to another.

_____ 14. The object of a novation is to effect a substitution of an item in a contract.

_____ 15. It is possible to exchange real estate for real estate without paying a capital gains tax on the gain.

FILL-INS. Fill in the blanks with the appropriate words or phrases.

16. Upon the final payment of a contract for deed, the buyer should receive a _____ _____ .

17. With an option goes the right but not the _____ to buy.

18. The best way to free oneself of an obligation is to obtain a _____ from the lender.

19. Rights to use leased property may be transferred through a(n) _____ _____ .

20. When mortgaged real estate is being exchanged and mortgages will be assumed by new owners, the _____ for both properties should be evaluated to determined whether the exchange is a fair trade.

ANSWERS

1. C	6. B	11. F	16. deed
2. D	7. B	12. T	17. obligation
3. B	8. C	13. F	18. novation
4. C	9. A	14. T	19. assignment
5. D	10. B	15. T	20. equities

Chapter 14/Mortgages and Finance

Most real estate professionals learn very early in their careers that borrowed money is the very lifeblood of the real estate business, because nearly all real estate purchases are made with borrowed funds. In addition, most real estate development and construction uses borrowed money. Without access to such funds, these aspects of the real estate business dry up quickly; this has happened several times in the past, during periods of "tight" money, when interest rates were high and loanable funds were scarce.

There are several reasons for this dependence on borrowed money in the real estate business. Perhaps the most significant reason is that real estate is *expensive*. Even a modest home costs tens of thousands of dollars; apartment projects, office buildings, shopping complexes, and the like often cost in the millions. Very few of the better than 60 percent of American families that own their own homes could do so if they had not been able to borrow a significant portion of the price at the time of purchase. Quite simply, very few families have the kind of ready cash necessary to buy a home without borrowing. Similarly, very few real estate developers or builders have enough cash on hand to finance completely the ventures they engage in.

Another reason that contributes to the importance of borrowed money in the real estate business is that real estate is *very good collateral* for loans. It lasts a long time and so can be used to back up loans that have very long repayment terms (such as the twenty to thirty years typical of most home mortgage loans). This enables real estate owners to spread the cost of the asset over a long payment term, and so makes it possible for them to afford more expensive units, as well as to spread the payment over the time they expect to use it.

Real estate is *stable in value*. Of course, some real estate values are more stable than others, but generally a lender can expect that real estate collateral will not depreciate quickly and may indeed rise in value.

Real estate investors like to borrow money to buy real estate because it gives them leverage. As a simple example, suppose someone buys an apartment complex costing $500,000 by putting up $100,000 of his own money and getting a mortgage loan for the other $400,000. In effect, he has gained "control" of a $500,000 property but has used only $100,000 to do it. By borrowing he is able to buy considerably more than if he used only his own money; if he is wise in his choices of the real estate to buy, he may improve his investment profits considerably by borrowing.

Mortgages and Notes

In the financing of real estate, two important documents are employed: the *loan*, which is evidenced by a *note* or *bond,* and the *mortgage,* which is a pledge of property as security for a debt. A simplified sample of a note and a mortgage is shown below.

NOTE	MORTGAGE
Date	Date
I owe you $10,000, payable at the rate of $80 per month for 20 years, beginning next month. Signed, T. Borrower	If I don't pay on the attached note, you can take 34 Spring Street, Hometown, U.S.A. Signed, T. Borrower

Since the borrower gives the note and mortgage to the lender, the borrower is the mortga*gor*. The lender is the mortga*gee*. (Always remember that the suffix *-or* signifies the giver, whereas *-ee* describes the receiver.)

A mortgage and a note are both contracts. Any provisions that are agreed upon may be written into either contract, so long as such provisions are legal. The essential elements of a note are (a) a promise to pay at (b) a fixed or determinable time (c) a certain sum of money (d) to a payee or to bearer, (e) signed by the borrower.

Title and Lien Theory

Mortgages (also called *trust deeds* in several states) are viewed either as transfers of property (title theory) or as the creation of a lien (lien theory). Title theory holds that the property is transferred to the lender subject to an automatic return of the property to the borrower upon payment of the loan. Lien theory holds that a mortgage gives the lender a lien on property, but not title.

Mortgage Loan Classification

Mortgages are often classified or described according to particular provisions. Some such provisions follow.

VA MORTGAGES (ALSO KNOWN AS GI MORTGAGES)

The Veterans Administration guarantees to private lenders that, in the event of default, the VA will make restitution for the default. The VA guarantee is good for up to 60 percent of the original loan or $25,000, whichever is less. These guarantees are helpful to both lenders and eligible borrowers.

VA borrowers need not make a down payment; that is their principal advantage. Lenders have greater security. They may look to the borrower, the VA, and/or the property in the event of default.

For example: suppose that someone borrows $25,000 on a VA mortgage, reduces it to $24,000, and then defaults. The property is foreclosed and sold for $20,000. The VA will repay the lender $4000 (the outstanding balance less the amount realized at foreclosure) plus expenses of foreclosure. Though only a qualified veteran may originate a VA loan, the loan may be assumed by a non-veteran at a later date.

FHA MORTGAGES

The Federal Housing Administration (FHA), which is now a part of the Department of Housing and Urban Development (HUD), has many programs that help to provide housing. They insure single-family and multi-family housing loans, nursing home mortgage loans, and loans on mobile homes and other properties. Some FHA loans provide subsidies to eligible borrowers. FHA-insured loans require only a small down payment, which is their principal advantage to borrowers. Borrowers need their own cash only for the down payment and closing costs. One half of 1 percent is added to the interest rate on FHA loans for an insurance fund. The main attraction to lenders is the insurance of the loan principal balance. In addition, borrowers, property, and lenders must all meet FHA standards.

CONVENTIONAL MORTGAGES

Conventional mortgage loans are those that are neither guaranteed by the Veterans Administration (VA) nor insured by the Federal Housing Administration (FHA). These mortgages may be insured by private mortgage insurers.

PURCHASE MONEY MORTGAGES

Sometimes a *seller* provides financing for a purchaser by accepting a mortage loan in lieu of cash for all or part of the purchase price. When the seller accepts such a mortgage loan, it is called a purchase money mortgage. The seller effectively gives purchase money to the buyer.

CONSTRUCTION LOANS AND PERMANENT MORTGAGES

Construction loans are used by builders or developers to improve land. Construction loan advances are permitted as construction progresses. When commercial property is completed, a *permanent* loan is used to pay off completely the construction loan. Construction loans on single-family homes usually continue until a residence is sold and the occupant arranges permanent financing.

The word *permanent* as it is used in real estate financing is a misnomer. Permanent mortgage loans seldom have terms beyond 30 years. Most will be repaid prior to their full term. Recent experience has shown that the typical mortgage loan is outstanding for about twelve years.

TERM LOANS, AMORTIZING LOANS, AND BALLOON PAYMENTS

A *term loan* is one that requires only interest payments until maturity. At the end of the maturity term, the *entire* principal balance is due.

Amortizing loans require regular, periodic payments. Each payment is greater than the interest charged for that period so that the loan principal amount is reduced at least slightly with each payment. The amount of the monthly payment for an amortizing loan is calculated to be adequate to retire the *entire* debt over the amortization period.

A *balloon payment loan* requires interest and some principal to be repaid during its term, but the debt is not fully liquidated. Upon its maturity, there is still a balance to be repaid.

FIRST, SECOND, AND JUNIOR MORTGAGES

Mortgages may be recorded at county courthouses to give notice of their existence. The mortgage loan that is recorded in the courthouse first against property remains a *first mortgage* until it is fully paid off. In the event of default and foreclosure, the lender who holds the first mortgage receives payment in full *before* other mortgage lenders receive anything.

Any mortgage recorded after the first mortgage is called a *junior mortgage*. Junior mortgages are further described as *second, third, fourth*, etc., depending upon the time they were recorded in relation to other mortgage loans on the same property. The earlier a mortgage is recorded, the earlier the mortgagee's claim in a foreclosure action.

BUDGET MORTGAGES

Budget mortgages require a homeowner to pay, in addition to monthly interest and principal payments, $1/12$ of the estimated taxes and insurance into an escrow account. These mortgages reduce a lender's risk, for the lender is thus assured that adequate cash will be available when an annual tax or insurance bill comes due.

PACKAGE MORTGAGE

Package mortgages include appliances, drapes, and other items of personal property in the amount loaned. The lender tends to exercise more control over a borrower's monthly obligations, and the borrower is able to spread the payment for such items over a lengthy period.

CHATTEL MORTGAGE

A chattel mortgage is one on personal property. The property may be a car, boat, furniture, etc.

BLANKET MORTGAGE

A blanket mortgage covers more than one parcel of real estate. *Release provisions* are usually included to allow individual parcels to be released from the mortgage upon payment of part of the mortgage principal.

ALTERNATIVE MORTGAGE INSTRUMENTS

A variety of mortgage repayment plans, called *Alternative Mortgage Instruments* (AMIs), are available in most parts of the United States and Canada. Some were developed in response to borrowers' needs for affordable payments, others in response to lenders who were financially damaged by holding long-term fixed rate loans during a period of rising interest rates. There are many variations of AMIs and technical changes in them occurred rapidly during the 1980s. The best known ones are:

1. Graduated Payment Mortgages (GPM); also Flexible Payment Mortgages (FPM or FLEXI)

2. Price Level Adjusted Mortgages (PLAM)

3. Adjustable Rate Mortgages (ARM)

4. Reverse Annuity Mortgages (RAM)

1. Graduated Payment Mortgages and Flexible Payment Mortgages offer borrowers lower monthly payments in the early years of the loan as compared to the standard payment loan. Payments in the first year for GPMs and FPMs are as much as 15 to 30 percent lower. But payments increase for each subsequent year by $2\frac{1}{2}$ to $7\frac{1}{2}$ percent for 5 to 10 years, then remain level for the remaining term of the loan. For example, the popular plan III of the FHA's Section 245 calls for payments to rise by steps of $7\frac{1}{2}$ percent per year for 5 years. Beginning with the sixth year of the loan, payments are level and will amortize the loan over the 25 remaining years of its term. During the first few years, however, payments are less than the interest required so there is *negative amortization*, meaning that the loan balance actually increases.

FPMs work much the same way. Some require a *pledged savings account*. The borrower, in addition to paying the downpayment on the home, also deposits money in a special interest-bearing savings account. Monthly payments on the mortgage, which are tailored to fit the borrower's budget, are supplemented by withdrawals from the savings account. This supplement reduces the amount of negative amortization and may result in positive amortization. When the special savings account is depleted, the homeowner's required monthly payment is increased.

2. Price Level Adjusted Mortgages have principal balances that rise with inflation. Initially, monthly payments are quite low since they are based on a 3 to 4 percent interest rate. Each year the principal balance on the loan increases with inflation so monthly payments in subsequent years will rise. The use of PLAMs is not widespread because of the uncertainty that they create for both lenders and borrowers.

3. Adjustable Rate Mortgages allow periodic adjustments to interest rates. The frequency of adjustment (i.e., every 6 months or every year) varies with each loan program. Some programs include a *cap* restriction that interest rates cannot change more than a certain percentage each period (i.e., a 2 percent maximum rise each year) and/or a ceiling cap on the maximum change over the life of the loan. Some

ARMs allow the payment to remain the same upon moderate interest rate increases, which causes the loan term to be extended. These types of loans are especially popular with lenders when interest rates are fluctuating widely.

In any given year, ARMs will represent 25% to over half of all new home mortgage loans originated. Specific terms can vary in detail, though the general outline presented here will describe nearly all of them. Most ARMs are assumable (while most new fixed-rate conventional loans are not.) Also, many ARMs have a feature which allows the borrower to "lock in" the interest rate (i.e., convert the ARM to a fixed-rate loan at the rate currently in effect) early in the loan period. Generally, this option is not allowed until the loan is at least three years old. Some loans with this feature have an additional charge that must be paid if and when the borrower elects to "lock" the interest rate.

4. Under a Reverse Annuity Mortgage a lender gradually advances money to a (typically elderly) homeowner. The amounts advanced, plus interest, become the principal of the loan. Payments to the lender are deferred until a sale of the property, the death of the homeowner, or a time when the balance owed approaches the market value of the home. RAMs also can be arranged whereby money, borrowed against the home, is used to purchase an annuity contract that will pay the homeowner for life. The homeowner then pays the mortgage interest with income from the annuity.

Lenders

The following organizations are active in real estate financing:

SAVINGS AND LOAN ASSOCIATIONS

These institutions hold about 45 percent of all residential mortgages in the United States. Savings and loan associations keep most (about 75 percent) of their funds invested in residential mortgages, and almost 90 percent of their mortgages are conventional ones.

COMMERCIAL BANKS

These banks hold about 15 percent of all residential mortgages; they are more active in the construction loan field and in other types of lending. They have a great deal of latitude in the types of activity in which they are engaged, but strict limitations are imposed for each type. Only about 10 percent of their assets is invested in residential mortgages; of those, about 85 percent are conventional loans.

MUTUAL SAVINGS BANKS

Mutual savings banks have no stockholders; they operate for the benefit of depositors. Over half of their assets is invested in residential mortgages; of those mortgages, slightly over half are conventional loans. Mutual savings banks hold about 12 percent of all residential mortgages.

LIFE INSURANCE COMPANIES

Life insurance companies invest about 15 percent of their total assets in residential mortgage loans and hold about 7½ percent of all residential mortgages. About two thirds of their mortgages are conventional loans; the balance are FHA or VA loans. Life insurance companies are quite active in permanent mortgage loans on income-producing property, including apartments, shopping centers, and office buildings.

FEDERAL NATIONAL MORTGAGE ASSOCIATION

The *Federal National Mortgage Association* (also known as *FNMA* or *"Fanny Mae"*) is a federally chartered, privately owned and managed corporation. It does not make direct loans to homeowners; rather, it purchases first mortgage loans, originated by others, in the secondary mortgage market. FNMA thereby aids in the liquidity of mortgage investments, making mortgages more attractive investments. FNMA presently owns about 6 percent of all residential mortgages.

MORTGAGE BROKERS

These brokers bring borrowers and lenders together, receiving a commission as compensation for their efforts.

MORTGAGE BANKERS

Mortgage bankers also bring borrowers and lenders together, for fees. They also service the loans, for a fee, by collecting payments and remitting them to lenders.

Features of Mortgage Loans

INTEREST RATES AND DISCOUNT POINTS

Interest rates for conventional loans are set in the capital markets and based on the supply of and demand for funds. Interest is rent for the use of money. Ceiling interest rates on VA loans are established by VA and change from time to time, and are often below the rate charged on conventional loans.

Lenders, in an effort to equate interest rates of VA loans with those of conventional loans, will often *discount* the VA loan. Each discount *point* is equal to 1 percent of the loan, which the lender does not advance. For example, suppose that the VA ceiling interest rate is 12 percent at a time when conventional loan interest rates are 12.5 percent. A lender may offer the 12 percent rate on a VA loan but withhold four discount points. If a $20,000 loan is applied for, the VA lender will advance $19,200 ($20,000 less 4 percent of $20,000). This raises the effective interest rate on the 12 percent face rate VA loan to 12.5 percent. Discount points ($800 in this case) must be supplied by a property seller for VA loans. Discount points may also be required for conventional loans, in which case either buyer or seller may pay them.

Discounts sometimes also will be charged on conventional and FHA loans. The effect here is the same; to "pay" for a lower contract rate of interest on the loan itself. However, while VA borrowers may not pay discounts on their loans, FHA and conventional borrowers are allowed to. Actually, who does pay these discounts (if any) is a subject for negotiation between buyer and seller when the purchase is arranged.

Because some non-VA loans may have discounts, lenders usually will provide potential borrowers with a selection of interest rates — and associated discounts. For example, the lender may offer 10% interest with a 5-point discount, 10.5% with a 3-point discount, and 11% with no discount at all. Discounts also are used as *buydowns*, often in association with *teaser* interest rates. Buydowns substitute an initial charge for interest later in the loan. Most often they are used to provide an unusually low interest rate during the early period of a loan. For example, if the "normal" rate of interest is 11%, a lender may offer a buydown (for a fee of about 5.5% of the loan amount) which will give the loan an interest rate of 8% the first year, 9% the second and 10% the third. After the third year, the interest rate will be 11% for the remainder of the loan period. The low interest rates in the early period of the loan are called teaser rates.

PREPAYMENT PENALTIES AND PRIVILEGES

Some mortgage loans allow the borrower to pay off the principal balance at any time. Others require a penalty, such as 3 percent of the outstanding balance, for early debt retirement.

ACCELERATION CLAUSES

An *acceleration clause* states that the full principal balance becomes due upon certain default. So if one or more payments are past due (depending on the agreement), the entire loan becomes due.

LOAN ASSUMPTION

Property offered for sale may be encumbered by a loan bearing a low interest rate, which makes it attractive to the real estate purchaser. The buyer may pay the seller for his equity (the difference between the property value if free and clear and the amount of debt) and then *assume* the loan. The purchaser then becomes liable for the loan and its required payments. Yet this does not automatically free the original borrower from his obligation. The original borrower may ask the lender for a *novation,* which serves to release him from responsibility, and then substitute the new property owner as the sole debtor. In the absence of a novation, the lender may look to the property and to both the original borrower and the subsequent purchaser for repayment.

Rather than assume a loan, a purchaser may agree to take the property *subject to* a mortgage loan. In doing so, the buyer acknowledges the debt, but it does not become his personal liability. In the event of default, he stands to lose no more than his investment.

CREATIVE FINANCING

In recent years mortgage interest rates have risen to very high levels. Whereas 5 percent interest was common in the 1950s, 6 percent to 7 percent in the 1960s, and 7 to 10 percent in the 1970s, the 1980s have seen increases in interest rates to nearly 20 percent! Naturally, homebuyers would prefer lower interest rates for the money they need to borrow, since this will make the monthly payment lower, or will enable them to borrow more money (and buy more house) with a given monthly payment.

When interest rates went well into the teens, buyers became quite interested in buying homes which already had lower-interest loans on them, made when the seller had originally purchased the home at a time when interest rates were lower. If the seller was willing, the buyer could assume the low-interest loan and, so, borrow money at a much lower rate by taking over the existing loan.

Two problems occur in loan assumption deals. The first is that the loan may have a "due-on-sale" clause. The second problem is that the price of the home may have gone up since the seller originally purchased it, and so, the buyer would have to make a large down payment to pay the seller's equity if he or she were to assume the old loan.

A due-on-sale clause is a form of acceleration clause which states that if the borrower sells the property which is mortgaged, then the entire loan becomes due and payable at the time of sale. This, naturally, would make assumption of the loan impossible without the permission of the lender. And, if the lender could get, say, 12 percent interest in the current market there is little incentive for him to allow someone to assume and continue a loan which is paying him only, say, 9 percent interest. One way out of this problem is for the buyer of the property to agree to pay a higher interest rate than was originally on the loan. This is nice for the lender, but not so nice for the buyer since it removes some or all of the attractiveness of the low-interest loan assumption.

In some states, state-chartered lenders are effectively prohibited by state law from enforcing due-on-sale clauses, even though such language may be included in the original mortgage loan contract. In these states such loans may be assumed without any change in the interest rate at the time of assumption. You should check the situation in your state.

Note that FHA and VA loans are always assumable and at no increase in the original interest rate. Also, in many states there was a spate of "bond-money" loans in the 1979–1981 period. These were loans made from the proceeds of state and local federally tax-exempt bonds. These loans usually carried a lower than normal rate of interest, and in many states these loans may be assumed without any change in the interest rate.

If a loan can be assumed at an attractive interest rate, there still remains the problem that the owner's equity in the property may be too high for most buyers to pay. As an example, the owner may have bought the house in 1978 for $60,000. Today it is worth $110,000. Even if the owner had financed the house completely with a VA loan of $60,000 when he bought it, and even though there still may be $50,000 of the loan left to pay off today, that still means that a buyer would have to pay $60,000 in cash to the owner in order to assume the loan and give the owner full value.

This type of problem has led to what is now being called *creative financing*. Suppose that our owner's 1978 loan carries an interest rate of 9 percent and that today's interest rate is 14 percent. Clearly, buyers would much rather pay 9 percent interest! In fact, very few would be willing to pay 14 percent interest, and so, if the owner insists that a buyer either come up with the full $51,000 in cash or get a new loan, he may find no buyers at all for his property. Very few buyers of a home costing $110,000 will have a handy $50,000 or so to put up, either.

If the owner is willing, there is the creative financing solution. In this situation, the owner allows the buyer to assume his low-interest loan and the buyer makes a more normal down payment—say $25,000. This leaves the seller $26,000 short, so he executes a second mortgage of $26,000 payable to the buyer. The buyer then makes payments to this second mortgage as well as to the first mortgage which he assumed. This is an advantage to the buyer, since he did not have to come up with a lot of cash and presumably is making monthly payments that he can afford. Also, $59,000 of what he owes on his new home carries a very favorable rate of interest. The seller may not be so happy, since he did not receive his entire equity in cash, but if the buyer is a good credit risk, the seller can be well assured of getting it eventually and in the meantime he will receive interest on it. These *creative* second mortgages usually are designed to come due in a relatively few years, by which time the buyer may be able to refinance the entire house at an interest rate more favorable than the current one.

USURY

Every state has laws prescribing maximum permitted interest rates. Charging a higher interest rate than that permitted by law is considered *usury*. Penalties for usury differ widely from state to state.

ESTOPPEL CERTIFICATE

An *estoppel certificate* is a statement that prevents its issuer from later asserting different facts. For example, a mortgage originator may wish to sell the mortgage loan (the right to collect payments) to another. The loan purchaser may ask for an estoppel certificate, whereby the borrower states the amount he owes. Later, the borrower is stopped from asserting that he owed less at the time he signed the estoppel certificate.

RELEASING MORTGAGES FROM PROPERTY

Four methods by which property may be released from mortgages are:

1. *Satisfaction piece.* This is a document from a lender stating that the loan is paid off and that he (the lender) releases property from the lien.
2. *Parcel or land release.* This releases part of mortgaged property from the mortgage, usually upon payment of part of the debt.
3. *Postponement of lien.* The lien is not satisfied but subordinated, meaning that it assumes a lower priority.
4. *Foreclosure.* This is described in detail below.

FORECLOSURE, DEFICIENCY JUDGMENTS, AND EQUITY OF REDEMPTION

Upon certain default, a lender may be allowed to go through an authorized procedure to have the property applied to the payment of the debt. This is known as *foreclosure*. Should the property sell at foreclosure for more than the unpaid first mortgage loan plus expenses of the foreclosure action, the excess belongs to the junior lenders, if any. After all lenders have received full payment, any excess funds go to the borrower.

It is more likely that the proceeds from a foreclosure will be inadequate to pay mortgage indebtedness. In this case, the lender may attempt to get a *deficiency judgment* for the amount of the loan that remains unpaid. This requires the borrower to pay the deficiency personally. Deficiency judgments are difficult to establish in many jurisdictions. Commercial property mortgagors are frequently able to negotiate *exculpatory* clauses in their loans. Exculpatory clauses cause loans to be *nonrecourse;* when such clauses exist, a defaulting borrower may lose the real estate that he has pledged, but he is not personally liable for the debt. The lender may look only to the property as collateral for the debt.

Should property be foreclosed, borrowers have the right to redeem the property by repaying in full the principal owed. This is known as the *equity of redemption* and must be exercised within the time period prescribed by state law. In some states, the right must be exercised before the actual foreclosure sale; in others, the right remains for up to two years after such a sale.

QUESTIONS TO ANSWER ABOUT YOUR STATE

Is your state a
- ☐ title theory state?
- ☐ lien theory state?
- ☐ other (explain): _____

_____

Does your state allow equity of redemption?
- ☐ No
- ☐ Yes (explain the conditions): _____

_____

Questions on Chapter 14_____

1. The major source of single-family home mortgage loan funds is
   - (A) mortgage bankers
   - (B) commercial banks
   - (C) savings and loan associations
   - (D) the Federal National Mortgage Association (FNMA)

2. A conventional mortgage is
   - (A) amortizing
   - (B) guaranteed by FHA
   - (C) not guaranteed by a government agency
   - (D) approved by the VA

3. A chattel mortgage is usually given in connection with
   - (A) realty
   - (B) farms
   - (C) personal property
   - (D) commercial property

4. The lending of money at a rate of interest above the legal rate is
   - (A) speculating
   - (B) usury
   - (C) both A and B
   - (D) neither A nor B

5. One discount point is equal to
   - (A) 1 percent of the sales price
   - (B) 1 percent of the interest rate
   - (C) 1 percent of the loan amount
   - (D) none of the above

6. Discount points in FHA and VA loans are generally paid by the
   - (A) lender
   - (B) purchaser
   - (C) seller
   - (D) broker

7. The main appeal of VA mortgages to borrowers lies in
   (A) low interest rates
   (B) minimum down payments
   (C) an unlimited mortgage ceiling
   (D) easy availability

8. When a loan is assumed on property that is sold,
   (A) the original borrower is relieved of further responsibility
   (B) the purchaser becomes liable for the debt
   (C) the purchaser must obtain a certificate of eligibility
   (D) all of the above

9. An estoppel certificate is required when the
   (A) mortgage is sold to an investor
   (B) property is sold
   (C) property is being foreclosed
   (D) mortgage is assumed

10. An owner who seeks a mortgage loan and offers three properties as security will give a(n)
    (A) blanket mortgage
    (B) FHA mortgage
    (C) conventional mortgage
    (D) chattel mortgage

11. A clause in a mortgage or accompanying note that permits the creditor to declare the entire principal balance due upon certain default of the debtor is
    (A) an acceleration clause
    (B) an escalation clause
    (C) a forfeiture clause
    (D) an excelerator clause

12. Which of the following statements is (are) false?
    (A) VA loans are insured loans.
    (B) FHA loans are guaranteed loans.
    (C) Both A and B
    (D) Neither A nor B

13. A second mortgage is
    (A) a lien on real estate that has a prior mortgage on it
    (B) the first mortgage recorded
    (C) always made by the seller
    (D) smaller in amount than a first mortgage

14. A large final payment on a mortgage loan is a(n)
    (A) escalator
    (B) balloon
    (C) amortize
    (D) package

15. A requirement of a borrower under an FHA-insured loan is that he
    (A) not be eligible for a VA or conventional loan
    (B) have cash for the down payment and closing costs
    (C) have his wife sign as co-borrower
    (D) certify that he is receiving welfare payments

16. A mortgaged property can
    (A) be sold without the consent of the mortgagee
    (B) be conveyed by the grantor making a deed to the grantee
    (C) both A and B
    (D) neither A nor B

17. In the absence of an agreement to the contrary, the mortgage normally having priority will be the one
    (A) for the greatest amount
    (B) that is a permanent mortgage
    (C) that was recorded first
    (D) that is a construction loan mortgage

18. The mortgagor's right to reestablish ownership after delinquency is known as
   (A) reestablishment   (C) equity of redemption
   (B) satisfaction   (D) acceleration

19. The Federal National Mortgage Association is active in the
   (A) principal mortgage market   (C) term mortgage market
   (B) secondary mortgage market   (D) second mortgage market

20. The money for making FHA loans is provided by
   (A) qualified lending institutions
   (B) the Department of Housing and Urban Development
   (C) the Federal Housing Administration
   (D) the Federal Savings and Loan Insurance Corporation

21. Amortization is best defined as
   (A) liquidation of a debt   (C) winding up a business
   (B) depreciation of a tangible asset   (D) payment of interest

22. A mortgage is usually released of record by a
   (A) general warranty deed   (C) satisfaction piece
   (B) quitclaim deed   (D) court decree

23. Loans from savings and loan associations may be secured by mortgages on
   (A) real estate   (C) both A and B
   (B) mobile homes   (D) neither A nor B

24. The borrower is the
   (A) mortgagee   (C) mortgagor
   (B) creditor   (D) A and B

25. In an amortizing mortgage, the
   (A) principal is reduced periodically along with the payment of interest for that period
   (B) principal is paid at the end of the term
   (C) lenders have greater security compared to an unamortizing mortgage
   (D) loan-to-value ratio does not exceed 30 percent

26. A term mortgage is characterized by
   (A) level payments toward principal
   (B) interest-only payments until maturity
   (C) variable payments
   (D) fixed payments including both principal and interest

27. Mortgage bankers
   (A) are subject to regulations of the Federal Reserve System
   (B) are regulated by Federal, not state, corporation laws
   (C) act as primary lenders
   (D) earn fees paid by new borrowers and lenders

28. The seller of realty takes a mortgage as partial payment. The mortgage is called
   (A) sales financing
   (B) note toting
   (C) primary mortgage
   (D) purchase money mortgage

29. A state in which a borrower retains title to the real property pledged as security for a debt is a
   (A) lien theory state   (C) creditor state
   (B) title theory state   (D) community property state

30. A state in which a mortgage conveys title to the lender is known as a
   (A) lien theory state   (C) conveyance state
   (B) title theory state   (D) community property state

31. The Renegotiated Rate Mortgage is one that requires
   (A) monthly payments to increase by predetermined steps each year
   (B) fixed interest rates for 3- to 5-year intervals
   (C) lender sharing profits from resale
   (D) none of the above

32. The use of Price Level Adjusted Mortgages (PLAMs) is
   (A) widespread because of inflation
   (B) infrequent because of the uncertainty they cause
   (C) losing importance with inflation
   (D) none of the above

TRUE — FALSE. Mark *T* for true, *F* for false.

____ 33. When interest rates fluctuate widely, lenders prefer fixed rate loans because of their certainty.

____ 34. The Reverse Annuity Mortgage is generally intended for young people who need more income.

____ 35. Most Shared Appreciation Mortgages require a share of the appreciation to be paid to the lender in exchange for an interest rate reduction.

____ 36. The guarantee on a VA loan is 60 percent of the loan amount, but no more than $25,000.00.

____ 37. A VA, or GI, loan may be assumed only by a qualified veteran.

____ 38. A purchase money mortgage is a mortgage loan made by a financial institution for the purpose of purchasing real estate.

____ 39. A conventional mortgage loan is one that is not guaranteed by the VA or insured by the FHA.

____ 40. Permanent loans are loans with terms in excess of 30 years.

____ 41. A mortgage that covers more than one real property is called a blanket mortgage.

____ 42. Discounts or points are charged on loans that have interest rates set below the prevailing market rate of interest.

____ 43. Sellers must pay discounts, or points, on FHA/VA loans because it is illegal for these fees to be charged to borrowers.

____ 44. A satisfaction piece is a document that states that the FHA or VA is satisfied with the fairness of the price charged for a particular property.

____ 45. If a borrower misses a payment on his mortgage loan, he will be evicted immediately.

FILL-INS. Fill in the blanks with the appropriate words or phrases.

46. A state in which a mortgage is considered to be a transfer of title to the lender is called a _____ state.

47. If, after foreclosure, the proceeds from the sale of foreclosed property are not enough to pay the debt owed, the lender may secure a _____ for the unpaid balance, which requires the borrower to pay the unrecovered amount.

48. When a loan is assumed, the original borrower may ask the lender for a(n) _____ _____ to release him from any further obligation for the loan.

49. Charging an interest rate higher than that permitted by law is _____ .

50. A clause that states that a mortgage loan becomes fully due and payable upon default is called a(n) _____ .

51. "Fanny Mae" is really the _____ .

52. A mortgage that covers personal property as well as real property is called a(n) _____ .

53. A loan requiring periodic payments that will pay the loan partly or fully by the time the loan term ends is called a(n) _____ loan.

54. A mortgage loan payable by a buyer of property to the seller of that same property is called a(n) _____ .

55. The lender of a mortgage loan is called the _____ .

56. When loan balances increase it is called _____ .

57. A clause in a mortgage that allows the loan to be called payable upon the sale of property is a _____ _____ .

ANSWERS

1. C	15. B	29. A	43. T
2. C	16. C	30. B	44. F
3. C	17. C	31. B	45. F
4. B	18. C	32. B	46. title theory
5. C	19. B	33. F	47. deficiency judgment
6. C	20. A	34. F	48. novation
7. B	21. A	35. T	49. usury
8. B	22. C	36. T	50. acceleration clause
9. A	23. C	37. F	51. Federal National
10. A	24. C	38. F	Mortgage Association
11. A	25. A	39. T	52. package mortgage
12. C	26. B	40. F	53. amortizing
13. A	27. D	41. T	54. purchase money mortgage
14. B	28. D	42. T	55. mortgagee
			56. negative amortization
			57. due on sale

Chapter 15 / *Valuation and Appraisal*

Value

An *appraisal* is an estimate or opinion of value. Since *value* can be modified by many adjectives (*market, insurance, use, investment, salvage, objective, speculative, assessed, book*, etc.), an appraiser, in undertaking an appraisal, must determine the purpose of the appraisal and the type of value sought. He can then define the problem, plan the appraisal, and gather and analyze the data.

MARKET VALUE

In most appraisal situations, the type of value sought is *market value*. One definition of market value is:

> the highest cash price that property will bring in a competitive market under all conditions requisite to a fair sale, the buyer and seller each acting prudently and in their own interests and without undue stimulus.

Another definition of market value is:

> the highest price a buyer is willing, but not compelled, to pay, and the lowest price a seller is willing, but not compelled, to accept.

Implicit in the definition of market value are the following:
1. Buyer and seller are typically motivated.
2. Both parties are well informed and acting in their own best interests.
3. A reasonable time is allowed for exposure in the market.
4. Payment is in cash or its equivalent.
5. Financing, if any, is on terms generally available in that geographical area.

The selling price of real estate is usually based on its market value. *Price* is a historical fact, whereas market value is a justifiable estimate of value. Price and value are not the same.

FORCES AFFECTING VALUE AS OF A GIVEN DATE

Since the market value of a property may vary from time to time, an appraisal is made "as of" a given date to indicate the market conditions and forces influencing the property at that time. Forces that may influence the value of property are:
1. Physical: size, shape, topography, soil, construction quality
2. Economic-financial: type of industry in the area, employment and unemployment, interest rates, per capita and household income, stability
3. Political-governmental: schools, police, fire, sanitation, utilities, zoning, building codes, taxes, and the like
4. Social: population and its density, household size, education level, housing tastes

HIGHEST AND BEST USE

The highest and best use of real estate is that reasonable, possible, and probable use that will yield the highest land value. In considering the value of land, whether it is improved or not, an appraiser should estimate such value on the highest and best use of the land, even though it is not currently being used in that manner.

Approaches to Appraisal

There are three approaches to the appraisal of real property:
1. Market data (sales comparison)
2. Cost (summation)
3. Income (capitalization)

MARKET DATA APPROACH

The market data approach is predicated on the assumption that the value of a property can be estimated on the basis of the actual selling price of similar (comparable) properties. In applying the market data approach, a careful, thorough search is performed to discover and verify the sales price and features of properties that have characteristics similar to those of the property being appraised. Then the actual sales price of each comparable property is adjusted upward or downward to account for the *contribution* to value of features that are different from those of the subject. The result is an estimate of the amount that each comparable property would have sold for had it possessed the same salient characteristics as the property being appraised. With adequate and reliable information concerning adjusted sales prices of comparable properties, a judgment can be made concerning the market value of the subject being appraised.

The market data approach is commonly used, particularly for single-family homes, land, and certain other types of property. The reliability of this approach is limited to situations where there is an adequate number of comparable sales. When the market is inactive, the reliability of the market data approach is limited.

COST APPROACH

The cost approach to appraising is predicated on the assumption that the value of a structure does not exceed the current cost of producing a replica of it. This tends to hold true when a site is improved with a new structure that represents the highest and best use of the site.

Typically, an appraiser estimates the reproduction cost[1] of the *subject property*, then subtracts for depreciation. The market value of the site (land prepared for use) is then added to the depreciated reproduction cost to arrive at a final estimate of value. This approach is also called the "summation approach."

Four methods of measuring reproduction cost are:
1. *Quantity survey*, whereby each type of material in a structure is itemized and costed-out (the price of each nail, brick, etc., is reflected). Overhead, insurance, and profit are added as a lump sum.
2. *Unit-in-place*, whereby the installed unit cost of each component is measured (e.g., exterior walls, including gypsum board, plaster, paint, wallpaper, and labor). Equipment and fixtures are added as a lump sum.
3. *Segregated cost* or *trade breakdown*, which is similar to the unit-in-place method except that units are major functional parts of the structure, such as foundation, floor, ceiling, roof, heating system, etc. Fixtures and equipment are added as a lump sum.
4. *Comparative unit*, whereby all components of a structure are lumped together on a unit basis to total the cost per square foot or cubic foot. Costs include materials, installation, and builder's overhead and profit.

---

[1] *Reproduction cost* is the cost of building a replica, whereas *replacement cost* is the cost of replacing the subject with one that has equivalent utility but is built with modern materials and to current standards of design and function.

Depreciation (diminished utility), which is subtracted from reproduction cost new, is broken down into three categories:

1. *Physical deterioration* (wear and tear, such as peeling paint, broken windows, a leaking roof)
2. *Functional obsolescence* (loss of efficiency in comparison to modern structures caused by changing tastes and standards, e.g., poor floor plan, inadequate wiring, air conditioning in Alaska, lack of elevators in a highrise building, etc.)
3. *Economic obsolescence* (loss of value due to locational or environmental factors external to the property, such as a nearby jetport or industrial plant, or the loss of a mining industry creating a "ghost town")

Physical deterioration and functional obsolescence are further classified as curable or incurable. The test of curability is whether the cost to cure is less than the value that would be added if the deficiency were remedied. Economic obsolescence is never curable, since the cost of changing the environment cannot be recovered by the added value in the subject property.

The cost approach to appraisal can be useful for new construction, proposed construction, highest and best use analysis, and appraisal of specialty buildings (auto assembly plant, post office, courthouse). Its reliability is limited, however, for existing structures, especially those older structures having many functional deficiencies. In such cases, reproduction is unlikely, and depreciation is difficult to measure.

INCOME APPROACH

The income approach to appraisal is predicated on the assumption that a lump sum present value can be estimated for an anticipated stream of income. The income most commonly used is called *net operating income*, and it is found for rental properties as follows:

1. Estimate potential gross income (the rental collected if all units are rented for an entire year).
2. Subtract a vacancy and collection allowance.
3. Subtract operating expenses. These include insurance, maintenance and repairs, real estate taxes, utilities, and other expenses essential to the operation of the property. *Not included* are interest and principal payments or depreciation.

The result — (1) minus (2) and (3) — is net operating income. Net operating income is then divided by a capitalization rate, which is the rate used to convert an income stream into a lump sum capital value.

The capitalization rate must be adequate to provide for a return on the entire investment as well as a recovery of the portion of the property that is subject to depreciation. The rate of return on the entire investment can be estimated as in the following example:

Safe, liquid rate (U.S. Government bonds, insured savings)	5%[1]
Provision for illiquidity	1%
Provision for investment management	1%
Provision for risk	2%
Rate of return on investment	9%
Plus, capital recovery: 80% of cost represented by improvements, which are subject to a forty-year life = 80% × 2½% (straight-line annual depreciation)[2]	2%
Capitalization rate	11%

If net operating income is estimated at $100,000, the resulting value is $100,000 ÷ .11 = $909,091, rounded to $910,000. This employs the formula:

$$\text{Value} = \frac{\text{Income}}{\text{Capitalization Rate}}$$

[1]These rates will vary from time to time, depending on economic or other conditions.

[2]The Ellwood, Hoskold, and other sophisticated techniques are also used by professional appraisers to arrive at an appropriate capital recovery rate.

The higher the capitalization rate, the lower the resulting estimate of value.

Another method of arriving at a capitalization rate for net operating income is called the "band of investment." It presumes that a typical portion of the property will be financed with a mortgage loan at the going rate of return and the balance financed by the equity owner at the going rate.

Suppose that 75 percent of the purchase price will be raised with a 9 percent interest rate mortgage and 25 percent with equity that seeks a 13 percent rate. The band of investment rate is computed by weighting these amounts and providing for capital recovery.

Type of Interest	Purchase Capital Contributed		Rate		Weighted
Mortgage	75%	×	9%	=	6.75%
Equity	25%	×	13%	=	3.25%
Annual required return on investment					10.00%
Add: Annual recovery of investment (= 80% depreciable × 2½%)					2.00%
Overall capitalization rate					12.00%

A third method of arriving at an overall rate is to examine market data. For example, if properties in the same area that generate the same type of income stream have sold for a 12 percent overall rate, then 12 percent would be a market rate. **Example:**

$$\text{If net operating income} = \$12{,}000 \text{ then}$$
$$\text{sales price} = \$100{,}000$$
$$\text{rate} = \frac{\$12{,}000}{\$100{,}000} = 12 \text{ percent}$$

The income approach to appraisal is useful for income-producing property, including office buildings, shopping centers, hotels, warehouses, etc. When applying this approach, an appraiser must exercise great care in selecting the capitalization rate and in estimating net operating income.

GROSS RENT MULTIPLIER (GRM)

A *gross rent multiplier* is computed as follows: sales price ÷ market rental = GRM. A $40,000 house that rents for $400 monthly has a GRM of 100 ($40,000 ÷ $400). Sometimes the GRM is expressed in terms of annual rental income. Although the GRM applies market prices to market rental rates, it is considered an income approach for single-family residences.

Value Conclusion

A professional appraiser estimates value using all three approaches (market data, cost, and income) whenever practical and then arrives at a final value estimate by evaluating, choosing, and weighting each of the indicators of value, using justifiable, definable proportions. Weights assigned are chosen subjectively, considering the market behavior, the relevance of each approach, and the quality of the data. This process is called *reconciliation of value estimates*. An example follows:

Approach	Value Estimate	×	Weight Assigned	=	Weighted Amount
Market data	$41,000	×	50%	=	$20,500
Cost	$41,500	×	35%	=	$14,525
Income	$39,700	×	15%	=	$ 5,955
			Weighted amount	=	$40,980
			Final value estimate (rounded)	=	$41,000

Types of Reports

Four types of reports are available to an appraiser:
1. *Demonstration narrative:* a most thorough report, presented by a candidate for a professional appraisal designation to show proficiency in appraisal and reporting
2. *Narrative report:* a report that explains value estimate and appraiser's reasons
3. *Form report:* standardized forms widely used in residential appraisals
4. *Letter report:* a written opinion of value, not necessarily including supporting evidence

Basic Elements of Value

Four basic elements must be present before a thing has value in exchange. They are:
1. *Utility:* the object must have some usefulness. Useless objects or things that get in the way (dust, smoke, soot, etc.) do not have a positive value. But even a pet rock is perceived to have some utility.
2. *Scarcity:* the object must have some degree of rarity. Air certainly has utility — we cannot live without breathing it — but, since it is plentiful, there is no market for air. Ice may be a "hot seller" on the beach but not at the South Pole.
3. *Demand:* the object must be wanted and the want coupled with purchasing power. Unless enough people want and can afford to fly to the moon for a vacation, there is no point or profit in building a hotel on the moon.
4. *Transferability:* the object or the use of it must be transferable. Surgeons have yet to accomplish a brain transplant. So, although you may be a genius, your brain has no value in exchange for goods. Of course, you can sell services generated by your mind. Virtually all real estate interests are transferable unless the conveyance specifically prohibits their transfer to or use by a party other than the specifically designated party.

The actual value of a commodity or service is based on the available supply or the supply of similar, substitutable goods, and the demand for the product. The four items noted must be present to command a price.

Questions on Chapter 15

1. An appraisal is a(n)
   (A) forecast of value
   (B) estimate of value
   (C) prediction of value
   (D) precise statement of value

2. Which of the following is *not* an appraisal approach?
   (A) Cost
   (B) Market
   (C) Income
   (D) Trade

3. The usefulness of the cost approach may be limited if the subject is
   (A) a new structure
   (B) in an inactive market
   (C) proposed construction
   (D) an old structure with many functional deficiencies

4. The direct sales comparison approach may be unreliable in a(n)
   (A) period of hyper-inflation
   (B) inactive market
   (C) "bedroom" community
   (D) area where there is new construction

5. Value is determined by
   (A) intrinsic forces
   (B) supply and demand
   (C) asking prices
   (D) active brokers

6. An appraisal is made as of a given date to indicate
   (A) when the property was inspected
   (B) the number of days required to prepare the report
   (C) the market conditions influencing the property at that time
   (D) when the appraiser completed the report

7. Which of the following is *not* a type of depreciation (decrease in value)?
   (A) Physical deterioration
   (B) Psychological obsolescence
   (C) Functional obsolescence
   (D) Economic obsolescence

8. Market value appraisals assume that
   (A) the purchaser pays all cash (no mortgage financing)
   (B) FHA or VA financing is employed
   (C) the appraiser can determine the types of financing involved
   (D) financing, if any, is on terms generally available in the area

9. The·adjustment process in the direct sales comparison approach involves the principle of
   (A) contribution
   (B) diminishing returns
   (C) variable proportions
   (D) anticipation

10. Replacement cost is the
    (A) cost of building a property of equivalent utility with modern materials
    (B) cost of building an exact replica of the subject
    (C) original cost adjusted for inflation
    (D) cost of purchasing an equally desirable property

11. The process by which the appraiser evaluates and selects among two or more alternatives is called
    (A) analysis
    (B) reconciliation
    (C) averaging
    (D) appraisal

12. When changing tastes and standards cause an existing house to lose value, there is
    (A) physical deterioration
    (B) economic obsolescence
    (C) functional obsolescence
    (D) all of the above

13. When changed surroundings cause an existing house to lose value, there is
    (A) physical deterioration
    (B) economic obsolescence
    (C) functional obsolescence
    (D) all of the above

14. One type of depreciation is generally not curable. It is
    (A) physical deterioration
    (B) functional obsolescence
    (C) deferred maintenance
    (D) economic obsolescence

15. The four general groups of forces that affect the value of a given property are
    (A) population, natural resources, prices, and social forces
    (B) money and credit, zoning, building ordinances, and social forces
    (C) economic, social, physical, and political forces
    (D) natural, economic, social, and physical forces

16. The first thing an appraiser should know in undertaking an appraisal is
    (A) how he or she is getting paid
    (B) the selling price of the property
    (C) the purpose of the appraisal
    (D) what property has sold for recently in the area

17. The income approach would be most suitable for
    (A) a newly opened subdivision
    (B) commercial and investment property
    (C) property heavily mortgaged
    (D) property heavily insured

18. Depreciation can be caused by which of the following factors?
    (A) Physical deterioration   (C) Economic obsolescence
    (B) Functional obsolescence   (D) All of the above

19. The selling price of real estate is usually based on its
    (A) intrinsic value   (C) exchange value
    (B) speculative value   (D) market value

20. The highest price a buyer is willing, but not compelled, to pay and the lowest price a seller is willing, but not compelled, to accept is
    (A) estimated value   (C) marginal value
    (B) economic value   (D) market value

21. A "rule of thumb" method for determining the price a wage earner can afford to pay for a home is to multiply his annual income by
    (A) 1½   (C) 4
    (B) 2½   (D) 6

22. Capitalization is a process used to
    (A) convert an income stream into a lump sum capital value
    (B) determine cost
    (C) establish depreciation
    (D) determine potential future value

23. A specific parcel of real estate has been assessed at a value of $6500. The local tax rate is 30 mills. What is the amount of the tax?
    (A) $19.50   (C) $195.00
    (B) $182.50   (D) $205.00

24. Highest and best use is
    (A) single-family property zoned for industrial use
    (B) property purchased for owner use
    (C) the use which the purchaser intends when he purchases the property
    (D) the reasonable, possible, and probable use of the property that will yield the highest return on investment

25. In the direct sales comparison approach, the *adjusted* sales price of a comparable property is
    (A) the amount that the comparable property sold for
    (B) the amount that the comparable property would have sold for
    (C) an estimate of the comparable's sale price, had it possessed the same important characteristics as the subject
    (D) the market value of the subject property

26. In the application of the income approach to appraising, which of the following statements is (are) true?
    (A) The higher the capitalization rate, the lower the appraised value
    (B) The higher the capitalization rate, the higher the appraised value
    (C) Both A and B
    (D) Neither A nor B

27. The livable square footage of a single-family residence is usually measured from the
    (A) interior   (C) interior plus basement
    (B) inside rooms   (D) exterior

28. The number of square feet in one acre is
    (A) 64,000   (C) 440
    (B) 460   (D) 43,560

TRUE — FALSE. Mark *T* if the statement is true, *F* if it is false.

_____ 29. Price and value are the same thing.

_____ 30. The objective of an appraisal is to estimate the cost of a new building similar to the one being appraised.

_____ 31. The market value of a particular property may vary from time to time.

_____ 32. The highest and best use of real estate is the use that will show an increase in value over a short time.

_____ 33. Functional obsolescence is exemplified by a building becoming out-of-date or out of style.

_____ 34. The capitalization approach attempts to place a value on the right to acquire today the right to receive the income a property will generate in the future.

_____ 35. GRM stands for Great Reproduction Method.

_____ 36. An object cannot have a market value if it cannot be transferred from someone who has it to someone who does not.

FILL-INS. Fill in the blanks with the appropriate words or phrases.

37. The three approaches to appraisal are _____ , _____ _____ , and _____ .

38. The three kinds of depreciation that appraisers recognize in real estate are _____ _____ , _____ , and _____ _____ .

39. If the capitalization rate is raised, the resultant value will _____ _____ .

40. The value that an appraiser usually seeks is _____ .

ANSWERS

1. B	12. C	23. C	34. T
2. D	13. B	24. D	35. F
3. D	14. D	25. C	36. T
4. B	15. C	26. A	37. income, market (replace-
5. B	16. C	27. D	ment), cost or summation
6. C	17. B	28. D	38. physical deterioration,
7. B	18. D	29. F	functional obsolescence,
8. D	19. D	30. F	economic obsolescence
9. A	20. D	31. T	39. fall (be less, decrease)
10. A	21. B	32. F	40. market value
11. B	22. A	33. T	

Chapter 16/*Taxation and Assessment*

Real estate has been subject to tax for nearly all of human history. This is because it is valuable and also hard to hide. Consequently, it is easy for officials to assess taxes on it. The property tax is an *ad valorem* tax; this means that it is based on the *value* of the thing being taxed. In effect, then, the tax bill on a large, valuable property should be more than the bill on a small, relatively low-valued one.

The property tax usually is the major source of income for city and county governments. In a sense, this may be just, because the real estate that provides the bulk of the taxes collected also benefits greatly from many of the services local government pays for with the property taxes it collects. Most important of these is fire protection, which accrues almost exclusively to real estate. Police protection and the provision and maintenance of local streets and roads also provide obvious benefits. Nearby, locally provided public developments such as schools and parks make many kinds of real estate more valuable. The control of real estate development through zoning and building codes also tends to preserve values of existing real estate improvements, as does the provision of planning services. Local courthouses store the records that are so necessary for the documentation of title to real estate.

Tax Assessment

Real estate taxation is relatively straightforward, but there can be some fairly confusing elements unless the process is studied carefully.

The tax is based upon the value of the real estate; therefore, some method must be available for determining the values of all parcels of real estate in the taxing jurisdiction. For this purpose, local governments usually have a *tax assessor's* office, although it often goes by a different name. The function of the office is to set a valuation upon each parcel of taxable property in the jurisdiction. Sometimes this is done by actually undertaking an appraisal of each property, but this is very expensive except for the most valuable properties. More often, the assessment is arrived at by simpler means. Frequently the indication of value made when property is sold will be used to determine the sale price, which, it is assumed, is very close to the true value. (In states that use documentary stamps or deed transfer taxes the approximate sale price often can be deduced from the value of stamps affixed to the deed or from the amount of transfer tax paid.) Often all assessments will be adjusted by some specific formula each year to take account of inflation, or other reasons for overall value changes. Building permits serve to pinpoint new construction and additions to existing buildings; aerial photography accomplishes the same objective.

More often than not a single property will be in *more* than one taxing jurisdiction. Most commonly, a property might be in a particular county, as well as in a specific city or town, and each may levy taxes. Many areas have independent school districts as well. Furthermore, there can be a multiplicity of other kinds of taxing districts, depending upon what state and local laws will allow and provide for. Usually, however, a single assessing agency will be used to provide a valuation for all taxing jurisdictions that affect a given property; this is because assessment is an expensive process and duplication of effort is avoided.

Every jurisdiction will provide some means whereby property owners can appeal assessments they consider unjust. The exact method of appeal varies considerably across the country.

Exemption from Property Taxes

Not all real estate is subject to the real property tax; some of it is *exempt*. Exactly what is exempt and what is not is a matter decided by both state and local law. However, some kinds of property are exempt almost everywhere. Primary among these is any property owned by government. This seems to make sense: it would be peculiar for the government to pay taxes to itself. Of course, there are several governments and it is conceivable that they could pay taxes to one another, but they usually don't. Therefore, *all* government-owned property, no matter which government owns it, is exempt from property taxes. In some areas, where a very large proportion of the property is government-owned, this can work a hardship upon local taxpayer-owners of property, especially where the government-owned property receives a large quantity of the services paid for by local taxes. Examples of such "problem" areas are state capitals, Washington, D.C., and many small cities and towns that provide school and other services for large government (usually military) establishments. In cases such as this, the benefiting branch of government often will provide some direct grant of money to the affected local government to make up for the property tax it does not pay.

Some privately owned property may also be exempt from tax. Most areas will exempt certain kinds of land uses that would seem to provide other benefits to the community, making them desirable even when exempt from property tax. These usually include churches, nonprofit private schools, and some other charitable organizations. In some localities, *all* property owned by such organizations is exempt from tax; however, the current trend is toward granting the exemption only to property that actually is used by the organization for its basic purposes. In such an area, then, a church building used for religious purposes might be exempt, but an apartment project owned by the congregation would not be — even if all its profits went to the church.

Payment of Taxes

Past-due property taxes automatically become a lien on the property so affected. If the taxes still are not paid, the taxing government eventually will be able to foreclose and have the property sold in order to pay the taxes. A tax lien takes priority over all other liens, including mortgages, even though they may have been entered on the records before the tax lien.

Normally, a property owner has a considerable period of time between the time the taxes actually are levied and the date payment is due. The specific schedule followed varies from state to state and sometimes even among localities within a state. As a matter of fact, a property owner whose land falls into more than one single taxing district may find that the various districts have differing collection schedules.

Homeowners often are spared the chore of remembering when taxes are due, because their mortgage lenders require them to make a supplemental payment into an escrow account with each monthly payment. This money mounts up to create a fund from which the lender pays taxes (and, usually, insurance) when they are due. Generally the lender is contractually responsible to the borrower for paying the taxes out of these funds; if a mistake is made, or a penalty is required for late payment, the lender can be held liable to the borrower.

Calculation of Property Taxes

(NOTE: The following section assumes that you have enough arithmetic knowledge to handle percents and decimals. If you feel that your arithmetic is rusty, you should turn to Chapter 17, "Arithmetic Review," before reading the remainder of this chapter.)

When you calculate property taxes, three figures are necessary: the *appraised valuation* of the property, *the assessment ratio*, and the *tax rate*. The assessment ratio is applied to the appraised valuation, resulting in *assessed value*. Then, the tax rate is applied to the assessed value in order to find the tax due. In effect, the tax rate will be a certain proportion of the assessed valuation, such as 7.66% of assessed valuation, or $7.66 per $1000 of valuation, or 76.6 *mills* per dollar of assessed valuation. All three of these represent the same tax rate, but they are expressed in three different ways.

To determine the tax rate, it usually is easiest to turn the rate into a percentage figure, because that can be easily applied to the assessed valuation through simple arithmetic procedures. Rarely, however, is the tax rate expressed as a percentage. Instead, it usually is expressed as a *millage rate*. A millage rate specifies how many *mills* must be paid for each *dollar* of assessed valuation. A *mill* is ¹/₁₀ of a cent; therefore, there are 1000 mills in one dollar. The millage rate, then, shows how many *thousandths* of the assessed valuation must be paid in tax.

Millage rates are easy to convert to percents: percents measure hundredths, so to change a millage rate to a percentage rate *move the decimal point one place to the left*. This is the same as dividing by 10, since there are 10 thousandths in each hundredth. Consequently, a millage rate of 77.6 is the same as 7.76%. Sometimes the millage rate is expressed as so many dollars per thousand dollars of assessed valuation. In either case, the figure is in thousandths, so the numerical value is the same: 77.6 mills per dollar is the same as $77.60 per thousand dollars.

Once the tax rate is expressed as a percent, the next step is to determine the assessed valuation to which it must be applied. In some states and localities, the assessed valuation is the same as the market value of the property as estimated by the tax assessor. In others, however, only part of the market value is subject to tax. Sometimes the taxable amount is fixed by state law; in other localities, the local government itself determines the taxable portion of the estimated value. Often the figure so arrived at will be altered even further. Many states have a *homestead exemption* which exempts a certain proportion of the assessed valuation from taxation. Often older homeowners get special exemptions, as do poor homeowners in a few areas. Once these exemptions are determined, they are subtracted from the assessed valuation to arrive at the net figure upon which the tax is based. However, a further element of confusion can enter the picture: many properties are subject to tax by more than one jurisdiction, and the method of calculating assessed valuation, and the exemptions that may be allowed, can vary among them.

When the assessed valuation subject to tax has been determined, the tax rate is applied to it to determine the tax to be paid. For example, let us assume that a property has a taxable assessed valuation of $20,000, and the millage rate is 77.6. The millage rate, then, is 7.76%, so we want to find 7.76% of $20,000, which will be the tax to be paid. This is found by changing the percentage into a decimal and multiplying 0.0776 x $20,000 = $1552. The tax, then, is $1552.

SAMPLE PROPERTY TAX PROBLEM

Following is an example of calculation of property tax. This problem is for illustrative purposes, so it may be somewhat more complicated than what you are likely to encounter, either on licensing examinations or in actual practice.

Jones wishes to determine what the tax will be on his home. He just bought it for $39,500. Current practice in his area is for the assessor to estimate the value of newly sold property as 95% of the sale price. Taxes are levied on 30% of estimated value. There is a homestead exemption of $3000 of taxable value. The city tax rate is 21.1 mills. County taxes that Jones's property is subject to are 14.5 mills. In addition, the city school system levies a 34.8 mill tax. There is a state tax of 0.5 mills. The homestead exemption does *not* apply to county taxes. The city allows an additional $2000 exemption on its taxes for the elderly; Jones is 72 years old, so he qualifies for this exemption.

(1) The first step is to determine the assessed valuation. First we find 95% of $39,500 to get the estimated value.

$$0.95 \times \$39,500 = \$37,525 \text{ estimated value}$$

The assessed valuation is 30% of this figure:

$$0.30 \times \$37,525.00 = \$11,257.50 \text{ assessed valuation}$$

(2) Actually, there are four separate taxes: city, county, school, and state. They can be computed separately; however, the school and state tax are computed on the same base, so they can be combined for efficiency. We will show both ways, however. First, the school tax (34.8 mills) is applied to the assessed valuation ($11,257.50) minus the $3000 homestead exemption ($8.257.50 tax base). A rate of 34.8 mills is 3.48%, or 0.0348. Therefore, to calculate the school tax:

$$0.0348 \times \$8257.50 = \$287.36 \text{ school tax}$$

The state tax is calculated on the same base of $8257.50. The tax rate is 0.5 mills which is 0.05% or 0.0005:

$$0.0005 \times \$8257.50 = \$4.13 \text{ state tax}$$

These two taxes add up to $291.49. This total could have been arrived at by adding the two tax rates and applying the total to the assessed valuation of $8257.50:

$$34.8 \text{ mills} + 0.5 \text{ mills} = 35.3 \text{ mills combined tax rate} = 3.53\% = 0.0353$$
$$0.0353 \times \$8257.50 = \$291.49 \text{ combined state and school taxes}$$

(3) Now the city tax must be calculated. Since the city has the extra $2000 exemption for the elderly, for which Jones qualifies, this tax is applied to a base calculated by adjusting the assessed valuation to reflect the homestead exemption and the exemption for the elderly:

$$\$11,257.50 - (\$3000 + \$2000) = \$6257.50 \text{ tax base}$$

The city tax rate is 21.1 mills, which is 2.11% or 0.0211. So the tax is:

$$0.0211 \times \$6257.50 = \$132.03 \text{ city tax}$$

(4) The county tax is on a third base, because the homestead exemption does not apply. Consequently, the county tax is based on the full assessed valuation of $11,257.50. The county tax rate is 14.5 mills, which is 1.45% or 0.0145. The county tax is calculated as follows:

$$0.0145 \times \$11,257.50 = \$163.23$$

(5) Now that the four separate taxes have been calculated, they are added to arrive at the total property tax on Jones's house:

$287.36	school tax
4.13	state tax
132.03	city tax
163.23	county tax
$586.75	total property tax

Checklist for Your State's and Locality's Property Taxation Practices_____

Obtain the answers to the following questions from the literature supplied by your state's licensing agency or from the local tax assessor's office in your area.

What proportion of the estimated market value is subject to tax? _____%

Are any of the following exemptions applicable to the tax base?
☐ Homestead exemption
☐ Old-age exemption
☐ Exemption for the poor
☐ Other(s): _____

Is it possible for a property to be subject to taxes by more than one governmental body?

☐ No; taxes are levied only by _____

☐ Yes; these include:

   ☐ State government

   ☐ County (parish) government

   ☐ City (township) government

   ☐ School district

   ☐ Special assessment district

   ☐ Improvement district

   ☐ Other(s): _____

Questions on Chapter 16

1. An *ad valorem* tax is one which is based on
   (A) income earned
   (B) the value of the thing being taxed
   (C) the size of the thing being taxed
   (D) something other than A, B, or C

2. The property tax is a form of
   (A) sales tax
   (B) *ad valorem* tax
   (C) income tax
   (D) excise tax

3. The major source of income for local government usually is
   (A) income taxes
   (B) licenses and fees
   (C) property taxes
   (D) parking meters

4. Which of the following always is (are) exempt from real property taxes?
   I. Income-producing property owned by a church
   II. Government-owned property
   (A) I only
   (B) II only
   (C) I and II
   (D) Neither I nor II

5. A millage rate of 84.5 mills is the same as
   I. $84.50 per $1000
   II. 8.45%
   (A) I only
   (B) II only
   (C) I and II
   (D) Neither I nor II

6. If a property is assessed at $60,000 and the millage rate is 32.5, the tax is
   (A) $19.50
   (B) $195.00
   (C) $1950
   (D) $19,500

7. The appraised valuation is $25,000. The property tax is based on 20% of appraised valuation. The city tax is 50 mills; the county tax is 40 mills. Which of the following is true?
   I. The city tax is $1250.
   II. The county tax is $2000.
   (A) I only
   (B) II only
   (C) I and II
   (D) Neither I nor II

8. A lien for unpaid property taxes
   (A) can be sold at auction
   (B) takes priority over all other liens
   (C) cannot exist unless taxes are at least 36 months overdue
   (D) is a form of adverse possession

9. Which of the following is *not* a good reason why real property taxes are so popular?
   (A) Real estate ownership is easy to hide.
   (B) Real estate is valuable.
   (C) Real estate is easy to find.
   (D) Real estate can be foreclosed to provide payment of unpaid tax levies.

10. Real property taxes are justifiable because
   I. real property benefits from many of the services provided by the government entities that collect real property taxes
   II. real property owners all are rich and can afford to pay taxes
   (A) I only   (C) I and II
   (B) II only   (D) Neither I nor II

TRUE — FALSE. Write *T* for true, *F* for false.

_____ 11. There is no way that a property owner can appeal an assessment he considers incorrect.

_____ 12. A tax lien takes priority over all other liens.

_____ 13. The property tax rate is always applied to the market value of the property.

_____ 14. Real estate owners benefit from many of the services provided by local government with the money collected from real property taxes.

_____ 15. Some properties may be subject to real property taxes levied by more than one jurisdiction.

FILL-INS. Fill in the blanks with the proper word or phrase.

16. Unpaid and overdue property taxes become a _____ on the property.

17. If the assessed valuation is $40,000 and the tax rate is 77 mills, the tax is _____ .

18. A *mill* is an amount of money equal to _____ .

19. A millage rate can also be expressed as so many dollars per _____ .

20. The property tax is based on the value of the thing taxed, so it is a form of _____ _____ tax.

ANSWERS

1.	B	6.	C	11.	F	16.	lien
2.	B	7.	D	12.	T	17.	$3080
3.	C	8.	B	13.	F	18.	$1/10$ of a cent
4.	B	9.	A	14.	T	19.	thousand dollars
5.	C	10.	A	15.	T	20.	*ad valorem*

Chapter 17/ *Arithmetic Review*

Arithmetic Is Familiar

Many applicants for real estate license examinations worry about the part of the examination that features "mathematics." Actually, the science of mathematics encompasses such things as algebra, calculus, and a variety of exotic fields of study, NONE of which appears on real estate license examinations. It would be better, and less frightening, to refer to the real estate mathematics as real estate *arithmetic*, because that is actually what it is.

You have been through all the necessary arithmetic before! Every state requires applicants for real estate licenses to have a high school education or the equivalent. The "mathematics" you will encounter on the licensing examination is the kind of arithmetic taught in the sixth and seventh grades, so you should have been exposed to it at least that one time if you are eligible to take the licensing examination in your state. Of course, the arithmetic problems in elementary and junior high school probably didn't deal with real estate situations, but the arithmetic used (the manipulation of numbers) is similar to that required on the licensing examination.

To pass the licensing examination, you should know:

> *Basic manipulations:*
> addition
> subtraction
> multiplication
> division
>
> *How to work with:*
> fractions
> decimals
> percentages
>
> *How to figure areas of simple figures:*
> quadrilaterals (four-sided figures, including squares and rectangles)
> triangles
> circles

That pretty much sums it up. Sometimes there may be a problem involving simple volumes (how much concrete will fill a box of such-and-such a size?); therefore, we will also include a section on that.

If your own day-to-day activities have not required you to keep up-to-date on all the arithmetic skills you learned in school (whether long ago or recently), and if you feel a bit rusty on some points, this chapter is for you. In Chapter 18 we will apply these arithmetic skills to the various kinds of *real estate* problems you are likely to encounter on the examination, but for now we will concentrate on basic arithmetic procedures.

If you think your arithmetic ability is adequate, you can skip this chapter. But before you do, why not try a few problems from each of the Problem Sets (A through O) and check your answers with the key at the end of the chapter? The Problem Sets combine all the arithmetic skills you will require on licensing examinations, so if you can do well on them you are indeed mathematically competent.

As you go through this review, you will probably be surprised at how simple the arithmetic is. Remember, all you really have to be able to do is to add, subtract, multiply, and divide accurately. We must assume that you can indeed do that; *our* job will be to show you WHEN to do each of these things in the various problems. If you can do the basic arithmetic manipulations, then all you have to know is *when* to apply them, and to *what* numbers.

Every day you may work with many of the necessary arithmetic concepts, even though you may not actually realize it:

- You work with *decimals* whenever you deal with money. Decimals show numbers in tenths, hundredths, thousandths, etc. The sum $17.62 is seventeen dollars and sixty-two cents. It is also 17.62 dollars, or seventeen and sixty-two one-hundredths dollars. You add and subtract decimals whenever you check a restaurant bill, balance your checkbook, or count a pocket full of loose change. You multiply with decimals when you figure how much it will cost to buy four paperback books, if each costs $1.39. You divide with decimals when the store is selling mousetraps at 3 for $1.99 and you want to buy only one.

- You work with *percentages* when you try to figure out sales taxes on purchases you make, or when you figure out your income tax. You do also when you try to determine what something costs if the store sign says that everything is 40% off the price marked. If you work on a commission basis you almost certainly work with percentages, since commission payments (including those in the real estate business) are nearly always expressed as a percentage of sales. Finally, if you ever try to compute the interest on a loan, once again you will be manipulating percentages.

- You work with *fractions* when you follow a recipe that calls for $1\frac{1}{3}$ cups of this and $2\frac{1}{2}$ teaspoons of that, and you want to make three times as much because you're having a lot of people over for a party. Often when you're dealing with percentages and decimals you are also dealing with fractions, because fractions, decimals, and percents are just three different ways of saying basically the same thing. Don't forget that in your pocket you may have a *half*-dollar or a *quarter*.

- You may even work with *areas* more than you think. Wrapping paper, paper towels, tissue, and the like all are measured in square feet or square inches. Wallpaper, carpeting, and the size of your house are all measured in terms of area, as is any land you may own.

So let's begin our review. First we will go over fractions, then decimals, followed by percents. This chapter includes many examples and a variety of practice problems as well. We will work on handling "word problems" also and will look at examples of common kinds of arithmetic problems that involve the concepts we are dealing with.

Working With Fractions

Fractions are numbers that look like these:

$$\frac{1}{2} \qquad \frac{4}{19} \qquad \frac{6}{11} \qquad \frac{2}{3} \qquad \frac{345}{346} \qquad \frac{2180}{5881} \ldots \text{etc.}$$

The top number in a fraction is called the *numerator,* and the bottom number is called the *denominator.* A fraction represents the division of the number 1 into a certain quantity of equal parts, shown by the denominator. The numerator tells us how many of these equal parts are included in a particular fraction. As an example, the number $\frac{1}{6}$ is read as "one sixth." It means that the number 1 has been divided into six equal parts, and this number represents one of the parts. The number $\frac{5}{6}$ (five sixths) represents five of the six parts of the number 1.

Whole numbers are numbers without fractions. These are whole numbers:

3   5   234   486   1189   234,564   1,000,000,000

Consider this number: $\frac{3}{5}$. It is read as "three fifths." What it means is that the number 1 has been divided into five equal parts and that three of them are represented by this number. Suppose there are five people in the Smith family, but that Mr. Smith and little Kenneth are out at a ball game, leaving Mrs. Smith, Bobby, and Jennifer at home. This would mean that $\frac{3}{5}$ of the people in the Smith family are at home. Also, $\frac{2}{5}$ of them are at the ball game. When Mr. Smith and Kenneth get home, the entire Smith family will be at home: $\frac{5}{5}$ or, in other words, 1 entire Smith family will be at home.

The number $\frac{5}{5}$ means that all of the five equal parts are included; thus, a number like $\frac{5}{5}$ means the same thing as the number 1. This also tells us that $\frac{3}{5} + \frac{2}{5} = 1$. (This is read: "Three fifths *plus* two fifths *equals* one.")

This should tell us something else, too: if $\frac{3}{5}$ and $\frac{2}{5}$ *add up* to 1, then each of those fractions separately ought to be *less than* 1. In fact, **any fraction which has a numerator (top number) smaller than its denominator (bottom number) must be less than 1.** All these fractions are *less than* 1:

$$\frac{2}{5} \qquad \frac{3}{5} \qquad \frac{4}{7} \qquad \frac{28}{29} \qquad \frac{1}{16} \qquad \frac{3}{4} \qquad \frac{2}{3} \qquad \frac{19,732}{19,733}$$

If the numerator and the denominator are exactly the same, then the fraction is equal exactly to 1. All these fractions are *equal to* 1:

$$\frac{5}{5} \qquad \frac{7}{7} \qquad \frac{29}{29} \qquad \frac{16}{16} \qquad \frac{4}{4} \qquad \frac{3}{3} \qquad \frac{19,733}{19,733}$$

If the numerator is a higher number than the denominator, then the fraction is greater than 1. All these fractions are *greater than* 1:

$$\frac{7}{5} \qquad \frac{11}{7} \qquad \frac{36}{29} \qquad \frac{23}{16} \qquad \frac{11}{4} \qquad \frac{7}{3} \qquad \frac{19,734}{19,733}$$

Fractions like these (which are greater than 1) are called *improper fractions* because they can also be expressed as mixed numbers.

CHANGING IMPROPER FRACTIONS TO MIXED NUMBERS

A mixed number is a number that contains both a whole number and a fraction. These are mixed numbers:

$$3\frac{1}{2} \qquad 47\frac{3}{4} \qquad 1\frac{276}{383} \qquad 46\frac{1}{10} \qquad 3,827,483\frac{1}{2} \qquad 11\frac{466}{467}$$

Any improper fraction can be changed to a mixed number. The procedure is very simple:

(a) *Divide* the denominator (bottom) *into* the numerator (top).
(b) The *whole number* part of the resulting mixed number will be equal to the number of times that the denominator divides into the numerator *evenly*.
(c) For the *fraction* part of the mixed number, the *denominator* is the same as in the improper fraction. The *numerator* will be the *remainder* from the division performed in step (a). (If there is *no remainder*, then the improper fraction is one that converts to a *whole number*.)

As an example, let's change the improper fraction $\frac{233}{6}$ into a mixed number.

(a) We divide 6 *into* 233:

$$
\begin{array}{r}
38 \\
6\,\overline{)\,233} \\
-18 \\
\hline
53 \\
-48 \\
\hline
5 \text{ remainder}
\end{array}
$$

Thus, 6 goes into 233 a total of 38 times, with a remainder of 5.

(b) Our whole number part of the resulting mixed number is 38.

(c) The denominator of the fraction part of the mixed number will be 6, just as in our original improper fraction ($\frac{233}{6}$). The numerator will be the remainder of 5, so the fraction part must be $\frac{5}{6}$.

Therefore, $\frac{233}{6}$ is the same as the mixed number $38\frac{5}{6}$.

Look over these examples:

(1) Change $\frac{36}{5}$ into a mixed number.

Answer:

$$
\begin{array}{r}
7 \\
5\,\overline{)\,36} \\
-35 \\
\hline
1 \text{ remainder}
\end{array}
$$

So, $\frac{36}{5} = 7\frac{1}{5}$.

(2) Change $\frac{3,822,409}{23}$ into a mixed number.

Answer:

$$
\begin{array}{r}
166191 \\
23\,\overline{)\,3822409} \\
-23 \\
\hline
152 \\
-138 \\
\hline
142 \\
-138 \\
\hline
44 \\
-23 \\
\hline
210 \\
-207 \\
\hline
39 \\
-23 \\
\hline
16 \text{ remainder}
\end{array}
$$

So, $\frac{3,822,409}{23} = 166,191\frac{16}{23}$.

(3) Change $\frac{42}{3}$ into a mixed number.

Answer:

$$
\begin{array}{r}
14 \\
3\,\overline{)\,42} \\
-3 \\
\hline
12 \\
-12 \\
\hline
0 \text{ remainder}
\end{array}
$$

In this case, there is no remainder, so instead of writing the answer as $14\frac{0}{3}$, we just write 14. **Any fraction whose numerator (top number) is 0 is equal to 0.**

On page 148 we listed a few sample improper fractions. Here are their mixed number equivalents. Check each of these, using the steps we have just outlined, to be sure you understand how they were arrived at:

$$\frac{7}{5} = 1\frac{2}{5} \qquad \frac{11}{7} = 1\frac{4}{7} \qquad \frac{36}{29} = 1\frac{7}{29} \qquad \frac{23}{16} = 1\frac{7}{16}$$

$$\frac{11}{4} = 2\frac{3}{4} \qquad \frac{7}{3} = 2\frac{1}{3} \qquad \frac{19,734}{19,733} = 1\frac{1}{19,733}$$

Now try the following problems. The answers are at the end of the chapter.

Problem Set A

Change the following improper fractions into mixed numbers:

1. $\frac{48}{11}$ 6. $\frac{114}{13}$

2. $\frac{322}{19}$ 7. $\frac{24,877}{3321}$

3. $\frac{426}{7}$ 8. $\frac{46}{5}$

4. $\frac{7}{2}$ 9. $\frac{132,763}{51,111}$

5. $\frac{2423}{108}$ 10. $\frac{79}{5}$

MULTIPLYING FRACTIONS

Multiplication of fractions is the easiest fraction operation to remember:
(a) Multiply the numerators to get the numerator (top) of the answer.
(b) Multiply the denominators to get the denominator (bottom) of the answer.

For example, multiply $\frac{3}{8}$ by $\frac{5}{11}$. According to what we've just said, the answer is as follows. (The symbol × means "multiplied by.")

$$\frac{3}{8} \times \frac{5}{11} = \frac{3 \times 5}{8 \times 11} = \frac{15}{88}$$

That's basically it, except that answers to fractional multiplication problems often can be *reduced*. Reducing will be discussed a few sections from now, so there is no need to worry about it yet.

Let's multiply some more fractions for practice:

(1) $\frac{2}{9} \times \frac{2}{9} = \frac{2 \times 2}{9 \times 9} = \frac{4}{81}$

(2) $\frac{3}{7} \times \frac{3}{5} = \frac{3 \times 3}{7 \times 5} = \frac{9}{35}$

(3) $\frac{41}{165} \times \frac{11}{23} = \frac{41 \times 11}{165 \times 23} = \frac{451}{3795}$

In the following examples, we have not shown the middle step. Do it yourself, following the rules just given, to make sure you understand how fractions are multiplied:

$$\frac{23}{38} \times \frac{1}{4} = \frac{23}{152} \qquad \frac{17}{18} \times \frac{2}{3} = \frac{34}{54} \qquad \frac{1}{2} \times \frac{1}{2} = \frac{1}{4}$$

$$\frac{1}{4} \times \frac{1}{4} = \frac{1}{16} \qquad \frac{1}{8} \times \frac{1}{2} = \frac{1}{16} \qquad \frac{6}{19} \times \frac{21}{382} = \frac{126}{7258}$$

$$\frac{1}{2} \times \frac{1}{4} \times \frac{2}{3} = \frac{2}{24}$$

Now try the following practice problems. The answers are at the end of the chapter.

Problem Set B

Multiply the following fractions:

1. $\frac{3}{8} \times \frac{2}{9}$

2. $\frac{11}{16} \times \frac{2}{13}$

3. $\frac{3}{5} \times \frac{2}{5}$

4. $\frac{21}{22} \times \frac{21}{22}$

5. $\frac{12}{19} \times \frac{14}{19}$

6. $\frac{127}{386} \times \frac{41}{2192}$

7. $\frac{271}{273} \times \frac{336}{33661}$

8. $\frac{2}{7} \times \frac{4}{5} \times \frac{3}{8}$

9. $\frac{8}{15} \times \frac{13}{14} \times \frac{6}{7}$

10. $\frac{12}{19} \times \frac{435}{502} \times \frac{2876}{4883}$

DIVIDING FRACTIONS

A division problem with fractions usually is written like this:

$$\frac{4}{5} \div \frac{7}{8}$$

The symbol ÷ means *divided by*. Written to look like a division problem, the same problem would be:

$$\frac{7}{8} \overline{)\, \frac{4}{5}}$$

However, that looks terribly awkward, and our regular rules of long division would work very clumsily here. Fortunately, the technique for dividing fractions is just as easy as it is for multiplying them, except that you have to start with a special step. Remember, first of all, to write all division of fraction problems like our first example above. Then:

(a) *invert* the *second* fraction in the problem

(b) proceed just as in multiplication of fractions

Inverting a fraction means to "turn it upside down"; that is, you substitute the numerator for the denominator, and the denominator for the numerator. Or put still another way, just switch the numerator and the denominator with one another.

Here are some examples of inverting fractions:

If you invert $\frac{3}{5}$ you get $\frac{5}{3}$.

If you invert $\frac{478}{569}$ you get $\frac{569}{478}$.

If you invert $\frac{1}{8}$ you get $\frac{8}{1}$.

However, any fraction that has the number 1 as the denominator (bottom number) is actually the same as the whole number represented by the numerator. So, $\frac{8}{1} = 8$. In the same way, $\frac{13}{1} = 13$; $\frac{6}{1} = 6$; etc.

When you're doing fraction division, though, don't bother to change these kinds of numbers to whole numbers. Also, when you invert fractions you will get improper fractions (unless you started out with them to begin with), but for division purposes leave them that way rather than change them to mixed numbers.

Let's use the example we started with:

$$\frac{4}{5} \div \frac{7}{8}$$

First we invert the second fraction in the problem and get $\frac{8}{7}$ instead of $\frac{7}{8}$. Then we go ahead and *multiply* the two numbers we now have. Therefore, $\frac{4}{5} \div \frac{7}{8}$ becomes

$$\frac{4}{5} \times \frac{8}{7} = \frac{4 \times 8}{5 \times 7} = \frac{32}{35}$$

Here are a few more examples:

$$\frac{33}{39} \div \frac{657}{822} \text{ becomes: } \frac{33}{39} \times \frac{822}{657} = \frac{33 \times 822}{39 \times 657} = \frac{27,126}{25,623} = 1\frac{1503}{25,623}$$

$$\frac{3}{4} \div \frac{2}{3} \text{ becomes: } \frac{3}{4} \times \frac{3}{2} = \frac{3 \times 3}{4 \times 2} = \frac{9}{8} = 1\frac{1}{8}$$

$$\frac{3}{16} \div \frac{11}{12} \text{ becomes: } \frac{3}{16} \times \frac{12}{11} = \frac{3 \times 12}{16 \times 11} = \frac{36}{176}$$

Now we'll show some more problems and answers, but with the intermediate steps left out. Do these steps yourself, to make sure you understand how to divide with fractions.

$$\frac{2}{3} \div \frac{4}{5} = \frac{10}{12} \qquad\qquad \frac{23}{47} \div \frac{565}{566} = \frac{13,018}{26,555} \qquad\qquad \frac{7}{8} \div \frac{1}{206} = 180\frac{2}{8}$$

$$\frac{13}{16} \div \frac{3}{4} = 1\frac{4}{48} \qquad\qquad \frac{26}{27} \div \frac{27}{26} = \frac{676}{729} \qquad\qquad \frac{37}{43} \div \frac{2}{7} = 3\frac{1}{86}$$

$$\frac{1}{287,314} \div \frac{1}{143,657} = \frac{1}{2}$$

Here is a set of fraction division problems for you to work yourself. The answers are at the end of the chapter.

Problem Set C

Divide the following fractions:

1. $\frac{7}{8} \div \frac{8}{9}$

2. $\frac{13}{15} \div \frac{1}{5}$

3. $\frac{2}{3} \div \frac{4}{7}$

4. $\frac{3}{8} \div \frac{1}{4}$

5. $\frac{4}{5} \div \frac{11}{19}$

6. $\frac{36}{39} \div \frac{54}{99}$

7. $\frac{11}{76} \div \frac{4}{9}$

8. $\frac{218}{1007} \div \frac{3,164}{4,899}$

9. $\frac{1165}{1166} \div \frac{21,088}{22,001}$

10. $\frac{1}{9,999} \div \frac{138}{145}$

ADDING AND SUBTRACTING FRACTIONS

Addition and subtraction of fractions is more complicated than division or multiplication, because *you cannot add or subtract fractions unless they have the same denominator*. Therefore, most problems will require you to adjust at least one of the fractions in order to get both (or all) of them to have the same denominator. This is called finding a *common denominator*.

The simplest way to find common denominators in problems involving the addition or subtraction of two fractions is to *multiply* both the numerator and denominator of each fraction by the *denominator* of the other. For example, let's find a common denominator for these two fractions: $\frac{2}{3}$ and $\frac{3}{8}$. We multiply the numerator and denominator of each fraction by the denominator of the other:

$$\frac{2}{3}: \frac{2 \times 8}{3 \times 8} = \frac{16}{24} \qquad\qquad \frac{3}{8}: \frac{3 \times 3}{8 \times 3} = \frac{9}{24}$$

In this manner, we have converted both fractions so that they are expressed in 24ths, instead of 3rds and 8ths. Now we can add or subtract easily, using the following rule:

Fractions with the same denominator can be added or subtracted simply by performing the appropriate operation on the numerators of the fractions and using the result as the numerator of the answer, over the common denominator.

Thus:

$$\frac{2}{3} + \frac{3}{8} = \frac{2 \times 8}{3 \times 8} + \frac{3 \times 3}{8 \times 3} = \frac{16 + 9}{24} = \frac{25}{24} = 1\frac{1}{24}$$

$$\frac{2}{3} - \frac{3}{8} = \frac{2 \times 8}{3 \times 8} - \frac{3 \times 3}{8 \times 3} = \frac{16 - 9}{24} = \frac{7}{24}$$

$$\frac{11}{16} + \frac{7}{15} = \frac{11 \times 15}{16 \times 15} + \frac{7 \times 16}{15 \times 16} = \frac{165 + 112}{240} = \frac{277}{240} = 1\frac{37}{240}$$

$$\frac{11}{16} - \frac{7}{15} = \frac{11 \times 15}{16 \times 15} - \frac{7 \times 16}{15 \times 16} = \frac{165 - 112}{240} = \frac{53}{240}$$

Here are some problems with the intermediate steps omitted. Do them all the way through for practice, to be sure you understand addition and subtraction of fractions.

$$\frac{1}{2} + \frac{1}{4} = \frac{6}{8} \qquad \frac{8}{9} + \frac{11}{13} = 1\frac{86}{117} \qquad \frac{13}{33} + \frac{116}{347} = \frac{8,339}{11,451}$$

$$\frac{4}{7} + \frac{5}{11} = 1\frac{2}{77} \qquad \frac{1}{2} - \frac{1}{4} = \frac{2}{8} \qquad \frac{8}{9} - \frac{11}{13} = \frac{5}{117}$$

$$\frac{13}{33} - \frac{116}{347} = \frac{683}{11,451} \qquad \frac{4}{7} - \frac{5}{11} = \frac{9}{77}$$

Here is a set of fraction addition and subtraction problems for you to work out. The answers are at the end of the chapter.

Problem Set D

Solve the following addition and subtraction problems involving fractions:

1. $\frac{6}{7} - \frac{1}{8}$

2. $\frac{1}{2} + \frac{2}{3}$

3. $\frac{4}{17} - \frac{1}{100}$

4. $\frac{9}{10} + \frac{3}{10}$

5. $\frac{2}{3} - \frac{5}{11}$

6. $\frac{3}{4} + \frac{7}{8}$

7. $\dfrac{11}{12} - \dfrac{2}{9}$ 9. $\dfrac{155}{188} + \dfrac{208}{467}$

8. $\dfrac{7}{8} - \dfrac{6}{137}$ 10. $\dfrac{16}{161} - \dfrac{2}{163}$

REDUCING FRACTIONS

Reducing fractions means trying to express them in a simpler way. Not all fractions can be reduced, but many can — especially fractions that result from some kind of arithmetic manipulation. Here is our rule for reducing fractions:

A fraction can be *reduced* if both the numerator and the denominator can be *divided* by the *same number*.

A fraction whose numerator and denominator *cannot* be divided by one single number is said to be *reduced to lowest terms*.

Let's illustrate what we mean. Consider the fraction $\dfrac{10}{12}$. It is fairly obvious that both the numerator and denominator of this fraction can be divided by the number 2:

$$\frac{10}{12} = \frac{10 \div 2}{12 \div 2} = \frac{5}{6}$$

In other words, the fraction $\dfrac{10}{12}$ can be reduced to the fraction $\dfrac{5}{6}$ by dividing both numerator and denominator by 2. Actually, $\dfrac{10}{12}$ and $\dfrac{5}{6}$ represent *exactly the same quantity*. When you reduce a fraction you do not change its value at all. You just make it into a simpler-looking number.

Can the fraction $\dfrac{5}{6}$ be reduced further? No, it cannot, because there is no number that will divide into both 5 and 6 (except for the number 1, but if we divide both numbers by 1 we end up with exactly the same numbers as before; therefore, when we reduce we look for numbers *other* than 1 as common divisors to the numbers in our fractions).

There is no surefire way to find numbers that will divide into both the numerator and denominator of any fraction you may happen to come up with. However, there are a few guidelines you can use to make this trial and error method a little more efficient.

(a) If your fraction is composed of small numbers (and most of the ones you will encounter are likely to be), then you can often tell, just by looking, whether it can be reduced.

(b) If both numbers in your fraction are *even* (end in 0, 2, 4, 6, or 8), then they can be divided by 2.

(c) If the numbers in your fraction end in 0 or 5, then they both can be divided by 5.

In many cases, though, you will just have to experiment to make sure that your fraction is reduced to lowest terms.

Here are some examples of reducing fractions to lowest terms:

$\dfrac{11}{33} = \dfrac{1}{3}$, because both are divisible by 11.

$\dfrac{6}{9} = \dfrac{2}{3}$, because both are divisible by 3.

$\dfrac{4}{8} = \dfrac{1}{2}$, because both are divisible by 4.

$\dfrac{21}{70} = \dfrac{3}{10}$, because both are divisible by 7.

$\dfrac{15}{45} = \dfrac{1}{3}$, and $\dfrac{35}{80} = \dfrac{7}{16}$. All are divisible by 5.

$\dfrac{1008}{1288} = \dfrac{18}{23}$, because both are divisible by 56.   (!)

$\dfrac{1025}{1288}$ cannot be reduced. There is no number that can divide both numbers evenly.

Now for some practice problems for you to do. Up to this point we have not bothered reducing fractions in the answers to earlier practice problems, so all of the following problems use answers to problems in Problem Sets A, B, C, and D that were not reduced. (Be careful: We've thrown in a couple of ringers that *can't* be reduced, just to keep you on your toes.) The numbers in parentheses (A-1, B-7, etc.) show which problems and sets these are the answers to. The correct answers are at the end of the chapter.

Problem Set E

Reduce these numbers to lowest terms:

1.	(A-1) $4\dfrac{4}{11}$	7.	(B-9) $\dfrac{624}{1470}$	13.	(C-6) $1\dfrac{1458}{2106}$
2.	(B-1) $\dfrac{6}{72}$	8.	(B-10) $\dfrac{15,012,720}{46,574,054}$	14.	(D-1) $\dfrac{41}{56}$
3.	(B-2) $\dfrac{22}{208}$	9.	(C-2) $4\dfrac{5}{15}$	15.	(D-4) $1\dfrac{20}{100}$
4.	(B-3) $\dfrac{6}{25}$	10.	(C-3) $1\dfrac{2}{12}$	16.	(D-5) $\dfrac{7}{33}$
5.	(B-7) $\dfrac{91,056}{9,189,453}$	11.	(C-4) $1\dfrac{4}{8}$	17.	(D-6) $1\dfrac{20}{32}$
6.	(B-8) $\dfrac{24}{280}$	12.	(C-5) $\dfrac{76}{55}$	18.	(D-7) $\dfrac{75}{108}$

DEALING WITH MIXED NUMBERS IN PROBLEMS

So far, all of our problems have involved plain fractions, proper and improper. However, quite frequently you will have to work problems that involve mixed numbers. Consider these problems:

$$4\dfrac{1}{3} \div 6\dfrac{6}{7} \qquad 11\dfrac{7}{8} + 2\dfrac{1}{9} \qquad 3\dfrac{1}{2} \times 4 \qquad 6 - 3\dfrac{26}{29}$$

In order to do these operations most easily, you should convert mixed numbers and whole numbers into *improper fractions*. Then go ahead and work the problem according to the rules laid out in earlier sections. When you are through with your computations, change any improper fractions in your answer to mixed numbers or whole numbers, and be sure to reduce your answers to lowest terms.

Here are the rules for making improper fractions out of whole numbers and mixed numbers:

(a) To change a *whole number* into an improper fraction, use the whole number as the *numerator* of a fraction having 1 as the denominator.

$$5 = \dfrac{5}{1} \qquad 73 = \dfrac{73}{1} \qquad 8 = \dfrac{8}{1} \qquad 136,908,457 = \dfrac{136,908,457}{1}$$

(b) To change a *mixed number* into an improper fraction, multiply the whole number part of the mixed number by the denominator of the fraction part. Add this result to the numerator of the fraction part, using the original denominator.

As an example:

To change $11\dfrac{7}{8}$ into an improper fraction, we multiply 11 by the denominator of the fraction part, which is 8: $11 \times 8 = 88$. We add 88 to the numerator (7) of the fraction:

$88 + 7 = 95$. We use the original denominator, so our improper fraction will be $\frac{95}{8}$; that is, $11\frac{7}{8} = \frac{95}{8}$. Now some others:

$$22\frac{1}{2} = \frac{(22 \times 2) + 1}{2} = \frac{44 + 1}{2} = \frac{45}{2}$$

$$17\frac{11}{12} = \frac{(17 \times 12) + 11}{12} = \frac{204 + 11}{12} = \frac{215}{12}$$

$$6\frac{1}{8} = \frac{(6 \times 8) + 1}{8} = \frac{48 + 1}{8} = \frac{49}{8}$$

Once you have changed the whole or mixed numbers in your problem to improper fractions, you can perform the necessary operations just as already outlined. As examples, let's do the four problems from the beginning of this section. We are leaving out some intermediate steps, but you should do them yourself, to be sure that you know how to manipulate whole numbers and mixed numbers along with fractions.

(1) $4\frac{1}{3} \div 6\frac{6}{7}$ is the same as $\frac{13}{3} \div \frac{48}{7}$. In order to divide, we must invert the second fraction: $\frac{13}{3} \times \frac{7}{48} = \frac{91}{144}$.

(2) $3\frac{1}{2} \times 4$ is the same as $\frac{7}{2} \times \frac{4}{1} = 14$, when reduced.

(3) $11\frac{7}{8} + 2\frac{1}{9}$ is the same as $\frac{95}{8} + \frac{19}{9} = 13\frac{71}{72}$.

(4) $6 - 3\frac{26}{29}$ is the same as $\frac{6}{1} - \frac{113}{29} = 2\frac{3}{29}$.

Here is a set of practice problems. The answers are at the end of the chapter.

Problem Set F

Change the following numbers into improper fractions:

1. 17	6. $42\frac{5}{6}$	11. $13\frac{3}{11}$
2. $4\frac{1}{3}$	7. $8\frac{3}{8}$	12. 2
3. $174\frac{1}{2}$	8. $22\frac{15}{16}$	13. $53\frac{3}{4}$
4. 36	9. $36\frac{1}{100}$	14. $1,882,675\frac{11}{12}$
5. $7\frac{46}{1017}$	10. $36\frac{8}{100}$	15. $1,882,675$

Following is a set of practice problems using all the various methods of manipulating fractions. In these problems you will encounter addition, subtraction, multiplication, division, reducing, and changing whole numbers and mixed numbers into improper fractions, as well as changing improper fractions into mixed and whole numbers. Answers to these problems are at the end of the chapter.

Problem Set G

Solve the following arithmetic problems, which involve fractions.

1. $4 \times \frac{4}{5}$	3. $3\frac{3}{8} \times 17\frac{1}{4}$	5. $15 - \frac{3}{8}$
2. $\frac{56}{57} + 32\frac{3}{4}$	4. $2\frac{1}{2} \div 3\frac{7}{9}$	6. $11\frac{3}{4} + 4\frac{5}{6}$

7. $11\frac{3}{4} - 4\frac{5}{6}$ 12. $27\frac{5}{12} + 13\frac{1}{5}$ 17. $32\frac{1}{2} + 11\frac{6}{7}$

8. $11\frac{3}{4} \times 4\frac{5}{6}$ 13. $55\frac{55}{56} - 55\frac{7}{8}$ 18. $7 \div \frac{1}{7}$

9. $11\frac{3}{4} \div 4\frac{5}{6}$ 14. $\frac{1}{8} \div 16$ 19. $26\frac{789}{899} + \frac{1}{2}$

10. $3\frac{67}{100} + 9\frac{1}{10}$ 15. $5 \times 33\frac{1}{3}$ 20. $3\frac{2}{3} \times 4\frac{11}{14}$

11. $13\frac{1}{7} \div 4\frac{3}{7}$ 16. $2\frac{7}{12} - 1\frac{8}{9}$

Working With Decimals

Decimals are a special kind of fraction, expressed in a special way that makes them much easier to work with than fractions. These are decimal numbers:

21.6   133.6785   288.11   3830.1   0.0001

The decimal point (the dot) in these numbers separates the "whole number" part from the "fraction" part. Decimals actually are fractions, expressed in tenths, hundredths, thousandths, etc. Each of the numbers above can be expressed as a fraction as well:

$$21.6 = 21\frac{6}{10} \qquad 133.6785 = 133\frac{6785}{10,000} \qquad 288.11 = 288\frac{11}{100}$$

$$3830.1 = 3830\frac{1}{10} \qquad 0.0001 = \frac{1}{10,000}$$

Remember, prices, bills, debts, and any other thing expressed in dollars and cents is actually a decimal number, since one cent is $\frac{1}{100}$ of a dollar.

The big advantage to using decimal numbers is that they are so easy to work with. You add, subtract, multiply, and divide them almost as though the decimal point were not even there — all you have to do that is special is to *remember where the decimal point goes in your answer.*

ADDING AND SUBTRACTING DECIMAL NUMBERS

The only thing you have to do before you add or subtract decimal numbers is to line the decimal points in the numbers one beneath the other. For example, to add the following problem,

$$
\begin{array}{r}
118.6 \\
+ \quad 3.38 \\
+ \ 10.882 \\
+ \quad 6.6 \\
\hline
? \\
\end{array}
$$

just adjust the numbers to align the *decimal points* directly under one another, like this:

$$
\begin{array}{r}
118.6 \\
+ \quad 3.38 \\
+ \ 10.882 \\
+ \quad 6.6 \\
\hline
139.462 \\
\end{array}
$$

There is an additional trick you can do that may make it easier to add up long columns of decimal numbers. In any decimal number, you can add zeroes at the right end, AFTER the decimal point, without changing the value of the number. In other words, all these numbers are equal:

$$118.6 = 118.60 = 118.600 = 118.6000 = 118.60000 \quad \text{etc.}$$

If you add enough zeroes to each number so that all the sums have the same number of digits AFTER the decimal point, you can line them up a bit more easily:

$$
\begin{array}{r}
118.600 \\
+ \quad 3.380 \\
+ \quad 10.882 \\
+ \quad 6.600 \\
\hline
139.462
\end{array}
$$

What happens if you have included in your problem some numbers that don't have decimal points (that is to say, whole numbers)? No problem. In any *whole number*, the decimal point goes *at the end*:

$$22 = 22.0 \qquad 6 = 6.0 \qquad 1{,}887{,}654 = 1{,}887{,}654.0 \quad \text{etc.}$$

As with decimal numbers, you can tack on as many zeroes as you like without changing the value of the number.

In subtracting decimals, follow exactly the same rule: keep the decimal points under one another. The trick of adding zeroes often comes in particularly handy in subtraction.

$$
\begin{array}{r}
113.677 \\
- \quad 21.1 \\
\hline
92.577
\end{array}
\quad \text{or} \quad
\begin{array}{r}
113.677 \\
- \quad 21.100 \\
\hline
92.577
\end{array}
\qquad
\begin{array}{r}
28.6 \\
- \quad 11.822 \\
\hline
16.778
\end{array}
\quad \text{or} \quad
\begin{array}{r}
28.600 \\
- \quad 11.822 \\
\hline
16.778
\end{array}
$$

Notice that in both addition and subtraction of decimals the decimal point in the answer comes *directly under* the decimal points in the other numbers. So, for adding and subtracting decimal numbers, remember these rules:

(a) Line up the decimal points. If a number is a whole number, the decimal point goes at the end.
(b) Add zeroes, if it makes the problem easier to handle.
(c) Proceed just as if the decimal point were not there.
(d) The decimal point in the answer goes directly beneath the ones in the other numbers.

Here are some practice problems in addition and subtraction of decimals. The answers to these problems are at the end of the chapter.

Problem Set H

Perform the operation indicated.

1. $33.6 - 31.87$

2. $1.87 + 11.55 + 6$

3. $22.8 + 18.987 + 1.1$

4. $16.6 - 3.875$

5. $28.11 + 6.6667$

6. $486 + 11.8876 + 32.8 + 0.001$

7. $0.18001 - 0.08$

8. $11.19 + 16.667 + 20$

9. $27.65 - 13.119805$

10. $665 - 322.583$

MULTIPLYING DECIMAL NUMBERS

Multiplication of decimal numbers is very easy. First, perform the operation as if the decimal points were not there; then follow this simple rule for positioning the decimal point in the answer:

The answer to a decimal multiplication problem has as many decimal places as the two multiplied numbers put together.

Here is an example: $24.6 \times 3.54 = 87.084$

Note that the answer (87.084) has *three* digits after the decimal point. The two numbers that were multiplied to get this answer have *one* (24.6) and *two* (3.54) (a *total* of *three* decimal places), so the answer will have *three*. Therefore, to position the decimal point you count back three spaces from the end of the answer.

The rules for multiplying decimal numbers are:

(a) Multiply the numbers as if the decimal points weren't there.
(b) Count the digits to the *right* of the decimal points in each of the two numbers you multiplied.
(c) Count off that many digits to lie to the right of the decimal point in the answer.

Here are some examples (with intermediate steps omitted):

146.832	15.55	48.82	3476
× 1.11	× 23.8	× 117	× 0.56
162.98352	370.09	5711.94	1946.56

The following set of problems will give you practice in multiplication of decimal numbers. The answers are at the end of the chapter.

Problem Set I

Multiply the following sets of decimal numbers:

1. 34.34×28.119
2. 55×0.18
3. 6×0.0008
4. 18.887×54.3
5. 76.897×8.33
6. 0.008×0.0191
7. $54.678 \times 18,198.34$
8. 42.8×1.0001
9. 56.66×7.4
10. 99.99×0.98

DIVIDING DECIMAL NUMBERS

Division of decimal numbers is a bit more complicated than the other operations. As far as the *arithmetic* manipulations are concerned, they are exactly the same as they are in numbers without decimals. However, the placement of the decimal point in the answer requires more elaborate preparation.

When you divide two numbers, you divide one number *into* another. When these are decimal numbers, you want to "rearrange" them so that the number being divided *into the other* has *no decimal point*. It is done very simply: you **move the decimal point in BOTH numbers enough spaces to the right to drop it entirely *out* of the first number.** Here is an example:

We want to divide 44.6 by 22.3, or $44.6 \div 22.3$. We set the problem up like this: $22.3\,)\,\overline{44.6}$. Then we move the decimal point *one* space to the *right* in each number. Now we have $223\,)\,\overline{446}$ and can go on with the division to get our answer, which is 2. Here is another example:

$$11.66\,)\,\overline{456.872} \qquad 11.66\,)\,\overline{456.87.2} \qquad 1166\,)\,\overline{45687.2}$$

Suppose the first number has more decimal places than the second? Then we just add zeroes to the second number, before moving the decimal points. If the second number turns out to be a whole number (no decimal point), then put the decimal point at the end of it and add enough zeroes so that the decimal point can be moved far enough to eliminate the point in the other number. If the number that is being divided *into the other* already is a whole number, then you don't have to move a decimal point at all. Here are examples of various situations:

$$283.667 \overline{)433.01} \text{ becomes } 283667 \overline{)433010}$$
$$14.1 \overline{)17.66} \text{ becomes } 141 \overline{)176.6}$$
$$14.65 \overline{)361} \text{ becomes } 1465 \overline{)36100}$$
$$23.45 \overline{)567.8799} \text{ becomes } 2345 \overline{)56787.99}$$

$380 \overline{)3476.899}$ doesn't change, because the first number already is a whole number.

Once the decimal points have been moved properly, you divide to get your result. The decimal point in your answer goes *directly* above the one in the number below it, like this:

$$11.87 \overline{)39.8832} \qquad 11.87. \overline{)39.88.32} \qquad 1187 \overline{)3988.32}$$

$$\begin{array}{r} 3.36 \\ 1187 \overline{)3988.32} \\ -3561 \\ \hline 427.3 \\ -356.1 \\ \hline 71.22 \\ -71.22 \\ \hline 0 \end{array}$$

With decimal division problems, often you can continue on for as many places as you like; instead of leaving a remainder, you can add more zeroes and keep going on with the problem, adding more and more numbers to the right of the decimal point in your answer. This can become a problem, too: when should you stop? That all depends on the amount of accuracy you want. The further to the right of the decimal point you go, the smaller the value of the numbers located there. Consider these numbers:

$$0.1 \qquad 0.01 \qquad 0.001 \qquad 0.0001 \qquad 0.00001 \qquad 0.000001 \text{ etc.}$$

Translated into fractions, they become:

$$\frac{1}{10} \qquad \frac{1}{100} \qquad \frac{1}{1000} \qquad \frac{1}{10,000} \qquad \frac{1}{100,000} \qquad \frac{1}{1,000,000} \text{ etc.}$$

As you can see, they get pretty small after a while; usually the accuracy needed in most real estate problems doesn't require more than three or four places. In the section on rounding we will explain how you can achieve maximum accuracy without having to extend your answer to a large number of decimal places. In the meantime, here are some decimal division problems to practice on. The answers are at the end of the chapter.

Problem Set J

Solve the following decimal division problems; carry them to five places.

1. $4.55 \div 13.6$
2. $11.784 \div 4$
3. $46.8 \div 0.11$
4. $235.01 \div 9$
5. $67.5 \div 0.5$

6. $163 \div 4.889$
7. $1 \div 3$
8. $16 \div 16.5$
9. $6.1 \div 0.066$
10. $14.8 \div 0.01$

CONVERTING FRACTIONS INTO DECIMALS

As we said at the beginning of the section on decimals, these numbers are really a special way of expressing fractions. As a matter of fact, ANY fraction can be made into a decimal by following a very simple procedure:

To change a fraction into a decimal, divide the denominator into the numerator.

It's as simple as that. So, to get the decimal equivalent of, say, $\frac{1}{3}$ we just divide 3 into 1 like this:

$$3 \overline{)1.00000} \quad .33333 \ldots$$

Remember, now that you can work with decimals you don't have to worry about dividing a number into a smaller one; just put your decimal point in the right place and keep on going.

Here are some other fractions converted into decimals:

$$\frac{11}{12} \text{ becomes } 12\overline{)11.0000} \quad .9166\ldots \qquad \frac{1}{2} \text{ becomes } 2\overline{)1.0} \quad .5$$

$$\frac{3}{4} \text{ becomes } 4\overline{)3.00} \quad .75 \qquad \frac{7}{8} \text{ becomes } 8\overline{)7.000} \quad .875$$

This process works quite well with mixed numbers too. If you want, you can change the mixed number into an improper fraction and proceed from there. However, a good short-cut is just to perform the operation on the *fraction* part of the mixed number; attach the resulting decimal number to the whole number part and you have solved the problem. So,

$$37\frac{11}{12} \text{ becomes } 37.91666\ldots \qquad 4\frac{1}{2} \text{ becomes } 4.5$$

$$283\frac{3}{4} \text{ becomes } 283.75 \qquad 21\frac{7}{8} \text{ becomes } 21.875$$

When you change a fraction into a decimal, you will get one of three kinds of results: (1) You may get a result that comes out even. This will happen with fractions like $\frac{1}{2}$ (0.5) and $\frac{3}{4}$ (0.75). (2) You may get what is known as a *repeating decimal*. A repeating decimal has no end to it because it doesn't come out even, but it does have a pattern of repeating the same number or numbers. Probably the most common repeating decimals are $\frac{1}{3}$ (0.33333 . . .) and $\frac{2}{3}$ (0.66666 . . .), but there are many others, such as $\frac{1}{11}$ (0.090909 . . .), etc. A very elaborate one is $\frac{1}{7}$, where the repetition occurs in groups of six numbers: 0.142857142857 . . .

TABLE 17-1.
DECIMAL EQUIVALENTS OF COMMON FRACTIONS*

DENOMINATOR	NUMERATOR										
	1	2	3	4	5	6	7	8	9	10	11
12	.08333	⅙	¼	⅓	.41666	½	.58333	⅔	¾	⅚	.91666
11	.09090	.18181	.27272	.36363	.45454	.54545	.63636	.72727	.81818	.90909	—
10	.1	.2	.3	.4	.5	.6	.7	.8	.9	—	—
9	.11111	.22222	.33333	.44444	.55555	.66666	.77777	.88888	—	—	—
8	.125	¼	.375	½	.625	¾	.875	—	—	—	—
7	.14285	.28571	.42857	.57142	.71428	.85714	—	—	—	—	—
6	.16666	⅓	½	⅔	.83333	—	—	—	—	—	—
5	.2	.4	.6	.8	—	—	—	—	—	—	—
4	.25	½	.75	—	—	—	—	—	—	—	—
3	.33333	.66666	—	—	—	—	—	—	—	—	—
2	.5										

*To use this table, first find the denominator of your fraction in the column at the extreme left. Then move over to the column under the number representing the numerator of your fraction to find the decimal equivalent. For fractions that are not in lowest terms, the *reduced fractional equivalent* is shown; the decimal equivalent can be found by looking up this reduced equivalent. (This has not been done for fractions in tenths, since it is common practice to speak of such unreduced tenths fractions as ⁴/₁₀, ⁶/₁₀, etc.) Repeating or irrational fractions are shown by a rule beneath the digits given.

(3) You may get what is known as an *irrational number*. This is one that goes on and on but has no pattern to it. These irrational numbers usually occur with fairly elaborate fractions such as $\frac{121}{201}$ (0.60199004 . . .).

The best way to handle repeating and irrational decimals is to round them off; rounding will be discussed further on. Rounding may also be necessary with some even decimal fractions, if they happen to extend many places. (An example would be $\frac{1}{64}$, which becomes 0.015625; it comes out even but still takes up six places.)

Table 17-1 shows decimal equivalents for the common fractions having denominators from 2 to 12. Many of these you may already know, and you will soon keep many of them handy in your mind as you become more used to working with these kinds of numbers. In common practice you should be able to remember instantly the following decimal equivalents:

$\frac{1}{2} = 0.5$; $\frac{1}{3} = 0.3333$. . .; $\frac{2}{3} = 0.6666$. . .; $\frac{1}{4} = 0.25$; $\frac{3}{4} = 0.75$; $\frac{1}{5} = 0.2$; $\frac{1}{10} = 0.1$; etc.

Here are some problems in converting fractions to decimals. The answers are at the end of the chapter.

Problem Set K

Convert the following fractions to decimals. Carry your answer to five decimal places.

1.	$\frac{11}{13}$	6.	$\frac{7}{20}$
2.	$\frac{8}{17}$	7.	$\frac{7}{8}$
3.	$\frac{43}{101}$	8.	$\frac{9}{16}$
4.	$\frac{27}{28}$	9.	$\frac{15}{32}$
5.	$\frac{566}{569}$	10.	$\frac{27}{41}$

As you will learn in the next section, many of the answers to the last two problem sets can be *rounded*. However, the answers given for Problem Sets J and K are *not* rounded.

Rounding

Rounding is a process whereby we take a number with many decimal places (or *significant digits* — see page 163) and reduce it to a more manageable size. Suppose, for example, that you have very carefully measured a house and, according to your calculations, it has 1378.872698543 square feet. Is that elaborate decimal number really necessary? After all, one square foot is only a bit larger than this page (which is about $\frac{2}{3}$ square foot), so the fact that there is 0.872698543 square foot more than 1378 may not be worth all the trouble it took to find it out. One letter on this page occupies about 0.00005 square foot; the number 1378.872698543 is far more precise than that, since it purports to measure to the nearest 0.000000001 square foot — a particle of space too small to see without a magnifying glass.

In fact, for nearly all purposes, measurement of a house to the "nearest" $\frac{1}{10}$ or $\frac{1}{100}$ (0.1 or 0.01) square foot is plenty. The measurement 0.01 square foot is only slightly larger than a square inch. Then, how would we adjust our long number above to get the desired level of accuracy? To do this, we would *round off* the number.

Rounding is very simple. We **look at the number that occupies the space representing the desired degree of accuracy. If the number to the *right* of it is 4 or less, drop that number and all the others. If the number to the *right* of the desired number is 5 or higher, *raise* the desired number by 1 and drop all the rest.**

Let's go back to the number we started with: 1378.872698543. To round it to the nearest 0.01, we look at the number in the *second* decimal place, because to round to the nearest 0.01 we will end up with a number having *two* decimal places. The number occupying this space is 7. The number to the *right* of this one is 2. Therefore, we leave the 7 as it is and drop *all* the numbers to the right of it. Rounded to the nearest 0.01, then, the number 1378.872698543 becomes 1378.87. Now, if we round it only to the nearest 0.1, we look at the number in the *first* decimal place; it is 8. The number to the right of it is 7; 7 is greater than 5, so we *round up*. This means that we change the 8 to a 9 and then drop all the numbers to the right of it. Consequently, 1378.872698543 rounded to the nearest 0.1 becomes 1378.9.

Here, then, are our rounding rules:

(a) After determining the degree of accuracy desired, locate the number occupying the space representing that degree of accuracy.

(b) If the number to the right of it is 4 or less, *round down*.

(c) If the number to the right of it is 5 or larger, *round up*.

(Rounding *down* means to drop all the numbers beyond the significant place without changing the number *in* the significant place. Rounding *up* means to change the number in the significant place to the next highest number and then drop the numbers beyond the significant place.)

What happens if the number in the significant place is 9 and you have to round it up? Then you change the 9 to a 0 and round up the number to the *left* of the place the 9 occupied. If that number, too, is a 9, you just repeat the process until you encounter a number that is not a 9. Therefore, the number 1.01999 rounded to three places becomes 1.02. As a matter of fact, this number will be 1.02, whether it is rounded to 2, 3, or 4 places.

Here is a practice set of numbers to round. The answers will be found at the end of the chapter.

Problem Set L

Round each of these numbers to *two*, *three*, and *four* decimal places.

1.	11.879456	6.	0.00016
2.	23.050567	7.	0.998356
3.	11.00019	8.	1.11896
4.	0.098765	9.	0.7654329
5.	31.00008	10.	5.76009

SIGNIFICANT DIGITS

Sometimes you will encounter instructions that require you to round to a certain number of *significant digits*, rather than to a specific place. Significant digits are those that actually express quantity in a number. In effect, all digits in a number are significant *except* strings of zeroes on either side of the decimal point. Both of these numbers have four significant digits:

1,198,000,000,000   0.0000000001198

The function of the zeroes in these numbers is to show *magnitude* — whether we are dealing in trillions or trillionths.

These numbers have 13 significant digits each:

1,198,000,000,001   0.1000000001198

The difference here is that these numbers do *not* have a string of zeroes beginning *right next* to the decimal point. They have strings of zeroes, all right, but the zeroes are separated from the decimal point by at least one nonzero digit.

Significant digits represent numbers that are important to the people using them. 1,198,000,000,000 might be a number the federal government uses; say, a measure of earned incomes in the nation or something like that. A stray billion or two doesn't mean a whole lot in this context (one billion dollars spread evenly among all Americans would be less than five dollars apiece), so the accuracy needed is adequately satisfied by measuring to the nearest billion. The decimal number might be used by physicists measuring the size of some atomic particle.

When you work a problem, your answer should contain *no more* significant digits than the factor you used with the least; that is, 23.8×44.8765 should be rounded to 3 digits, because 23.8 has only 3. This rule does not apply when changing fractions to decimals, when using numbers like 3, 4, etc., or when using numbers which you know are *exact*.

(1) $38 \times 54.7 = 2100$ (rounded to 2 digits because 38 has only 2)

(2) $381 \times 547.13 = 208,000$ (rounded to 3, since 381 has 3)

(3) $0.0131 \times 0.000567 = 0.00000743$ (carried to 3, since 0.0131 has 3)

(4) $\frac{1}{7} = 0.142857142857142857 \ldots$ (carried to 4 digits is 0.1429)

(5) $\frac{1}{13} = 0.07692307 \ldots$ (carried to 6 digits is 0.076923)

(6) $200 \times 1.733 = 346.6$ (use all 4 significant digits if you know that the figure 200 is *exact* and not an approximation.)

Here are some exercises in using significant digits. Answers are given at the end of the chapter.

Problem Set M

In the following problems, carry all answers to five significant digits, when warranted.

1. Decimal equivalent of $3\frac{18}{19}$

2. $42.1 \div 56.88$

3. 0.008×1.9866

4. $1.1187 \div 467$

5. 0.0009×0.00098

6. 1.188×3.66

7. Decimal equivalent of $\frac{16}{33}$

8. $5664 \div 0.00046$

9. $5.19 \div 1.004$

10. 6.16×0.00055

Dealing With Percents

"Per cent" is Latin for "per hundred." A percent is a special way of writing decimal numbers, expressed in hundredths. **To convert percents into decimals, you move the decimal point TWO SPACES TO THE LEFT. To convert decimals into percents, you move the decimal point TWO SPACES TO THE RIGHT.** Here are some examples of percent numbers and their *decimal equivalents*.

$$6\% = 0.06 \quad 11\% = 0.11 \quad 115\% = 1.15 \quad 2\frac{1}{2}\% = 0.025 \quad 8\frac{3}{4}\% = 0.0875$$

You will encounter percentages throughout your real estate career. Two of the most important numerical concepts used in the real estate business almost always are expressed in percentage terms: sales commissions and interest rates on mortgage loans. Other frequently encountered concepts that you will find expressed in percents are down payments, loan-to-value ratios, the rates of commission split between brokers cooperating on a sale, and the rate of commissions brought in that is retained by the broker. Generally speaking, whenever you encounter anything expressed as a *rate*, be on the lookout for a percentage figure lurking somewhere.

Arithmetic with percentages is just the same as it is with decimals, with two important additional steps:

(a) At the beginning of the problem, convert all percent numbers into their decimal equivalents. Then perform all the necessary operations on the decimal numbers you have produced.

(b) At the end of the problem, be sure to convert back to percentage numbers all those that should properly be expressed in percentage terms.

Here is an elaborate problem that requires a lot of converting back and forth between decimals and percents:

Jones, a salesman for Mr. Goodguy, the broker, sells a house that had been listed by Smith, a salesman for Mrs. Dearlady, another broker. Mrs. Dearlady's listing had specified a 6% commission, and she and Mr. Goodguy have agreed to split that commission between their two firms. Jones's agreement with Goodguy is that he receives $42\frac{1}{2}\%$ of the total commission he brings in. Smith's agreement with Mrs. Dearlady is that he gets a flat $1000 fee for every listing he brings in that is successfully sold. The house was sold for $60,000.

(a) How much was Jones' commission?

(b) What was Smith's rate of the total commission?

This is a pretty elaborate problem, but now that we're almost at the end of our chapter on computation, we ought to be able to do it. The way to tackle any problem like this is to find out:

(1) What is the information I have to get?   (2) How do I solve the problem?

For question (a) we want to know how much Jones's commission was. Note that the question doesn't ask "How many dollars?" but that's what it means. To answer this question, we must find out the following things: (1) What was the total commission on the house? (2) How much of that went to Mr. Goodguy's brokerage? (3) Of that amount, how much did Jones get?

First, compute the commission on the sale. It was 6% of $60,000. We convert 6% to a decimal by moving the decimal place two spaces LEFT: 6% = 0.06. The commission on the house, then, was 0.06 × $60,000 = $3600.

Second, we must determine how much of the $3600 went to Mr. Goodguy's firm. In the language of this problem, you interpret the word *split* to mean an even split, so each firm would get half. Therefore, Mr. Goodguy's firm got $\frac{1}{2}$ of $3600 or $1800.

Third, we know that Jones gets $42\frac{1}{2}\%$ of the commissions he brings in, so he gets $42\frac{1}{2}\%$ of the $1800. We change $42\frac{1}{2}\%$ into a decimal by moving the decimal point two spaces to the left and get 0.425. Therefore, Jones's commission was 0.425 × $1800 = $765.

The second part of the problem is to find Smith's *rate* of commission. In effect, we have just the opposite task from Jones's problem; there we knew his rate of commission and had to find out the dollar amount. Here we know the dollar amount and need to find out the rate. We know from the work we already have done that Smith got $1000 of the total of $3600 split between Goodguy and Mrs. Dearlady. Consequently, Smith got $\frac{1000}{3600}$ of the commission. We can express it that way, because it is obvious that of the 3600 dollars of the total commission, Smith got 1000, or 1000-3600ths of them. To find the rate of commission that Smith got, we change $\frac{1000}{3600}$ first to a decimal and then to a percent. So,

$$\frac{1000}{3600} = \frac{5}{18} = 0.277777 \ldots = 27.78\% \text{ (rounded)}$$

Therefore, Smith got 27.78% of the total commission.

Problems using percentages generally deal with three numbers:

(a) The first is the percentage number itself. We will call it the *rate*.
(b) The second is the number the percentage is based upon. We will call it the *base*.
(c) The third is the number that represents the proportion of the base specified by the rate. We will call it the *product*.

Here are some examples:

5 is 50% of 100. 5 is the *product*. 50% is the *rate*. 10 is the *base*.

$3600 is 6% of $60,000. $3600 is the *product*. 6% is the *rate*. $60,000 is the *base*.

Remembering that you have to convert into decimals to do the arithmetic, and back again to percents to express your answer, you can solve any percentage problem so long as you have *two* of the three parts: base, rate, or product. Here's how:

(a) Product = Rate × Base $3600 =   0.06 × $60,000
(b)   Rate = Product ÷ Base   0.06 = $3600 ÷ $60,000
(c)   Base = Product ÷ Rate $60,000 = $3600 ÷ 0.06

Here are some examples of questions that would fit each of the three types of solution arrangements.

(a) Mr. Quagmeyer's house was sold for $60,000 and the broker received a 6% commission. What commission was paid?
(b) Mr. Quagmeyer's house was sold for $60,000 and the broker received a commission of $3600. What was the rate of commission?
(c) Mr. Quagmeyer's house was sold, and the broker was paid a 6% commission that came to $3600. What was the sale price of the house?

Let us use the letter P for product, R for rate, and B for base. Their relationship can conveniently be expressed as follows:

$$P \text{ is } R\% \text{ of } B. \qquad P = R \times B. \qquad R = \frac{P}{B}. \qquad B = \frac{P}{R}.$$

To find P, multiply R and B.

To find R or B, divide P by the other factor. (If you know P and one of the other factors, divide that other factor into P to find the missing one.)

Now here are some problems involving percentages. Remember your two sets of rules: (a) how to convert decimals into percent numbers, and vice versa, and (b) how to handle percent problems involving P, R, and B.

Problem Set N

Perform the indicated computations involving percentages.

1. Calculate the following:

   a. 15% of 250

   b. 22.6% of 3

   c. $8\frac{3}{4}$% of $33,668

   d. $48\frac{1}{2}$% of 110

   e. 6% of $37,950

   f. 11% of 45,560

2. Calculate the correct number to fill the blank spaces:

   a. 46 is _____% of 200.

   b. 67 is _____% of 6911.

   c. 196 is _____% of 8.

   d. 39.6 is _____% of 55.

   e. 11 is _____% of 22.

   f. 2.11 is _____% of 1000.

3. Calculate the correct number to fill the blank spaces:

   a. 1096 is 56% of _____.

   b. 56 is 56% of _____.

   c. 7 is 70% of _____.

   d. 345 is 0.2% of _____.

   e. 117 is 2367% of _____.

   f. 56 is $18\frac{2}{3}$% of _____.

PERCENTAGE — FRACTION EQUIVALENTS

Remember, just like decimals, percentage numbers can have fractional equivalents. Here is a list of common percentage-fraction equivalents.

$$10\% = \frac{1}{10} \qquad 30\% = \frac{3}{10} \qquad 60\% = \frac{3}{5} \qquad 80\% = \frac{4}{5}$$

$$12\frac{1}{2}\% = \frac{1}{8} \qquad 33\frac{1}{3}\% = \frac{1}{3} \qquad 62\frac{1}{2}\% = \frac{5}{8} \qquad 83\frac{1}{3}\% = \frac{5}{6}$$

$$16\frac{2}{3}\% = \frac{1}{6} \qquad 37\frac{1}{2}\% = \frac{3}{8} \qquad 66\frac{2}{3}\% = \frac{2}{3} \qquad 87\frac{1}{2}\% = \frac{7}{8}$$

$$20\% = \frac{1}{5} \qquad 40\% = \frac{2}{5} \qquad 70\% = \frac{7}{10} \qquad 90\% = \frac{9}{10}$$

$$25\% = \frac{1}{4} \qquad 50\% = \frac{1}{2} \qquad 75\% = \frac{3}{4}$$

Calculating Areas

Figuring the *area* of a particular space is important in the real estate business, because so much real estate is measured, bought, and sold by area. It costs so-much *per square foot* to build a house or to rent office space. Much land is priced on a *per-acre* basis. Nearly everyone who deals in real estate wants to know *how much* land or floor space he is dealing with, and this must be expressed in units of area.

MEASUREMENT OF AREAS

Area is measured in *square measures* and in some special measurements as well. Square measures are measures such as *square inches, square feet, square miles,* etc. In land measurement we also make frequent use of the *acre,* which is 43,560 square feet; this measure is a very ancient one, and it would take too much space to describe how this peculiar area measurement came into common use. But, remember that it *is* widely used.

Square measures sometimes are hard to visualize. This page, for example, has an area of about 94 square inches, or about $\frac{2}{3}$ square foot. If you took approximately 67,000 of these pages and very carefully laid them out next to each other so that they didn't overlap and no space showed between any of them, you would have covered an area of about one acre. An acre might be easier to visualize if you think of a square plot of land a little over 208 feet on a side.

Remember also that a square measure does not actually have to be an area that is square. This confusing statement really means that a figure can have an area of, say, one square inch without actually being a square with sides one inch long. In Figure 17-1 we have drawn a number of figures. Each may look different from the others, but they all have one thing in common: each of them encompasses an area of one square inch. The measurements of each are shown, and as we go through the ways of figuring areas of various kinds of figures in the next pages, you can return to these drawings and verify that each of them has exactly one square inch.

COMPARATIVE MEASURES

We have spoken of inches and feet; in real estate there are some other measures that are used infrequently but should be remembered for future reference. It is also possible that some license examination questions may require you to know these measures. We divide them into *linear measures* and *square measures*. Square measures we have already defined; linear measures simply are measurements of distance from one point to another. Here the linear and square measures are compared:

LINEAR MEASURE	SQUARE MEASURE
12 inches = 1 foot	144 square inches = 1 square foot
16½ feet = 1 rod	272.25 square feet = 1 square rod
66 feet = 4 rods = 1 chain	16 square rods = 1 square chain
320 rods = 1 mile	4356 square feet = 1 square chain
80 chains = 1 mile	10 square chains = 1 acre
5280 feet = 1 mile	43,560 square feet = 1 acre
	640 acres = 1 square mile

"Feet," "inches," "miles," and "acres" are familiar terms, but "rods" and "chains" are less so. Remember them, though, since they are occasionally used in land measurement. They also appear fairly often on licensing examinations, since they are specialized terms exclusive to real estate.

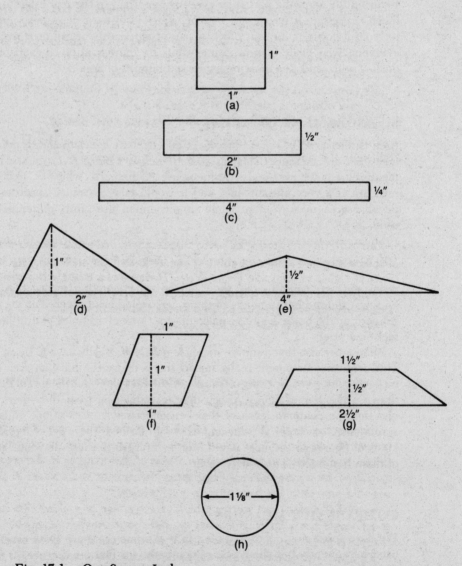

Fig. 17-1. One Square Inch

COMMON GEOMETRIC SHAPES

Licensing examinations are likely to require you to be able to figure the areas of certain *shapes*. These shapes would most likely be triangles, most four-sided figures, and circles.

Triangles are three-sided figures. In Figure 17–1, (d) and (e) are triangles. Mathematicians have given special names to several different kinds of triangles: a triangle with two sides the same length is an *isosceles* triangle, and the one with all three sides the same length is called an *equilateral* triangle. However, the most significant special kind of triangle for real estate purposes is the *right* triangle; this is a triangle with one *right angle*. A right angle is a 90° angle, or one that makes a square corner. The corners of this page are right angles. As a matter of fact, if you draw a line between two opposite corners (upper right and lower left, for example), you will divide the page into two right triangles.

Quadrilaterals are four-sided figures. In Figure 17–1, (a), (b), (c), (f), and (g) all are quadrilaterals. Quadrilaterals fall into three major groups; the area of each kind is calculated in a different way.

(1) *Parallelograms* are figures whose opposite sides are *parallel*. Lines are parallel when they always remain the same distance apart. The rails on a railroad track are an example of parallel lines. The left and right edges of this page are parallel to each other, and so are the top and bottom edges; therefore this page is a parallelogram.

A parallelogram whose corners all are right angles is called a *rectangle*. This page also is a rectangle, since it has square corners. A rectangle with all four sides the same length is a *square*. In Figure 17–1, (a) is a square (as well as a rectangle and a parallelogram). Both (b) and (c) are rectangles (and parallelograms). Shape (f) is a parallelogram only. Shape (g) is *not* a parallelogram; although the top and bottom sides are parallel, the left and right sides are not.

(2) *Trapezoid* is the name given to figures like (g). In these kinds of figures, one opposite pair of sides is parallel but the other is not.

(3) *Irregular quadrilaterals* are all other four-sided figures.

Circles, of course, are familiar figures, whose area you should be able to determine, following the simple directions given later in this section.

AREA OF TRIANGLES

As we will discover, triangles occur frequently in real estate measurement, mainly because the best way to determine the area of an irregular figure is to cut it up into triangles, get the area of each one, and add them all up. The area of a triangle is derived as follows:

To find the area of a triangle, multiply the length of one side by the distance from that side to the corner opposite it; then divide this result by two.

We can state this rule in a formula, too:

$$A = B \times H \times \frac{1}{2}$$

In this formula, *A* means *area*, *B* means *base*, and *H* means *height*. Note that to multiply something by $\frac{1}{2}$ is exactly the same as dividing it by 2.

Finding the *height* (*H*) in this calculation is not always easy. Usually on a license examination the height will be given to you, or there will be an easy way of finding it. The height is the *shortest distance* from a side of the triangle to the corner opposite it. It is measured by a *perpendicular* line from the side to the corner. A perpendicular line is one that intersects the base to form a right angle.

Note that it does not matter which side you use in making this calculation; each side of a triangle has a different corner opposite to it. Always remember that the height of a triangle is the distance from the *specific* side you are using to the *single corner opposite* it. In Figure 17–2 we have drawn the same triangle three times to show that the same answer is arrived at when calculating area, no matter which side is used.

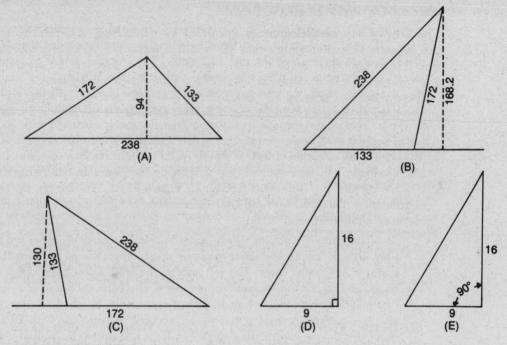

Fig. 17-2.   Triangles

Illustration (A) uses the side with the length of 238. The broken line represents the height to the corner opposite the side. This length is 94. According to our formula, the *base* is 238, and the height is 94. Therefore:

$$A = 238 \times 94 \times \frac{1}{2}$$

$$= 22{,}372 \times \frac{1}{2}$$

$$= 11{,}186 = 11{,}000 \text{ (2 significant digits)}$$

We show the same triangle in illustration (B), but have rotated it so that another side is on the bottom. Notice that this side is so short that the corner opposite it is nowhere directly above it. That doesn't matter; we just "extend" the side far enough that we can measure a perpendicular line from it to the opposite corner. Here, then, we have a base of 133 and a height of 168. Using our formula gives us an area of 11,172, which is 11,000, rounded to 2 significant digits.

Illustration (C) shows the same triangle being measured from the third side of 172, with a height of 130. This gives 11,180, which, once again, rounds to 11,000. We have omitted the calculations for illustrations (B) and (C) so that you may practice them yourself to see if you get the right answers.

Triangles (d) and (e) in Figure 17–1 can be used for practice also, to see if you can calculate the correct area of one square inch for each of them.

A special case when you figure areas of triangles is the *right triangle*. Remember that the right triangle is one that contains a right angle, which is an angle of 90 degrees, or a square corner.

Illustrations (D) and (E) in Figure 17–2 are right triangles. Usually a square corner, or 90° angle, is indicated in one of the two ways shown in these figures: either the symbol "90°" appears or a little square is drawn in the corner of the right angle. These indications may occur in other figures besides triangles.

The interesting thing about a right triangle, is that the two sides next to the right angle are the respective *heights* for each other. The height, as we remember, is the perpendicular distance from a side to the corner opposite it. The two sides by the right angle are perpendicular to each other because there is a right angle between them. Therefore, each must represent the height figure for the other. So, when you are given a right triangle, you don't have to calculate the height, since it is given by the length of one of the sides.

AREAS OF PARALLELOGRAMS

The area of any parallelogram is calculated by multiplying one side by the height to the *opposite* side. Remember that the height is measured by a perpendicular line from one side to the other. Since the two sides are parallel, they are the same distance apart everywhere, so it doesn't matter where the measurement takes place.

Illustration (f) in Figure 17-1 is a parallelogram; its base is 1 in. long, and the height, represented by the dotted line, is also 1 in. Our formula for the area of a parallelogram is

$$A = B \times H$$

so in this case the area of the parallelogram is 1×1, or 1 sq. in.

For simple parallelograms you have to measure the height and this may cause problems, just as with triangles. However, rectangles and squares are much easier to work with, because the sides adjacent to the base *are* the height. Remember, the height of a parallelogram is the perpendicular distance between two opposite sides. A perpendicular is a line that intersects are a right angle. The sides of a square or a rectangle *all* are perpendicular to the ones next to them — in fact, that is the precise definition of those figures. Therefore, the area of a *rectangle* is the length of one *long side multiplied by* the length of a *short side*. In Figure 17-1, (b) and (c) are rectangles, of one square inch each. The area of (b) is $\frac{1}{2}$ in. $\times$ 2 in. = 1 sq. in.; (c) is $\frac{1}{4}$ in. $\times$ 4 in., or 1 sq. in.

The area of a square is even easier to measure. Since all the sides are the same length, you just have to measure one and you know them all. Therefore, the area of a square is the length of *one side, multiplied by itself*. Illustration (a) in Figure 17-1 is a square with a one-inch side; 1 in. $\times$ 1 in. = 1 sq. in.

In Figure 17-3 are some parallelograms. The area of the square is 25; of the rectangles, 18 and $31\frac{1}{2}$; and of the other parallelogram, 36. We will leave it to you to determine which is which and to go through the calculations yourself to see how the areas were arrived at.

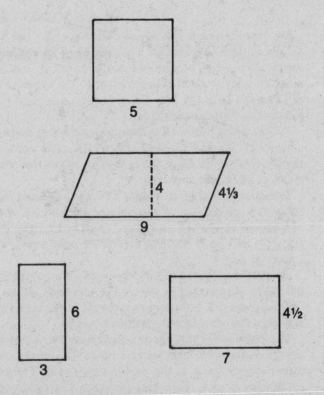

Fig. 17-3.   Parallelograms

AREAS OF TRAPEZOIDS

A trapezoid is a four-sided figure with two sides parallel and two sides not parallel. Illustration (g) in Figure 17-1 is a trapezoid. To find the area of these figures, you do the following:

The area of a trapezoid is calculated by (1) adding the lengths of the two *parallel* sides, (2) dividing this sum by 2, and (3) multiplying this result by the *height*, which is the distance between the two parallel sides. As a formula, this is

$$A = \frac{B_1 + B_2}{2} \times H$$

That formula looks pretty imposing, but it really isn't. B_1 and B_2 are the two parallel sides (bases) of the trapezoid; H is the height. Let's apply this method to (g) in Figure 17-2. The two parallel sides are $1\frac{1}{2}$ in. and $2\frac{1}{2}$ in., which add up to 4 in. The height is $\frac{1}{2}$ in., which multiplied by 4 in. gives 2 sq. in. Since the area of a trapezoid is *half* this amount, the correct answer is 1 sq. in.

Figure 17-4 has an illustration of a trapezoid whose area is 168. See if you can arrive at this same result.

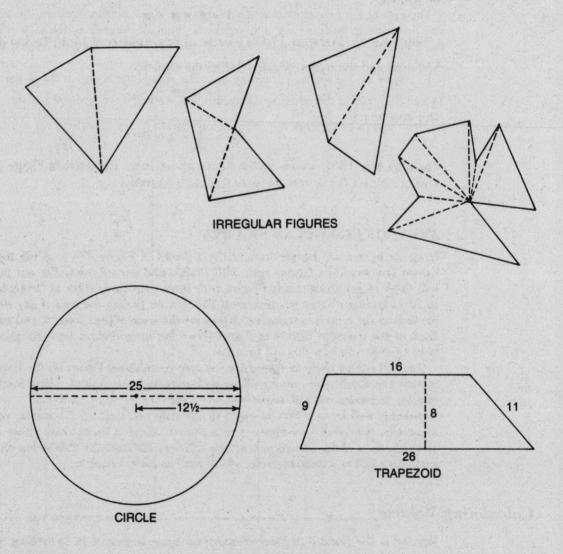

Fig. 17-4. Trapezoids, Circles, and Irregular Figures

AREAS OF CIRCLES

A circle, as you know, is a figure that is perfectly round. The formal mathematical definition is that it is a figure whose edge is always exactly the same distance from its center; all U.S. coins are in the shape of a circle.

There are three important terms concerning the circle that you must know: (1) The *radius* of the circle is the distance from the center to the edge. (2) The *diameter* of the circle is the distance across the circle, going through the center. It would be, therefore, exactly twice as long as the radius. (3) The third term you must know is π. This is the Greek letter *pi* (pronounced "pie") and is the symbol that mathematicians use to denote "the ratio of the circumference of a circle to its diameter." This means that if you multiply the diameter of any circle by the number π the result will be the distance *around* the circle. Here is the actual value of π:

$$\pi = 3.14159 \ldots$$

Therefore, if you have a circle with a diameter of 30 ft., then the distance around the outside of the circle would be $\pi \times 30$ ft., or 3.14159×30 ft., or about $94\frac{1}{4}$ ft.

The symbol π is also used when calculating the *area* of the circle. To find the area of a circle, multiply the *radius* by itself and multiply that result by π. The formula would be written:

$$A = R \times R \times \pi$$

Illustration (h) in Figure 17-1 is a circle, with a diameter of $1\frac{1}{8}$ in. To find the area, we first must find the radius, which is half of the diameter:

$$\frac{1}{2} \times 1\frac{1}{8} = \frac{9}{16}$$

Our area then is:

$$\frac{9}{16} \times \frac{9}{16} \times 3.14159$$

The answer is 0.991, which rounds to one square inch. The circle in Figure 17-4 has an area of 491; see if you can calculate this result correctly.

AREAS OF IRREGULAR FIGURES

Irregular figures are figures such as those shown in Figure 17–4, at the top. Irregular figures also would be figures with both straight and curved sides. For our purposes, we will think of any straight-sided figure with more than three sides as "irregular," at least so far as finding its area is concerned. The rule for finding the area of any *straight-sided* figure is to cut it up into triangles, determine the areas of the triangles, and add them up. Each of the irregular figures in Figure 17–4 has been divided into triangles by broken lines to show you how this can be done.

You will not be likely to encounter any *very* complicated figures on the licensing examination nor should you encounter any with partially curved sides. These kinds of figures require trigonometry and sometimes even calculus to solve, and that is mathematical knowledge well beyond that assumed in any state examination. Of course, you *may* find a question that involves a figure with a curved side, but in that case either you will be given the area of the curved part or you will very obviously be able to lop off the curved part into a half or a quarter circle, which you can easily calculate.

Calculating Volume

Volume is the amount of three-dimensional space contained in something. If this page has so and so many square inches, a bucket would be said to contain so and so many *cubic* inches. Volume, therefore, is measured in *cubic measures*.

In real estate, relatively few volume measurements are made. Houses are sometimes measured in cubic feet, but this convention is much less popular than it used to be. Concrete is measured in cubic feet or yards.

On an examination, you probably won't encounter any volume questions; if you happen to, they will almost certainly involve only *rectangular solids*. A rectangular solid is a box. It is a solid figure with six sides, with the sides opposite each other being identical, and with all sides perpendicular to the ones next to them. Look at any normal box, and you will see that this is a proper description.

A box has three measurements: length, width, and height. (A rectangle, remember, had two measurements.) Figure 17-5 shows a rectangular solid, with length (L), width (W), and height (H) marked. The broken lines represent the back sides of the solid (or box), which are hidden by the front. The volume of any rectangular solid is easy to calculate: Multiply the length times the width, and then multiply the answer by the height. Or,

$$V = L \times W \times H$$

VOLUME

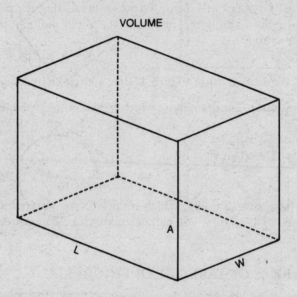

Fig. 17-5.   Rectangular Solid

Let us suppose that our box has the three measurements of 12 in., 8 in., and 6 in. Then its volume is $12 \times 8 \times 6$, or 576 *cubic* inches. How many cubic *feet* would that be? First we must figure out how many cubic inches are in a cubic foot. There are 12 in. in a foot and 12×12 (or 144) sq. in. in a sq. ft. A cu. ft. is a volume that would be represented by a box with each edge (L, W, and H) being 1 ft., or 12 in., long. Therefore, a cubic foot contains $12 \times 12 \times 12$ cu. in., or 1728 cu. in. Our box contained 576 cu. in., so it also contains $\frac{576}{1728}$ cu. ft. This reduces to $\frac{1}{3}$ cu. ft.

Here are some cubic measure equivalents:

$$1 \text{ cu. ft.} = 12 \times 12 \times 12 \text{ cu. in.} = 1728 \text{ cu. in.}$$

$$1 \text{ cu. yd.} = 3 \times 3 \times 3 \text{ cu. ft.} = 27 \text{ cu. ft.}$$

$$1 \text{ cu. yd.} = 27 \times 1728 \text{ cu. in.} = 46,656 \text{ cu. in.}$$

Practice problems involving volume are in the "Real Estate Mathematics" chapter (Chapter 18) that follows.

Problem Set O

Calculate the areas of the following figures:

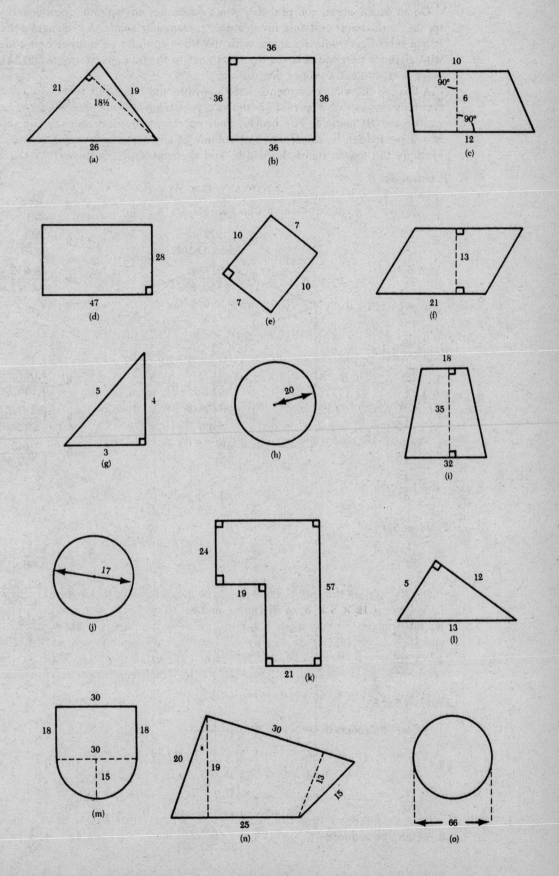

ANSWERS

Problem Set A

1. $4\frac{4}{11}$

2. $16\frac{18}{19}$

3. $60\frac{6}{7}$

4. $3\frac{1}{2}$

5. $22\frac{47}{108}$

6. $8\frac{10}{13}$

7. $7\frac{1630}{3321}$

8. $9\frac{1}{5}$

9. $2\frac{30,541}{51,111}$

10. $15\frac{4}{5}$

Problem Set B

1. $\frac{6}{72}$

2. $\frac{22}{208}$

3. $\frac{6}{25}$

4. $\frac{441}{484}$

5. $\frac{168}{361}$

6. $\frac{5207}{846,112}$

7. $\frac{91,056}{9,189,453}$

8. $\frac{24}{280}$

9. $\frac{624}{1470}$

10. $\frac{15,012,720}{46,574,054}$

Problem Set C

1. $\frac{63}{64}$

2. $4\frac{5}{15}$

3. $1\frac{2}{12}$

4. $1\frac{4}{8}$

5. $1\frac{21}{55}$

6. $1\frac{1458}{2106}$

7. $\frac{99}{304}$

8. $\frac{1,067,982}{3,186,148}$

9. $1\frac{1,042,557}{24,588,608}$

10. $\frac{145}{1,379,862}$

Problem Set D

1. $\frac{41}{56}$

2. $1\frac{1}{6}$

3. $\frac{383}{1700}$

4. $1\frac{20}{100}$

5. $\frac{7}{33}$

6. $1\frac{20}{32}$

7. $\frac{75}{108}$

8. $\frac{911}{1096}$

9. $1\frac{23,693}{87,796}$

10. $\frac{2286}{26,243}$

Problem Set E

1. Can't be reduced

2. $\frac{1}{12}$

3. $\frac{11}{104}$

4. Can't be reduced

5. $\frac{4336}{437,593}$

6. $\frac{3}{35}$

7. $\frac{104}{245}$

8. $\frac{7,506,360}{23,287,027}$

9. $4\frac{1}{3}$

10. $1\frac{1}{6}$

11. $1\frac{1}{2}$

12. $1\frac{21}{55}$

13. $1\frac{9}{13}$ 15. $1\frac{1}{5}$ 17. $1\frac{5}{8}$

14. Can't be reduced   16. Can't be reduced   18. $\frac{25}{36}$

Problem Set F

1. $\frac{17}{1}$ 6. $\frac{257}{6}$ 11. $\frac{146}{11}$

2. $\frac{13}{3}$ 7. $\frac{67}{8}$ 12. $\frac{2}{1}$

3. $\frac{349}{2}$ 8. $\frac{367}{16}$ 13. $\frac{215}{4}$

4. $\frac{36}{1}$ 9. $\frac{3601}{100}$ 14. $\frac{22,592,111}{12}$

5. $\frac{7165}{1017}$ 10. $\frac{3608}{100}$ 15. $\frac{1,882,675}{1}$

Problem Set G

1. $3\frac{1}{5}$ 8. $56\frac{19}{24}$ 15. $166\frac{2}{3}$

2. $33\frac{167}{228}$ 9. $2\frac{25}{58}$ 16. $\frac{25}{36}$

3. $58\frac{7}{32}$ 10. $12\frac{77}{100}$ 17. $44\frac{5}{14}$

4. $\frac{45}{68}$ 11. $2\frac{30}{31}$ 18. 49

5. $14\frac{5}{8}$ 12. $40\frac{37}{60}$ 19. $27\frac{679}{1798}$

6. $16\frac{7}{12}$ 13. $\frac{3}{28}$ 20. $17\frac{23}{42}$

7. $6\frac{11}{12}$ 14. $\frac{1}{128}$

Problem Set H

1. 1.73   5. 34.7767   8. 47.857

2. 19.42   6. 530.6886   9. 14.530195

3. 42.887   7. 0.10001   10. 342.417

4. 12.725

Problem Set I

1. 965.60646   5. 640.55201   8. 42.80428

2. 9.9   6. 0.0001528   9. 419.284

3. 0.0048   7. 995,048.83452   10. 97.9902

4. 1025.5641

Problem Set J

1. 0.33455   5. 135   8. 0.96969

2. 2.946   6. 33.34015   9. 92.42424

3. 425.45454   7. 0.33333   10. 1480

4. 26.11222

Problem Set K

1.	0.84615	5.	0.99472	8.	0.5625
2.	0.47058	6.	0.35	9.	0.46875
3.	0.42574	7.	0.875	10.	0.65853
4.	0.96428				

Problem Set L

Answers are shown to 2, 3, and 4 places, as instructed.

1.	11.88 11.879 11.8795	5.	31 31 31.0001	8.	1.12 1.119 1.1190
2.	23.05 23.051 23.0506	6.	0 0 0.0002	9.	0.77 0.765 0.7654
3.	11 11 11.0002	7.	1. 0.998 0.9984	10.	5.76 5.76 5.7601
4.	0.1 0.099 0.0988				

Problem Set M

1.	3.947	5.	0.0000009	8.	12,000,000
2.	0.740	6.	4.35	9.	5.17
3.	0.159	7.	0.48485	10.	0.0034
4.	0.00240				

Problem Set N

1.	a.	37.5	b.	0.678	c.	$2945.95	d.	53.35	e.	$2277	f.	5011.6
2.	a.	23%	b.	0.9695%	c.	2450%	d.	72%	e.	50%	f.	0.211%
3.	a.	1957.1428	b.	100	c.	10	d.	172,500	e.	4.943	f.	300

Problem Set O

a.	$194\frac{1}{4}$	b.	1296	c.	66	d.	1316	e.	70
f.	273	g.	6	h.	1256.6	i.	875	j.	227

k. 1653 (NOTE: This figure can be divided into two rectangles, 19 × 24 and 21 × 57. Calculate the area of each and add them: 456 + 1197 = 1653.)

l. 30

m. 893 (NOTE: This figure is a rectangle, 30 × 18, attached to half a circle with a radius of 15.)

n. 432.5 (NOTE: This figure is irregular, but it can be split into triangles. If you draw a line from the upper *left* corner to the lower *right*, you will easily see the two triangles, with the heights given by the broken lines. The areas are 195 + 237.5 = 432.5.)

o. 3421

Chapter 18/Real Estate Mathematics and Problem Solving

The mathematics problems you will encounter on the licensing examination are most likely to be in the form of *word problems*. Word problems are problems that describe a situation in which you have to find a mathematical answer. Here is an example of a simple word problem:

I have three apples. John has four apples. How many apples do John and I have together?

Here is an example of a very complicated word problem:

Jones owns a building that is rectangular in shape: 40 ft. × 66 ft. 3 in. He wishes to construct a sidewalk around the perimeter of the building. The sidewalk will be made of concrete and crushed stone. It will be 4 ft. wide and will be poured to a depth of 3½ in. The composition will be 85% concrete and 15% crushed stone. Concrete costs $313.00 per cu. yd. Crushed stone is $27.83 per ton; 1 cu. yd. of crushed stone weighs 3282 lb. 15 oz. Labor required to construct the sidewalk is $19 per hour; in 1 hour the laborer can finish 188 sq. ft. of sidewalk. The laborer must be paid for at least 4 hours every time he works, even if it takes him less time to finish the job. How much will the sidewalk cost?

In spite of the complicated appearance of the second problem, the process for solving it is basically the same as the process for solving the first:

1. *Read* the question.
2. Determine *what* is being asked for.
3. Determine *how* to arrive at the answer.
4. *Calculate* the answer.
5. *Check* the answer.

The last step is particularly important, especially when the problem is a complicated one; you have to make sure that you did all the calculations correctly or your answer will be wrong. On most examinations, knowing *how* to do a problem will get you no credit at all; you must provide the *correct answer* as evidence you know how to do a particular problem. You should be aware of one more thing: on mathematics questions offered in a multiple-choice format you have both an advantage and a possible disadvantage. The advantage, which is always present, is that *you are given the correct answer to the problem!* Obviously, it *must* be among the ones you are to choose from; all you have to do is to figure out *which* one it is.

A possible disadvantage is that some of the *incorrect* answers may be answers you would arrive at by making common mistakes. If you do that, you may be lulled into choosing the incorrect answer by assuming that, since your calculations got you an answer that is among the ones you must choose from, then you *must* have done it correctly. You should especially be on your guard if one of the answers given is something like "none of the above" or "none of the other answers is correct." If this kind of answer is on the list of answers it may mean that none of the answers is correct, but it may also be included as a red herring.

Mistakes on mathematics problems may result from:

1. Incorrect reading of the problem. *Solution:* Read carefully!
2. Misunderstanding what is being asked for. *Solution:* Read carefully and slowly; you have plenty of time, so don't rush!
3. Not knowing how to do the problem correctly. *Solution:* Study this chapter carefully, so that you know how to approach all kinds of problems.
4. Incorrect calculation of the answer. *Solution:* Study the methods of calculation of all kinds of real estate problems, as outlined in this chapter.
5. Mistakes in arithmetic. *Solution:* Check your work, to make sure that you did your arithmetic correctly.

Note that these five common errors can be controlled by applying the five steps in problem solving offered in the beginning of this chapter.

Now let us discuss the various kinds of real estate mathematics problems. Remember, we are going to assume in this chapter that you have an adequate knowledge of basic arithmetic. If you feel your arithmetic skills are rusty, be sure to read Chapter 17 ("Arithmetic Review") before you go any further. If you feel confident about your arithmetic but later have trouble with some specific steps in the solution processes we offer, then turn back to Chapter 17 and read over and practice the *specific* arithmetic processes that you need to review. The best step would be to read all of Chapter 17 if you have any doubts at all about your arithmetic ability. It won't hurt to read over material that you already know; in the process you may discover some things you had forgotten.

Lengths, Areas, and Measures

Quite a number of real estate problems involve measurement of lengths and areas. You will be presumed to know certain relationships involving length and area, which are detailed in Chapter 17, page 167. You also have to know certain volume measures, as shown in Chapter 17, page 173. This information you *must* know when you go in to take the examination; almost certainly they will *not* tell you how many inches are in a foot, how many acres are in a square mile, etc. You must know these relationships or must know how to calculate them if you need them.

Also, you must know the following special terms used in real estate measurement; these are illustrated in Figure 18–1.

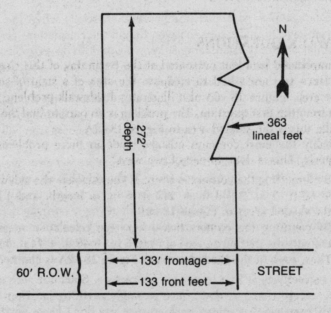

Fig. 18-1. Real Estate Measurement

Depth refers to the straight-line distance from the front lot line to the rear lot line. If these lot lines aren't parallel, the term *depth* will refer to the *longest* straight-line distance between them. The lot shown in Figure 18–1 has a depth of 272 feet.

Frontage is the *lineal distance* (see *lineal feet* below) of the lot line that is also a part of a public street or other right-of-way. Frontage of corner lots usually is expressed as separate figures for the distance fronting on each of the streets the lot bounds. This would also apply to very deep lots that border streets at both ends, etc. The frontage of the lot in Figure 18–1 is 133 feet.

Front foot refers to the distance that a lot borders on a street. In the case of the lot illustrated in Figure 18–1, we can say the lot has *133 feet of frontage* or we can say that the lot has *133 front feet*. (To say that the lot has 133 front feet of frontage is redundant.)

Lineal foot refers to the distance between two particular spots. Note that lineal feet need not be a *straight* measure; rather, the term refers to the number of feet traveled while following a *particular path connecting the particular points involved*. In real estate, this term is used normally to describe irregular lot sides (such as the east side of the lot in Figure 18–1, which is 363 lineal feet on a lot that has only 272 feet of depth) or irregular paths along roads, etc.

Right-of-way, or *R.O.W.*, refers to the area owned by the government within which a road is located. On maps, plats, etc., the term R.O.W. usually refers to the width of the right-of-way area (which usually exceeds *pavement* width).

The basic methods of calculating distance, area, and volume are discussed in Chapter 17; here we will confine ourselves to particular kinds of real estate problems that you will encounter. Most of them can be characterized as specific *forms* of problems that are easy to recognize; we will discuss them and show how to deal with them.

Before doing so, however, we should pass on one very crucial hint for solving these kinds of problems:

Draw a picture of the problem, if you possibly can. Then, with the picture as your guide, go through the problem step-by-step.

We cannot stress this process too much. By drawing a picture of the problem, you can *look* at it. A picture really is valuable, especially if it helps you to visualize a problem. (Sometimes, of course, the problem on the exam will include a picture or diagram. But if it doesn't, supply your own!) Then when you do the problem, work it very carefully, and step-by-step. Even if you feel you can take some shortcuts, or do part of it in your head, DON'T! Solving problems this way may be boring or tedious but it works, because it helps to eliminate mistakes.

SIDEWALK QUESTIONS

The complicated problem presented at the beginning of this chapter is a "sidewalk question." Here you are asked to compute the area of a strip of something that *surrounds* another area. Figure 18–2A also illustrates a sidewalk problem, using some of the information from the first question. The problem is (in part) to find the area of the surface of the sidewalk; this is the shaded area in Figure 18–2A.

Probably the most common mistake made in these problems is to treat the *corners* improperly. This is done in one of two ways:

(a) By forgetting the corners entirely: if you calculate the sidewalk as 66 ft. 3 in. + 40 ft. + 66 ft. 3 in. + 40 ft. = 212 ft. 6 in. in length, and 4 ft. wide, you get all *but* the shaded areas in Figure 18–2B.

(b) By counting the corners *twice*: here the calculation measures the sidewalk along the outside, getting an area of 74 ft. 3 in. + 48 ft. + 74 ft. 3 in. + 48 ft. = 244 ft. 6 in. Thus, each of the shaded areas in Figure 18–2A is counted *twice*.

The correct way is first to *draw* your picture. Start out with an illustration like Figure 18–2A, except that you don't have to shade anything in. Then divide the sidewalk area into easily measured sections, making sure you don't leave anything out. The best way is to divide it into a set of rectangles; one way of doing that is shown in Figure 18–2C. Here we have two rectangles that are 74 ft. 3 in. × 4 ft., and two that are 40 ft. × 4 ft. To solve the problem of finding the area of the sidewalk, we do the following:

$$Area = [(74.25 \text{ ft.} \times 4 \text{ ft.}) + (40 \text{ ft.} \times 4 \text{ ft.})] \times 2$$
$$= (297 + 160) \times 2$$
$$= 914 \text{ sq. ft.}$$

Of course there are other ways of dividing the sidewalk into easily computed rectangular areas. Once you have finished such a problem, you should choose a different way of dividing up the sidewalk and then use that way as a *check* on your answer.

Note that sidewalk problems don't always involve sidewalks. You would use the same technique to find the area of a yard surrounding a house, the area of a field surrounding a lake, the area of a parking lot surrounding a building, etc.

Sometimes it may be easier to use a second method of solving sidewalk problems, especially when there is a fairly small area inside a fairly large one. Here you simply figure the area of the small space and *subtract* it from the area of the large one. To refer to the problem we just did, the large area is the area covered by the building *and* the sidewalk. The small area inside it is the area of the building alone. Obviously, if you subtract the area of the

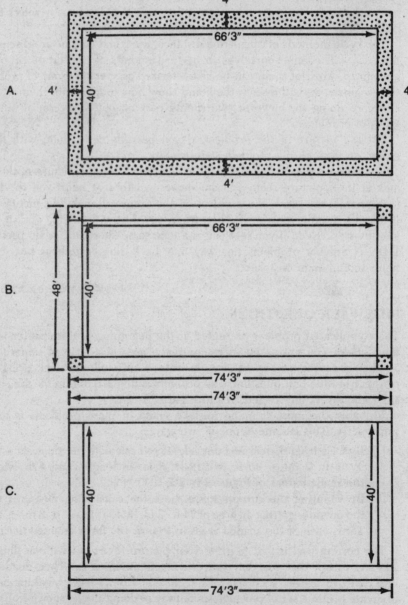

Fig. 18-2. Sidewalks

building from the area of the *building and the sidewalk*, what you'll have left is the area of the *sidewalk* alone. Again let's use the problem from Figure 18–2. The outside area is 74.25 ft. × 48 ft. = 3564 sq. ft.; the inside area is 66.25 ft. × 40 ft. = 2650 sq. ft. Subtracting the area of the building from the area of the building and sidewalk we get 3564 − 2650 = 914 sq. ft. This is the same answer we got previously. If you wish, you can use both methods when you solve a sidewalk problem, using one as a check against the other.

ROAD PROBLEMS

Road problems are a lot like sidewalk problems in that the most common mistake is to forget the corners. In a road problem, all or part of it involves finding the area of a road that usually has one or more corners or bends to it. An example is shown in Figure 18–3A; here we have a *two-step* problem in that we have to do some initial calculations before we can get to the calculations that produce our final result.

The lot shown in Figure 18–3A is exactly square and is ¼ sq. mi. in area. The road passing through it has a right-of-way 150 ft. wide. All corners are right angles. What is the road's area?

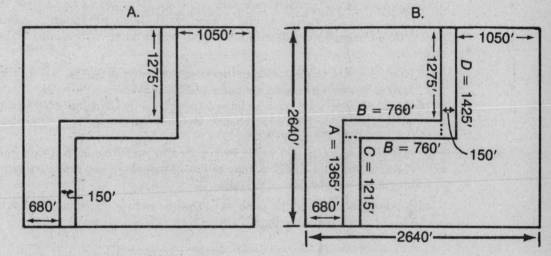

Fig. 18-3.   Roads

Step One: Find the remaining measurements of the road so we can calculate its area. The way to do this is to find the measurements of the lot. We have a major clue: it is square, so all its sides are the same length. Since it contains ¼ sq. mi., it must be ½ mi. on a side: ½ × ½ = ¼. We know that ½ mi. = 2640 ft.; therefore the lot is 2640 ft. on a side. Now we can get the measurements we need by subtraction; the necessary ones are all shown in Figure 18–3B. Here is how they were found:

(a) 2640 ft. − 1275 ft. = 1365 ft.
(b) 2640 ft. − (680 ft. + 150 ft. + 1050 ft.) = 760 ft.   Here we have to remember the width of the road when we make our calculations! It is 680 ft. from the west side of the lot to the right-of-way of the road; the road is 150 ft. wide. At the top of the lot, it is 1050 ft. from *the other side of the road* to the east side of the lot. Between its turns, therefore, the road actually traverses only 760 ft.
(c) is the side of the road opposite (a); it should be 150 ft. *shorter* than (a) because of the turn in the road: 1365 ft. − 150 ft. = 1215 ft.
(d) is the side of the road opposite the one side for which measurement was given; because of the turn in the road, it should be 150 ft. longer: 1275 ft. + 150 ft. = 1425 ft.

Given all this information, we now can proceed to step two, using the same method as in the sidewalk questions: Divide the area of the road into easily calculated rectangles, making sure no part of the road is left out. Then calculate the areas of each of the rectangles and add them.

The dotted lines in Figure 18–3B show one suggested way of dividing the road; we have three rectangles, each of which is 150 ft. wide. The three are 760 ft., 1215 ft., and 1425 ft. in length. The total area of the road, then, is as follows:

$$150 \text{ ft. } \times 760 \text{ ft. } = 114{,}000 \text{ sq. ft.}$$
$$150 \text{ ft. } \times 1215 \text{ ft. } = 182{,}250 \text{ sq. ft.}$$
$$150 \text{ ft. } \times 1425 \text{ ft. } = 213{,}750 \text{ sq. ft.}$$
$$114{,}000 \text{ sq. ft. } + 182{,}250 \text{ sq. ft. } + 213{,}750 \text{ sq. ft. } = 510{,}000 \text{ sq. ft.}$$
$$510{,}000 \text{ sq. ft. } \div 43{,}560 \text{ sq. ft. } = 11.708 \text{ acres, the area of the road.}$$

To check such a problem, divide the road into different rectangles and do the problem again.

You should be aware of a special way that such a problem can be stated: the lot within which the road appears can be described, using a *legal description*. This is particularly tempting for examination officials in states that use the Government Rectangular Survey description, since descriptions can be given very briefly and usually will be of fairly regular-shaped lots. Other times, you may be given an entire plat of a subdivision, with lot dimensions and directions all spelled out. As part of the analysis of such a plat, you may get a road problem.

An outgrowth of road problems are *path* problems. Here you are being asked the *straight-line* distance from one specified point to another. These usually appear in connection with plats or Government Survey descriptions. Some sample questions that need not be answered here are:

(1) How far would a rabbit have to hop from the center of NW¼, NW¼, Sec. 22, T3N, R4W to get to the eastern boundary of T3N, R5W?

(2) If I start at a point on the base line and travel exactly 155.6 miles in a straight line *due north*, how many townships (checks, sections) will I cross over completely? Identify the *section* in which I will stop.

(3) (Referring to a plat that would be supplied to you) How far is it from the northeast corner of A Street and B Avenue to Lake Mudhole, if you are to travel in a straight line to the *nearest* part of the lake?

All of these are answered the same way: *Draw a picture.* Once you do that, the answer can be found quite mechanically.

FENCE PROBLEMS

Fence problems are usually stated like this example:

Jones has a lot 50 ft. by 90 ft. He wants to build a fence all the way around the lot. It will be 4 ft. high. Fence posts have to be put in every 10 ft. Special posts are used at the corners. There will be one gate assembly; the gate is 10 ft. wide, between 2 regular posts. Fence posts cost $10 each. Corner posts cost $22 each. The gate costs $125. Fence fabric costs 27¢ per sq. ft. The gate requires no fabric. How much will the materials for the fence cost?

A similar type of problem would be to find the area of (or the cost of the materials for) the sides of a house or other structure. A variation of the problem has a fence that does not go all the way around the property.

Once again, the way to do this is to *draw a picture* first because you have to know how many fence posts and corner posts and how much material to buy. The question tells you that there will be only one gate.

Figure 18–4 shows you one way of drawing the picture. Of course, during the examination you don't have to be as neat so long as what you draw makes sense to you. Here is how we would get the answer to our problem.

(A) We need one gate, because that's what we're told.

(B) We need four corner posts, because the lot is rectangular.

(C) We need 24 fence posts. We can calculate this simply by counting the fence posts in our drawing. A shortcut method would be to count the posts on one side and the bottom and multiply by 2, since the other side and the top would use the same

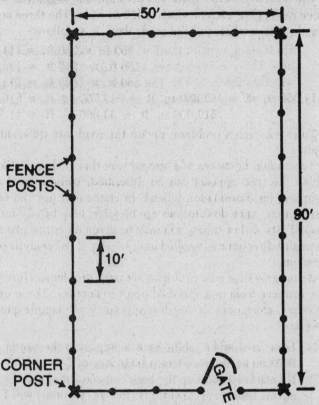

Fig. 18-4.   Fences

amount. Notice something important: each side uses only 8 fence posts, even though the side is 90 ft. long and we use a post every 10 ft. This occurs because there is a corner post at each end of the side, so fence posts are only needed *between* them.

(D) There will have to be 1080 sq. ft. of fence fabric. This is found as follows: each side is 90 ft. long, the top is 50 ft., and the bottom is only 40 ft., because 10 ft. is taken up by the *gate*. This adds up to 270 lineal ft. of fence. The fence is 4 ft. high, so the area of the fence is 4 ft. × 270 ft. = 1080 sq. ft.

A slightly different way would have been to figure the full perimeter of the lot as 280 ft., and then subtract 10 ft. for the gate, to get the 270 lineal ft. of fence.

Now we can calculate the cost of the fence:

1 gate @ $125	$125.00
4 corner posts @ $22	88.00
24 fence posts @ $10	240.00
1080 sq. ft. fence fabric @ 27¢	291.60
TOTAL	$744.60

Remember, the key element to solving this kind of measurement problem is to draw a picture of the problem and to reason from there. Note that this example was fairly comprehensive, in that you had to calculate the total cost of the materials used to build the fence. Some problems may be fairly simple, asking only how much fence fabric is necessary or how much the fence fabric alone would cost. A variation of the fence problem would be a question asking how much paint would be necessary to paint the outside of a house. Here you would be careful to note any mention of windows and glass in doors, since these are spaces that would *not* be painted. (The problem we just did had a similar situation with the gate.) This sort of question could ask how much paint would be needed, by telling how many square feet of surface a given amount of paint will cover. It could ask the cost of the paint needed, by including the price of a given amount of paint.

Problem Set A

Following are some problems dealing with lengths, areas, and measures. Answers, along with the method of solution, appear at the end of the chapter. Use the space below each question to work it out.

1. Brown's home measures 55 ft. long and 30 ft. wide. The outside walls are 8½ ft. high. He is going to paint these walls and wants to know how much the paint is going to cost him. There are two doors, each 3 ft. × 7½ ft., one picture window 12 ft. × 5 ft., and 6 windows 2½ ft. × 4 ft. The doors and windows will not be painted. Each gallon can of paint will cover 320 sq. ft. and will cost $9.98.

2. Jones wishes to subdivide his 76-acre tract into building lots. He will have to use 665,000 sq. ft. of land for streets, roads, parks, etc. If the zoning code requires that lots have at least 7500 sq. ft., what is the *maximum* number of lots that he can develop out of this land?

3. Smith has a building that measures 65 ft. long × 35 ft. deep. One of the 65 ft. sides fronts directly on the sidewalk; he wants to build a sidewalk 8 ft. wide to surround the building on the other 3 sides. If the sidewalk costs $1.15 per sq. ft. to build, what will be the total cost?

4. Johnson's lot is rectangular and contains 313 sq. yd. If the frontage is 41 ft., how deep is the lot?

5. A triangular plot of land is 500 ft. wide at the base and 650 ft. deep to the point of the triangle. What is the value of this lot, at $600 per acre?

6. *If your state uses Government Survey, do this problem:*
Smith purchased the NW¼ of the SE¼ of a section of land. A road 66 ft. wide goes due north-south through the parcel, splitting it into two pieces. Smith did *not* acquire title to the road. How much land did he get?

Percent Problems

A great many real estate problems involve percents; these include commissions, interest, mortgage payments, loan discounts (points), depreciation, profit and loss, and return on investment. We will discuss each of these, but it should be remembered that the mathematics involved are the same in all of them: you will be looking for one of three things — a base, a rate, or a result.

If you are rusty on percents, you should read the appropriate part of Chapter 17 before proceeding further.

All percent problems can be stated in one of three variations on the following statement:

$$A \text{ is } B \text{ percent of } C.$$

Examples of such a statement are "14 is 50 percent of 28," or "63 is 90 percent of 70." Of course, if you know all three numbers, then you don't have a problem.

All percent problems are like the statement above, except that one of the numbers is missing: the "problem" is to find that missing number.

Type #1	A is B percent of ?	(C is missing.)
Type #2	A is ? percent of C	(B is missing.)
Type #3	? is B percent of C	(A is missing.)

The solutions to these problems are as follows:

$$A = B \times C$$
$$B = A \div C$$
$$C = A \div B$$

An easy way to remember these is that A is B multiplied by C. To find either B or C, you divide A by the other. Here are some examples illustrating the three variations of the percent problem.

1. *What is 88.5% of 326?*   (? is B percent of C.)
2. *16 is what % of 440?*   (A is ? percent of C.)
3. *43 is 86% of what?*   (A is B percent of ?.)

The solutions to these are as follows:

1. The missing item is A. $A = B \times C$. $A = 0.885 \times 326$. $A = 288.51$.
2. The missing item is B. $B = A \div C$. $B = 16 \div 440$. $B = 0.0363636 \ldots$
3. The missing item is C. $C = A \div B$. $C = 43 \div 0.86$. $C = 50$.

COMMISSION PROBLEMS

Commission problems naturally are very popular on real estate examinations because most licensees are paid in commission form. A real estate commission is simply what the employer pays the agent for performing his duty. Most often, the commission is a portion of the sale price received by a seller because of the efforts of the agent to secure a buyer. Typical commission rates vary from as low as 1 percent or less to over 10 percent, depending on the kind of property, prevailing custom in the area, and the success of the agent, or the employer, in negotiating the listing contract.

The simplest commission problems are like this one:

Jones sells Smith's house for $55,900. Jones's commission is 7% of the sale price. What is his commission, in dollars?

Here the solution is to find 7% of $55,900: $0.07 \times \$55,900 = \$3913$.

This *same* problem, which is the type #1 described previously, can also be stated as a type #2 or type #3:

Type 2:   Jones sells Smith's house for $55,900 and receives a commission of $3913. What is his commission rate?

Type 3:   Jones sells Smith's house and receives a commission of $3913, which is 7% of the sale price. What was the sale price?

These problems are simple. To make them more "interesting," they are often expanded in one of two ways. The first way is to make them more complicated, and there are two methods of doing that. The second way is to develop the question *backwards;* this often traps many unwary examinees, but if you pay attention it won't trap you.

First, let us look at the more elaborate kinds of commission problems. The two methods used are (a) to have you calculate the salesperson's share of a total commission and (b) to make the means of determining the commission more complicated.

Here (a) is illustrated:

Jones sells Smith's house for $42,750. The commission is 6½% of the sale price: Jones' broker receives 45% of this amount from the listing broker as the selling broker's share. Jones himself is entitled to 60% of all commissions that he is responsible for bringing in. How much does Jones get?

This may look complicated, but it is just three consecutive simple percent problems.

(1) How much was the total commission? A is 6½% of $42,750.00; A = $2778.75.
(2) Jones's broker received 45% of this amount. A is 45% of $2778.75 = $1250.44.
(3) Jones gets 60% of that amount. A is 60% of $1250.44 = $750.26.

This is the second kind (b):

Albertson sold Harding's house for $115,000. The commission rate as 7% of the first $50,000 of the sale price, 4% of the next $50,000, and 1½% of everything over that. What was Albertson's total commission?

Once again, we have several simple percentages to calculate: 7% of the first $50,000 is $3500; 4% of the next $50,000 is $2000; adding $2000 to $3500 yields a commission of $5500 on the first $100,000 (or $50,000 + $50,000). This leaves a balance of $15,000, to which we apply the commission rate of 1½% to get another $225 of commission, for a total commission of $5725.

This question could have been complicated by going one step further and asking, *What was the effective commission rate on the sale?* Here the question is, "What percent of the sale price is the actual commission?" First we say, $5725 is ?% of $115,000. Then we take the additional step: $B = 5725 \div 115,000 = 0.0498$, percentage = 4.98%.

Now let us turn to the other general category of complicated commission problems — that of developing the question *backwards.* Here the question is phrased like this:

Jones sold his house; after paying a 7% commission he had $37,153.50 left. What was the sale price of the house?

A lot of people will find 7% of $37,153.50, add it on, and GET THE WRONG ANSWER!! Their mistake is that the commission should be figured on the *sale price,* and they are figuring it on what the seller had left *after* the commission was paid. The way to solve these problems is simple: If Jones paid a 7% commission, then *what he had left* was 93% (or 100% − 7%) of the sale price. Now the problem becomes a familiar variation: $37,153.50 is 93% of ? C = $37,153.50 ÷ 0.93 = $39,950.00.

As you can see, this question is "backwards" in that you don't actually have to figure the dollar amount of the commission at all. On your examination be sure to look out for·these kinds of problems; the best way to spot them is to follow the rule of *reading* the question and *then* trying to determine what you are being asked to do.

You should be aware of the terminology used in commission figuring. The *commission* is the dollar amount you arrive at by applying the *commission rate* to the *sale price.* If you are asked for the "commission," you are being asked to tell *how many dollars and cents* the commission payment was. If you are asked for the "commission rate," or the "rate," you are being asked to provide the *percent rate* of the commission.

INTEREST PROBLEMS

Interest is money paid to "rent" money from others. It is typically expressed as an annual percentage rate; that is, for each year that the money is borrowed, a certain percentage of the loan amount is charged as interest. Interest will most often be stated in annual percentage terms even for loans that have a duration of much less than one year. As an example, the "interest rate" on charge accounts, credit card accounts, etc., may be charged monthly, and the bill may be due within a month, but the interest rate still is expressed as an annual rate. This practice is becoming even more prevalent as a result of Federal truth-in-lending laws, which *require* that the annual percentage rate (APR) be stated. Usually, for short-term arrangements a monthly or quarterly rate will also be stated. If you are given only an annual rate and are required to calculate based on a monthly or quarterly rate, simply divide the annual rate by 12 to get the monthly rate; divide the annual rate by 4 to get the quarterly rate. If a problem should give a monthly or quarterly rate, multiply a monthly rate by 12 or a quarterly rate by 4 to get the annual rate. As examples:

> A rate of 12% annually is 1% monthly and 3% quarterly.
> A rate of 9½% annually is 2.375% quarterly or 0.791666 . . .% monthly.
> A rate of 0.6% monthly is 1.8% quarterly or 7.2% annually.

Interest is calculated in two ways, *simple* and *compound*.

Simple interest is calculated quite straightforwardly. To determine the interest charge for any period of time, calculate the proportional interest, based on the annual rate. If the annual rate is 12%, interest for two years would be 24%, interest for six months would be 6%, etc.

When *compound interest* is used, interest is charged on unpaid interest, as well as on the unpaid debt. This adds a complicating element to the calculation, since now some sort of adjustment may be necessary to allow for the fact that interest is not being paid periodically, but is being allowed to accumulate over all or part of the term of the debt. Since most debts are paid in monthly installments in real life, one does not frequently encounter interest compounding in the payment of debts. One *does* encounter it in savings accounts, where one well-advertised feature is that if you do not withdraw the interest your deposit earns, it is added to your balance and begins to earn interest too.

Before compound interest can be calculated, the compounding frequency must be given. This is expressed in units of time. Compounding can be daily, quarterly, semiannually, annually — indeed it can be over any period of time, even "continuously." Given a compounding term, interest is figured by first deriving an interest rate for the term involved. Then interest is calculated for *each* term, taking into account the fact that some or all of the interest earned so far may not have been paid out. Here is an example:

Jones borrows $1000 at 8% annual interest. The interest is compounded quarterly. How much interest will Jones owe after nine months?

First we must change the annual rate to a quarterly rate: 8 ÷ 4 = 2, so the quarterly interest rate is 2%.

For the first quarter, interest is 2% of $1000, or $20.

To calculate interest for the second quarter, we add the first quarter's interest to the balance to get $1020, upon which interest for the second quarter is due. Therefore, the second quarter's interest is 2% of $1020.00, or $20.40. In effect, for the second quarter there is $20 interest, again, on the initial balance of $1000, plus another 40¢ interest on the unpaid $20 of interest earned in the first quarter.

Interest for the third quarter of the nine-month period will be based on a balance of $1040.40, which is the original balance plus the interest accumulated in the first two quarters. Therefore, interest for the third quarter is 2% of $1040.40, or $20.81. The total interest for the nine months (three quarters) will be $20.00 + $20.40 + $20.81, or $61.21.

Notice that compounded interest will be *more* than simple interest, if the interest period extends over more than one compounding term. We can show this with the same problem, this time assuming that simple interest is paid. In this case, the interest is $20 each quarter, for a total of only $60, compared to the $61.21 charged under compound interest. The reason for this is that, with simple interest, interest is calculated only on the original loan balance. Compound interest includes interest on earned but unpaid interest as well as on the original principal, so a larger amount becomes subject to interest once one compounding term has passed.

In real estate problems, interest questions usually involve *mortgage loans* and *loan discounts*, or *points*.

Mortgage Loans

Mortgage loans are like any other loans in that interest is charged for the use of someone else's money. Usually these loans require monthly payments, with part of the payment used to pay the interest due since the last payment and the remainder used to reduce the amount of the loan (the *principal*). Eventually, in this manner the loan will be fully paid off.

A very common question on this type of loan concerns the interest payable in any given month. This requires you to calculate the loan balance for that month before you can find the interest payment due. Here is an example:

Smith borrows $30,000 on a 30-year mortgage loan, payable at 9% interest per year. Payments are $241.55 per month. How much interest is to be charged in each of the first three months?

The first step in the solution is to determine the *monthly* interest rate, since mortgage interest payments are made monthly. Therefore, we divide the annual rate of 9% by 12 and get an interest rate of ¾% per month.

Now we can find the interest payable in the first month, which is 0.0075 × $30,000.00 = $225.00. The total monthly payment is $241.55, so after the $225.00 interest is paid, there remains $241.55 − $225.00 = $16.55 to be used to reduce the loan. This means that the loan balance for the second month is $30,000.00 − $16.55 = $29,983.45.

Now we calculate interest for the second month: 0.0075 × $29,983.45 = $224.88. This means that in the second month $241.55 − $224.88 = $16.67 is used to reduce the loan, leaving a balance of $29,983.45 − $16.67 = $29,966.78 for the third month.

The third month's interest, then, will be 0.0075 × $29,966.88 = $224.75. We can tabulate these results as follows:

Month	Loan Balance	Loan Payment	Interest	Loan Payoff
1	$30,000.00	$241.55	$225.00	$16.55
2	29,983.45	241.55	224.88	16.67
3	29,966.78	241.55	224.75	16.80
4	29,949.98	......	......	......

This kind of loan is called *self-amortizing, equal payment*. The monthly payments are equal. However, as the loan balance is reduced a little each month, the portion of the payment representing interest decreases each month, while the portion going to reduce the loan increases each month.

Some loans are called level principal payment loans. These are loans where the loan amount is reduced the *same* amount with each payment. This means that the payments themselves get smaller each time, as the interest due decreases because the loan balance is decreasing. Here is an example:

Smith borrows $24,000 for 10 years at an annual rate of interest of 12%. He pays it back in level principal payment manner each month. What will be his payments for the first, fourth, and tenth months?

The first thing we must do here is to calculate the amount of the monthly level principal payment. Since 10 years is 120 months, the monthly principal payment is $24,000 ÷ 120 = $200. The monthly interest rate is 12% ÷ 12 = 1%.

In the first month, the entire $24,000 is on loan, so the payment is the level $200 payment plus 1% of $24,000, which is another $240. Therefore, the first month's total payment is $200 + $240 = $440.

For the fourth month, he will owe the original balance of $24,000 *less* the $200 payments that have been made for each of the first three months. That amount totals $600, so for the fourth month he owes $24,000 − $600 = $23,400. Then, 1% of $23,400 is $234; this added to the level payment of $200 gives a payment of $434 for the fourth month.

The payment for the tenth month is calculated the same way. At that time, nine payments will have been made, so the loan will have been reduced by 9 × $200 = $1800, leaving a loan amount of $22,200. Since 1% of that amount is $222, the full payment for the tenth month would be $422.

Loan Discounts

The purpose of loan discounts is briefly explained in Chapter 14 ("Mortgages and Finance"). They are very simple to calculate, since they are merely a given percentage of the loan amount. You should be aware of the terminology, though, since these discounts often are referred to as "points." One discount point is the same as a charge of 1 percent of the loan amount. Therefore, a discount of three points (often just referred to as "three points") is 3 percent of the loan amount. Frequently, a problem involving discounts will require you first to determine the loan amount; this can trap the unwary examinee, who makes the mistake of calculating the discount based on the purchase price instead of the *loan amount*. Here is an example:

> *Murgatroyd bought a home costing $54,900. He got a 95% loan, on which there was a charge of 3¾ points. What was the discount in dollars and cents?*

First we calculate the loan amount, which is 95% of $54,900: $0.95 \times \$54,900 = \$52,155$. Now we can calculate the discount, which is 3¾ points, or 3¾% of the loan amount: $0.0375 \times \$52,155 = \$1955.81$.

DEPRECIATION

While the tax laws allow all sorts of complicated ways to calculate depreciation, the only one you have to worry about on licensing examinations is the simplest one, which is called *straight-line depreciation*. Straight-line depreciation assumes that the property depreciates an *equal* amount each year.

We will not argue, here, whether or not real estate does, in fact, depreciate. Some does and some does not seem to. However, there are many reasons why one should be aware of the possibility of depreciation, not the least of which is that in the long run a real estate asset *will* wear out. The 50-year old house that is being offered for ten times the original cost of construction also has a new roof, modernized heating and air-conditioning, new wiring, carpeting, kitchen installations, and plumbing. Nearly every visible surface has been repainted and remodeled.

When calculating depreciation, you must know the *useful life* of the property. (Sometimes this is referred to as *economic life*, or just plain *life*.) Once you know this, you can calculate an annual *depreciation rate*. Doing that is quite simple: you divide the useful life, in years, *into* 100% to get the percent rate of depreciation per year. For example:

10-year life: 100% ÷ 10 = 10% depreciation per year
50-year life: 100% ÷ 50 = 2% depreciation per year
35-year life: 100% ÷ 35 = 2.857% depreciation per year

Once this has been done, most depreciation problems become only slightly elaborated versions of the standard three types of percentage problems:

(a) *Madison owns a building for which he paid $55,000. If it has a total useful life of 30 years, what is its value after 5 years?*

(b) *Madison owns a building for which he paid $55,000. If it has a 40-year life, in how many years will it be worth $42,625?*

(c) *Madison owns a building worth $55,000. If it depreciates to $44,000 in 9 years, what is the total useful life?*

(d) *If a building depreciates at 2½% per year, in how many years will it be worth 85% of its original value?*

Here is how the answers to each of these is found:

(a) Here you are being asked to determine the value after 5 years, so you must determine how much the building depreciates each year. A 30-year life yields 3⅓% depreciation per year. Five years' depreciation, then, is 16⅔%. Therefore, in 5 years the building will be worth 83⅓% (100% − 16⅔%) of its original value: 0.8333 × $55,000.00 = $45,833.33, its value after 5 years.

(b) Here you want to know how long it takes for a certain depreciation to take place. A 40-year life is depreciation at 2½% per year. $42,625 is 77½% of $55,000 (42,625 ÷ 55,000). 100% − 77½% = 22½% total depreciation. At 2½% per year, that would take 9 years to accumulate (22.5 ÷ 2.5 = 9).

(c) Here you have to determine the useful life. $44,000 is 80% of $55,000 (44,000 ÷ 55,000 = 0.80). Therefore, the building depreciates 20% in 9 years, or 2.2222 . . . % per year. Divide this figure into 100% to get the total number of years required for the building to depreciate fully: 100 ÷ 2.2222 = 45. Thus, the useful life is 45 years.

(d) In this problem you don't have to calculate the depreciation rate, since it is given to you (2½% per year). If it depreciates to 85% of its original value, it will have depreciated 15%. 15% ÷ 2½% = 6 years' worth of depreciation.

PROFIT AND LOSS

Calculation of profit and loss is another slightly altered version of the three types of percentage problems. The important thing to remember is that profit and loss are always expressed as a percentage of *cost*. Cost is the original price that the seller paid for the property when he acquired it. If *his* selling price is higher than cost, he has a profit. If it is lower, he has a loss.

The *dollar value* of profit or loss is the difference between purchase price and sale price. The *rate* of profit or loss is the percentage relationship between the purchase price and the dollar value of profit or loss.

Here are some examples:

(a) *Martin bought his house for $44,950 and sold it later for $55,900. What was his rate of profit?*

(b) *Samson Wrecking Company mistakenly tore down part of Smith's home. Before the home was damaged it was worth $75,000. Afterward, it had sustained a 28% loss. What was its value after the wrecking?*

(c) *Harrison sold his home for $42,050 and made a 45% profit. What had he paid for the home?*

Here are the solutions:

(a) First, determine the dollar value of the profit: $55,900 − $44,950 = $10,950. Then determine what percentage proportion the dollar value is of the *purchase price* ($10,950 is ?% of $44,950). 10,950 ÷ 44,950 = 24.36%.

(b) The loss was 28% of the original value of $75,000: 0.28 × $75,000 = $21,000. $75,000 − $21,000 = $54,000 value afterward.

(c) The original price of the house, plus 45%, is now equal to $42,050. Therefore, $42,050 is 145% of the original price of the home (? is 145% of $42,050). 42,050 ÷ 1.45 = $29,000. As a check, his profit is $13,050 ($42,050 less $29,000), which is 45% of $29,000 ($13,050 ÷ $29,000 = 0.45).

RETURN ON INVESTMENT

The concept of return on investment is very similar to the concept of interest payments on loans. In the investment case, an investor spends money to buy an income-producing asset. He wants to make money at it; otherwise there is no point to the investment. He calculates his return and expresses it as a *percentage* of his investment being paid back to him each year. In a sense, he can be thought of as "lending" his money to the investment and having it "pay" him "interest" on his money.

It is possible to make deceptively simple-sounding investment questions so complicated that they can best be answered with the aid of a computer or a very sophisticated calculator. This needn't concern you, though. On licensing examinations the questions are kept simple enough that they can be calculated quickly by hand or, in those states that allow their use, with simple, hand-held calculators that do no more than add, subtract, multiply, and divide.

If you think of return on investment problems as similar to interest problems, you should have no trouble with them. Here are some examples:

(a) *Bennett owns a building that cost him $65,000. How much income should the building produce annually to give Bennett a 15% return on his money?*

(b) *Maximilian paid $43,500 for a triplex apartment building. All units are identical. He lives in one unit and rents the other two. The total net income per month from rentals is $355. What annual rate of return is he getting on his investment in the rental units?*

(c) *What monthly income should a building costing $38,500 produce if the annual return is to be 15%?*

Here are the solutions:

(a) The building should produce an income each year of 15% of $65,000: 0.15 × $65,000 = $9750.

(b) This problem has a lot of steps, but they are simple ones. First we must determine how much of the purchase price should be allocated to the two rental units. Since all three are the same, then ⅓ of the purchase price ought to be allocated to each. This means that ⅔ of the price should be allocated to the two rental units: ⅔ × $43,500 = $29,000. Now we must determine the annual dollar amount of income received. The monthly income is $355, so the annual income is $355 × 12 = $4260. Now we must find out what percent $4260 is of $29,000 ($4260 is ?% of $29,000). $4260 ÷ $29,000 = 14.69%, the annual rate of return.

(c) Here we must calculate a monthly dollar income. The annual income must be 15% of $38,500.00 or $5775.00. The monthly income is 1/12 of that amount, or $481.25.

Problem Set B

Here are some practice questions concerning percent problems. They include all of the kinds we have just discussed, including common variations.

1. Smith sold his home for $49,700 and made a 42% profit. How much did he pay for the home?

2. Jones's home cost $49,900. He financed the purchase with a 90% loan. The discount was three points. How much was the dollar amount of discount?

3. Going back to question #2, assume that the interest rate on Jones's loan was 8½% per year and that the loan was for a 25-year period. How much interest would be payable with the first payment?

4. Jones sold his building for $48,443.75. He had owned it for seven years and had originally paid $57,500.00 for it. What was his annual rate of depreciation?

5. Sam Zealous, the real estate agent, sold I. M. Sellar's home for him. After paying Zealous a commission of 7½% of the sale price, Sellar ended up with $18,490.75. What was the sale price?

6. Winken, Blinken, and Nod are partners in the ownership of a certain property worth $44,000. The property produces a 21% return per year, in income collected monthly. Winken owns a 37% share of the building. How much is Winken's monthly income from the property?

7. In problem #6, Blinken owns a 22% share and Nod owns the rest. If $19,800 originally was paid for the property, what would be the dollar value of Nod's share of the profit, if they were to sell it today for its current value? What rate of profit does this represent?

8. Bernie is a real estate salesman for Gettum Realty, Inc. Bernie gets 52½% of all real estate commissions he brings into the firm. Bernie just sold Fred's home for $44,750. Fred had listed the home with a different broker in the same Multilist group as Bernie's broker. According to the Multilist rules, the listing broker received 40% of the commission, the selling broker received the rest after a fee of 3% of the commission was paid to the Multilist group to cover its expenses. How much (dollar amount) of the 6½% commission on this sale was paid to Bernie?

9. Mr. Selkirk borrowed $5000 to install a new kitchen in his home. The loan was for one year, with no payments to principal to be made until the loan term was past. The interest rate was 10½% per year, with the interest payable quarterly. How much was the quarterly interest payment? If the interest had been allowed to compound quarterly, how much *extra* interest would Mr. Selkirk have had to pay in excess of simple quarterly interest?

10. Mr. Lucky just sold his building for $62,500. He had bought it eight years earlier for $93,000. What is the percent rate of his loss? What is the annual rate of depreciation he sustained?

Proration

Proration is a topic that normally will come up only on examinations for broker's licenses, as it is a necessary input into the calculation of closing statements. If you are seeking a salesperson's license, and not a brokerage license, you need not cover the material in this section of the chapter.

There are two kinds of prorating methods in common use. The most widely used one employs the *statutory year;* the other uses the *actual year.*

The function of proration is to distribute equitably the costs of a particular charge that two or more people must share. In real estate, these costs usually are created by transactions associated with a title closing, in which allocations are made for charges that apply over the period in which both buyer and seller own the property. Most commonly prorated items are:

Real property taxes
Property insurance
Interest on assumed mortgage loans
Prepaid or later-paid rentals

Property taxes are usually paid by the year; when a transaction occurs in the middle of a year, part of that year's property tax usually will be deemed, by the parties to the sale, payable by each one. Note that the government that collects the taxes does *not* prorate them; it collects the *full* tax bill from whomever owns the property at the time the taxes are due. If, when the sale occurs, the year's property taxes *already* have been paid, then the seller will have paid them and the buyer must recompense the seller for the portion of the taxes that apply to that portion of the year when the buyer will own the property. Similarly, if the taxes are due *after* the close of the sale, when they come due the buyer will have to pay them in full for the entire year. So at the closing the seller pays the buyer for the share that applies during the period of the tax year when the seller owned the property.

Insurance usually is paid in advance. Often insurance policies are multiyear policies, although the premiums generally are payable annually. However, on licensing examinations the closing problems often assume that the entire multiyear premium was paid at once when the policy was purchased; this is a device to see if examinees are on their toes and read the questions completely. Since insurance usually is paid in advance, the buyer, if he assumes the existing insurance policy, recompenses the seller for the prepaid unused portion of the policy that the buyer gets from him.

When the buyer assumes the seller's mortgage loan, and the closing date is not the day after the loan payment is due and paid, then the month's interest must be prorated between buyer and seller. Loan payments are due at the end of the monthly payment period, so when the next payment is due, the buyer will have to pay it in full, including the interest for an entire month during which he actually owned the property only part of the time. Therefore, the seller will have to pay the buyer for his share of the mortgage interest.

Rents work the other way, since they are payments *to* the owner rather than *by* the owner. Rent usually is paid in advance, but you should read the problem carefully because it is possible to have a situation where rent is paid at the *end* of the month or lease period. If rent is paid in advance, then the seller will have been paid a full month's rent for the month in which the closing occurs; he must pay the buyer his prorated share of that month's rent already received. If the rent is paid at the end of the month, then the buyer will get a full month's rent covering the month of sale, and he must recompense the seller for the period during which the seller owned the property.

COMPUTING PRORATIONS

In order to compute prorations you must know three things: (1) How much — in money — is the item to be prorated? (2) To whom is payment to be made? (3) How much time is involved?

The discussion above covered the question of who pays whom what charges, but in summary we can state two easily remembered rules.

(1) If the item was paid *before* closing, the buyer recompenses the seller.

(2) If the item will be paid *after* closing, the seller recompenses the buyer.

This is so, because the seller had to pay all items due before closing, and the buyer will have to pay everything coming due after closing.

Calculation of the amount of money due in the payment will vary, depending on the complexity of the problem. Sometimes the amount is specified exactly; other times it will have to be calculated. It is quite popular in licensing examinations to require the examinee to calculate the property tax bill before he can begin to prorate it (see Chapter 16). Usually the insurance premium and rentals will be given, inasmuch as there is rarely a sensible calculation method for them that can be incorporated into a problem. Interest on assumed mortgages is another favorite candidate for calculation before it can be prorated.

Calculation of the proration itself includes apportioning the time involved among the parties. Rent and interest usually are apportioned over one month, taxes over a year, and insurance over one or more years. When the items are apportioned, the day of closing is considered to be the seller's.

The Statutory Year

Prorating items over a full year can involve very messy calculations, since everything has to be divided by 365 (or 366), the number of days in a year. Many banks and other financial institutions therefore have substituted the 360-day "statutory year" as a means of simplifying calculation. This system assumes the year to be made up of twelve 30-day months. Numbers such as 360 and 30, while large, can be divided easily by many other numbers and so calculations involving them are less cumbersome.

For items paid monthly, such as interest and rent, the statutory year rarely is used, since its use can create visible distortion in 31-day months and, especially, in February. However, spread over a year or more the error introduced with the statutory year becomes very small, so it is frequently used for calculation of prorated taxes and insurance. To prorate an item using the statutory year, first the full period's payment is found. Then the payment is divided by the number of months in the period to get the monthly cost. The monthly cost is divided by 30 to get the daily cost. Then it is determined who pays whom, and for what length of time. From that information, the prorated payment can be calculated.

The Actual Year

If using the statutory year is forbidden, then the actual year must be used. In this case, you must calculate how many days of the period must be paid for. This sum then is multiplied by the *daily* cost of the item to get the prorated payment. The difficulty comes in the fact that to get the daily rate you must divide the annual rate by 365, or 366 in leap years. Further, it often is confusing to try to count days elapsed in a significant part of a year, especially when dealing with odd beginning and ending dates. It is bad enough to try to figure how many days elapse between January 1 and July 26 of a given year; it is a lot worse to have to calculate the number of days elapsed from, say, October 23 of one year to March 14 of the following year. If you must use the actual year, you have no alternative; you have to remember the number of days in each month and whether or not you're dealing with a leap year.

Calculating Time With The Statutory Year

The statutory year lends itself well to calculation of elapsed time. In this type of calculation you want to find out how many days have elapsed between two dates, one of which is usually the closing date. To do this, write each date *numerically* as follows: YEAR — MONTH — DATE. June 17, 1941, would be 41 — 6 — 17. July 4, 1986, would be 86 — 7 — 4. To find the elapsed time,"subtract" the earlier date from the later one. Remember you can "borrow" from adjacent left-hand columns just as you do in normal arithmetic subtraction. Also remember that you're borrowing months and years, not digits. Each month has 30 days, and each year has 12 months. Here is an example, to find the elapsed time between December 28, 1988, and March 19, 1989:

$$89 - 3 - 19$$
$$- 88 - 12 - 28$$
$$?\quad ?\quad ?$$

First, we find the number of days; here we would have to subtract 28 from 19, and you can't do that. We must borrow a month (30 days) from the month column, to change the 19 to 49. 49 − 28 = 21. So we have:

$$\overset{2}{\quad}\quad\overset{49}{\quad}$$
$$89 - 3 - 19$$
$$- 88 - 12 - 28$$
$$?\quad ?\quad 21$$

Now we look to the months; we must subtract 12 from 2. We can't do that, so we borrow a year, or 12 months, from the year column, and subtract 12 from 14:

$$\overset{88}{89} - \overset{\overset{14}{2}}{\cancel{3}} - \overset{49}{\cancel{19}}$$
$$- 88 - 12 - 28$$
$$0 - 2 - 21$$

88 subtracted from 88 leaves 0, so the elapsed time between December 28, 1988, and March 19, 1989, is 2 months and 21 days.

Rounding In Proration

One very important warning must be given here. When you are calculating prorations, always carry your intermediate results (i.e., daily and monthly charges) to *at least two decimal places beyond the pennies*. Do *not* round to even cents until you have arrived at your *final* answer, because when you round you introduce a tiny error. This is all right with respect to your final answer, but intermediate answers will later be operated on, including multiplication by fairly large numbers. Each time a rounded number is multiplied, the rounding error is multiplied also! To keep this from affecting your final results, always carry intermediate steps two extra decimal places beyond what your final answer will carry.

PRORATION EXAMPLES

Here are examples of prorating each of the four common prorated items: rent, interest, taxes, insurance.

Rent

Rent usually is paid in advance. As an example:

We have a closing date of May 19, 1988, and rent is payable for the calendar month on the first of each month. Who pays whom what in the proration of rent of $265 per month?

Since the seller received the May rent payment on May 1, he should pay the buyer the portion of rent covering the part of the month *after* the closing date. May has 31 days; the closing date is May 19. Therefore, the buyer will own the property for 31 − 19 = 12 days during May. The daily rent for May is $1/31$ of the monthly rent, since there are 31 days: $265.00 ÷ 31 = $8.5484. (Remember to carry to two extra decimal places.) The buyer's share of the rent, then, is 12 × $8.5484 = $102.5808, which rounds to $102.58.

(Note that if you had rounded the daily rental to $8.55 and then multiplied by the 12 days, your result would have been $102.60, or 2¢ off.)

Interest

Interest is paid after it has accrued. Normally, the interest period ends the day *before* a payment is due — that is, a payment due on the first of the month covers the previous month; one due on the 18th of the month covers the period from the 18th of the previous month through the 17th of the current one.

The closing date is September 22, 1983. Interest is payable with the payment on the 16th of the month. The loan amount as of September 16, 1983, is $44,881.10. The interest rate is 9¼ % per year. If the loan is assumed, who pays whom what for prorated interest?

We have to calculate the monthly interest due and to determine how much of that amount is paid by whom. First, the dollar amount of interest — this is $1/12$ of 9¼% of the loan balance of $44,881.10: $1/12 \times 0.0925 \times \$44,881.10 = \$345.96$. Note that you rounded off the monthly interest, because the lender does that, too, each month.

The period involved here is 30 days, since September has that length. The seller will have to pay the buyer for all of the interest between September 16 and September 22, since on October 16 the buyer is going to have to pay the full month's interest. The seller will own the property for 7 days of that time. (At a glance, this appears incorrect since $22 - 16 = 6$. However, the seller owns the property on both the 16th and the 22nd, so we must add a day. Another way is to count the days on your fingers, starting with the 16th and ending with the 22nd.)

Now we must determine the daily interest charge, which is $\$345.96 \div 30 = \$11.5320$. We multiply this by 7 to get the seller's share for 7 days: $\$11.5320 \times 7 = \$80.724 = \$80.72$ rounded off.

Taxes

Taxes are usually assessed for a full year, so we would use the statutory year for calculation, if permitted.

The closing date is April 27, 1988. Taxes are $1188.54 per year. The tax year is March 1 to February 28 (or 29) of following year. Who pays whom how much in prorated taxes? Use both the statutory and the actual year, assuming (a) that taxes are paid on June 1 and (b) that taxes are paid on March 15 of the tax year.

This sample problem is likely to be more complex than any you will encounter on a licensing examination, but it demonstrates all the possibilities.

In situation (a) the seller pays his share to the buyer, since the taxes are due after the closing date and so must be paid by the buyer. In situation (b) the buyer pays the seller his share, because the taxes for the full tax year had already been paid by the seller before the closing date.

Statutory year calculations. The closing date is April 27, 1988, and the tax year begins March 1, 1988. Therefore the seller owns the property for 1 month and 27 days:

$$
\begin{array}{rrr}
88 & 4 & 28 \\
-88 & 3 & 1 \\
\hline
 & 1 & 27
\end{array}
$$

Note that we did not use April 27, the closing date, in this calculation, because we must consider the closing date as belonging to the seller. April 28, then, is the first day that the seller does *not* own the property, and so we must count from that day.

The seller's share, then, is for 1 month and 27 days. The total tax payment is $1188.54 per year. Dividing by 12 yields a monthly tax charge of $99.0450. Dividing this amount by 30 yields a daily tax charge of $3.3015.

$$
\begin{array}{lcr}
1 \text{ month @ } \$99.0450 & = & \$99.0450 \\
+ \ 27 \text{ days @ } \$3.3015 & = & + \ 89.1405 \\
\hline
\text{Total seller's charge} & & \$188.1855 = \$188.19
\end{array}
$$

The seller's share is $188.19, so the buyer's share is the rest, or $1188.54 - $188.19 = $1000.35.

In situation (a), then, the seller pays the buyer $188.19.

In situation (b) the buyer pays the seller $1000.35.

Actual Year Calculations. When calculating using the actual year, we reduce every-thing to days. The year has 365 days, so, using the same problem, the daily tax charge is $1188.54 ÷ 365 = $3.25627. The seller owns the property for a total of 58 days: 31 days of March and 27 days of April of the tax year. Therefore the seller's share is 58 × $3.25627 = $188.8654 = $188.87. The buyer's share would be $1188.54 − $188.87 = $999.67.

In situation (a) — taxes are paid on June 1 — the seller pays the buyer $188.87.

In situation (b) — taxes are paid on March 15 — the buyer pays the seller $999.67.

Note two things about this calculation. First, it comes out 68¢ different from the statutory year method; this occurs because of the different calculation technique. Second, when the daily charge was calculated it was carried to *three* extra decimal places. In the actual year calculation, you could multiply by a number as large as 365 and so multiply the rounding error by that much. Carrying to three extra decimal places reduces this error.

Insurance

A three-year insurance policy, dated October 22, 1982, is assumed on the closing date of August 11, 1984. The full three-year premium of $559.75 was paid at the time the policy was bought. Who pays whom what if this policy is prorated?

First we calculate the monthly insurance charge, which is $1/36$ (three years, remember) of the premium of $559.75: $559.75 ÷ 36 = $15.5486. The daily charge is $1/30$ of that amount: $15.5486 ÷ 30 = $0.5183.

Now we must calculate how long the buyer will use the policy. If the policy is dated October 22, 1982, then it expires on October 21 (at midnight) of 1985.

$$\begin{array}{r} 89 \quad 10 \quad 21 \\ - \ 88 \quad \ 8 \quad 11 \\ \hline 1 \quad \ 2 \quad 10 \end{array}$$

The buyer will own the policy for 1 year, 2 months, and 10 days. He will pay the seller the prorated share, since the seller paid for the full 3 years when he bought the policy. (Note that now we just go ahead and figure 1 year and 2 months to be 14 months, to save the problem of calculating the annual premium.)

14 months @ $15.5486	=	$217.6804
10 days @ $0.5183	= +	5.1830
Total payable to seller		$222.8634 = $222.86

Calculating insurance according to the actual year can be cumbersome. To do this we ought to calculate first the annual premium, which is $1/3$ of $559.75 = $186.58333. The daily premium charge is this amount divided by 365: $186.58333 ÷ 365 = $0.51119. Note that once again we are carrying actual year calculations to an extra *three* decimal places.

Figuring the time of ownership by the buyer is a lot more trouble. From October 22, 1988, to October 21, 1989, is one full year. From August 11, 1988, to October 21, 1988, is an additional 71 days — 20 in August, plus 30 in September and 21 in October.

1 year @ $186.58333	=	$186.58333
71 days @ $0.51119	= +	36.29449
Total payable to seller		$222.87782 = $222.88

Problem Set C

Here are some proration problems for you to practice with:

1. The closing date is June 26, 1988. Taxes are collected on a calendar year basis and are payable on June 1 of each year. Taxes for the year are $779.90. A two-year insurance policy, dated May 2, 1988, is to be assumed. A full two-year premium of $345.76 was paid when policy was issued. A mortgage loan of $28,883.00 as of June 1, 1988, will be assumed. Its interest rate is 7¾ % per year, payable at the first of each month. Part

of the property is rented, with rent of $125.00 per month payable in advance. Use the statutory year. Who pays whom what at closing?

2. The closing date is December 15, 1989. Taxes are $982, and cover the period from May 1, 1989, to April 30, 1990; they are not due and payable until the last day of the tax year. An insurance policy of one year, dated March 19, 1984, and costing $360, is to be assumed. The property is not rented and the loan is not to be assumed. Use the *actual* year. Who pays who what?

3. Use the statutory year for insurance and taxes. The closing date is April 20, 1988. Taxes are $1188.00 per year and are payable in four quarterly installments due March 31, June 30, September 30, and December 31 of each year. Quarterly tax payments are equal. An insurance policy costing $1046.55 for five years, dated July 16, 1985, is to be assumed. The property is not rented. Who pays whom what?

4. The closing date is September 25; you are to use the statutory year. In this area, two property taxes are paid. A $555.10 *city* tax must be paid by August 15, while a $303.25 *county* tax must be paid by October 15. Taxes cover the calendar year in which they are paid. What is the *net* amount payable? Who pays it to whom?

Hints On Handling Mathematical Problems On Examinations _____

Now that we have discussed the different kinds of mathematics problems that appear on licensing examinations, a few remarks dealing with the proper ways to approach them are in order.

You should remember that your objective on the examination is to get a passing grade. It is *not* necessary that you get 100% — only enough to pass. Mathematical problems can be terrible time-consumers; therefore you should devote your time at the outset to doing those problems that do not take up a lot of time. Save the really cumbersome ones for later, when you have had the chance to answer all the "easy" questions on the examination. A lot of people determinedly tackle the mathematics first or spend tremendous amounts of time on a very few problems, only to find later in the examination that they have to rush just to have a chance of getting to every question on the examination.

Always try to determine just how long it will take to do a problem *before* you tackle it. If it's going to take a lot of time, postpone doing it. Then when you get back to the time-consuming ones, do those first that are worth the most points. This may mean that you will turn in your examination without finishing one or two of the arithmetic problems simply because they were too long. That doesn't mean you're stupid — it means you're smart. Instead of slaving away over the few points these unfinished problems represented, you used your time to rack up points on the other parts of the examination that could be answered quickly. However, before turning in your test paper, try to mark an answer for *all* questions, even math problems not attempted. You might just guess the right answer!

Another point concerning arithmetic questions is that you may not need all the information given in the problem. After you read the question and determine just what it is you are being asked to do, then you will begin to search for the information you need to provide the answer. Do not assume that just because some information is included you must find some way of using it in your solution to the problem. It is fairly common to find that extra information has been included just to sidetrack or worry those whose arithmetic skills make them unsure of themselves.

ANSWERS

Before getting into Problem Set A, let us finish doing the problem that appears at the beginning of the chapter. This is the very complicated "sidewalk question," which was partially answered in association with Figures 18–2 (A), (B), and (C). We got as far as calculating the area of the sidewalk to be 914 sq. ft.

(1) Calculate the *volume* of the sidewalk, given that its area is 914 sq. ft. and the depth is 3½ in.
First, convert everything into inches: 1 sq. ft. = 144 sq. in.
914 × 144 sq. in. = 131,616 sq. in.
Now we can find the volume, in cubic inches, of the sidewalk.
$$\text{Volume} = 3\tfrac{1}{2} \times 131,616 \text{ sq. in.} = 460,656 \text{ cu. in.}$$

(2) Change the cubic inches into cubic yards: 1 cu. yd. = 36 × 36 × 36 cu. in., or 46,656 cu. in.
$$460,656 \text{ cu. in.} \div 46,656 \text{ cu. in.} = 9.87346 \text{ cu. yd.}$$

(3) Figure out how much stone and concrete are necessary.
Concrete is 85% of the sidewalk. 0.85 × 9.87346 cu. yd. = 8.39244 cu. yd. of concrete.
Stone is 15% of the walk. 0.15 × 9.87346 cu. yd. = 1.48102 cu. yd. of stone.

(4) Figure out how many tons of stone: 1 cu. yd. of stone weighs 3282 lb. 15 oz. (Change the 15 oz. to $^{15}/_{16}$ lb., or 0.9375 lb., to get 3282.9375 lb.) Since we are using 1.48102 cu. yd. of stone, there will be
$$1.48102 \text{ cu. yd.} \times 3282.9375 \text{ lb.} = 4862.0961 \text{ lb. of stone.}$$
One ton is 2000 lb. Therefore, we will use
$$4862.0961 \div 2000 = 2.43105 \text{ tons of stone.}$$

(5) Figure out how much labor is necessary. A worker can do 188 sq. ft. of walk per hour; we have 914 sq. ft. So we will use
$$914 \text{ sq. ft.} \div 188 \text{ sq. ft.} = 4.862 \text{ hours of labor.}$$

(6) Now (finally!) we can figure out the cost of the walk:

8.39244 cu. yd. of concrete @ $313 per cu. yd.	$2626.83
2.43105 tons of stone @ $27.83 per ton	67.66
4.862 hours of labor @ $19 per hour	92.38
TOTAL COST OF SIDEWALK	$2786.87

Problem Set A

1. **$39.92** total cost
The house is 55 ft. × 30 ft., or 170 ft. around. Since it is 8½ ft. high, the total wall area is
$$170 \text{ ft.} \times 8.5 \text{ ft.} = 1445 \text{ sq. ft.}$$
Now we must subtract for doors, the picture window, and other windows:
Doors: 3 ft. × 7.5 ft. = 22.5 sq. ft. each
Picture window: 12 ft. × 5 ft. = 60 sq. ft.
Windows: 2.5 ft. × 4 ft. = 10 sq. ft. each

Total unpainted area:

2 doors @ 2.5 sq. ft.	45 sq. ft.
Picture window	60 sq. ft.
6 windows @ 10 sq. ft.	60 sq. ft.
TOTAL UNPAINTED	165 sq. ft.

If 165 sq. ft. is unpainted, then 1280 sq. ft. (1445 − 165) must be painted. A gallon of paint covers 320 sq. ft. Therefore, we will need:
$$1280 \text{ sq. ft.} \div 320 \text{ sq. ft.} = 4 \text{ gal. of paint @ } \$9.98 = \mathbf{\$39.92} \text{ total cost}$$

2. **352** lots
76 acres is 3,310,560 sq. ft. (76 × 43,560). Taking out 665,000 sq. ft. for roads, parks,

etc., leaves 2,645,560 sq. ft. to be devoted to lots. Each lot must be 7500 sq. ft.

$$2,645,560 \text{ sq. ft.} \div 7500 \text{ sq. ft.} = 352.74$$

Therefore, he can get no more than **352** lots out of the land.

3. **$1389.20** total cost

Refer to the following picture and you will see that the walk can be divided into two parts, each 43 ft. × 8 ft., and one part 65 ft. × 8 ft. These contain 344 + 344 + 520 = 1208 sq. ft. If 1 sq. ft. costs $1.15, then 1208 sq. ft. cost 1208 × $1.15 = **$1389.20**.

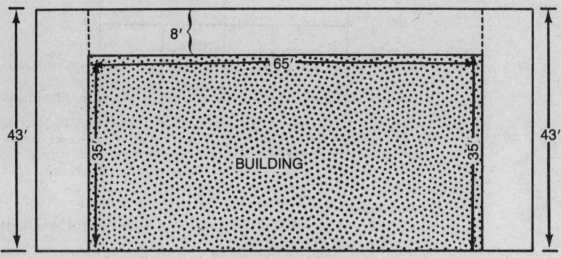

EXISTING SIDEWALK

4. **68.707** ft.

There are 9 sq. ft. in a sq. yd., so the lot contains 313 × 9 = 2817 sq. ft. If the plot is rectangular, with frontage of 41 ft. the depth must be

$$2817 \text{ sq. ft.} \div 41 \text{ ft.} = \textbf{68.707 ft.}$$

5. **$2238.29** total value

The formula for the area of a triangle is $A = \frac{1}{2} \times B \times H$. The base is 500 ft.; the height (depth) is 650 ft.

$$500 \text{ ft.} \times 650 \text{ ft.} = 325,000 \text{ sq. ft.}$$
$$325,000 \text{ sq. ft.} \times \frac{1}{2} = 162,500 \text{ sq. ft.}$$
$$162,500 \text{ sq. ft.} \div 43,560 \text{ sq. ft.} = 3.73049 \text{ acres}$$

The land is valued at $600 per acre, so the total value is

$$\$600 \times 3.73049 \text{ acres} = \textbf{\$2238.29}$$

6. **38** acres

One section (a square mile) contains 640 acres. You have to know that fact. The NW¼ of the SE¼ of a section, then, contains

$$\frac{1}{4} \times \frac{1}{4} \times 640 = 40 \text{ acres}$$

Now we must determine how much of that 40-acre tract is taken up by the road. The road is 66 ft. wide. The 40-acre tract is ¼ mi. on a side (draw a diagram, if necessary, as shown); ¼ mi. is 1320 ft. (or 5280 ft. ÷ 4). Therefore, the road is 66 ft. × 1320 ft., since it crosses the entire tract.

$$1320 \text{ ft.} \times 66 \text{ ft.} = 87,120 \text{ sq. ft.}$$
$$87,120 \text{ sq. ft.} \div 43,560 \text{ sq. ft.} = 2 \text{ acres}$$

If the road contains 2 acres, then Smith ended up with the rest of the 40 acres, or 38 acres.

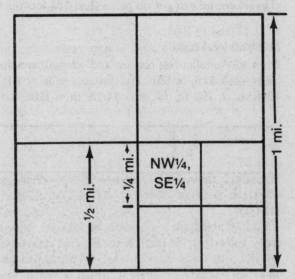

Problem Set B

1. **$35,000 purchase price**
   If Smith sold his home for $49,700 and made a 42% profit, then $49,700 is 142% of his purchase price: $49,700 ÷ 1.42 = **$35,000** purchase price.

2. **$1347.30 discount on loan**
   First the amount of the loan: 90% of $49,900 is $44,910. The three-point discount is 3% of the loan amount: 0.03 × $44,910 = **$1347.30** discount.

3. **$318.11 interest the first month**
   The interest for the first month will be $1/12$ of the annual interest on the full loan amount, since none of it will have been paid back during the first month of the loan. 0.085 × $44,910.00 = $3817.35 annual interest. $3817.35 ÷ 12 = **$318.11** interest the first month.

4. **2¼% depreciation per year**
   The building had depreciated a total of $57,500.00 − $48,443.75 = $9056.25. Next we determine what percentage $9056.25 is of $57,500.00: 9056.25 ÷ 57,500 = 15¾%. This had occurred over seven years, to give an annual rate of 15¾% ÷ 7 = **2¼%** depreciation per year.

5. **$19,990 sale price**
   If Sellar paid a 7½% commission, his $18,490.75 represents 92½% of the sale price (100% − 7½% = 92½%). $18,490.75 is 92.5% of _?_. $18,490.75 ÷ 0.925 = **$19,990.00** sale price.

6. **$284.90 is Winken's share of the monthly income.**
   The building produces an annual income of 21% of $44,000.00: 0.21 × $44,000.00 = $9240.00 annual income. $9240 ÷ 12 = $770 monthly income to the building. Winken gets 37% of this: 0.37 × $770.00 = **$284.90** monthly income going to Winken.

7. **$9922 Nod's share; 122.22% rate of profit**
   Since Winken owns 37% and Blinken owns 22%, that leaves 41% for Nod. The total profit is $44,000 − $19,800 = $24,200. Nod's share is 41% of this: 0.41 × $24,200 = **$9922**. Note that the *rate* of profit for the entire building is the same as the rate of profit for each of the three investors. This just means that each of them experienced the same growth in wealth as did the entire investment. If you are skeptical about this, work it out for each of the investors. For the entire building, the profit of $24,200 is

122.222...% of the original purchase price of $19,880. For Nod's share, we can calculate his original share as 41% of the $19,800 purchase price: 0.41 × $19,800 = $8118. **$9922** is 122.22...% of $8118 (9922 ÷ 8118).

8. **$870.44** paid to Bernie
This problem is elaborate and time consuming, but not difficult at all. First we determine what percentage of the total commission goes to Bernie's broker. If the other broker gets 40% and the Multilist group gets 3%, that leaves 57% for Bernie's broker. Second, we figure the dollar amount of Bernie's broker's share of the commission. The total commission is 6½% of $44,750: 0.065 × $44,750.00 = $2908.75. Bernie's broker gets 57% of that amount: 0.57 × $2908.75 = $1657.99. Bernie gets 52½% of that: 0.525 × $1657.99 = **$870.44**.

9. **$131.25** quarterly payment; **$21.06** more per year for compounding
The simple interest due quarterly is ¼ of the annual interest, which is 10½% of $5000, or 0.105 × $5000 = $525. The quarterly simple interest is $525 ÷ 4 = **$131.25**.

To find accumulated compound interest requires additional computation. We already know that the interest for the first quarter is $131.25 from the calculations we just did. For the second quarter, then, we will have $5000.00 + $131.25 = $5131.25 on which to calculate interest. Thus, ¼ × 0.105 × $5131.25 = $134.70, the interest due for the *second* quarter. At this point, a total of $265.95 of unpaid interest has accrued ($131.25 + $134.70), so for the third quarter interest must be calculated on $5265.95: ¼ × 0.105 × $5265.95 = $138.23. This means that at the end of the third quarter a total of $404.18 in unpaid interest has accrued ($265.95 + $138.23); therefore, for the fourth quarter interest will be calculated on $5404.18. The interest for the fourth quarter is ¼ × 0.105 × $5404.18 = $141.86. This gives a total interest for the year of $546.04 ($404.18 + $141.86).

Simple interest would have been 4 × $131.35 = $525.00, so with compound interest a total of **$21.04** more is paid ($546.04 − $525).

10. **32.8% loss; 4.1%** annual depreciation rate
The total amount of the loss is $93,000 − $62,500 = $30,500. This is **32.8%** of $93,000 ($30,500 ÷ $93,000 = 0.328). Remember that profit and loss are calculated based on the *purchase* price originally paid. Since this depreciation occurred over an eight-year period, the annual depreciation rate is 32.8% ÷ 8 = **4.1%**.

Problem Set C

1. Taxes: **$398.62** payable to seller
Insurance: **$319.35** payable to seller
Interest: **$161.67** payable to buyer
Rent: **$16.67** payable to buyer
Taxes: June 26 represents 5 months and 26 days that the seller will own the property during the year; he has already paid the taxes, since they are due June 1. Therefore, the buyer must pay the seller for the 6 months and 4 days that he will own the property during the tax year. One month's tax charge is $779.90 ÷ 12 = $64.9917. One day's tax charge is $64.9917 ÷ 30 = $2.1664.

6 months @ $64.9917 =	$389.9502	
4 days @ $2.1664 =	+ 8.6656	
Total taxes payable to seller	$398.6158 = **$398.62**	

Insurance: The policy expires May 1, 1990, so the buyer will own it for 1 year, 10 months, and 5 days. The yearly charge is $345.76 ÷ 2 = $172.88. The monthly charge is $172.88 ÷ 12 = $14.4067. The daily charge is $14.4067 ÷ 30 = $0.4802.

One year @ $172.88 =	$172.88	
10 months @ $14.4067 =	144.0670	
5 days @ $0.4802 =	+ 2.4010	
Total due seller for insurance	$319.3480 = **$319.35**	

Interest: The payment date is July 1, covering all of June. The seller owns the property for 26 days of June, so he pays $^{26}/_{30}$ of the interest charge for that month to the buyer. The monthly interest charge is $^{1}/_{12} \times 0.0775 \times \$28,883.00 = \$186.5360$. One day's interest is $\$186.5360 \div 30 = \$6.2179$. The seller's portion of the interest is $\$6.2179 \times 26 = \$161.6654 = \mathbf{\$161.67}$ payable to the buyer.

Rent: The seller has been paid for the entire month a total of \$125.00; 4 days of that is due to the buyer. One day's rent proration is $\$125.00 \div 30 = \$4.1667$; $4 \times \$4.1667 = \$16.6668 = \mathbf{\$16.67}$ payable to the buyer.

2. Taxes: **\$616.10** payable to buyer
Insurance: **\$91.73** payable to seller

Taxes: The taxes due cover from May 1 to December 15 for the seller, who has to pay his share to the buyer at closing, since the buyer will be liable for the entire year's tax bill at the end of the tax year. One day's tax charge is $\$982.00 \div 365 = \$2.69041$. The seller owns the property for 229 days (31 days each in May, July, August, and October; 30 days each in June, September, and November; and 15 days in December): $229 \times \$2.69041 = \$616.10389 = \mathbf{\$616.10}$ payable to the buyer.

Insurance: One day's insurance is $\$360 \div 365 = \$0.98630$. The buyer must pay the seller, since the seller paid the full premium when the policy was bought. The buyer will own the property from December 16 (the day after closing, for prorating purposes!) through the expiration of the policy on March 18. He will own it for 93 days (16 in December, 31 in January, 28 in February, 18 in March): $93 \times \$0.98630 = \$91.7259 = \mathbf{\$91.73}$ payable to the seller.

3. Taxes: **\$66** due to buyer
Insurance: **\$468.04** due to seller

Taxes: Taxes here are paid quarterly and not annually. The closing date is April 20, so the March 31 payment already has been made. The only payment that must be prorated is the June 30 payment, since it covers a period in which both buyer and seller will own the property. Quarterly taxes are $\$1188.00 \div 4 = \$297.00$. Monthly taxes are $\$297.00 \div 3 = \$99.00$. Daily taxes are $\$99.00 \div 30 = \$3.30$. These numbers all come out even, so no extra decimal places are necessary since no rounding will be necessary.

The seller will own the property for the 20 days of April during the second quarter. Therefore, he must pay the buyer $20 \times \$3.30 = \mathbf{\$66}$ for his share of the second quarter's taxes.

Insurance: The five-year policy cost \$1046.55; one year's insurance charge is $\$1046.55 \div 5 = \$209.31$. One month's charge is $\$209.31 \div 12 = \$17.4425$. One day's charge is $\$17.4425 \div 30 = \$0.5814$. The policy expires July 15, 1990.

$$
\begin{array}{r r r}
 & \overset{6}{\cancel{7}} & \overset{4\ 5}{\cancel{15}} \\
85 & & \\
- \ 83 & 4 & 20 \\
\hline
2 & 2 & 25
\end{array}
$$

The buyer will own the policy for 2 years, 2 months, and 25 days.

2 years @ \$209.31	=	\$418.62
2 months @ \$17.4425	=	34.885
25 days @ \$0.5814	=	+ 14.535
Total due seller for insurance		**\$468.04**

4. Seller owes **\$76.75** to buyer.
In this problem, part of the tax is payable before the closing (by the seller) and part is payable after the closing (by the buyer). The seller owns the property for 8 months and 25 days of the year; the buyer owns it for 3 months and 5 days.

City tax: This is payable by the buyer to the seller, since it was paid August 15. One month's tax is $555.10 ÷ 12 = $46.2583; one day's tax is $46.2583 ÷ 30 = $1.5419. The seller receives payment for 3 months and 5 days, or $146.48 from the buyer.

County tax: This is payable by the seller to the buyer, since it is due *after* closing. The tax is $303.25 ÷ 12 = $25.2708 monthly; daily it is $25.2708 ÷ 30 = $0.8424. The seller owes a total of $223.23 to the buyer. Therefore, the seller owes a net of $223.23 − $146.48 = **$76.75** to the buyer.

Chapter 19/*Closing Statements*

In most states real estate brokers, not their salespersons, are responsible for preparing closing statements. Consequently, only *broker* licensing examinations involve questions concerning closing statements. (Note that in some states closing statements are called "settlement statements.")

Closing Statements — Purpose

Closing statements provide an accounting of all funds involved in a real estate transaction. These statements show the amount that the buyer must pay and that the seller will receive from the transaction. Buyer and seller each are given an accounting of all items they must pay for or are credited with in the transaction. Brokers should prepare a reconciliation as well, to "button up" the statements.

Debits and Credits

You need not be a bookkeeper to understand closing statements. Two columns are shown for the buyer and two for the seller. The two columns for each party are debit column and credit column. Totals of debit and credit columns must agree with each other.

Listed in the debit column are amounts that the party being considered is charged for. Listed in the credit column are those that the party will receive credit for. Cash is needed to balance.

As a simple example, assume the sale of a $40,000 house on January 30, 1988. The seller has already paid taxes for the entire 1988 calendar year, which amounted to $730. The seller should be credited with the $40,000 house plus $670 prepaid taxes for the remainder of the year. Cash will be the offsetting debit. The buyer will be debited for the house and paid-up taxes; cash is the offsetting credit. The closing statements would appear as follows:

	Seller		Buyer	
	Debit	Credit	Debit	Credit
Real property		$40,000	$40,000	
Prepaid taxes		670	670	
Cash paid by buyer to close				$40,670
Cash received by seller	$40,670			
Totals	$40,670	$40,670	$40,670	$40,670

Suppose that a broker was involved who earned a $2400 commission from the sale. The seller is to pay for the commission, so the seller would be debited with the $2400 fee. Assume further, that the buyer must pay $75 for a survey. Then he would be debited for

215

that amount. The closing statements would be as follows:

	Seller		Buyer	
	Debit	Credit	Debit	Credit
Real property		$40,000	$40,000	
Prepaid taxes		670	670	
Sales commission	$ 2,400			
Survey fee			75	
Cash paid by buyer to close				$40,745
Cash received by seller	38,270			
Totals	$40,670	$40,670	$40,745	$40,745

Items that affect only one party will be shown as a debit or a credit *only on the statement of the party affected*. For example, if the sales commission is paid by the seller, the amount will appear only on the seller's closing statement. If the buyer pays for a survey, it will appear only as a debit to him.

Those items of value that are sold, exchanged, or transferred between buyer and seller will be shown in *opposite* columns of *both* parties. For example, the transferred property is shown as a credit to the seller *and* as a debit to the buyer. Never should an item transferred, exchanged, or taken over be shown as a credit to both parties or as a debit to both. If an item is transferred, sold, or exchanged, it will be a debit to one party and a credit to the other.

Items usually *debited* (charged) to the buyer that are likely to be encountered include the following:

1. Purchase price of the real property
2. Purchase price of personal property
3. Deed recording fees
4. Title examination
5. Title insurance
6. Hazard insurance
7. Survey
8. Appraisal fee (sometimes charged to seller)
9. Prepaid taxes
10. Loan assumption fees

Items that are likely to be *credited* to the buyer are:

1. Earnest money deposits
2. Proceeds of a loan he borrows
3. Assumption of a loan
4. Mortgage to the seller (purchase money)
5. Current taxes unpaid to closing
6. Tenant rents paid in advance (the seller collected these)
7. Balance due from purchaser to close (paid by buyer to close)

Items likely to be *debited* to a seller are:

1. Sales commission
2. Current but unpaid taxes
3. Existing debt — whether assumed or to be paid off
4. Loan prepayment penalties
5. Discount points for buyer's VA or FHA loan. Discount points on *conventional* loans may be charged to buyer or to seller depending on contractual arrangements, custom in the area, local law, etc.
6. Rent received in advance
7. Deed preparation

Items usually *credited* to a seller are:

1. Sales price of real property
2. Sales price of personal property

3. Prepaid taxes
4. Prepaid insurance (only if policy is assumed by buyer)
5. Escrow balance held by lender

COMPREHENSIVE SAMPLE PROBLEM

Abe Seller and Will Buyer are to close on Seller's House on January 30, 1983. The purchase price is $40,000. In addition, Buyer will pay $650 for appliances. Seller is to pay a 6 percent commission on the real estate to the Alternative Real Estate, Inc., brokers. County taxes for the 1983 calendar year were $730, due on January 15, 1983. They were paid in full on that date by Mr. Seller. Since it is an unincorporated area, there are no city taxes.

The property was occupied by Mr. Happy Tenant, whose lease survives the sale. His monthly rental is $310 paid the first of each month. Rent is to be prorated to the date of closing.

Abe Seller owes $24,000 on a 6 percent mortgage, which must be paid at closing, plus interest for the entire month of January. He will also incur a 1 percent mortgage prepayment penalty. In addition, he has agreed to pay two discount points on Mr. Buyer's $33,000 VA mortgage loan.

Mr. Buyer will take over Mr. Seller's hazard insurance policy. The policy anniversary date is January 26, 1983. But Mr. Seller has not yet paid the $182.50 premium.

Mr. Seller owes $25 for a termite inspection, which will be paid by the Alternative Real Estate, Inc. Mr. Buyer will pay $75 for a survey, $50 for a credit report, $66 for mortgage recording fees, and $12 to record the deed. He will also pay $198 for title insurance. He will give Mr. Seller a $1500 second purchase money mortgage at closing. A $400 earnest money check being held in escrow by the broker will be turned over to Mr. Seller at closing. Complete the closing statements (see figures 19–1 and 19–2).

SETTLEMENT STATEMENT WORKSHEET

SETTLEMENT DATE:	BUYER'S STATEMENT		SELLER'S STATEMENT	
	DEBIT	CREDIT	DEBIT	CREDIT

Fig. 19-1.

SETTLEMENT STATEMENT WORKSHEET

SETTLEMENT DATE:	BUYER'S STATEMENT		SELLER'S STATEMENT	
	DEBIT	CREDIT	DEBIT	CREDIT
PURCHASE PRICE	40,000.00			40,000.00
EARNEST MONEY		400.00		
MORTGAGE LOAN		33,000.00		
SECOND MORTGAGE LOAN		1,500.00	1,500.00	
PRORATED TAXES	670.00			670.00
PRORATED INSURANCE		2.00	2.00	
PRORATED RENT		10.00	10.00	
PURCHASE OF PERSONAL PROPERTY	650.00			650.00
MORTGAGE LOAN PAYOFF			24,000.00	
ACCRUED MORTGAGE INTEREST			120.00	
PREPAYMENT PENALTY			240.10	
BROKERAGE COMMISSION			2,400.00	
DISCOUNT POINTS			660.10	
TERMITE INSPECTION			25.00	
DEED RECORDING	12.00			
MORTGAGE RECORDING	66.00			
SURVEY	75.00			
CREDIT REPORT	125.00			
TITLE INSURANCE	198.00			
DUE FROM BUYER / TO SELLER		6,884.00	12,363.00	
	41,796.00	41,796.00	41,320.00	41,320.00

Broker's Reconciliation

A broker's reconciliation worksheet is used to assure that all cash receipts and disbursements are accounted for properly. Like a closing statement, it has two columns, which can be described as "cash receipts" and "cash disbursements," respectively. The totals of the two columns must agree.

The reconciliation can be prepared using the following steps:

1. Go down the debit column of the purchaser's closing statement.
    A. List the items that the broker will pay for the purchaser's account in the "disbursements" column of the reconciliation.
    B. On a separate worksheet called "Loan Proceeds," list the items that the new mortgage lender will receive directly from the buyer or withhold from the loan amount.
2. Go down the credit column of the buyer's closing statement.
    A. List on the broker's reconciliation, as a receipt, all cash paid by the buyer. Be sure to include the earnest money and cash paid at closing.
    B. On the top of the loan proceeds worksheet, list the amounts of mortgage money supplied at closing. Do not include assumed mortgages or those taken by the seller in partial payment.
3. Go down the debit column of the seller's closing statement.
    A. List any amounts to be paid by the broker on behalf of the seller as a "disbursement" on the broker's reconciliation.
    B. List the sales commission as a disbursement on the broker's reconciliation.

BROKER'S CASH RECONCILATION STATEMENT

Address: 1999 Somewhere Parkway   Closing Date: January 30, 1988

Mr. Abe Seller   Mr. Will Buyer
(Seller)   (Buyer)

	Receipts	Disbursements
From Buyer		
Earnest Money Deposited	400	
Check for Balance	6,884	
To Seller		
Check for Balance		12,363
Expenses		
Real Estate Commission		2,400
Preparation of Warranty Deed		
Preparation of Security Deed and Promissory Notes		
Title Fees		
Recording Mortgage ~~Security Deed~~		66
Recording Warranty Deed		12
Survey		75
Special Assessments		
First Mortgage Proceeds	7,980*	
Survey and Credit Report		125
Termite Inspection		25
Title Insurance		198
	15,264	15,264

*See worksheet attached

Fig. 19-2.

C. On the loan proceeds worksheet, list the balance of loans to be paid off, accrued interest, prepayment penalties, and discount points charged to the seller.

4. Go down the credit column of the seller's statement. If the seller has paid cash and not received something from the buyer in return, it must be reconciled.

5. Items not selected in steps 1–4 include the property being sold and prorated charges. These items will not appear on the broker's reconciliation.

6. On the loan proceeds worksheet, sum all items, excluding the principal of the new loan, which was written on top of the page. Subtract the sum from the new loan principal to get the loan proceeds. That amount is inserted as a receipt on the broker's reconciliation.

7. Total the receipts and the disbursements columns of the reconciliation. They should agree, to complete the reconciliation.

8. Amounts shown in each column should be received/disbursed by the broker who has earned a commission.

LOAN PROCEEDS WORKSHEET

Amount borrowed on new loan		$33,000.00
Less: Discount points	$ 660.00	
Existing mortgage loan payoff	24,000.00	
Prepayment penalty	240.00	
Accrued interest payable	120.00	
	$25,020.00	− 25,020.00
Loan proceeds		$ 7,980.00

Real Estate Settlement Procedures Act

The *Real Estate Settlement Procedures Act* (RESPA) covers most residential mortgage loans used to finance the purchase of one- to four-family properties. It includes a house, a condominium or cooperative apartment unit, a lot with a mobile home, or a lot on which a house will be built or a mobile home placed using the proceeds of a loan.

PURPOSE OF RESPA

The purpose of RESPA is to provide potential borrowers with information concerning the settlement (closing) process to enable one to shop for settlement services and make informed decisions. RESPA does not set the prices for services; its purpose is merely to provide information about settlement (closing) and costs.

MATERIALS TO BE RECEIVED UNDER RESPA

Under RESPA, one who files a loan application for property covered must receive from the lending agency a pamphlet titled *Settlement Costs and You* and a good faith estimate of the costs of settlement services. The lender has three business days after receiving a loan application to mail these materials. From that time until settlement, the loan applicant has an opportunity to shop for loan settlement services. One business day before settlement, if the borrower requests, the loan applicant has the right to inspect a Uniform Settlement Statement, which shows whatever figures are available at that time for settlement charges. At settlement the completed Uniform Settlement Statement is given to the borrower or his agent. Where there is no actual settlement meeting, the Uniform Settlement Statement is mailed.

SETTLEMENT COSTS AND YOU

The pamphlet *Settlement Costs and You* must be given by lending agencies to borrowers within three days after they apply for loans covered by RESPA. It contains information concerning shopping for services, homebuyer's rights, and homebuyer's obligations. It also includes a sample Uniform Settlement Statement form and describes specific settlement services. It provides information concerning a comparison of lender costs and describes reserve accounts and adjustments between buyer and seller.

REPORTING TO IRS

While this is not a part of RESPA, the Federal Tax Reform Act of 1986 created a new requirement that brokers and/or settlement agents report the details of some real estate transactions to the U.S. Internal Revenue Service. The primary responsibility lies with the settlement agent, whoever actually handles the closing. Thus, brokers who handle closings must abide by this new requirement.

If there is no settlement agent, then the responsibility rests with the buyer's broker and the seller's broker, in that order. Not all transactions need be reported.

Checklist for Your State's Practices

(1) Does your state have a deed transfer (documentary) tax?
☐ No
☐ Yes. How is it calculated? _____
Who pays it?   ☐ Buyer   ☐ Seller

(2) How are property taxes assessed in your state? (See checklist for Chapter 16, "Taxation and Assessment.") _____
_____

Questions on Chapter 19

1. The purchase price would be shown on the purchaser's closing statement as
(A) a debit
(B) a credit
(C) both A and B
(D) neither A nor B

2. The purchaser's earnest money held by a broker until closing would be shown as
(A) a debit to the purchaser
(B) a credit to the seller
(C) both A and B
(D) neither A nor B

3. Property taxes for the current year have not yet been paid. They should be shown as
(A) a credit to the buyer
(B) a debit to the seller
(C) both A and B
(D) neither A nor B

4. A tenant paid rent at the beginning of the month. The sale takes place during the middle of the month. To prorate rent,
(A) credit the seller
(B) debit the buyer
(C) both A and B
(D) neither A nor B

5. The buyer has arranged new financing for property. Closing statements, with respect to the mortgage principal, should show
(A) a credit to the buyer
(B) a debit to the seller
(C) both A and B
(D) neither A nor B

6. The seller will pay a broker's commission. The commission would be shown as
(A) a credit to the seller
(B) a debit to the seller
(C) a debit to the buyer
(D) A and C only

7. The buyer will take over the seller's insurance policy. The premium has been paid by the seller. The unexpired premium should be shown as
(A) a credit to the seller
(B) a debit to the buyer
(C) both A and B
(D) neither A nor B

8. The seller will accept a second mortgage from the buyer. The amount owed is shown as
   (A) a credit to the buyer
   (B) a debit to the seller
   (C) both A and B
   (D) neither A nor B

9. The sale price of personal property to be paid for at closing would be shown as
   (A) a credit to the buyer
   (B) a debit to the seller
   (C) both A and B
   (D) neither A nor B

10. An existing mortgage on the property is to be assumed by the buyer. The closing statements would show the mortgage principal as
    (A) a credit to the buyer
    (B) a debit to the seller
    (C) both A and B
    (D) neither A nor B

11. The buyer must pay $100 for a survey and credit report at closing. Settlement statements would show
    (A) a debit to the buyer
    (B) a credit to the seller
    (C) both A and B
    (D) neither A nor B

12. The buyer has arranged an 8 percent VA mortgage loan with two discount points. The discount points are shown as
    (A) a debit to the seller
    (B) a debit to the buyer
    (C) both A and B
    (D) neither A nor B

13. The buyer is to assume the seller's mortgage loan and must also maintain the tax and insurance escrow account held by the mortgage lender. The escrow account balance would be shown as a
    I. debit to the buyer
    II. credit to the seller
    (A) I only
    (B) II only
    (C) I and II
    (D) Neither I nor II

14. The tenant has a $250 security deposit in an account to be taken over by the buyer. At closing, the security deposit should be shown as a
    I. credit to the buyer
    II. debit to the seller
    (A) I only
    (B) II only
    (C) I and II
    (D) Neither I nor II

15. The seller incurs a prepayment penalty to pay off his mortgage loan. The penalty is shown as
    (A) a credit to the seller
    (B) a debit to the seller
    (C) a credit to the buyer
    (D) B and C only

16. The buyer, in connection with his new financing, must establish a $500 escrow account at closing, for taxes and insurance. The escrow deposit is shown as
    (A) a debit to the buyer
    (B) a credit to the buyer
    (C) a credit to the seller
    (D) A and C only

17. The buyer will pay for deed recording and title insurance at closing. These items are shown as
    (A) a credit to the buyer
    (B) a debit to the buyer
    (C) a credit to the seller
    (D) A and C only

18. RESPA is intended to
    (A) regulate charges for settlement services
    (B) provide information about settlement services to home loan applicants
    (C) both A and B
    (D) neither A nor B

19. After a home loan application is filed, a lender has _____ business day(s) to provide a good faith estimate of settlement charges.
   (A) one
   (B) two
   (C) three
   (D) fifteen

20. Upon the loan applicant's request, he has the right to inspect
   I. a final Uniform Settlement Statement
   II. a Uniform Settlement Statement with whatever figures are available
   (A) I only
   (B) II only
   (C) I and II
   (D) Neither I nor II

TRUE — FALSE. Mark *T* for true, *F* for false.

_____ 21. The purpose of a closing statement is to provide an accounting of all funds involved in a real estate transaction.

_____ 22. In a closing statement, entries for the buyer are called debits, while entries for the seller are called credits.

_____ 23. Items that affect only one party will be shown as a debit or credit only on the statement of the party affected.

_____ 24. Both the buyer and seller must make up their own closing statement and submit it to the broker at closing so the broker will know how to distribute the funds.

_____ 25. Earnest money is an item likely to be credited to the buyer.

_____ 26. Items of value that are sold, exchanged, or transferred between buyer and seller will be shown in opposite columns on each party's statement.

FILL-INS. Fill in the blanks with the appropriate words or phrases.

27. The purchase price of real property is likely to be a _____ to the buyer and a _____ to the seller.

28. Property taxes that are as yet unpaid as of the closing date are likely to be a _____ _____ to the buyer and a _____ to the seller.

29. Deed recording fees usually will *not* appear on the statement of the _____ .

30. Tenant rents paid in advance are a debit to the _____ .

31. The broker's commission usually is a _____ to the _____ _____ .

32. The term RESPA stands for _____ .

ANSWERS

1.	A	10.	C	18.	B	26.	T
2.	D	11.	A	19.	C	27.	debit, credit
3.	C	12.	A	20.	B	28.	credit, debit
4.	D	13.	C	21.	T	29.	seller
5.	A	14.	C	22.	F	30.	seller
6.	B	15.	B	23.	T	31.	debit, seller
7.	C	16.	A	24.	F	32.	Real Estate Settlement
8.	C	17.	B	25.	T		Procedures Act
9.	D						

PART V: FEDERAL LAW AFFECTING REAL ESTATE

Chapter 20/*Fair Housing Law*

The Federal "Fair Housing Act," Public Law 90–284, was enacted into law on April 11, 1968, as Title VIII of the Civil Rights Act of 1968.

Purpose

The purpose of the Fair Housing Act is expressed by Section 801 of the law, which states:

> It is the policy of the United States to provide, within constitutional limitations, for fair housing throughout the United States.

NEED FOR FAIR HOUSING

The following is quoted directly from *Understanding Fair Housing*, U.S. Commission on Civil Rights.[1]

> Housing is a key to improvement in a family's economic condition. Homeownership is one of the important ways in which Americans have traditionally acquired financial capital. Tax advantages, the accumulation of equity, and the increased value of real estate property enable homeowners to build economic assets. These assets can be used to educate one's children, to take advantage of business opportunities, to meet financial emergencies, and to provide for retirement. Nearly two of every three majority group families are homeowners, but less than two of every five nonwhite families own their homes. Consequently, the majority of nonwhite families are deprived of this advantage.
>
> Housing is essential to securing civil rights in other areas. Segregated residential patterns in metropolitan areas undermine efforts to assure equal opportunity in employment and education. While centers of employment have moved from the central cities to suburbs and outlying parts of metropolitan areas, minority group families remain confined to the central cities, and because they are confined, they are separated from employment opportunities. Despite a variety of laws against job discrimination, lack of access to housing in close proximity to available jobs is an effective barrier to equal employment.
>
> In addition, lack of equal housing opportunity decreases prospects for equal educational opportunity. The controversy over school busing is closely tied to the residential patterns of our cities and metropolitan areas. If schools in large urban centers are to be desegregated, transportation must be provided to convey children from segregated neighborhoods to integrated schools.
>
> Finally, if racial divisions are to be bridged, equal housing is an essential element. Our cities and metropolitan areas consist of separate societies increasingly hostile and distrustful of one another. Because minority and majority group families live apart, they are strangers to each other. By living as neighbors they would have an opportunity to learn to understand each other and to redeem the promise of America: that of "one Nation indivisible."

---

[1]From *Understanding Fair Housing*, U.S. Commission on Civil Rights, Clearinghouse Publication 42, February 1973, p. 1.

224

Property Covered

Upon its enactment, the 1968 Fair Housing Act prohibited discriminatory practices with respect to:

1. A. Dwellings owned or operated by the Federal Government.
   B. Dwellings provided in whole or in part with loans, grants, advances or contributions of the Federal Government, under agreements entered into after November 20, 1962.
   C. Dwellings provided in whole or part by Federally insured or guaranteed credit agreements (mortgages) entered into after November 20, 1962.
   D. Dwellings provided by the development or redevelopment of real estate purchased, leased, or otherwise obtained from a state or local agency that received Federal financial assistance for the project under an agreement entered into after November 20, 1962.

2. After December 31, 1968, to all dwellings covered above and to all other dwellings *except*
   A. A single-family house sold or rented by an owner provided that he:
      1) does not own more than three such houses at any one time, and
      2) was the current or most recent occupier or, if not, may sell only one house within any 24-month period, and
      3) is not under commitment to acquire more than a total of three houses at any time, and
      4) after December 31, 1969, does not utilize any services of a real estate broker and does not advertise for sale or rental in a discriminatory fashion.
   B. Rooms or dwelling units containing living quarters for four or fewer families, provided the owner lives in one of the units.

Discrimination in the Sale or Rental

Section 804 of the Fair Housing Act makes it unlawful to do any of the following:

(a) To refuse to sell or rent after the making of a bona fide offer, or to refuse to negotiate for the sale or rental of, or otherwise make unavailable or deny, a dwelling to any person because of race, color, religion, sex, or national origin.

(b) To discriminate against any person in the terms, conditions, or privileges of sale or rental of a dwelling, or in the provision of services or facilities in connection therewith, because of race, color, religion, sex, or national origin.

(c) To make, print, or publish, or cause to be made, printed, or published any notice, statement, or advertisement, with respect to the sale or rental of a dwelling that indicates any preference, limitation, or discrimination based on race, color, religion, sex, or national origin, or an intention to make any such preference, limitation, or discrimination.

(d) To represent to any person because of race, color, religion, sex, or national origin that any dwelling is not available for inspection, sale, or rental when such dwelling is in fact so available.

(e) For profit, to induce or attempt to induce any person to sell or rent any dwelling by representations regarding the entry or prospective entry into the neighborhood of a person or persons of a particular race, color, religion, sex, or national origin.

Discrimination in Financing

Section 805 of the Fair Housing Act applies to transactions after December 31, 1968. It states that it is unlawful for:

> any bank, building and loan association, insurance company or other corporation, association, firm or enterprise whose business consists in whole or in part in the making of commercial real estate loans, to deny a loan or other financial assistance to a person applying therefore for the purpose of purchasing, constructing, improving, repairing, or maintaining a dwelling, or to discriminate against him in the fixing of the amount, interest rate, duration, or other terms or conditions of such loan or other financial assistance, because of the race, color, religion, sex, or national origin of such person or of any person associated with him in connection with such loan or other financial assistance or the purposes of such loan or other financial assistance, or of the present or prospective owners, lessees, tenants, or occupants of the dwelling or dwellings in relation to which such loan or other financial assistance is to be made or given: *Provided,* That nothing contained in this section shall impair the scope or effectiveness of the exception contained in Section 803(b).

Section 803(b) exempts a single-family house sale or lease by owner, if certain provisions are met. This was described earlier.

Discrimination in Brokerage Services

Section 806 of the Fair Housing Act states:

> After December 31, 1968, it shall be unlawful to deny any person access to or membership or participation in any multiple-listing service, real estate brokers' organization or other service, organization, or facility relating to the business of selling or renting dwellings, or to discriminate against him in the terms or conditions of such access, membership, or participation, on account of race, color, religion, sex, or national origin.

Blockbusting

"Blockbusting" is prohibited. It is the soliciting of homeowners by unscrupulous real estate agents, brokers, or speculators who feed upon fears of homeowners. They attempt to buy property at very low prices from whites in racially transitional neighborhoods and broker or sell them to blacks at high prices. Some blockbusters deliberately incite panic and white flight to achieve their greedy, unlawful goal.

Specific Exemptions

There are two specific limited exemptions to Fair Housing Laws. One exemption allows a religious organization to discriminate with respect to its noncommercial property. It does not, however, allow this if the religion discriminates on the basis of race, color, sex, or national origin with respect to membership. The other exemption allows private clubs, which provide lodging as an incident to their main purpose, to give preferential treatment to club members.

Enforcement by HUD

Any person who claims to have been injured by a discriminatory housing practice or who believes that he will be irrevocably injured by a discriminatory housing practice that is about to occur (hereafter "person aggrieved") may file a complaint with the Secretary of the Department of Housing and Urban Development (HUD). Complaints must be in writing, state the facts, and be filed within 180 days after the alleged discriminatory housing practice occurred. The Attorney General conducts all litigation in which the Secretary of HUD participates as a party pursuant to the Fair Housing Act.

Enforcement by Private Persons

The rights granted to private persons by the Fair Housing Act may be enforced by civil action in appropriate U.S. district courts without regard to the amount in controversy and in appropriate state or local courts of general jurisdiction. A civil action shall be commenced within one hundred and eighty days after the alleged discriminatory housing practice occurred.

Upon application by the plaintiff and in such circumstances as the court may deem just, a court of the United States in which a civil action under this section has been brought may appoint an attorney for the plaintiff and may authorize the commencement of a civil action upon proper showing without the payment of fees, costs, or security. A court of a state or subdivision thereof may do likewise to the extent not inconsistent with the law or procedures of the State or subdivision.

The court may grant as relief, as it deems appropriate, any permanent or temporary injunction, temporary restraining order, or other order, and may award to the plaintiff actual damages and not more than $1000 punitive damages, together with court costs and reasonable attorney fees in the case of a prevailing plaintiff: *Provided,* That the said plaintiff in the opinion of the court is not financially able to assume said attorney's fees.

Preventing Intimidation

Under Section 901 of the Civil Rights Act of 1968 (Title IX) whoever:

A. Injures or threatens to injure or interfere with any person because of his race, religion, color, sex, or national origin and who is selling, leasing, occupying, financing, etc., property, or

B. Intimidates persons who deal with others in housing on account of race, religion, color, sex, or national origin, or

C. Discourages others from dealing with others in housing on account of race, religion, color, sex, or national origin.

Shall be fined up to $1000 or imprisoned for up to one year, or both. If bodily injury results, the fine is a $10,000 maximum or up to 10 years in prison, or both. If death results, he shall be imprisoned for any term of years or for life.

Other Fair Housing Laws

The Fair Housing Act was not the first law to prevent discriminatory practice in housing. The Supreme Court of the United States, in the 1917 *Buchanan* case, prohibited, on constitutional grounds, local governments from requiring residential segregation. This ruling is noteworthy because in 1896 the Supreme Court had established the doctrine that legally compelled segregation in such areas as public transportation and public education was constitutionally permissible. The *Buchanan* decision destroyed the doctrine as it applied to housing. In 1948, in *Shelley* v. *Kraemer,* the Supreme Court struck down as unconstitutional the legal enforcement of racially restrictive covenants.

The executive branch of the government took fair housing action for the first time in 1962, when President Kennedy issued an Executive order on equal opportunity in housing. While it represented a significant legal step forward, his Executive order was limited. Its guarantee of nondiscrimination was restricted largely to housing provided through the insurance and guaranty programs administered by FHA and its sister agency, the Veterans Administration

(VA). Housing financed through conventional loans was not covered by the President's order. The President's order applied only to FHA and VA housing insured or guaranteed after the date of the order's issuance (November 20, 1962). It left hundreds of thousands of existing housing units receiving FHA and VA assistance immune from the requirement of the nondiscrimination mandate. Barely 1 percent of the nation's housing was covered by President Kennedy's Executive order.

In 1964, Congress enacted Title VI of the Civil Rights Act of 1964, prohibiting discrimination in any program or activity receiving federal financial assistance. Among the principal programs affected by this law were low-rent public housing, a program directed to providing housing for the poor, and urban renewal. Like President Kennedy's Executive order, Title VI excluded conventionally financed housing. Title VI also excluded most FHA and VA housing, which the Executive order covered. Less than half of 1 percent of the nation's housing inventory was subject to the nondiscrimination requirement through Title VI.

In 1968, Congress enacted Title VIII of the Civil Rights Act of 1968, the Federal Fair Housing Law. This law prohibits the discriminatory practices of all real estate brokers, builders, and mortgage lenders and is the one described earlier.

In June 1968, two months after enactment of Title VIII, the Supreme Court of the United States, in the landmark case of *Jones* v. *Mayer*, ruled that an 1866 Civil Rights law passed under the authority of the Eighteenth Amendment (which outlawed slavery) bars all racial discrimination in housing, private as well as public.

Today, over 90 percent of all U.S. housing is subject to the Fair Housing Law.

Questions on Chapter 20

1. The 1968 Fair Housing Act provides against housing discrimination on the basis of
   (A) race and color
   (B) race, color, and religion
   (C) race, color, religion, and national origin
   (D) race, color, religion, national origin, and sex

2. The prohibitions of the 1968 Fair Housing Act apply to privately owned housing when
   (A) a broker or other person engaged in selling or renting dwellings is used
   (B) discriminatory advertising is used
   (C) both A and B
   (D) neither A nor B

3. These prohibitions of the 1968 Fair Housing Act apply to multifamily housing in cases of
   (A) multifamily dwellings of five or more units
   (B) multifamily dwellings of four or less units if the owner occupies one of the units
   (C) both A and B
   (D) neither A nor B

4. Single-family houses privately owned by an individual owning less than three such houses may be sold or rented without being subject to the provisions of the Fair Housing Act unless
   (A) a broker is used   (C) both A and B
   (B) discriminatory advertising is used   (D) neither A nor B

5. The limiting of sale, rental, or occupancy of dwellings owned or operated by a religious organization for noncommercial purposes, provided that membership in said religion is not based on race, color, or national origin,
   (A) is prohibited by the Fair Housing Act
   (B) is prohibited by the Civil Rights Act
   (C) both A and B
   (D) neither A nor B

6. Single-family houses privately owned by an individual owning less than three such houses may be sold or rented without being subject to the provisions of the Fair Housing Act if
   (A) no more than one such house is sold in any two-year period
   (B) a broker is employed to sell such a house
   (C) both A and B
   (D) neither A nor B

7. What are the broker's responsibilities under the 1968 Fair Housing Act?
   (A) To show all houses to all prospects
   (B) To treat all prospects equally
   (C) Both A and B
   (D) Neither A nor B

8. Complaints about discrimination may be brought
   (A) to the Secretary of Housing and Urban Development
   (B) directly to court
   (C) both A and B
   (D) neither A nor B

9. If a minority prospect asks to be shown homes in white neighborhoods, the broker
   (A) obliges and shows homes in white neighborhoods
   (B) responds and shows homes as requested
   (C) both A and B
   (D) neither A nor B

10. The 1968 Federal Fair Housing Law states that it is illegal to discriminate against any person because of race, color, religion, national origin, or sex
    (A) in the sale, rental, or financing of housing or residential lots
    (B) in advertising the sale or rental of housing
    (C) both A and B
    (D) neither A nor B

11. The broker's obligation in complying with equal opportunity in housing is
    (A) to replace white residents with minority homeowners
    (B) to avoid any acts that would make housing unavailable to someone on account of color
    (C) both A and B
    (D) neither A nor B

12. The Civil Rights Act of 1968
    (A) makes it illegal to intimidate, threaten, or interfere with a person buying, renting, or selling housing
    (B) provides criminal penalties and criminal prosecution if violence is threatened or used
    (C) both A and B
    (D) neither A nor B

13. Court action may be taken by an individual under the Fair Housing Act
    I. only if a complaint is filed with HUD
    II. if action is taken within 180 days of the alleged discriminatory act
    (A) I only
    (B) II only
    (C) I and II
    (D) Neither I nor II

14. For HUD to act on a housing discrimination complaint under the 1968 Fair Housing Act
    I. the complaint must be written within 180 days of the alleged discrimination
    II. the complaint must be telephoned within 30 days of the alleged discrimination
    (A) I only
    (B) II only
    (C) I and II
    (D) Neither I nor II

15. Blockbusting is
    I. unlawful
    II. an attempt by a broker to gain a financial advantage by promoting housing turn-over in a transitional neighborhood
    (A) I only   (C) I and II
    (B) II only   (D) Neither I nor II

TRUE — FALSE. Mark *T* for true, *F* for false.

_____ 16. The Fair Housing Act does not apply to an owner selling his own home, if it is the only home he owns.

_____ 17. The Fair Housing Act would not apply to a building containing three dwelling units, one of which is occupied by the owner.

_____ 18. It is illegal for someone to intimidate someone else into violating the Fair Housing Act.

_____ 19. Today over 90% of all housing in the U.S. is subject to the Fair Housing Act.

_____ 20. A part-time real estate salesperson is not required to abide by the Fair Housing Act.

FILL-INS. Fill in the blanks with the appropriate words or phrases.

21. The Federal Fair Housing Act was enacted in the year _____ .

22. A broker who solicits listings in a transitional area by trying to convince owners that values will decline because of the influx of people of another race, creed, color, or national origin is guilty of _____ .

ANSWERS

1. D	7. B	13. B	18. T
2. C	8. C	14. A	19. T
3. A	9. C	15. C	20. F
4. C	10. C	16. T	21. 1968
5. D	11. B	17. T	22. blockbusting
6. A	12. C		

Chapter 21/*Truth in Lending Law*

Regulation Z of the Federal Reserve System, known as the Truth in Lending Act, became effective on July 1, 1969. Amendments established on April 1, 1981, became mandatory on April 1, 1982. Those provisions affecting credit transactions in real estate are emphasized here, although the act covers other types of credit.

The purpose of Regulation Z is to let borrowers and consumers know the cost of credit so that they can compare costs among various credit sources and avoid the uninformed use of credit. Regulation Z also regulates issuance of credit cards and sets maximum liability for the unauthorized use of credit cards. In addition, it provides a procedure for resolving billing errors that occur in open end credit accounts. The Regulation does not set maximum or minimum interest rates or require any charge for credit.

Coverage

Generally, Regulation Z applies to each individual or business that offers or extends credit when four conditions are met:
1. The credit is offered or extended to consumers.
2. The offering or extension of credit is done regularly (see definition of *creditor*).
3. The credit is subject to a finance charge or is payable in a written agreement in more than four installments.
4. The credit is primarily for personal, family, or household purposes.

Creditors Defined

Creditors are those who must comply with Regulation Z. *Creditor* is defined for this purpose as a person who arranges or extends credit more than 25 times a year (or more than 5 times in a year in the case of transactions secured by a dwelling).

As of February 19, 1982, the term *creditor* does not include a person (such as a real estate broker) who arranges seller financing of a dwelling or real property. However, a real estate broker or salesperson is not exempt from coverage in all transactions. For example, a real estate broker may be a creditor in the following situations:
1. The broker acts as a loan broker to arrange for someone other than the seller to extend credit, provided that the extender of credit (the person to whom the obligation is initially payable) does not meet the *creditor* definition.
2. The broker extends credit itself, provided that the broker otherwise meets the *creditor* definition.

Penalties for Violation of Regulation Z

If lenders fail to make disclosures as required under the Truth in Lending Act, they may be sued for actual damages plus twice the amount of the finance charge, as well as court costs and attorneys' fees. The finance charge portion of damages is subject to a minimum of $100 and maximum of $1000. If lenders are convicted in a criminal action for willfully or knowingly disobeying the act or the regulation, they could be fined up to $5000 or imprisoned for up to one year, or both.

Exempt Transactions

1. Business, commercial, agricultural, or organizational credit.
2. Extension of credit to other than a natural person, including credit to government agencies.
3. Credit over $25,000 not secured by real property or a dwelling.
4. Extension of credit that involves public utility service.
5. Securities or commodities accounts.
6. Home fuel budget plans.

Annual Percentage Rate

Regulation Z takes ten printed pages to define *Annual Percentage Rate (APR)*. Briefly summarized, APR means the true interest rate charged for the use of money.

Finance Charge

The finance charge is the cost of consumer credit as a dollar amount. It includes any charge payable directly or indirectly by the consumer and imposed directly or indirectly by the creditor as an incident to or a condition of the extension of credit. It does not include any charge of a type payable in a comparable cash transaction.

EXAMPLES OF FINANCE CHARGES

1. Interest, time price differential, and any amount payable under an add-on or a discount system of additional charges.
2. Service, transaction, activity, and carrying charges, including any charge imposed on a checking or other transaction account to the extent that the charge exceeds the charge for a similar account without a credit feature.
3. Points, loan fees, assumption fees, finder's fees, and similar charges.
4. Appraisal, investigation, and credit report fees.
5. Premiums or other charges for any guarantee or insurance protecting the creditor against the consumer's default or other credit loss.
6. Charges imposed on a creditor by another person for purchasing or accepting a consumer's obligation, if the consumer is required to pay the charges in cash, as an addition to the obligation, or as a deduction from the proceeds of the obligation.
7. Premiums or other charges for credit life, accident, health, or loss-of-income insurance, written in connection with a credit transaction.
8. Premiums or other charges for insurance against loss of or damage to property, or against liability arising out of the ownership or use of property, written in connection with a credit transaction.
9. Discounts for the purpose of inducing payment by a means other than the use of credit.

The following charges are not finance charges:
1. Application fees charged to all applicants for credit, whether or not credit is actually extended.
2. Charges for actual unanticipated late payment, for exceeding a credit limit, or for delinquency, default, or a similar occurrence.
3. Charges imposed by a financial institution for paying items that overdraw an account, unless the payment of such items and the imposition of the charge were previously agreed upon in writing.

4. Fees charged for participation in a credit plan, whether assessed on an annual or other periodic basis.
5. Seller's points.
6. Interest forfeited as a result of an interest reduction required by law on a time deposit used as security for an extension of credit.
7. The following fees in a transaction secured by real property or in a residential mortgage transaction, if the fees are bona fide and reasonable in amount:
   a. Fees for title examination, abstract of title, title insurance, property survey, and similar purposes.
   b. Fees for preparing deeds, mortgages, and reconveyance, settlement, and similar documents.
   c. Notary, appraisal, and credit report fees.
   d. Amounts required to be paid into escrow or trustee accounts if the amounts would not otherwise be included in the finance charge.
8. Discounts offered to induce payment for a purchase by cash, check, or certain other means.

Premiums for certain types of insurance are excludable if certain conditions are met, and certain taxes and fees prescribed by law are excludable.

Content of Disclosures

The following are disclosure requirements for closed-end loans. Most real estate mortgages are considered closed-end because there are no subsequent credit advances. For each transaction, the creditor shall disclose the following information as applicable:

1. Creditor. The identity of the creditor making the disclosures.
2. Amount financed. The "amount financed," using that term, and a brief description such as "the amount of credit provided to you or on your behalf." The amount financed is calculated by:
   a. Determining the principal loan amount or the cash price (subtracting any downpayment);
   b. Adding any other amounts that are financed by the creditor and are not part of the finance charge; and
   c. Subtracting any prepaid finance charge.
3. Itemization of amount financed.
   a. A separate written itemization of the amount financed. (Good faith estimates of settlement costs for transactions subject to the Real Estate Settlement Procedures Act [RESPA] are acceptable substitutes.) These items include:
      i. The amount of any proceeds distributed directly to the consumer.
      ii. The amount credited to the consumer's account with the creditor.
      iii. Any amounts paid to other persons by the creditor on the consumer's behalf. The creditor shall identify those persons. (Generic names or general terms are acceptable for certain persons such as public officials, credit reporting agencies, appraisers, and insurance companies.)
      iv. The prepaid finance charge.
   b. The creditor need not comply with paragraph 3-a above if the creditor provides a statement that the consumer has the right to receive a written itemization of the amount financed, together with a space for the consumer to indicate whether it is desired, and the consumer does not request it.
4. Finance charge. The "finance charge," using that term, and a brief description such as "the dollar amount the credit will cost you."

5. Annual percentage rate. The "annual percentage rate," using that term, and a brief description such as "the cost of your credit as a yearly rate."

6. Variable rate. If the annual percentage rate may increase after consummation, the following disclosures must be included:
   a. The circumstances under which the rate may increase.
   b. Any limitations on the increase.
   c. The effect of an increase.
   d. An example of the payment terms that would result from an increase.

7. Payment schedule. The number, amounts, and timing of payments scheduled to repay the obligation.
   a. In a demand obligation with no alternate maturity date, the creditor may comply with this paragraph by disclosing the due dates or payment periods of any scheduled interest payments for the first year.
   b. In a transaction in which a series of payments varies because a finance charge is applied to the unpaid principal balance, the creditor may comply with this paragraph by disclosing the following information:
      i. The dollar amounts of the largest and smallest payments in the series.
      ii. A reference to the variations in the other payments in the series.

8. Total of payments. The "total of payments," using that term, and a descriptive explanation such as "the amount you will have paid when you have made all scheduled payments."

9. Demand feature. If the obligation has a demand feature, that fact shall be disclosed. When the disclosures are based on an assumed maturity of one year, that fact shall also be disclosed.

10. Total sale price. In a credit sale, the "total sale price," using that term, and a descriptive explanation (including the amount of any downpayment) such as "the total price of your purchase on credit, including your downpayment of $_____." The total sale price is the sum of the cash price, the items described in paragraph 2-b, and the finance charge disclosed under paragraph 4 above.

11. Prepayment.
    a. When an obligation includes a finance charge computed from time to time by application of a rate to the unpaid principal balance, a statement indicating whether or not a penalty may be imposed if the obligation is prepaid in full.
    b. When an obligation includes a finance charge other than the finance charge described in paragraph 11-a above, a statement indicating whether or not the consumer is entitled to a rebate of any finance charge if the obligation is prepaid in full.

12. Late payment. Any dollar or percentage charge that may be imposed before maturity due to a late payment, other than a deferral or extension charge.

13. Security interest. The fact that the creditor has or will acquire a security interest in the property purchased as part of the transaction, or in other property identified by item or type.

14. Insurance. The items required by law in order to exclude certain insurance premiums from the finance charge.

15. Certain security interest charges. The disclosures required by law in order to exclude from the finance charge certain fees prescribed by law or certain premiums for insurance in lieu of perfecting a security interest.

16. Contract reference. A statement that the consumer should refer to the appropriate contract document for information about nonpayment, default, the right to accelerate the maturity of the obligation, and prepayment rebates and penalties. At

the creditor's option, the statement may also include a reference to the contract for further information about security interests and, in a residential mortgage transaction, about the creditor's policy regarding assumption of the obligation.

17. Assumption policy. In a residential mortgage transaction, a statement as to whether or not a subsequent purchaser of the dwelling from the consumer may be permitted to assume the remaining obligation on its original terms.

18. Required deposit. If the creditor requires the consumer to maintain a deposit as a condition of the specific transaction, a statement that the annual percentage rate does not reflect the effect of the required deposit.

DISCLOSURE FOR CERTAIN RESIDENTIAL MORTGAGE TRANSACTIONS

1. Time of disclosure. In a residential mortgage transaction subject to the Real Estate Settlement Procedures Act the creditor shall make good faith estimates of the disclosures described above before consummation, or shall deliver or place them in the mail not later than three business days after the creditor receives the consumer's written application, whichever is earlier.

2. Redisclosure required. If the annual percentage rate in the consummated transaction varies from the annual percentage rate disclosed by more than ⅛ of 1 percentage point in a regular transaction or more than ¼ of 1 percentage point in an irregular transaction, the creditor shall disclose the changed terms no later than consummation or settlement.

SUBSEQUENT DISCLOSURE REQUIREMENTS

1. Refinancings. A refinancing occurs when an existing obligation that was subject to this part of Regulation Z is satisfied and replaced by a new obligation undertaken by the same consumer. A refinancing is a new transaction requiring new disclosures to the consumer. The new finance charge shall include any unearned portion of the old finance charge that is not credited to the existing obligation. The following shall not be treated as a refinancing:
   a. A renewal of a single payment obligation with no change in the original terms.
   b. A reduction in the annual percentage rate with a corresponding change in the payment schedule.
   c. An agreement involving a court proceeding.
   d. A change in the payment schedule or a change in collateral requirements as a result of the consumer's default or delinquency, unless the rate is increased, or the new amount financed exceeds the unpaid balance plus earned finance charge and premiums for continuation of insurance of certain types.
   e. The renewal of optional insurance purchased by the consumer and added to an existing transaction, if disclosures relating to the initial purchase were provided as required by this subpart.

2. Assumptions. An assumption occurs when a creditor expressly agrees in writing with a subsequent consumer to accept that consumer as a primary obligor on an existing residential mortgage transaction. Before the assumption occurs, the creditor shall make new disclosures to the subsequent consumer, based on the remaining obligation. If the finance charge originally imposed on the existing obligation was an add-on or a discount finance charge, the creditor need only disclose:
   a. The unpaid balance of the obligation assumed.
   b. The total charges imposed by the creditor in connection with the assumption.

c. The information required to be disclosed under section 226.18(k), (l), (m), and (n) of Regulation Z.
d. The annual percentage rate originally imposed on the obligation.
e. The payment schedule under section 226.18(g) and the total of payments under section 226.18(h), based on the remaining obligation.

Rescission

A borrower does *not* have the right to rescind a *residential mortgage transaction*. That includes a mortgage, deed of trust, or equivalent security interest that is created or retained against the consumer's dwelling to finance the acquisition or initial construction. One cannot rescind a refinancing or consolidation (with no new advances) of the principal balance and accrued interest.

One has the right to rescind most other consumer credit transactions on real estate. To do so, the borrower may notify the creditor of the rescission by mail, telegram, or other written means of communication. Generally, the right to rescind expires on midnight of the third business day following the loan transaction, delivery by the creditor of the notice of the right to rescind, or delivery of all material disclosures, whichever occurs last.

EFFECT OF RESCISSION

When a consumer exercises his right to rescind he is not liable for any finance or other charge, and any security interest becomes void upon such a rescission. Within 20 days after receipt of a notice of rescission, the creditor shall return to the consumer any money or property given as earnest money, down payment, or otherwise, and shall take any action necessary or appropriate to reflect the termination of any security interest created under the transaction. If the creditor has delivered any money or property to the consumer, the consumer may retain possession of it until the performance of the creditor's obligations under this section. Then the consumer shall tender the property to the creditor, except that if return of the property in kind would be impracticable or inequitable, the consumer shall tender its reasonable value. Tender of property shall be made at the location of the property or at the residence of the consumer, at the option of the consumer. Tender of money shall be at the creditor's place of business. If the creditor does not take possession of the property within 20 days after tender by the consumer, ownership of the property vests in the consumer without obligation on his part to pay for it.

Residential Mortgage Transactions: Summary of Distinctions

There are six parts of Regulation Z that provide different treatment for residential mortgage loans compared to other types of credit. These are as follows:

1. Certain fees in connection with a residential mortgage can be excluded from finance charges. These are for title examination, title insurance, title abstract, survey, preparing deeds and mortgage documents, notary, appraisal and credit report, and amounts paid into an escrow account if amounts are not otherwise included in a finance charge.

2. The right to rescind a loan does not apply to a residential mortgage transaction.

3. In a residential mortgage transaction, the creditor must include a statement as to whether a subsequent purchaser of the dwelling may assume the remaining obligation on its original terms.

4. The timing of disclosure under Regulation Z for residential mortgage transactions, which are also covered by the Real Estate Settlement Procedures Act (RESPA), coincide with RESPA's requirements.

5. When a mortgage loan is assumed, the creditor must look at the intentions of the party assuming it to determine the required disclosures. If such party will use the property as a principal dwelling, disclosures applicable for such use are necessary, even if the original borrower did not use the property for that purpose.

6. A transaction to construct or acquire a principal dwelling is not eligible for the right of rescission. The lien status (first or junior mortgage) does not matter. However, a transaction that is separate from the purchase, such as one to improve a residence, is covered by the right of rescission.

Mortgage Savings and Loan Assoc.

Date:

ANNUAL PERCENTAGE RATE The cost of your credit as a yearly rate.	FINANCE CHARGE The dollar amount the credit will cost you.	Amount Financed The amount of credit provided to you or on your behalf.	Total of Payments The amount you will have paid after you have made all payments as scheduled.
10.85 %	#106,500.74	#44,605.66	$151,106.40

Your payment schedule will be:

Number of Payments	Amount of Payments	When Payments Are Due
360	#419.74	Monthly beginning 6/1/88

This obligation has a demand feature.

You may obtain property insurance from anyone you want that is acceptable to Mortgage Savings and Loan Assoc. If you get the insurance from Mortgage Savings and Loan Assoc. you will pay $ 150-/year

Security: You are giving a security interest in:
☒ the goods or property being purchased.
☐ _____

Late Charge: If a payment is late, you will be charged $ N/A   5 % of the payment.

Prepayment: If you pay off early, you may have to pay a penalty.

Assumption: Someone buying your house may, subject to conditions, be allowed to assume the remainder of the mortgage on the original terms.

See your contract documents for any additional information about nonpayment, default, any required repayment in full before the scheduled date, and prepayment refunds and penalties.

e means an estimate

Fig. 21-1.   Sample of Mortgage with Demand Feature

State Savings and Loan Assoc.   Account number

ANNUAL PERCENTAGE RATE The cost of your credit as a yearly rate.	FINANCE CHARGE The dollar amount the credit will cost you.	Amount Financed The amount of credit provided to you or on your behalf.	Total of Payments The amount you will have paid after you have made all payments as scheduled.
9.00 %	$83,452.22	$44,000.00	$127,452.22

Your payment schedule will be:

Number of Payments	Amount of Payments	When Payments Are Due
360	$354.03	Monthly beginning 6-1-88

Variable Rate

The annual percentage rate may increase during the term of this transaction if the prime rate of State Savings and Loan Assoc. increases. The rate may not increase more often than once a year, and may not increase by more than 1% annually.

The interest rate will not increase above _15.00_ %. Any increase will take the form of higher payment amounts. If the interest rate increases by _1_ % in _one year_ , your regular payment would increase to $ _385.64_ .

Security: You are giving a security interest in the property being purchased.

Late Charge: If a payment is late, you will be charged 5% of the payment.

Prepayment: If you pay off early, you ☐ may ☐ will not have to pay a penalty.

Assumption: Someone buying your house may, subject to conditions, be allowed to assume the remainder of the mortgage on the original terms.

See your contract documents for any additional information about nonpayment, default, any required repayment in full before the scheduled date, and prepayment refunds and penalties.

e means an estimate

Fig. 21-2.   Sample of Variable-Rate Mortgage

| **Convenient Savings and Loan** | | | Account number: |

ANNUAL PERCENTAGE RATE The cost of your credit as a yearly rate.	**FINANCE CHARGE** The dollar amount the credit will cost you.	**Amount Financed** The amount of credit provided to you or on your behalf.	**Total of Payments** The amount you will have paid after you have made all payments as scheduled.
15.37%	$177,970.44	$43,777	$221,548.44

Your payment schedule will be:

Number of Payments	Amount of Payments	When Payments Are Due	
12	$446.62	Monthly beginning	6/1/88
12	$479.67	" "	6/1/89
12	$515.11	" "	6/1/90
12	$553.13	" "	6/1/91
12	$593.91	" "	6/1/92
300	varying from $637.68 to $627.37	" "	6/1/93

Security: You are giving a security interest in the property being purchased.

Late Charge: If a payment is late, you will be charged 5% of the payment.

Prepayment: If you pay off early, you
☒ may ☐ will not have to pay a penalty.
☒ may ☐ will not be entitled to a refund of part of the finance charge.

Assumption: Someone buying your home cannot assume the remainder of the mortgage on the original terms.

See your contract documents for any additional information about nonpayment, default, any required repayment in full before the scheduled date, and prepayment refunds and penalties.

---
e means an estimate

Fig. 21-3. Sample of Graduated-Payment Mortgage

Questions on Chapter 21

1. The purpose of Regulation Z is to
   (A) set the maximum interest rates that may be charged
   (B) let borrowers know the cost of credit
   (C) both A and B
   (D) neither A nor B

2. Regulation Z applies to
   I. all real estate salespersons
   II. all retail stores
   (A) I only   (C) I and II
   (B) II only   (D) Neither I nor II

3. Regulation Z covers
   I. credit extended to people for personal use, under $25,000
   II. all real estate credit transactions
   (A) I only   (C) I and II
   (B) II only   (D) Neither I nor II

4. Under Regulation Z, borrowers must be told in writing of
   I. the total dollar amount of the finance charge, except in the case of a credit transaction to finance the purchase of a dwelling
   II. the annual percentage rate
   (A) I only
   (B) II only
   (C) I and II
   (D) Neither I nor II

5. Which of the following must be included as a "finance charge" for real property credit transactions?
   (A) Fee for title insurance
   (B) Fee for deed preparation
   (C) Monthly payment, in dollars
   (D) None of the above

6. The Annual Percentage Rate (APR) means the
   (A) true interest rate charged
   (B) total dollar amount of finance charges
   (C) monthly payment, in dollars
   (D) percentage of loan paid off each year

7. Under Regulation Z, a borrower may have the right to cancel, within three days, a
   (A) second mortgage used to improve his dwelling
   (B) first mortgage loan used to purchase his dwelling
   (C) home-improvement loan over one year old
   (D) none of the above

8. To cancel a credit transaction, the borrower must inform the lender, within three days,
   (A) by phone
   (B) in writing
   (C) both A and B
   (D) neither A nor B

9. If a borrower cancels the contract within the three-day period, he is responsible for a
   (A) 10 percent finance charge
   (B) 1 percent finance charge
   (C) three days' interest
   (D) none of the above

10. The maximum penalty for conviction, in a criminal action, for willfully disobeying Regulation Z is up to
    (A) a $5000 fine
    (B) one year's imprisonment
    (C) both A and B
    (D) neither A nor B

TRUE — FALSE. Mark *T* for true, *F* for false.

_____ 11. The purpose of the Truth in Lending Act is to make sure that borrowers know only how much their monthly payment is to be on a loan.

_____ 12. The only lender who is obliged to provide all the information required under Truth in Lending is the lender who charges the highest rate of interest.

_____ 13. All real estate credit transactions, except agricultural credit, are covered under the Truth in Lending Act.

_____ 14. Appraisal fees are not considered as finance charges in real estate credit transactions.

_____ 15. Loan discounts are considered a finance charge in real estate credit transactions.

_____ 16. Charges or premiums for credit life insurance required by the lender are considered finance charges.

_____ 17. If lenders fail to make required disclosures, they may be sued for actual damages, plus twice the amount of the finance charge as well as court costs and attorneys' fees.

FILL-INS. Fill in the blanks with the appropriate words or phrases.

18. The Truth in Lending Act is enforced through application of Regulation _____ .

19. If a residence is used as collateral for a loan covered by Regulation Z that is not a mortgage loan used to construct or purchase one's dwelling, the borrower has _____ business days in which he can cancel the transaction.

20. The term APR stands for _____ .

21. In a residential mortgage transaction, the borrower must be informed of whether the mortgage can be assumed on the _____ terms.

22. The time of disclosure under Regulation Z for residential mortgage transactions that are subject to RESPA are the same as required by _____ .

ANSWERS

1. B	6. A	11. F	16. T
2. D	7. A	12. F	17. T
3. C	8. B	13. T	18. Z
4. C	9. D	14. T	19. three
5. D	10. C	15. T	20. Annual Percentage Rate
			21. Original (or same)
			22. RESPA

PART VI: REAL ESTATE LICENSE EXAMINATIONS

Chapter 22/*Preparing for the Examination*

Each state's real estate licensing examination falls into one of four categories:
  (1) The Uniform Real Estate Licensing Examination, administered by the Educational Testing Service (ETS).
  (2) The National Real Estate Examination, administered by American College Testing Program, Inc. (ACT).
  (3) The Real Estate Assessment for Licensure, administered by Assessment Systems, Inc. (ASI).
  (4) Examinations prepared and administered by individual states.

The three nationally administered exams (ETS, ACT and ASI: 1, 2, and 3 above) each are in two parts. There is a long (80 to 100 questions) *general* real estate examination, appropriate to all states, Then there is a shorter (30 to 50 questions) *state* examination, made up for each state separately. The state portion of the examination covers the state's real estate license law and specific matters of real estate law and practice as they apply in that state.

You should find out which examination your state uses. All three national examination administrations provide brochures which describe the exams; some also provide sample examinations which you can order for a small fee. States which produce their own examinations also provide descriptive materials. Whatever the situation in your state, be sure to obtain all materials that you can about the exam that is used.

Preparing For The Examination

Obviously the most important step in preparing for the examination is reading this book. You should also study the license law of your particular state, as well as any other material that your state *requires* you to know. This last will vary from state to state. Many states only require you to read and understand the license law, and to be knowledgeable about basic real estate principles, which is information you will get from this book. But some also provide other literature that they want you to read. This would especially be the case if your state has some unusual laws that you would have to know and that would not usually be covered in a book of real estate principles. So be sure that you understand, when you make inquiries about becoming licensed in your state, just what will be required of you and what you are expected to know. When you contact your state licensing agency to find out how to apply for the exam, where to go to take it, etc., at the same time you can get all the other information you will need. Remember, it probably would be better for you to telephone the office instead of writing. You may have to write anyway, in order to send money for any materials for which payment is required, but by telephoning you can immediately get the answers you need.

Here is a checklist of information you should get as soon as possible.
  (1) You should have copies of the following:
      (a) Your state's real estate license laws
      (b) Any other material that your state requires, or suggests that you read and know
  (2) When and where will the examinations be given?

(3) How do you apply for the exam?

(4) When is the deadline for application?

(5) How much does it cost —

    (a) At the time you apply to take the exam?

    (b) At the time you actually take the exam?

    (c) At the time your license is issued?

    (d) On a regular annual (or otherwise periodic) basis thereafter?

(6) Do you need a broker or anyone else to:

    (a) Sponsor you to take the exam?

    (b) Attest to your good character on your application?

    (c) Put up any bond in your behalf?

(7) Must you submit any photographs? (If so, get them ready SOON.)

(8) Do you have to submit documents of any kind, such as:

    (a) Proof of graduation from high school/college?

    (b) Birth certificate; other proof of age?

    (c) Proof of financial responsibility?

    (d) Proof of having passed any special educational requirements (such as certain real estate courses required by some states)?

    (e) Proof of veteran or disabled veteran status?

(9) Must any of the papers you have to submit be notarized?

(10) Just to be sure, does you state use:

    (a) The ETS Examination?

    (b) The ACT Examinaton?

    (c) The ASI Examination?

    (d) Its own examination

As for the examination itself, you should know the following:

(1) At what time does it start?

(2) Where will it be held?

(3) What MUST you bring with you?

    (a) Official papers that will let you in, such as your letter saying that you have been admitted to take the exam, etc.?

    (b) Pencils, scratch paper?

    (c) Money, check, etc., to pay exam fee, license fee, etc.?

    (d) Application papers, etc.?

(4) What must you NOT bring?

    (a) Anything at all; everything will be provided?

    (b) Electronic calculators?

    (c) Slide rules?

(5) What MAY you bring, if you want to?

    (a) Electronic calculators?

    (b) Pencils, blank paper?

    (c) Cigarettes?

(6) How will the exam be graded?

    (a) Is your score the sum of all the questions you get right, OR is a percentage of your wrong answers subtracted, to correct for guessing?

    (b) What is a passing grade?

    (c) Do you have to get a certain portion of EACH section correct in order to pass the examination, OR do they just add up your total score to determine if you pass?

    (d) How long does it take them to grade the exams and to report the results?

    (e) Are veterans or disabled veterans allowed bonus points or other preference?

(7) How are you notified of your performance on the exam?

    (a) Are you notified directly?

    (b) Is someone else notified (such as your sponsoring broker), whose responsibility it is to notify you?

(8) Are you told what your score was on the exam or just if you passed or failed?

(9) Can you call and ask for your grade?

(10) Will you have an opportunity to see your exam and find out where you did well and where you didn't?

(11) When you pass the examination, how do you get your license?

    (a) Is your license automatically issued when you pass?

    (b) Does passing the exam only make you *eligible* to apply for a license, and once you pass will you still have to make formal application for the license?

    (c) If you pass the exam, but decide not to get a license right away, does your eligibility for a license expire, or can you become licensed at a later time without having to take the exam again?

(12) How soon may people who fail the examination retake it?

When you have all this information, you're ready to get underway. First, you should decide which of the upcoming examinations you want to take. Some states offer examinations only a couple of times a year, and only in specific places (often the state capital), so you don't really have much choice where or when you'll take the examination. Other states may offer them frequently, perhaps at many different locations as well.

The next thing to do once you have all the necessary materials is to fill them out properly. Get everyone to sign them who has to, and get everything notarized that has to be. If photos are required, try to get fairly decent ones. The best to use, in terms of convenience, are Polaroid shots, especially the perfectly dry, uncoated ones you get with SX-70 or Pronto cameras. They're a lot cheaper than studio-posed portraits, and are quicker and more convenient to get than prints you have to develop.

Once all your application materials are prepared, submit them to the licensing agency of your state. If you live close enough to the office, try to deliver them yourself. If you don't, you'll have to mail them, so it will be wise to phone the agency a week or so afterward to make sure they have been received. Usually you will receive notification by mail that you have been registered to take a particular exam on a particular date.

Be sure to save every receipt and every letter that you receive from your state licensing agency. You never can tell when you will need them — except that if you lose them or throw them away you can almost be sure that you'll need them later on. Things always seem to work out like that.

Studying For The Exam

You can't expect to walk into the examination room cold and pass with flying colors. You have to be ready for the exam. This means more than just doing a lot of reading and trying to cram your head full of a certain group of facts. You have to be psychologically ready and properly prepared to take the examination so that you can *do your best* on it. To do this you have to acquire the following things:

(1) Information

(2) A positive attitude

(3) Knowledge about exam taking

(4) Confidence

(5) Rest

Let's take these things one by one:

(1) **Information.** Of course you have to have the *knowledge* to get through the examination; this means knowing the subject matter well, and you can accomplish that by studying this book and your state's license laws. Also, if your state provides special examination preparation materials, you must study those, too. You can't expect to be able to acquire this knowledge if you start in on it just a short while before the examination. You should have a *reasonable* study schedule to follow so that you will be at maximum readiness the day of the examination (see Chapter 1).

(2) **A positive attitude.** Your attitude should be one of confidence; after all, if you have

worked hard to learn all these real estate concepts, then you DO know the required material. The exam simply is the place where you get your chance to prove it.

(3) **Knowledge about exam taking.** Some people panic and end up doing badly because of it. This sort of thing does happen, but if you look at the examination in the proper perspective, it won't happen to you. If you are concerned about taking an examination after having been out of school for such a long time, the way to get over it is to practice: take the practice examinations after Chapter 23. Set up actual "examination conditions." Give yourself a time limit, and go right through each practice examination just as if it were the real thing. Use all the examination-taking techniques you'll read about in Chapter 23. Each of the practice examinations has a key at the end of the book so that you can grade your own performance. Note the areas where you did well and those where you did badly — this will guide your further study. Do this for *each* practice examination: first take the exam and grade it, then do some more studying in your weaker areas before you take the next one.

In this way you'll accomplish a number of important objectives. First, you'll get used to the examination situation. Second, you'll get practice in answering the kinds of questions featured on most real estate license examinations. Third, you'll be able to keep track of the subject areas where you need more study and practice.

(4) **Confidence.** These are the areas of subject matter that examinees worry most about: (A) arithmetic, (B) contracts, and (C) for broker examinees, closing statements. We have included elaborate sections on all of these, as well as on all other real estate subjects. The arithmetic you need to know is exactly the same sort of thing you had to do for homework in the sixth and seventh grades. Contracts inspire awe because they're supposed to be the province of lawyers. By now you know that a contract is just a piece of paper where people put down facts concerning an agreement they've made. All you have to be sure of is that you wrote what you were supposed to and that you were clear in what you said. Even property description doesn't have to look like mumbo-jumbo. Metes and bounds descriptions just have to tell you where the boundaries lie; government survey descriptions use a peculiar but very high-powered shorthand that's easy to learn; lot and block number descriptions are great because they're simple and explicit.

Closing statements worry broker examinees because they look so mysterious. Actually, they're nothing but a record of where people's money goes in a real estate transaction. Once again, the important thing here is accuracy. But if you think a bit about most of the items involved, it is easy to see if they should be paid by (or to) the seller or the buyer. All that's left is to line up all the numbers neatly so that they can be added easily. The tricky part about closing statements usually is the prorating of various items. There is nothing mysterious about prorating, but the calculations are long and clumsy, so there's room for error to sneak in if you're not careful.

Throughout this book an important aim of ours has been to explain everything thoroughly. If you understand the subjects we've discussed, then you have no confidence problem: you *know* the basic principles of real estate.

(5) **Rest.** Don't stay up studying the night before the exam! No one is at his best when he's tired or short of sleep. The day before the exam should be one of rest and relaxation.

You can even design a little last-minute study session that actually will help you, without disturbing your relaxation. Prepare a brief outline of the *important* points for which you know you need special effort. If arithmetic is your special problem, write down the basic rules from Chapter 17. If contracts bug you, make a list of all the contracts and a brief description of each. Study this material for one-half hour in the morning, one-half hour in the afternoon, and one-half hour in the evening, but finish your studying *at least* two hours before bedtime. That way you'll be strengthening your weaknesses, but you won't be spending so much time on your studying that it interferes with the really important task at hand: getting yourself relaxed. The morning of the examination, if you have time, you can spend another half hour going over those notes one last time.

Chapter 23/*Examination Strategy*

Your objective when you take any examination is to get as high a score as possible. The way to do that is to provide as many right answers as possible. This leads us directly to the most important rule of all in taking examinations.

ALWAYS ANSWER EVERY QUESTION. Even if you have to guess, write down an answer. If you leave the question blank you can be certain that it will be counted as wrong because a blank answer is a wrong answer. If you guess, and write down some sort of answer, there is always the chance that the guess will be correct. Boiled down, it is as simple as this: you know you will get the question wrong if you leave it blank, but if you guess at an answer you might guess the right one.

The second rule is SKIP THE HARD QUESTIONS AT FIRST AND SAVE THEM FOR LAST. Lots of people start at the beginning of an examination and work their way through, one question at a time, until they run out of time. If they run across a hard question, they battle with it for a long time and won't go on to the next question until they've licked it (or it has licked them). These people are lucky to get to the end of the exam before they run out of time; if they don't get to the end, then they never even see some of the questions — and they might have been able to answer enough of those questions to have earned a passing grade on the examination. On the ETS, ASI and ACT examinations, all questions are worth the same. Many independent states score their examination that way too. So what sense is there in spending 15 minutes or half an hour or more on a single question, when you might have used that same time to read and answer a couple of *dozen* questions correctly?

When you take the exam, start at the beginning. Read the instructions, then read the first question. Answer it, if you can, and then go on to number 2. Answer it, if you can, and then go on to the next and the next and the next. When you come across a question that is hard, that you have to think about a lot, or that will take a lot of time to answer even if you know exactly how to get the answer (some arithmetic problems can be like that), skip it for the time being. Come back to it later, after you have gone all the way through the exam and answered all the questions that you can do fairly quickly.

In order to know how to attack your state's particular examination, you have to know the special strategies for handling specific kinds of questions.

MULTIPLE-CHOICE QUESTIONS

This is a multiple-choice question:

The title of this chapter is
(A)   How to Hammer a Nail
(B)   Examination Strategy
(C)   I Was an Elephant for the FBI
(D)   None of the above

The ETS, ASI and ACT examinations are composed entirely of multiple-choice questions; many independent states use only this type of question, and several others use multiple-choice as well as other kinds. The essence of this kind of question is that you must choose one of the answers as the correct one.

Always remember that with a multiple-choice question you are looking at the right answer! You just have to pick it out. Your strategy for answering such questions is as follows:

1. Read the question. Many people miss those little key words like *if, not, but,* etc., that can completely change the meaning of a sentence. Be sure you read the question *completely* and *carefully*.

2. If the answer is obvious to you, mark it properly and go on to the next question. Then forget about the question you have just answered. An overwhelming part of the time the answer you pick first is the right one, and you will very rarely improve an answer by coming back to worry over it later.

3. If the answer is not obvious, it is time to begin the guesswork strategy. First look for all the choices that you know are wrong. You may not be sure of the right answer, but that doesn't mean you can't find some you know are wrong. Then guess an answer from the ones that are left.

   Remember to make your guesses educated. It is rare that you will not be able to guide your guesswork a little by using some of your knowledge. You may be able to decide that a certain answer is much more likely to be right than the others. Always be sure to eliminate those answers you *know* are wrong because that will improve your chances of guessing the right one. However, if it looks like it is going to take a long time to get at even a guesswork answer, skip the question and come back to it later when you know you have the time for it.

TRUE-FALSE QUESTIONS

This is a true-false question:

   T   F   Real estate is land and all attachments to it.

True-false questions are a guesser's paradise because you always have a fifty-fifty chance of getting them right even if you just answer at random. The rules for answering them are basically the same as for multiple-choice: read the question carefully, decide on the answer, and then mark your answer. Be very careful to read every word of the question. Those key words (*if, and, but, not, probably,* etc.) can make all the difference. Generally, the question must be absolutely true to be counted as true; otherwise it is false. However, it is almost always possible to think of outlandish exceptions to practically any statement, so be reasonable. As an example, the statement in the example above would be counted as true, even though there are some slight exceptions (such as seasonal crops, the tools of a lessee's trade). Nearly all true-false questions will be found to be very straightforward, once you have read them thoroughly. There are no true-false questions on ETS, ASI or ACT examinations.

FILL-IN QUESTIONS

This is a fill-in question.

   Real estate is _____ and all attachments to it.

Fill-in questions are less easy to guess because the answer is not shown to you as it is in multiple-choice and true-false. Usually these questions are easier to read because they generally don't make much use of the little key words that change meanings around. Essentially, most fill-in questions are various forms of definitions, for which you have to supply a missing part. Normally, you have to put in only one or two words; you aren't likely to be asked to write an entire sentence. There are no fill-in questions on ETS, ASI or ACT exams.

Fill-in questions are not popular with examiners because they are hard to grade; they can't be coded for computer answer forms, so they have to be read individually by people. However, if your examination features them, remember a few things:

1. Write very clearly. Try to use all capital letters because they are easy for the grader to read.

2. Answer every question, even if it means guessing. You are fighting longer odds when you guess on these questions, but remember that a blank space is always wrong and you *might* guess the right thing.

CONTRACTS

Many states require their examinees to show that they know and understand certain real estate contracts; usually they include listings and offer and acceptance contracts. Sometimes you are required actually to fill out such a contract, usually using the information from a narrative that describes a particular situation. You will find examples of such narratives and contract fill-ins in Chapter 12 and in Supplemental Examinations 1 and 2. Some states only require that you fill out the contract; the grader will look it over and determine how well you did. Others (especially when they use a computer grading form) will have you fill out the contract, and then, using the contract that you filled out as a reference, you will have to answer some specific questions.

Your strategy here is to read the narrative carefully, then look over the contract form entirely so as to get some familiarity with it. Then go over the narrative again; this time, write into the contract each item described in the narrative as you come to it. Check your contract carefully. Sometimes there will be blank spaces remaining, especially in listing contracts that have property description sections to them. There should be no blank spaces left in a contract of sale (offer and acceptance), deed, or the performance section of a listing. (This does not apply to large blanks into which you are instructed to put short entries. Examples would be of short property descriptions, or of only single parties, where space is provided for several to sign.) If your form has blank spaces left after you have filled it out, check to be sure that you haven't missed anything in the narrative.

USING COMPUTER ANSWER FORMS

Figure 23 – 1 is an example of a computer examination form. The use of these is very wide-spread; ETS, ASI and ACT examinations use them, and a great many of the states that examine independently use them also. The big advantage to these forms is that they are graded by a machine that can evaluate and grade thousands of examinations a day. This makes it much easier for the examining authority and also saves an enormous amount of time and labor.

If you have to use one of these answer forms, you will be given the form and a *test booklet*. The examination questions and instructions will be written in the test booklet; you will "code" your answers onto the answer sheet. Usually you will be asked to make no marks at all on the test booklet; you should put your name and any other identification asked for in the appropriate spaces on the answer sheet. Remember one critical thing: *Do not make any marks at all on either the test or the answer sheet unless and until you are instructed to.* Normally the test booklet will contain very detailed and specific instructions on how to enter the necessary information on the answer sheet; in addition, the people administering the examination will give an oral and visual presentation on the same thing.

Using these answer sheets is really quite simple. Below is an example of a set of answer spaces for three different questions:

1 :A:: :B:: :C:: :D::

2 :A:: :B:: :C:: :D::

3 :A:: :B:: :C:: :D::

For each question you get four answers to choose from: A, B, C, and D. When you have picked your answer, enter it on the examination form by *shading* the appropriate space with your pencil. Suppose, for example, you choose (C):

before shading   after shading

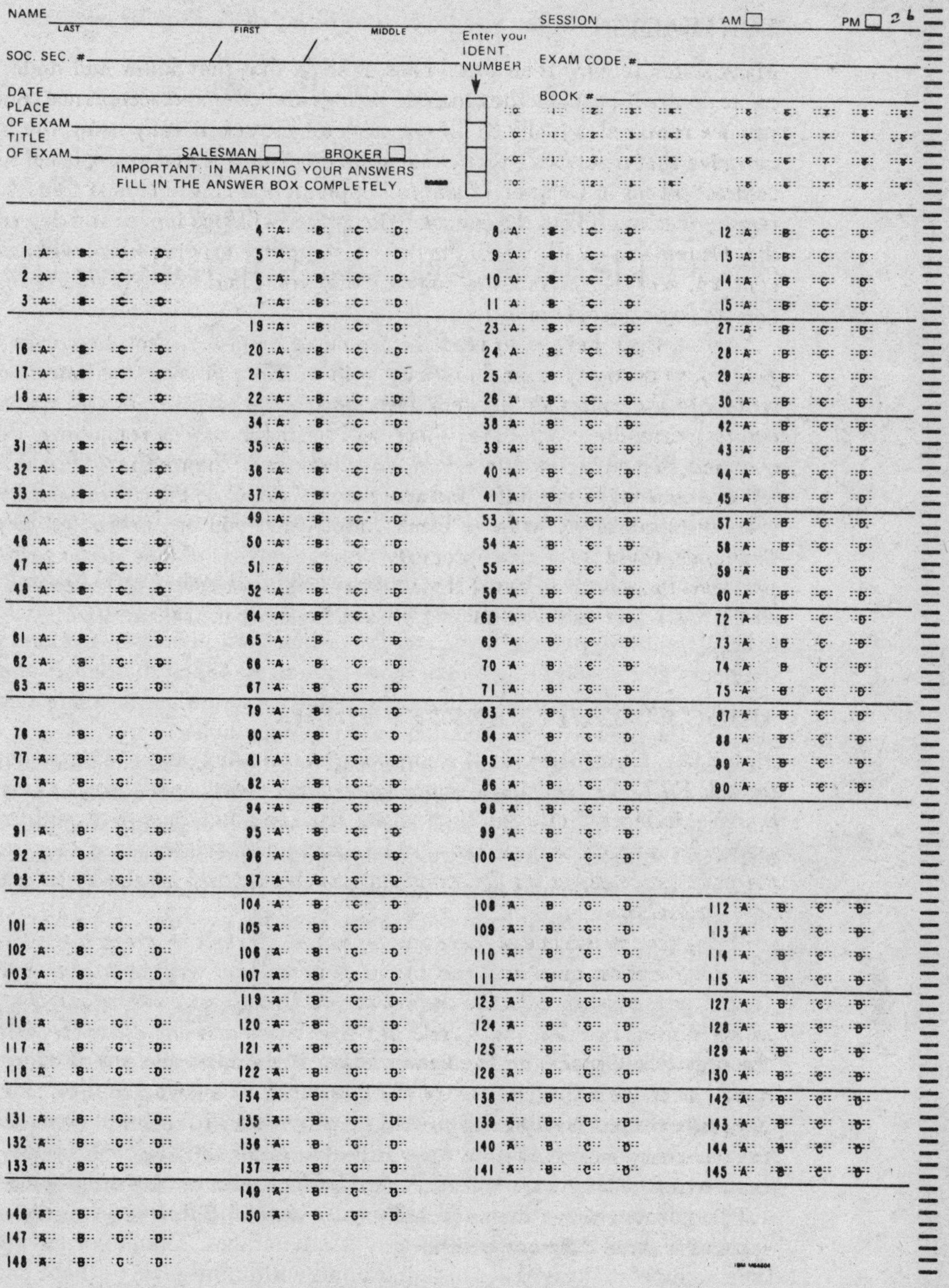

NAME _____   SESSION _____   AM ☐   PM ☐ 26

LAST   FIRST   MIDDLE

SOC. SEC. # _____ / _____ / _____   EXAM CODE # _____

Enter your IDENT NUMBER →

DATE _____
PLACE
OF EXAM _____   BOOK # _____
TITLE
OF EXAM _____ SALESMAN ☐   BROKER ☐

IMPORTANT: IN MARKING YOUR ANSWERS
FILL IN THE ANSWER BOX COMPLETELY

Fig. 23-1. Computer Examination Form

Here are three easy sample questions to use as examples. Answer them by shading the appropriate space in the sample answer set that follows.

1. If John has two apples and I have three, together we have
    (A) 4
    (B) 5
    (C) 6
    (D) 7

2. The capital of France is
    (A) London   (C) Paris
    (B) Washington   (D) Des Moines, Iowa

3. Those things in the middle of your face that you see through are
   (A) eyes   (C) nose
   (B) ears   (D) fingernails

```
1 :A::  :B::  :C::  :D::
2 :A::  :B::  :C::  :D::
3 :A::  :B::  :C::  :D::
```

The answers are obvious: 1 is (B), 2 is (C), 3 is (A). The properly marked answer form is as follows:

```
1 :A::  ■■  :C::  :D::
2 :A::  :B::  ■■  :D::
3 ■■  :B::  :C::  :D::
```

Model Examinations 1 and 2 in the next chapter can be applied to computer answer forms, and sample forms are included for your use. Chapter 26 provides the properly filled out computer answer forms for these two model examinations, as well as a regular key for each.

There are a couple of things you must be careful of with respect to using computer answer forms. First, make sure you have enough pencils. Be certain that you are or are not required to bring your own pencils; if you are, get ordinary #2 pencils — the kind you can get at any stationery store. And bring one of those little hand pencil sharpeners along, too. After you sharpen a pencil, be sure to blunt the point by scribbling on some scratch paper before marking the answer form. You don't want to poke holes in it.

Second, our strategy of skipping the hard questions and saving them to the last means that you have to *make absolutely certain that you are putting the answer in the right space for that question!* Be especially careful here. The computer is very stupid! — if you put answer marks in the wrong spaces, it won't know and will count them wrong.

By the way, you ought to remember that the computer form used on the exam you take may be slightly different from the sample form we use here. However, it will be used just the same way we use ours.

ON-SITE SCORING SYSTEMS (KEYPAD ANSWERING AND SCORING)

A new development in the examination is the introduction of computerized keypads, instead of answer sheets, for recording applicants' answers on licensing examinations. In states using these machines, you will be provided with a small terminal upon which you register your answers to questions. It is about half the size of this book, and has keys that you use to register your answers (A, B, C, D). It also has keys that allow you to "erase" an answer and insert another, and to "scroll" back and forth within the exam.

These devices have advantages and disadvantages. The major advantages are two: (1) The machines make is easier to skip around within the exam without losing track of where you are and without any risk that you will put your answers in the spaces for the wrong questions. (2) Most of the machines allow for instant scoring of your exam. When you are done, you "lock" the machine by pressing a special key. After that time, you no longer can enter or change answers. At that point, the administrators of the exam can instantly provide your exam score, since your answers are entered into the computer already. Usually you will be given a sheet that will tell you which answers you answered correctly and which you didn't. In some examining centers, if the exam isn't over yet, you may be allowed to check your answers against the exam you just took and, so, tell exactly where you went wrong on the questions you missed.

The disadvantage of the machine is that it is unfamiliar to most people. However, it is no more complicated to use than an ordinary calculator. Rest assured that if your examining center uses these machines, a very thorough explanation of them will be given before the exam starts, along with a brief practice session so that you can get familiar with it.

Chapter 24/*Model Examinations*

Following are seven different model examinations for you to take under examination conditions. At the end of the chapter are answer sheets that you can tear out and use for these examinations. The seven examinations include salesperson and broker facsimile examinations for ETS, ASI, and ACT examinations. The seventh examination contains true-false and fill-in questions for use in states that administer their own examinations and use these types of questions.

Many states that administer their own examinations use multiple-choice questions similar to the six national facsimile examinations presented here. If you live in one of those states, obtain the description of the examination provided by the state and determine which of the six facsimile exams presented here is most like the one you will be taking. Then take that exam.

Be sure to take the model examination that is similar to the exam you'll be taking. However, for practice and to brush up on your knowledge, you can also take the other six examinations. In fact, you should take those *first*, to get practice in examination conditions and to see what areas you need to concentrate on further. The last model examination you take should be the one most similar to the actual licensing examination that you'll be taking.

Note that there are no questions on license law or specific practices in your state, since these differ among the 50 states; for this subject matter, go over your notes and the questions in Chapter 5.

Chapter 25 provides special supplemental examinations concerning listing contracts, contracts of sale, Rectangular Survey descriptions, and closing statements. Take those that are necessary in your state.

Keys to all the examinations in Chapters 24 and 25 are found in Chapter 26. That chapter also contains explanations of the arithmetic questions on all examinations.

Where to Find the Model Examinations

Also, don't forget to review the Supplemental Examinations in Chapter 25. These cover contracts, settlement statements, and the rectangular survey. If your state requires you to fill out any contracts or settlement statements, or if it uses the rectangular survey (see Chapter 8), be sure to take the necessary supplemental examinations, too.

Model Examination 1

Salesperson (ETS)

The following sample examination is similar in format to the Uniform Real Estate Licensing Examination (RELE) for salespersons given in states that use ETS exams. The actual examination that you will take will include 80 questions on the Uniform (RELE) part and 30 to 40 questions on the State part. The state questions are designed especially to test for real estate law and practice in your state. This distribution of questions applies to both the salesperson and broker's examinations.

NOTE ALSO: If your state uses the Rectangular Survey (or Government Survey) method of land description, be sure to take Supplemental Examination 4 to practice this. This topic would appear on the state part of the examination.

Directions: Select the choice, marked A, B, C, or D, that best answers the question or completes the thought. Mark your answers clearly on the answer sheet.

1. If, upon receipt of an offer to purchase under certain terms, the seller makes a counter offer, the prospective purchaser is
   (A) bound by his original offer
   (B) bound to accept the counter offer
   (C) bound by the agent's decision
   (D) relieved of his original offer

2. If the broker makes profitable investments with earnest money deposits,
       I. he must share 50% of the profits with the owners of the money he used
       II. he has done something illegal
   (A) I only   (C) Both I and II
   (B) II only   (D) Neither I nor II

3. A real estate broker must comply with
       I. agency law
       II. his state's real estate license law
   (A) I only   (C) Both I and II
   (B) II only   (D) Neither I nor II

4. Smith makes an offer on Jones's property and states that the offer will remain open for three days. The next day Smith decides to withdraw the offer since Jones has neither rejected nor accepted it.
   (A) Smith cannot do this.
   (B) Smith can do this only if Jones was planning to reject the offer anyway.
   (C) Smith must give Jones at least half the remaining time to make a decision.
   (D) Smith may withdraw the offer.

5. In order to sell property belonging to a trust for which he is trustee, the trustee must have
   I. a broker's license
   II. a salesperson's license
   (A) I only   (C) Both I and II
   (B) II only   (D) Neither I nor II

6. Appraised valuation is $25,000. Tax is based on 20% of appraised valuation. City tax is 50 mills; county tax is 40 mills. Which of the following is true?
   I. City tax is $250.
   II. County tax is $2000.
   (A) I only   (C) Both I and II
   (B) II only   (D) Neither I nor II

7. Smith's building is 90 ft. by 60 ft. He wishes to build a sidewalk 5 ft. wide and 6 in. thick all around the outside of the building. How many cubic yards of concrete will be necessary?
   (A) 27.10   (C) 87.78
   (B) 29.63   (D) 263.34

8. In the absence of an agreement to the contrary, the mortgage normally having priority will be the one
   (A) for the greatest amount
   (B) that is a permanent mortgage
   (C) that was recorded first
   (D) that is a construction loan mortgage

9. A development in which one owns one's dwelling unit and, in common with other owners in the same project, owns common property is
   (A) a leased fee
   (B) a condominium
   (C) a homestead
   (D) none of the above

10. Which of the following is/are true?
    I. A condominium owner need not pay condominium fees which he feels are too high.
    II. Condominium units are attached housing units.
    (A) I only   (C) Neither I nor II
    (B) II only   (D) Both I and II are true

11. The money for making FHA loans is provided by
    (A) qualified lending institutions
    (B) the Department of Housing and Urban Development
    (C) the Federal Housing Administration
    (D) the Federal Savings and Loan Insurance Corporation

12. License law forbids
    I. soliciting for listings before one is licensed
    II. collecting a commission from more than one party to a transaction
    (A) I only   (C) Both I and II
    (B) II only   (D) Neither I nor II

13. The term REALTOR is
    I. a registered trademark
    II. one that can only be used by those licensed
    (A) I only   (C) Both I and II
    (B) II only   (D) Neither I nor II

14. Complaints about discrimination may be brought
    I. to the Secretary of Housing and Urban Development
    II. directly to court
    (A) I only
    (B) II only
    (C) Both I and II
    (D) Neither I nor II

15. Which of the following always is (are) exempt from real property taxes?
    I. Income-producing property owned by a church
    II. Government-owned property
    (A) I only
    (B) II only
    (C) Both I and II
    (D) Neither I nor II

16. Treasure Homes sold a lot to Mr. Kay under an installment land sales contract. Upon making the down payment, Mr. Kay is entitled to
    I. a warranty deed
    II. use of the property
    (A) I only
    (B) II only
    (C) Both I and II
    (D) Neither I nor II

17. To each sales agreement there must be
    I. an offer and an acceptance
    II. a mortgage loan
    (A) I only
    (B) II only
    (C) Both I and II
    (D) Neither I nor II

18. A licensee can lose his license for which of the following?
    I. Paying a commission to a nonlicensed person
    II. Using monies received as commissions to pay office help
    (A) I only
    (B) II only
    (C) Both I and II
    (D) Neither I nor II

19. A broker must keep all earnest money deposits in
    (A) his office safe
    (B) his business checking account
    (C) an escrow or trust account
    (D) a savings account

20. Eminent domain is
    (A) the right of the government to take private property for public use
    (B) the extent to which state boundaries reach out to sea
    (C) an ancient form of ownership not common today
    (D) the right of the Federal government to pass laws that supersede state law

21. An eight-year-old building was worth $19,000 after depreciating at a rate of 3% per year. What was its original value?
    (A) $19,570
    (B) $23,560
    (C) $25,000
    (D) $27,777

22. Smith's mortgage loan is for $40,000 and carries an annual interest rate of 9%. Monthly payments are $340. How much will the principal be reduced by the *second* monthly payment?
    (A) $40.00
    (B) $40.30
    (C) $299.70
    (D) $300.00

23. Smith signs a listing that guarantees the listing broker a commission payment if the sale is effected by any licensed agent. This is a(n)
    (A) open listing
    (B) exclusive agency listing
    (C) exclusive right to sell listing
    (D) net listing

24. Jones negotiates with Smith to list Smith's property once Jones is issued his real estate license. When the license is issued, Smith signs a listing with Jones.
    (A) The listing is valid.
    (B) The listing is invalid.
    (C) The listing is valid only at the listing price.
    (D) Jones can collect only half the normal commission.

25. A licensee can lose his license for
    I. selling properties quickly, at low prices
    II. buying property for his own use from his principal
    (A) I only   (C) Both I and II
    (B) II only   (D) Neither I nor II

26. The major source of single-family home mortgage loan funds is
    (A) mortgage bankers
    (B) commercial banks
    (C) savings and loan associations
    (D) the Federal National Mortgage Association (FNMA)

27. A conventional mortgage is
    (A) amortizing
    (B) guaranteed by FHA
    (C) not guaranteed by a government agency
    (D) approved by the VA

28. Among other things, the principal is obligated to
    I. compensate the agent for his services
    II. reimburse the agent for expenses incurred on behalf of the principal
    (A) I only   (C) Both I and II
    (B) II only   (D) Neither I nor II

29. Which of the following is not required to have a real estate license?
    (A) The resident manager of an apartment project
    (B) The resident manager of an apartment project who, for a fee, sells a house across the street
    (C) A student who sells houses as part of a research project
    (D) All of the above

30. Recordation of a deed is the responsibility of the
    (A) grantor   (C) both A and B
    (B) grantee   (D) neither A nor B

Questions 31–34 refer to the Far Hills Estates diagram.

31. Which of the following statements is (are) true?
    I. Four lots in Block E have frontage on two streets.
    II. Iron Road has more lots fronting on it than are shown for any of the other streets on the plat.
    (A) I only   (C) Both I and II
    (B) II only   (D) Neither I nor II

32. Which lot has the greatest footage on Wood Lane?
    (A) Lot 11, Block E   (C) Lot 1, Block L
    (B) Lot 12, Block E   (D) Lot 19, Block E

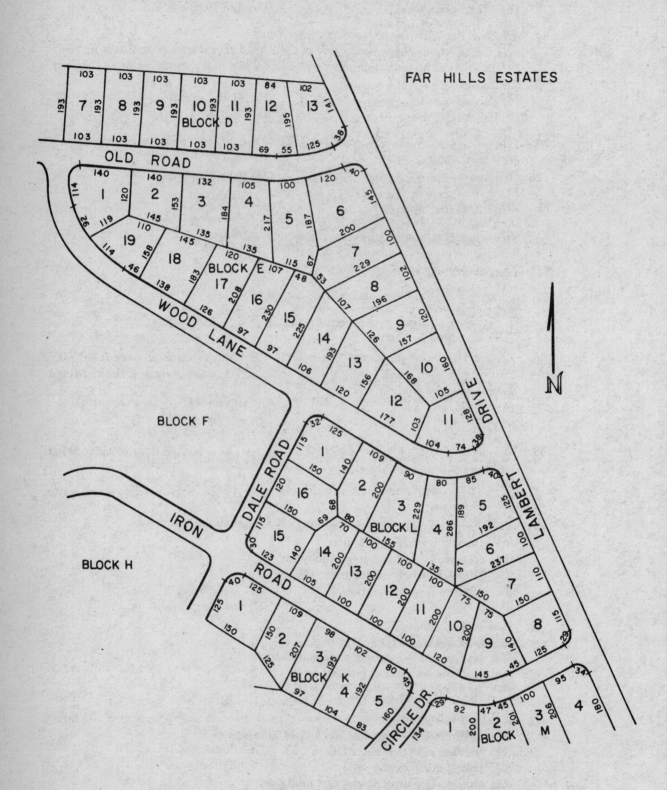

FAR HILLS ESTATES

33. Which lot has the greatest depth?
    (A) Lot 4, Block L   (C) Lot 5, Block E
    (B) Lot 7, Block E   (D) Lot 16, Block E

34. Which of the following statements is (are) true?
    I. The lots on the westerly side of Dale Road should appear on Sheet No. 3.
    II. There is no indication of where to find a plat of the easterly side of Lambert Drive.
    (A) I only   (C) Both I and II
    (B) II only   (D) Neither I nor II

35. The part of conveyance which defines or limits the quantity of the estate granted is
    (A) habendum   (C) equity
    (B) premises   (D) consideration

36. The Statute of Frauds Law
    (A) requires certain contracts to be in writing to be enforceable
    (B) requires a license to operate as broker or salesperson
    (C) regulates escrow accounts
    (D) regulates the estate owning real estate

37. A warranty deed protects the grantee against a loss by
    (A) casualty   (C) both A and B
    (B) defective title   (D) neither A nor B

38. Brown's building rents for $850 per month. The building's market value is $47,000. Taxes are 75 mills, based on 40% of market value. What percentage of the building's income must be paid out in tax?
    (A) 6.9%   (C) 13.8%
    (B) 10.7%   (D) 34.5%

39. Henderson bought a home for $42,000. Four years later he sold it for $59,900. What is the average annual rate of appreciation?
    (A) 9.92%   (C) 13.12%
    (B) 10.65%   (D) 42.62%

40. The income approach to appraisal would be most suitable for
    (A) a newly opened subdivision
    (B) commercial and investment property
    (C) property heavily mortgaged
    (D) property heavily insured

41. Real estate is defined as
    (A) land and buildings
    (B) land and all permanent attachments to it
    (C) land and everything growing on it
    (D) land only

42. A second mortgage is
    (A) a lien on real estate that has a prior mortgage on it
    (B) the first mortgage recorded
    (C) always made by the seller
    (D) smaller in amount than a first mortgage

43. Depreciation can be caused by
    (A) physical deterioration (C) economic obsolescence
    (B) functional obsolescence (D) all of the above

44. Regulation Z applies to
    I.   all real estate salespersons
    II. all retail stores
    (A) I only
    (B) II only
    (C) Both I and II
    (D) Neither I nor II

45. Perkins bought 11 lots for $2100 each. He keeps four and sells the remaining lots so as to receive a total of $2800 more than he originally paid for all of them. What was the average sale price of each lot that he sold?
    (A) $2100
    (B) $3300
    (C) $3700
    (D) $4900

46. One discount point is equal to
    (A) 1 percent of the sales price
    (B) 1 percent of the interest rate
    (C) 1 percent of the loan amount
    (D) none of the above

47. Which of the following is not realty?
    (A) Fee simple estate
    (B) Leasehold for indefinite duration
    (C) Lumber
    (D) Life estate

48. A lease can state that the rent is to be paid in
    (A) labor
    (B) crops
    (C) cash
    (D) any of the above

49. A mortgaged property can be
    I.   sold without the consent of the mortgagee
    II. conveyed by the grantor making a deed to the grantee
    (A) I only
    (B) II only
    (C) Both I and II
    (D) Neither I nor II

Diagram for questions 50 and 51

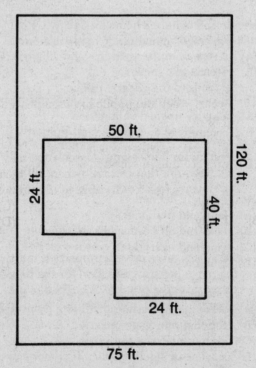

50. The above figure shows a diagram of a house and a lot. How many sq. ft. are there in the house?
    (A) 384
    (B) 1200
    (C) 1584
    (D) 2000

51. In the figure shown above, what percentage of the area of the lot is taken up by the house?
    (A) 13½%
    (B) 17.6%
    (C) 22.2%
    (D) 24.0%

52. Regulation Z covers
    I.   credit extended to people for personal use, under $25,000
    II. all real estate credit transactions
    (A) I only
    (B) II only
    (C) Both I and II
    (D) Neither I nor II

53. A contract that gives someone the right but not the obligation to buy at a specified price within a specified time is a(n)
    (A) contract of sale
    (B) option
    (C) agreement of sale
    (D) none of the above

54. The prohibitions of the 1968 Fair Housing Act apply to multi-family housing in cases of
    I.   multi-family dwellings of five or more units
    II. multi-family dwellings of four or less units if owner occupies one of the units
    (A) I only
    (B) II only
    (C) Both I and II
    (D) Neither I nor II

55. Consideration that has value only to the person receiving it is
    I.   good consideration
    II. valuable consideration
    (A) I only
    (B) II only
    (C) Both I and II
    (D) Neither I nor II

56. An easement in gross
    (A) covers an entire property and all parts of it
    (B) extends to one person only
    (C) extends to the general public
    (D) occurs when the public has used private land without hindrance for a certain period

57. A condominium homeowner's association may
    I.   require that certain owners sell their units and leave
    II. assess fees for the upkeep of common property
    (A) I only
    (B) II only
    (C) I and II
    (D) Neither I nor II

58. If government takes private property it must
    I.   make just compensation for the property taken
    II. require the property for a public use
    (A) I only
    (B) II only
    (C) I and II
    (D) Neither I nor II

Diagram for question 59

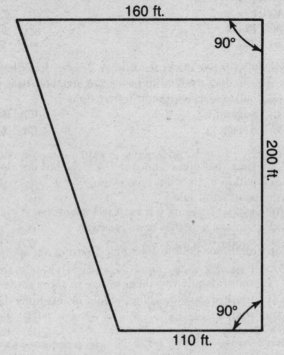

160 ft.

90°

200 ft.

90°

110 ft.

59. The lot shown above sold for $78,300. What was the price per sq. ft.?
   (A) $4.17
   (B) $3.56
   (C) $2.90
   (D) $2.45

60. A salesperson receives 60% of the total commission. The sale was for $63,000. The salesperson received $3024. What was the rate of commission?
   (A) 4.8%
   (B) 6%
   (C) 6¾%
   (D) 8%

61. A millage rate of 84.5 mills is the same as
   I. $84.50 per $1000
   II. 8.45%
   (A) I only
   (B) II only
   (C) Both I and II
   (D) Neither I nor II

62. A single-family house privately owned by an individual owning less than three such houses may be sold or rented without being subject to the provisions of the Fair Housing Act unless
   I.   a broker is used
   II. discriminatory advertising is used
   (A) I only
   (B) II only
   (C) Both I and II
   (D) Neither I nor II

63. When a tenant transfers certain rights and obligations of an existing lease to another tenant, it is called
   (A) assignment of lease
   (B) a release
   (C) subletting
   (D) an eviction

64. A "contract for deed" is also known as a(n)
   I.   installment land sales contract
   II. land contract
   (A) I only
   (B) II only
   (C) Both I and II
   (D) Neither I nor II

65. Smith buys a new home costing $47,000. Land value is 15% of total price. The home contains 1733 sq. ft. What is the cost per sq. ft. of the house alone (not including the land)?

   (A) $4.11   (C) $27.41
   (B) $23.05   (D) $31.80

66. Salesman Jones works for Broker Brown. Jones receives 42% of all commissions he brings in. Jones sells a home for $46,900, at a 6½% commission. What is the *broker's* share of the proceeds?

   (A) $1280.37   (C) $3048.50
   (B) $1768.13   (D) $469.00

67. Rent for a 90 ft. by 60 ft. office is $630 per month. What is the annual rent per sq. ft.?

   (A) $1.40   (C) 71½
   (B) $1.10   (D) 11⅔

68. An estoppel certificate is required when the

   (A) mortgage is sold to an investor   (C) property is being foreclosed
   (B) property is sold   (D) mortgage is assumed

69. An owner who seeks a mortgage loan and offers three properties as security will give a(n)

   (A) blanket mortgage   (C) conventional mortgage
   (B) FHA mortgage   (D) chattel mortgage

70. Jones bought a lot for $2000 in 1963 and spent $13,000 to build a house on it in 1965. Today the house has increased 40% in value while the lot has increased 800%. What is the combined value of house and lot today?

   (A) $18,000   (C) $21,000
   (B) $18,200   (D) $36,200

71. A contract that has no force or effect is said to be
   I. voidable
   II. void

   (A) I only   (C) Both I and II
   (B) II only   (D) Neither I nor II

72. Which of the following statements is (are) false?
   I. FHA loans are insured loans
   II. VA loans are guaranteed loans

   (A) I only   (C) Both I and II
   (B) II only   (D) Neither I nor II

73. A sales agreement to be enforceable must have
   (A) the signature of the wife of a married seller
   (B) an earnest money deposit
   (C) competent parties
   (D) witnesses

74. A broker listed a house for $35,000, at a 6% commission. The eventual sale price was $31,500. How much less was the broker's commission than it would have been if the house had sold at the listed price?

   (A) $21   (C) $1890
   (B) $210   (D) $3500

75. How many square feet are 1¼ acres?

   (A) 10,890   (C) 54,450
   (B) 44,649   (D) 152,460

76. Under Regulation Z, borrowers must be told in writing of
    I.   the total dollar amount of the finance charge, except in the case of a credit transaction to finance the purchase of a dwelling
    II. the annual percentage rate
    (A) I only
    (B) II only
    (C) Both I and II
    (D) Neither I nor II

77. An item of personalty that is affixed to realty so as to be used as a part of it is
    (A) a fixture
    (B) a chattel
    (C) personal property
    (D) encumbered

78. The requirement that all parties to the contract have an understanding of the conditions and stipulations of the agreement is
    I.   consenting realty
    II. a proper offer
    (A) I only
    (B) II only
    (C) Both I and II
    (D) Neither I nor II

79. A deed of conveyance must be signed by
    (A) grantee and grantor
    (B) only by the grantor
    (C) both A and B
    (D) neither A nor B

80. In the application of the income approach to appraising, which of the following statements is (are) true?
    I.   The higher the capitalization rate, the lower the appraised value
    II. The higher the capitalization rate, the higher the appraised value
    (A) I only
    (B) II only
    (C) Both I and II
    (D) Neither I nor II

Model Examination 2

Salesperson (ACT)

The following model examination includes 100 multiple-choice questions covering all aspects of real estate. For convenience, we have grouped all arithmetic questions at the end of the model examination (questions 91–100), but you may expect that in some states the questions may be scattered throughout the examination.

This model examination is similar in format to the National (ACT) examination. It can also be used as a good model in any state that uses the multiple-choice format, even if the state writes its own questions. However, remember that neither National states nor independent states will necessarily use a 100-question examination; they may use more or they may use fewer.

Directions: Select the choice, marked A, B, C, or D, that best answers the question or completes the thought. Mark your answers clearly on the answer sheet.

1. Jackson's will left to Mrs. Jackson the right to use, occupy, and enjoy Jackson's real estate until her death. At that time the real estate will become the property of their children. Mrs. Jackson is a
   (A) remainderman
   (B) life tenant
   (C) joint tenant
   (D) tenant in common

2. To prove his right to a commission the broker must show
   (A) that he was licensed throughout the transaction
   (B) that he had a contract of employment
   (C) that he was the "efficient and procuring cause" of the sale
   (D) all of the above

3. Contracts made by a minor are
   (A) enforceable at all times
   (B) void
   (C) voidable by either party
   (D) voidable only by the minor

4. Mr. Beans owns land worth $5000; Mr. Pork owns a house worth $30,000, subject to a $20,000 mortgage, which Beans will assume. For a fair trade,
   (A) Pork should pay $5000 cash in addition
   (B) Beans should pay $5000 cash in addition
   (C) they may trade properties evenly
   (D) none of the above

5. From the standpoint of the grantor, which of the following types of deed creates the least liability?
   (A) Special warranty
   (B) General warranty
   (C) Bargain and sale
   (D) Quit claim

6. The lending of money at a rate of interest above the legal rate is
   (A) speculating
   (B) usury
   (C) both A and B
   (D) neither A nor B

7. A licensee's license must be
   (A) carried in his (her) wallet at all times
   (B) posted in a public place in the broker's office
   (C) kept on the wall at the licensee's home
   (D) kept on the wall at the Real Estate Commission

8. The parties to a deed are the
   (A) vendor and vendee
   (B) grantor and grantee
   (C) offeror and offeree
   (D) acceptor and acceptee

9. A person must be licensed if he is to sell
   (A) his home
   (B) property belonging to an estate for which he is executor
   (C) property belonging to other clients who pay him a commission
   (D) property which he has inherited

10. Which of the following is NOT an appraisal approach?
    (A) Cost
    (B) Market
    (C) Income
    (D) Trade

11. The most comprehensive ownership of land at law is known as
    (A) estate for years
    (B) life estate
    (C) fee simple
    (D) defeasible title

12. Each of the following pairs of words or phrases has the same meaning EXCEPT
    (A) 1 acre — 43,560 square feet
    (B) 1 mile — 5,280 feet
    (C) 1 square mile — 460 acres
    (D) 1 section — 640 acres

13. In order to sell property, one must
    (A) have a REALTOR®'s license
    (B) belong to a REALTOR®'s association
    (C) hire only REALTORS®
    (D) none of the above

14. What are the broker's responsibilities under the 1968 Fair Housing Act?
    (A) To show all houses to all prospects
    (B) To treat all prospects equally
    (C) Both A and B
    (D) Neither A nor B

15. In order to record a deed, it must be in writing and must
    (A) be signed by grantee
    (B) recite the actual purchase price
    (C) be acknowledged
    (D) be free of all liens

16. Which of the following is not a good reason why real property taxes are so popular?
    (A) Real estate ownership is easy to hide.
    (B) Real estate is valuable.
    (C) Real estate is easy to find.
    (D) Real estate can be foreclosed to provide payment of unpaid tax levies.

17. The purpose of Regulation Z is to
    (A) set maximum interest rates that may be charged
    (B) let borrowers know the cost of credit
    (C) both A and B
    (D) neither A nor B

18. Which of the following contractual arrangements would be unenforceable?
    (A) A agrees to buy B's house.
    (B) A agrees with B that B shall steal money from C.
    (C) A agrees to find a buyer for B's car.
    (D) A agrees with B that B shall make restitution to C for money stolen by B.

19. The two parties to a lease contract are the
    (A) landlord and the serf   (C) lessor and the lessee
    (B) rentor and the rentee   (D) grantor and the grantee

20. When one deliberately lies in order to mislead a fellow party to a contract, it is
    (A) fraud
    (B) misrepresentation
    (C) legal if no third parties
    (D) all right if it is not written into the contract

21. A contract that transfers possession but not ownership of property is a(n)
    (A) special warranty deed   (C) easement
    (B) option   (D) lease

22. Egbert owns a building in life estate. Upon Egbert's death, ownership of the building will go to Ethel. Ethel is a
    (A) remainderman   (C) common tenant
    (B) life tenant   (D) reversionary interest

23. One who owns an undivided interest in land with at least one other, and having the right of survivorship, is said to be a
    (A) tenant in common   (C) joint tenant
    (B) tenant at will   (D) tenant at sufferance

24. If one has some rights to use land, but not all possessory rights, one is said to have a(n)
    (A) interest in land   (C) life estate in land
    (B) estate in land   (D) tenancy in common

25. Which of the following is not corporeal property?
    (A) Fee simple real estate   (C) Easement
    (B) Leasehold   (D) Fixture

26. A listing contract that says the broker will receive a commission no matter who sells the property is called a(n)
    (A) open listing
    (B) net listing
    (C) exclusive agency listing
    (D) exclusive right to sell listing

27. Which of the following best describes an installment or land contract?
    (A) A contract to buy land only
    (B) A mortgage on land
    (C) A means of conveying title immediately while the purchaser pays for the property
    (D) A method of selling real estate whereby the purchaser pays for the property in regular installments while the seller retains title to the property

28. Mr. Smith has a three-month option on 20 acres at $200 per acre. Mr. Smith may
    (A) buy the property for $4000
    (B) sell the option to another
    (C) not buy the land
    (D) all of the above

29. The mortgagor's right to reestablish ownership after delinquency is known as
    (A) reestablishment
    (B) satisfaction
    (C) equity of redemption
    (D) acceleration

30. A broker must place funds belonging to others in
    (A) his office safe, to which only he knows the combination
    (B) a safety deposit box
    (C) an account maintained by the Real Estate Commission
    (D) a trust, or escrow, account

31. A licensee's license can be revoked for
    (A) closing a deal
    (B) intentionally misleading someone into signing a contract that he ordinarily would not sign
    (C) submitting a ridiculous offer to a seller
    (D) all of the above

32. Capitalization is a process used to
    (A) convert income stream into a lump sum capital value
    (B) determine cost
    (C) establish depreciation
    (D) determine potential future value

33. The number of square feet in one acre is
    (A) 64,000
    (B) 460
    (C) 440
    (D) 43,560

34. When changed surroundings cause an existing house to lose value, there is
    (A) physical deterioration
    (B) economic obsolescence
    (C) functional obsolescence
    (D) all of the above

35. An appraisal is a(n)
    (A) forecast of value
    (B) estimate of value
    (C) prediction of value
    (D) precise estimation of value

36. A lien for unpaid property taxes
    (A) can be sold at auction
    (B) takes priority over all other liens
    (C) cannot exist unless taxes are at least 36 months overdue
    (D) is a form of adverse possession

37. The prohibitions of the 1968 Fair Housing Act apply to privately owned housing when
    (A) a broker or other person engaged in selling or renting dwellings is used
    (B) discriminatory advertising is used
    (C) both A and B
    (D) neither A nor B

38. To cancel a credit transaction, the borrower must inform the lender, within three days, according to Regulation Z,
    (A) by phone
    (B) in writing
    (C) both A and B
    (D) neither A nor B

39. A agrees to trade his car to B in exchange for a vacant lot that B owns.
    (A) This is a valid contractual agreement.
    (B) This is not a contract because no money changes hands.
    (C) This is not a contract because you can't trade "unlike" items.
    (D) This is not a valid contract because the car is titled in A's name.

40. A percentage lease requires the tenant to pay
    (A) a percentage of taxes and insurance
    (B) a percentage of net income as rent
    (C) a percentage of sales as rent
    (D) none of the above

41. A seller of real estate is also known as the
    (A) vendee
    (B) grantor
    (C) vendor
    (D) grantee

42. An estate at will is a(n)
    (A) limited partnership
    (B) tenancy of uncertain duration
    (C) inheritance by will
    (D) life tenancy

43. A hands B a deed with the intent to pass title and orally requests B not to record the deed until he dies. When is the deed valid?
    (A) Immediately
    (B) When B records the deed
    (C) When A dies
    (D) Never

44. A quitclaim deed conveys only the interest of the
    (A) guaranteed
    (B) property
    (C) claimant
    (D) grantor

45. A gross lease requires the tenant to pay rent based on
    (A) gross sales
    (B) net sales
    (C) gross profit
    (D) none of the above

46. The recording of a deed
    (A) passes the title
    (B) insures the title
    (C) guarantees the title
    (D) gives constructive notice of ownership

47. The law that requires most real estate contracts to be written to be enforceable is the
    (A) Statute of Limitations
    (B) Statute of Frauds
    (C) Statute of Written Real Estate Agreements
    (D) Law of Property

48. In the absence of an agreement to the contrary, the mortgage normally having priority will be the one
    (A) for the greatest amount
    (B) that is a permanent mortgage
    (C) that was recorded first
    (D) that is a construction loan mortgage

49. A net listing is one
    (A) that requires the broker to seek a net price for the property
    (B) that is legal in all states
    (C) that most ethical brokers would prefer to use
    (D) in which the broker's commission is the amount by which the sale price exceeds the agreed-upon net price the seller desires

50. Under Regulation Z, a borrower may have the right to cancel, within three days
    (A) a second mortgage on his dwelling
    (B) a first mortgage loan used to purchase his dwelling
    (C) a home-improvement loan over one year old
    (D) none of the above

51. Which of the following does not terminate an agency relationship?
    (A) Making an offer
    (B) Death of either party
    (C) Resignation of agent
    (D) Destruction of subject matter

52. The 1968 Fair Housing Act protects against housing discrimination on the basis of
    (A) race and color
    (B) race, color, and religion
    (C) race, color, religion, and national origin
    (D) race, color, religion, national origin, and sex

53. One who dies leaving no will is said to have died
    (A) intestate   (C) unbequeathed
    (B) without heirs   (D) unwillingly

54. From the point of view of the grantee, the safest kind of deed that can be received is a
    (A) general warranty deed   (C) quitclaim or release deed
    (B) special warranty deed   (D) trustee's deed

55. What is *not* an essential element of a valid contract?
    (A) offer and acceptance   (C) without ambiguity
    (B) capacity of participants   (D) legal objective

56. A freehold estate is
    (A) one acquired without paying anything
    (B) any leasehold
    (C) any estate wherein one may use the property as one wishes
    (D) an estate of uncertain duration

57. In order to do business, a licensee must
    (A) make proper application for a license
    (B) pass a licensing examination
    (C) have a license issued by the appropriate state agency
    (D) all of the above

58. When a loan is assumed on property that is sold,
    (A) the original borrower is relieved of further responsibility
    (B) the purchaser becomes liable for the debt
    (C) the purchaser must obtain a certificate of eligibility
    (D) all of the above

59. An estoppel certificate is often required when the
    (A) mortgage is sold to an investor
    (B) property is sold
    (C) property is being foreclosed
    (D) mortgage is assumed

60. Which of the following will not terminate a lease?
    (A) Performance   (C) Surrender
    (B) Breach   (D) Vacancy

61. The adjustment process in the direct sales comparison approach involves the principle of
    (A) contribution   (C) variable proportions
    (B) diminishing returns   (D) anticipation

62. A contract in which A agrees to allow B to use A's real estate in return for periodic payments of money by B is a
    (A) deed
    (B) contract of sale
    (C) lease
    (D) mortgage

63. Dower rights are rights that assure
    (A) that a husband receives a certain portion of his deceased wife's estate
    (B) that wives and, in some states, children receive a certain portion of a deceased husband's (or father's) estate
    (C) a homeowner cannot lose his entire investment in his home
    (D) that husbands and wives share equally in property acquired during marriage

64. When an individual holds property past the expiration of a lease without the landlord's consent, the leasehold estate he has is a
    (A) tenancy at sufferance
    (B) freehold estate
    (C) common of pasturage
    (D) holdover tenant

65. A broker's unlicensed secretary
    (A) may sell property providing she does it under the broker's direct supervision
    (B) may sell or negotiate deals so long as she does not leave the office
    (C) may refer interested clients to the broker or his employed licensees
    (D) all of the above

66. Discount points in FHA and VA loans are generally paid by the
    (A) lender
    (B) purchaser
    (C) seller
    (D) broker

67. Which of the following is *not* required of an agent with respect to his principal?
    (A) Loyalty
    (B) To act in person
    (C) To account for the agent's own personal finances
    (D) To act in the principal's best interests

68. Tenancy in severalty refers to
    (A) ownership by one person only
    (B) ownership by two persons only
    (C) ownership by at least three persons
    (D) a special form of joint ownership available only to married couples

69. When one has permission to use land, but one has no other rights, one has
    (A) tenancy at sufferance
    (B) tenancy in common
    (C) license
    (D) fee simple estate

70. When tastes and standards cause an existing house to lose value, there is
    (A) physical deterioration
    (B) economic obsolescence
    (C) functional obsolescence
    (D) all of the above

71. A rule-of-thumb method for determining the price a wage earner can afford to pay for a home is to multiply his annual income by
    (A) 1½
    (B) 2½
    (C) 4
    (D) 6

72. Real estate licenses, once received,
    (A) remain in effect indefinitely
    (B) are good for a limited period of time
    (C) must be filed in county records
    (D) may be inherited by one's spouse

73. Which of the following is most nearly described as personal property?
    (A) A fixture
    (B) A chattel
    (C) An improvement
    (D) Realty

74. A real estate broker is a
   (A) general agent
   (B) special agent
   (C) secret agent
   (D) travel agent

75. A broker may use escrow monies held on behalf of others
   (A) for collateral for business loans
   (B) for collateral for personal loans
   (C) to make salary advances to licensees in his employ
   (D) none of the above

76. Which of the following forms of deeds have one or more guarantees of title?
   (A) Quitclaim deed
   (B) Executor's deed
   (C) Warranty deed
   (D) Special form deed

77. The highest price a buyer is willing, but not compelled, to pay and the lowest price a seller is willing, but not compelled, to accept is
   (A) estimated value
   (B) economic value
   (C) marginal value
   (D) market value

78. A deed to be valid need not necessarily be
   (A) signed
   (B) written
   (C) sealed
   (D) delivered

79. One who receives title to land by virtue of having used and occupied it for a certain period of time, without actually paying the previous owner for it, receives title by
   (A) will
   (B) descent
   (C) alienation
   (D) adverse possession

80. A conventional mortgage is
   (A) amortizing
   (B) guaranteed by FHA
   (C) not guaranteed by a government agency
   (D) approved by the VA

81. The party to whom a deed conveys real estate is the
   (A) grantee
   (B) grantor
   (C) beneficiary
   (D) recipient

82. Which is not considered a permanent attachment to land?
   (A) Anything growing on it
   (B) Fixtures
   (C) Chattels
   (D) Anything built upon the land

83. The main appeal of VA mortgages to borrowers lies in
   (A) low interest rates
   (B) minimum down payments
   (C) unlimited mortgage ceiling
   (D) easy availability

84. For which reason or reasons is a deed recorded?
   (A) To insure certain title
   (B) To give notice to the world
   (C) Because it is required by the state
   (D) To save title insurance cost

85. Ownership of real property is transferred
   (A) when grantor signs the deed
   (B) when grantor's signature has been notarized
   (C) when delivery of the deed is made
   (D) when the correct documentary stamps are put on the deed and canceled

86. A valid contract of purchase or sale of real property must be signed by the
    (A) broker
    (B) agent and seller
    (C) seller only
    (D) buyer and seller

87. A sublease is a
    (A) lease made by a lessor
    (B) lease made by a lessee and a third party
    (C) lease for basement space
    (D) condition of property

88. "Hand money" paid upon the signing of an agreement of sale is called
    (A) an option
    (B) a recognizance
    (C) earnest money
    (D) a freehold estate

89. Market value appraisals assume that
    (A) the purchaser pays all cash (no mortgage financing)
    (B) FHA or VA financing is employed
    (C) the appraiser can determine the types of financing involved
    (D) financing, if any, is on terms generally available in that area

90. A licensed salesperson
    (A) must be under the supervision of a broker
    (B) can only collect commission payments from his broker
    (C) must have his license held by his employing broker
    (D) all of the above

91. If the property is assessed at $60,000 and the millage rate is 32.5, the tax is
    (A) $19.50
    (B) $195.00
    (C) $1950.00
    (D) $19,500.00

92. Smith sold three lots for a total of $9000. The first lot sold for 1½ times the price of the second lot. The second lot sold for twice the price of the third lot. How much did the first lot sell for?
    (A) $1500
    (B) $3000
    (C) $4500
    (D) $9000

93. Jones owns a 44-acre tract of land. In order to develop it he must set aside 10% of the area for parks and must use 6.6 acres for streets, drainage, and other uses. If the minimum permissible lot size is 7500 sq. ft., what is the maximum possible number of lots Jones could lay out?
    (A) 191
    (B) 180
    (C) 293
    (D) 81

94. Smith borrowed $7500 for four years, paying interest every quarter. The total amount of interest he paid was $2700. What was the annual interest rate?
    (A) 9%
    (B) 10%
    (C) 27%
    (D) 36%

95. Jim sold a parcel of land for $164,450. He made a profit of 43%. What was his purchase price?
    (A) $82,755.00
    (B) $93,736.50
    (C) $115,000.00
    (D) $164,450.00

96. Bill referred a customer to Joe, who sold the customer a house for $46,500. Joe paid Bill a referral fee of 12% of Joe's commission. If Bill received $390.60, what was the rate of the commission on Joe's sale?
    (A) 5%
    (B) 6%
    (C) 6½%
    (D) 7%

97. What monthly rent must Sam get on his land in order to get an annual return of 11% on the $210,000 that he paid for the land? Assume that the tenant pays all property taxes.
   - (A) $275
   - (B) $1552
   - (C) $1925
   - (D) $23,100

98. Smith bought three lots for $1000 each. If they increase in value by 25% each year *compounded,* in how many years will he be able to sell one of the lots for as much as he originally paid for all three?
   - (A) 4
   - (B) 5
   - (C) 6
   - (D) 7

99. How many acres are contained in a rectangular tract of land measuring 1700 ft. by 2100 ft.?
   - (A) 81.96
   - (B) 92.91
   - (C) 112.01
   - (D) 115.00

100. A backyard for a home measures 100 ft. by 80 ft. The house is 40 ft. wide. A fence 4 ft. high is to be built around the yard, with the width of the house as part of the barrier. If fence fabric is $1.80 per sq. yd., how much will the necessary fence fabric cost?
   - (A) $64
   - (B) $256
   - (C) $288
   - (D) $2304

Model Examination 3

Salesperson (ASI)

The following examination is for use by sales license examinees in states that use the ASI examination. Note also that this examination may be useful for those taking sales license examinations in states that prepare their own exams and that use the multiple-choice format. However, examinations in such states may have more or fewer questions than the 80 that appear on the general portion of the ASI REAL (Real Estate Assessment for Licensure) salesperson examination.

If your state uses the Rectangular Survey *anywhere* in the state, be sure also to take Supplemental Examination 4 found in the next chapter. Although the ASI examination does not use questions that require you to fill out contracts or settlement forms, you may also want to take Supplemental Examinations 1, 2, and 3 in the next chapter for practice.

Directions: Select the choice, marked A, B, C, or D, that best answers the question or completes the thought. Mark your answers clearly on the answer sheet.

1. An appraisal is a(an)
   - (A) forecast of value
   - (B) prediction of value
   - (C) estimate of value
   - (D) statement of exact value

2. The number of sq. ft. in one acre is
   - (A) 640
   - (B) 45,630
   - (C) 43,560
   - (D) 53,460

3. How is the *gross rent multiplier* calculated?
   - (A) market value/market rental
   - (B) monthly payment/market rental
   - (C) market rental/market price
   - (D) sales price/market price

4. A tract of land contains exactly 10.6 acres. It is perfectly rectangular. The measurement on one side is 181 ft. To the nearest foot, how deep is the tract?
   (A) 255 ft.
   (B) 385 ft.
   (C) 1817 ft.
   (D) 2551 ft.

5. What is the maximum number of 8000 sq. ft. lots that could be platted from a 17.1-acre tract if 19% of the land must be used for streets and parks?
   (A) 17
   (B) 62
   (C) 75
   (D) 93

6. Laws that set minimum construction standards are
   (A) building codes
   (B) zoning codes
   (C) environmental laws
   (D) condemnation laws

7. Which of the following is not an appraisal approach?
   (A) cost
   (B) trade
   (C) market
   (D) income

8. Value is determined by
   (A) supply and demand
   (B) asking prices
   (C) interest rates
   (D) active brokers

9. Permission for land use not normally permitted by the zoning classification of the property is a(an)
   (A) differential
   (B) zone change
   (C) variance
   (D) egregement

10. Smith sells a tract of land 400 ft. by 665 ft. for $17,100. To the nearest dollar, what is the price per acre?
    (A) $2800
    (B) $2950
    (C) $3117
    (D) $3228

11. In Green's city, the property tax rate is 71 mills, based upon 30% of the market value of the property. Green just paid $42,500 for a home. What should the tax be?
    (A) $905.25
    (B) $1117.52
    (C) $1829.29
    (D) $3017.50

12. When changes in taste cause a house's neighborhood to become less valuable, there is
    (A) physical deterioration
    (B) functional obsolescence
    (C) economic obsolescence
    (D) all of the above

13. The income approach would generally be most suitable for appraising
    (A) commercial and investment property
    (B) single-family homes
    (C) heavily mortgaged property
    (D) heavily insured property

Questions 14, 15, and 16 concern the following situation:

Mr. Jones died, leaving Mrs. Jones the right to use, occupy, and enjoy his real estate until her death, at which time their son Willis would receive a fee simple estate in the real estate.

14. Mrs. Jones is a
    (A) remainderman
    (B) life tenant
    (C) joint tenant
    (D) tenant in common

15. Willis is a
    (A) remainderman
    (B) life tenant
    (C) joint tenant
    (D) tenant in common

16. Mrs. Jones has a
   (A) fee simple estate in joint tenancy with Willis
   (B) fee simple estate as tenant in common with Willis
   (C) life estate
   (D) reversionary interest

17. A building 40 ft. by 22 ft. has exterior walls 10 ft. high. There are 13 windows, 4 sq. ft. each, and a door measuring 48 sq. ft. One gallon of paint covers 400 sq. ft. If the door and the windows are not to be painted, how much paint is needed to give the walls *two* full coats?
   (A) 2.85 gal.   (C) 3.1 gal.
   (B) 5.7 gal.   (D) 6.2 gal.

18. Jackson borrows $12,000. He pays $330 each quarter in interest. What is the annual interest rate on this loan?
   (A) 2¾ %   (C) 11%
   (B) 8%   (D) 12%

19. A freehold estate is
   (A) acquired without paying anything for it
   (B) always acquired by adverse possession
   (C) an estate of uncertain duration
   (D any leasehold estate

20. One who appears to own a piece of real estate, but actually does not, has
   (A) good title   (C) constructive notice
   (B) recorded title   (D) color of title

21. A real estate broker is a(an)
   (A) general agent   (C) special agent
   (B) attorney-in-fact   (D) agent provocateur

22. Contracts made by a minor are
   (A) void   (C) voidable by all parties
   (B) voidable by the minor   (D) voidable by non-minor parties

23. The parties to a deed are
   (A) vendor and vendee   (C) grantor and grantee
   (B) testator and testatee   (D) offeror and offeree

24. Smith has the choice of renting a house for $225 per month, including utilities, or for $175 per month if he pays the utility bills himself. Average utility bills are $480 per year, but Smith feels he can reduce this by 35%. How much *per month* does he expect to save by paying the utility bills himself?
   (A) $0   (C) $18
   (B) $15   (D) $24

25. Salesman Jones gets 50% of the first $20,000 of commissions he brings in and 60% for all above that amount in one year. Last year he sold $1,100,000 of real estate, all at 7% commission. How much did Jones get to keep?
   (A) $77,000   (C) $44,200
   (B) $46,200   (D) $34,200

26. A quit claim deed conveys only the interest of the
   (A) grantor   (C) quittor
   (B) claimant   (D) property

27. Which of the following will not terminate a lease?
    (A) breach
    (B) performance
    (C) vacancy
    (D) surrender

28. One discount point is equal to
    (A) 1% of the sale price
    (B) 1% of the loan amount
    (C) 1% of the interest rate
    (D) none of the above

29. Which of the following is not covered by title insurance?
    (A) forged deed
    (B) deed by incompetent
    (C) tornado damage
    (D) undisclosed heirs

30. Ownership of realty by one person is
    (A) tenancy in severalty
    (B) conjoint tenancy
    (C) tenancy by the entirety
    (D) tenancy sole

31. Green made an offer to purchase real estate from Blue. The offer gave Blue seven days to consider it. Two days later, without hearing anything from Blue, Green found another property that he liked better. Green then wanted to withdraw his offer to Blue.
    (A) Green had to wait until the seven days had passed.
    (B) Green was required to notify Blue of his desire to withdraw the offer, and to give Blue "reasonable time" to accept or reject it.
    (C) Green could withdraw the offer immediately.
    (D) none of the above.

32. The secondary mortgage market is
    (A) the market for second mortgages
    (B) the market in which existing mortgages are bought and sold
    (C) the market in which junior mortgages are originated
    (D) the market for older, low interest loan assumptions

33. A landowner leases his land to a lessee, who in turn leases the land to a sublessee. Who holds the *sandwich lease?*
    (A) landowner
    (B) lessee
    (C) sublessee
    (D) none of the above

34. The covenant whereby one warrants that he is the possessor and owner of property being conveyed is the covenant of
    (A) seizin
    (B) habendum
    (C) possession
    (D) further assurance

35. Title to land passes
    (A) on the date shown on the deed
    (B) upon recordation of the deed
    (C) when the deed is signed
    (D) upon delivery of the deed

36. Provisions for defeat of the mortgage are found in the _____ clause.
    (A) alienation
    (B) acceleration
    (C) foreclosure
    (D) defeasance

37. All mortgages are
    (A) due on sale
    (B) liens
    (C) recorded
    (D) none of the above

38. A fixture is
   (A) anything that cannot be removed from the real estate without leaving a hole
   (B) anything the property owner says is a fixture
   (C) anything necessary to the proper and efficient use of the real estate
   (D) none of the above

39. Jones lives in an apartment owned by Smith. The lease has expired, but Jones has stayed on and continues to pay rent to Smith. This is an example of
   (A) tenancy by remainder   (C) tenancy at suffrance
   (B) tenancy at will   (D) tenancy in common

40. Which of the following is not real estate?
   (A) a flagpole affixed to a house   (C) a greenhouse
   (B) a tomato crop not ready for harvest   (D) All of the above *are* real estate.

41. The law that requires that all transfers of ownership rights to real estate be in writing is the
   (A) statute of frauds   (C) parol evidence rule
   (B) statute of limitations   (D) statute of liberties

42. After paying a 6½ % commission, Jackson received net proceeds of $33,613.25 on the sale of his home. What was the sale price?
   (A) $2184.86   (C) $35,950.00
   (B) $35,798.11   (D) $37,500.00

43. When a valid lease of real estate exists, and the rent is paid on time, which of the following is false?
   (A) The lessor cannot move in and use the property until the lease expires.
   (B) The lessee possesses the right of occupancy.
   (C) The lessee holds the fee to the real estate.
   (D) The lessor has a reversionary interest in the real estate.

44. The clause in a mortgage note that allows the lender to demand immediate payment in full of the remaining balance, if payment of the note is not made as contracted, is the _____ clause.
   (A) alienation   (C) foreclosure
   (B) acceleration   (D) amortization

45. All of the following should be recorded except
   (A) easement   (C) mortgage
   (B) 20-year lease   (D) 6-month lease

46. In a typical mortgage loan transaction, the mortgagee is the
   (A) lender   (C) appraiser
   (B) borrower   (D) closing agent

47. Which of the following has access to documents that have been recorded in the public records?
   (A) prospective buyers   (C) appraisers
   (B) prospective lenders   (D) all of the above

48. Anderson sold a tract of land. After paying a 9% commission and paying 3% of the selling price in taxes, fees, and closing costs, he ended up with $176,000. What was the sale price of the land?
   (A) $181,280   (C) 197,120
   (B) 191,840   (D) $200,000

49. Farley's warehouse measures 52 ft. by 36 ft. The walls are 9 in. thick, and there are 13 support pillars inside the building, each 6 in. by 6 in. What is the *net* interior floor space?
    - (A) 1739 sq. ft.
    - (B) 1742¼ sq. ft.
    - (C) 1803⁵/₁₆ sq. ft.
    - (D) 1806⁹/₁₆ sq. ft.

50. Title that establishes ownership of real estate in a reasonably clear manner upon examination of the public records is _____ title.
    - (A) owner's
    - (B) marketable
    - (C) equitable
    - (D) quiet

51. A certain property has no road frontage; however, there exists a recorded right of access across a neighboring parcel of land. This right is a(an)
    - (A) conditional title
    - (B) entroversion
    - (C) easement
    - (D) defeasance

52. An estate that may be terminated by any party at any time is an estate
    - (A) for years
    - (B) at will
    - (C) in possession
    - (D) in termination

53. If the commission in a listing contract is arranged such that the broker receives all of the purchase price in excess of a certain figure, the listing is a(an) _____ listing
    - (A) open
    - (B) net
    - (C) gross
    - (D) multiple

54. Which of the following does not have the right of survivorship?
    - (A) tenant in common
    - (B) joint tenant
    - (C) tenant by the entirety
    - (D) *All* have the right of survivorship.

55. In a VA loan transaction, to whom is the discount (if any) paid?
    - (A) VA
    - (B) lender
    - (C) broker
    - (D) buyer

56. In a VA loan transaction, who usually pays the discount (if any)?
    - (A) VA
    - (B) lender
    - (C) seller
    - (D) closing agent

57. Jones leases a building. An earthquake destroys it. Under common law,
    - (A) the lease is no longer enforceable
    - (B) Jones needn't pay rent until the building is rebuilt
    - (C) Jones must rebuild the building, but may deduct the cost from rent
    - (D) Jones must continue to pay rent until the lease expires

58. Which of the following is neither real estate nor a fixture?
    - (A) ceiling
    - (B) chandelier on ceiling
    - (C) light bulb in chandelier
    - (D) light switch

59. Real estate brokers and salespeople should be familiar with
    - (A) common law
    - (B) agency law
    - (C) license law
    - (D) all of the above

60. Which of the following is not always a right possessed by an owner of a fee simple estate?
    - (A) possession
    - (B) easement
    - (C) occupancy
    - (D) disposition

61. Which of the following would not be considered commercial real estate?
   (A) office building
   (B) condominium home
   (C) shopping center
   (D) doctors' office complex

62. Smith wishes to develop a subdivision containing 55 lots averaging 10,500 sq. ft. each. An average of 1380 sq. ft. of street, sidewalk, and other space must be provided for each lot. What is the minimum number of acres that Smith will need?
   (A) 12
   (B) 14
   (C) 15
   (D) 17

63. Which of the following instructions from a seller may not be complied with by a real estate broker?
   (A) not put up a for sale sign in yard
   (B) not present offers for less than listing price
   (C) not show the property to persons who do not speak English
   (D) not show property on religious holidays observed by seller

64. Real estate brokers' commissions usually are set by
   (A) the local board of REALTORS®
   (B) the laws of the state
   (C) agreement with other brokerage firms
   (D) agreement between property owner and broker

65. When a licensed salesperson advertises property for sale,
   (A) the name of the broker must be mentioned
   (B) only the salesperson's name must be mentioned
   (C) the name of the property owner must be revealed
   (D) the price must not be mentioned

66. Which form of listing does not allow the seller to sell his/her listed property by himself/herself without paying the listing broker a commission?
   (A) open listing
   (B) exclusive right-to-sell listing
   (C) multiple listing
   (D) exclusive agency lsiting

67. A broker has a listing the terms of which allow him to earn a commission only if he finds a buyer before the seller or another broker does. This is an example of a(an)
   (A) open listing
   (B) exclusive right-to-sell listing
   (C) net listing
   (D) exclusive agency listing

68. Sam builds an addition to his home, part of which turns out to be on land belonging to June. This is an example of
   (A) accretion
   (B) riparian
   (C) easement
   (D) encroachment

69. Sam has the legal right to use Fred's driveway for his lifetime. Sam has a(an)
   (A) life estate
   (B) easement in gross
   (C) license to use
   (D) riparian right

70. Simpson wishes to install wall-to-wall carpeting in his home, which measures 42 × 28 ft. The outside walls are 6 in. thick, and the interior walls are 4 in. thick. There are 135 linear ft. of wall inside the home. The two bathrooms (each with interior measurements of 9 ft. × 6 ft.) and the kitchen (12 ft. × 12 ft.) are not to be carpeted. If installed carpeting costs $13.95 per sq. yd., how much will the job cost?
   (A) $1255.50
   (B) $1222.95
   (C) $1506.60
   (D) $1715.85

71. Fred contracts to buy a house for $55,000. He pays $1500 in earnest money and applies for a 75% loan. How much more money will he need to make up the purchase price of the home?
    (A) $13,375
    (B) $12,250
    (C) $10,750
    (D) $4875

72. Leo allows Lemmie to stay in his (Leo's) house while Leo is on vacation, but Lemmie must leave when Leo returns. Lemmie has a(an)
    (A) short-term lease
    (B) proprietary right
    (C) license
    (D) easement

73. An estate that has an indefinite duration is a(an)
    (A) freehold estate
    (B) renewable leasehold
    (C) estate at suffrance
    (D) nonfreehold estate

74. How many 100 ft. × 100 ft. lots can be made out of a three-acre plot of land?
    (A) 6
    (B) 11
    (C) 13
    (D) 43

75. A lot sold for $225 a front ft. If the lot was 96 ft. deep and had an area of 6336 sq. ft., how much did the lot sell for?
    (A) $11,770
    (B) $14,256
    (C) $14,850
    (D) $21,600

76. A "legal description" of land must
    (A) be sufficient to identify the property
    (B) carry measurements to the nearest inch
    (C) show the area of the land being described
    (D) all of the above

77. Increase in the size of a plot of land because of soil deposited by the flow of a stream is called
    (A) accretion
    (B) riparian
    (C) depletion
    (D) amortization

78. If an offer is *rescinded*, it is
    (A) revised
    (B) altered
    (C) terminated
    (D) accepted

79. Which of the following is not necessarily required in a deed?
    (A) acknowledgement
    (B) grantee's signature
    (C) date
    (D) description of real estate

80. Government's right to regulate land use derives from
    (A) escheat
    (B) just compensation
    (C) police power
    (D) eminent domain

Model Examination 4

Broker (ETS)

The following examination is for use by broker license examinees in states that use the ETS examination. Note also that this examination may be useful for those taking broker license examinations in states that prepare their own exams and that use the multiple-choice format. However, examinations in such states may have more or fewer questions than the 80 that appear on the general portion of the ETS RELE (Real Estate Licensing Examination) broker examination. Also, few other examinations will use the "I only II only...etc." answer format used in ETS license examinations.

If your state uses the Rectangular Survey *anywhere* in the state, be sure also to take Supplemental Examination 4 found in the next chapter. Although the ETS examination does not use questions that require you to fill out contracts or settlement forms, you may also want to take Supplemental Examinations 1, 2, and 3 in the next chapter for practice.

Directions: Select the choice, marked A, B, C, or D, that best answers the question or completes the thought. Mark your answers clearly on the answer sheet.

1. The number of dollars remaining each year after deducting cash expenses from cash rent receipts and other property income is
   (A) cash-on-cash
   (B) cash depletion
   (C) cash amortization
   (D) cash flow

2. The market value of a house is $70,000. If property is assessed at 20% of market value and the annual tax rate is 80 mills, how much is the tax?
   (A) $1120
   (B) $2140
   (C) $3500
   (D) $5600

3. Loss of value because the property is located in a run-down neighborhood is known as
   (A) physical deterioration
   (B) functional obsolescence
   (C) economic obsolescence
   (D) none of the above

4. Which of the following is not realty?
   (A) 50-year lease
   (B) fee simple estate
   (C) easement in gross
   (D) life estate

5. Which of the following is adequate recitation of consideration in a deed?
   (A) "for ten dollars and other valuable consideration"
   (B) "for natural love and affection"
   (C) the actual amount of consideration paid
   (D) all of the above

6. One type of depreciation generally is not curable. This type of depreciation is
   (A) physical deterioration
   (B) functional obsolescence
   (C) economic obsolescence
   (D) all of the above

7. Which of the following can enter into a listing agreement, in his/her own name, to sell real estate for a fee?
   I. a licensed salesperson
   II. a licensed broker
   (A) I only
   (B) II only
   (C) both I and II
   (D) neither I nor II

8. A licensed salesperson wishes to sell his/her own property. He/she must
   I. list the property with his/her broker
   II. inform prospective purchasers that he/she is the owner
   (A) I only
   (B) II only
   (C) both I and II
   (D) neither I nor II

Questions 9 to 13 refer to the following situation:

Robby buys a house from Freddy. The price is $50,000. Robby gets a VA loan for 80% of the purchase price. The loan discount is three points. The broker's commission on the sale is 6%. The contract interest rate on the VA loan is 10%.

9. Assuming no closing costs other than those cited above, how much does Freddy end up with?
   (A) $36,400
   (B) $45,500
   (C) $45,800
   (D) $46,400

10. What is the dollar amount of the discount?
    (A) $780
    (B) $900
    (C) $1200
    (D) $1500

11. What is the lender's effective rate of return on the loan?
    (A) 13%
    (B) 10.375%
    (C) 10%
    (D) 9.625%

12. Who pays the discount on the VA loan?
    (A) Freddy
    (B) Robby
    (C) broker
    (D) VA

13. To whom is the discount paid?
    (A) broker
    (B) lender
    (C) VA
    (D) FHA

14. Igor has a one-year lease that says the rent is $400 per month. However, the lease does not say when the rent shall be paid. Igor has to pay
    (A) at the end of each month
    (B) at the beginning of each month
    (C) at the end of the lease period
    (D) at the beginning of the lease period

15. Which of the following both originate mortgage loans and service them?
    I. mortgage bankers
    II. savings and loan associations
    III. commercial banks
    (A) I only
    (B) I and II only
    (C) II and III only
    (D) I, II, and III

16. Which of the following can be used as security for the payment of a debt?
    I. mortgage
    II. deed of trust
    III. release of lien
    (A) I only
    (B) I and II only
    (C) I and III only
    (D) I, II, and III

17. A lender may refuse to make a mortgage loan because of
    I. inability of the borrower to repay
    II. location of the property
    (A) I only
    (B) II only
    (C) both I and II
    (D) neither I nor II

18. A mortgage held by the seller of the mortgaged property is
    I. a purchase money mortgage
    II. a satisfaction piece
    (A) I only
    (B) II only
    (C) both I and II
    (D) neither I nor II

19. A recorded instrument that concerns ownership rights to realty
    I. gives constructive notice
    II. notifies the public of the claims made in it
    (A) I only
    (B) II only
    (C) both I and II
    (D) neither I nor II

20. Jones acquires a fee simple estate to land belonging to Green because Jones used and occupied the land openly for a period of time, unmolested by Green. This is a(an)
 (A) easement in gross
 (B) adverse possession
 (C) estoppel
 (D) subrogation

21. One who has another's power of attorney is called a(an)
 (A) agent in place
 (B) real estate broker
 (C) lawyer
 (D) attorney-in-fact

22. The right of the state to take title to real estate for which no legal owner can be found is called
 (A) police power
 (B) tenancy
 (C) eminent domain
 (D) escheat

23. Zach dies without a will. According to the laws of the state, Zelda receives title to Zack's real estate. Zelda has received
 (A) title by descent
 (B) clouded title
 (C) an easement
 (D) legacy title

24. A person may void a contract if it was entered into
 I. under duress
 II. with a minor
 (A) I only
 (B) II only
 (C) both I and II
 (D) neither I nor II

25. Which of the following real estate contracts can be unilateral?
 I. lease
 II. contract of sale
 (A) I only
 (B) II only
 (C) both I and II
 (D) neither I nor II

26. Which of the following has no warranty?
 (A) executor's deed
 (B) quit claim
 (C) general warranty deed
 (D) trustee's deed

27. A workman who is not paid for work that improved real estate may file a
 (A) suit for quiet title
 (B) lis pendens
 (C) mechanic's lien
 (D) satisfaction piece

28. What is the cash-on-cash ratio for a property that has a cash flow of $16,900 and an initial investor's cash equity of $130,000?
 (A) 7.69%
 (B) 0.219
 (C) 0.12
 (D) 0.13

29. What percent of a square mile is 200 acres?
 (A) 27.5%
 (B) 43.478%
 (C) 31.25%
 (D) 10%

30. When a property is foreclosed, which claim takes first priority?
 (A) tax lien
 (B) first mortgage
 (C) second mortgage
 (D) mechanic's lien

31. A parcel of land is 440 ft. by 817 ft. How many acres does it contain?
 (A) 17
 (B) 8.25
 (C) 11.67
 (D) more than 75

32. Which of the following is a specific lien?
    I.   judgment
    II. mechanic's lien
    (A) I only   (C) both I and II
    (B) II only   (D) neither I nor II

33. Real estate is
    (A) land and buildings
    (B) land and all permanent attachments to it
    (C) land only
    (D) land and everything growing on it

34. In an agency relationship, the employer is called the
    (A) seller   (C) principal
    (B) buyer   (D) broker

35. Real estate licenses, once received, are
    (A) valid indefinitely   (C) inheritable
    (B) filed in county record office   (D) valid for a limited period

36. In a lease contract, the tenant is the
    (A) lessee   (C) leasee
    (B) lessor   (D) leasor

37. Consideration that has value only to the person receiving it is
    (A) no consideration   (C) valuable consideration
    (B) good consideration   (D) good and valuable consideration

38. A general warranty deed protects the grantee against a loss by
    I.   casualty
    II. defective title
    (A) I only   (C) both I and II
    (B) II only   (D) neither I nor II

39. A lease that requires the tenant to pay operating expenses of the property is a
    _____ lease.
    (A) gross   (C) net
    (B) flat   (D) step

40. A house is valued at $55,560 for tax purposes. This is the
    (A) assessed value   (C) market value
    (B) appraised value   (D) replacement value

41. Taxes are due on October 15 of the year in which they are assessed. Tax rate is 38 mills. Assessed value is $48,500. If a sale of the property is closed on July 15, then at settlement (using the statutory year)
    (A) seller owes buyer $998.29   (C) seller owes buyer $844.71
    (B) buyer owes seller $998.29   (D) seller owes buyer $1843.00

42. The mortgagor's right to reestablish ownership after foreclosure is called
    (A) acceleration   (C) equity of redemption
    (B) resatisfaction right   (D) redemption provenance

43. Regulation Z
   (A) sets maximum interest rates on mortgage loans
   (B) determines discounts on VA loans
   (C) allows borrowers to repay loans ahead of time without penalty
   (D) requires that borrowers be informed of the cost of credit

44. Which of the following statements is true?
   I. A tenancy at will may be terminated at any time by either tenant or landlord.
   II. GRM stands for *Gross Reproduction Method.*
   (A) I only   (C) both I and II
   (B) II only   (D) neither I nor II

45. Which of the following is (are) functional obsolescence?
   I. some rooms have no electrical outlets
   II. one bathroom in a twelve-room house
   (A) I only   (C) both I and II
   (B) II only   (D) neither I nor II

46. An appraisal is a(an)
   (A) forecast of value   (C) prediction of value
   (B) estimate of value   (D) statement of exact value

47. At settlement, the buyer paid the seller $250.16 toward the annual tax bill of $763.20. If taxes are assessed for the calendar year and must be paid by July 15, what was the date of the settlement?
   (A) April 28   (C) March 30
   (B) September 2   (D) can't be determined

48. Which of the following statements is (are) false?
   I. A tax lien takes priority over all other liens.
   II. In a closing statement, earnest money is an item likely to be credited to the buyer.
   (A) I only   (C) both I and II
   (B) II only   (D) neither I nor II

49. If a borrower defaults on the payments to a mortgage loan, which clause allows the lender to demand immediate payment in full of the entire remaining loan balance?
   (A) defeasance clause   (C) acceleration clause
   (B) subrogation clause   (D) due-on-sale clause

50. Which of the following has the right of survivorship?
   (A) joint tenant   (C) tenant in common
   (B) tenant in severalty   (D) life tenant

51. In the covenant of seizin
   (A) the mortgagee states that he/she is foreclosing
   (B) the lessor states that the lessee has not abided by the lease contract
   (C) the grantor states that he/she owns the estate being transferred
   (D) the lessee states that he/she is being evicted

52. Escheat is
   (A) the right to cross someone else's land to get to the road
   (B) a variety of fraud exclusive to real estate
   (C) the right to inherit if there is no will
   (D) none of the above

53. A lot is 75 ft. wide and contains 825 sq. yds. How deep is it?
   (A) 6 rods
   (B) 88 ft.
   (C) 32 yds.
   (D) 1/16 mile

54. A broker's license is suspended for six months. The broker's two salespersons
   (A) also lose their licenses for six months
   (B) may continue to operate the broker's business
   (C) may, upon proper application, transfer their licenses to another broker
   (D) must place their licenses on inactive status for six months

55. An acre is equal to
      I. 4840 sq. yds.
      II. 10 sq. chains
   (A) I only
   (B) II only
   (C) both I and II
   (D) neither I nor II

56. The largest "bundle of rights" to real estate is a _____ estate.
   (A) leasehold
   (B) fee simple
   (C) life
   (D) homestead

57. In an exclusive right-to-sell listing,
      I. only one broker is authorized to act as the seller's agent
      II. if the seller finds the buyer, he/she still must pay the broker a commission
   (A) I only
   (B) II only
   (C) both I and II
   (D) neither I nor II

58. Salesperson Lois sold a house for $66,000. If her broker received 60% of the commission, and Lois's 45% share of that amount was $1158.30, what was the commission rate charged on the sale?
   (A) 6%
   (B) 6.5%
   (C) 7%
   (D) 7.5%

59. A 1/4-acre lot sold for $12,000. What was the price per sq. ft.?
   (A) $1.10
   (B) 27.5 cents
   (C) $2.20
   (D) $1.82

60. To prove that he/she is entitled to a commission, a broker must show that
      I. he/she was licensed throughout the transaction
      II. the price was a fair one
   (A) I only
   (B) II only
   (C) both I and II
   (D) neither I nor II

61. A broker receives two offers on the same property at the same time. He/she should
   (A) submit both offers
   (B) submit the better offer while trying to improve the other one
   (C) submit the better offer and reject the other one
   (D) reject both offers

62. Since the broker is the seller's agent, he/she may
   (A) accept an offer on behalf of the seller
   (B) solicit offers for the seller's listed property
   (C) try to negotiate better terms before submitting an offer
   (D) work to get the buyer the best possible price

63. Which of the following is not an "improvement" to land?
   (A) building
   (B) driveway
   (C) orchard
   (D) tomato crop

64. Which of the following is (are) usually exempt from property taxes?
    I. post office   II. hospital   III. theater
    (A) I only
    (B) I and II only
    (C) II only
    (D) I, II, and III

65. Real estate brokers advertise the most in (on)
    (A) radio and TV
    (B) newspapers
    (C) magazines
    (D) billboards

66. Which of the following is (are) evidence of involuntary alienation?
    I. deed in foreclosure
    II. quit claim
    (A) I only
    (B) II only
    (C) both I and II
    (D) neither I nor II

67. Which of the following is a nonfreehold estate?
    (A) fee simple estate
    (B) leasehold estate
    (C) life estate
    (D) none of the above

68. Sam's land has an easement to cross Fred's land to get to the lake. Sam subdivides his land into two parcels and sells one to George.
    (A) The easement no longer exists.
    (B) Sam's remaining land retains the easement, but George's does not.
    (C) Both Sam's remaining land and George's land have the easement rights.
    (D) Land benefiting from an easement cannot be subdivided.

69. A lease that specifies certain increases in rent over the life of the lease is a _____ lease.
    (A) reappraisal
    (B) net
    (C) step
    (D) percentage

70. A lease in which the tenant's rent is based at least in part upon the tenant's gross business revenues is a _____ lease.
    (A) reappraisal
    (B) net
    (C) step
    (D) percentage

71. Which level of government does not usually enact zoning laws?
    (A) federal
    (B) state
    (C) county
    (D) city

72. A court will appoint a(an) _____ to settle and manage the estate of a person who dies intestate.
    (A) trustee
    (B) executor
    (C) administrator
    (D) attorney-in-fact

73. An unlicensed person who shares in a real estate commission may be in violation of
    (A) federal law
    (B) license law
    (C) zoning law
    (D) common law

74. Millie wants to buy a house costing $73,500. For the loan she wants, she needs a 10% down payment and must pay a 1% origination fee, 2 points discount, and an 0.5% PMI fee. How much money does she need to obtain this loan?
    (A) $7350
    (B) $9665.25
    (C) $9922.50
    (D) $12,642

75. The interest rate on a loan is 9%. The interest for the month of April was $468.75. What was the loan balance at the beginning of April?
    (A) $52,083
    (B) $55,799
    (C) $60,000
    (D) $62,500

76. Usury is defined as
    (A) collecting more interest that that allowed by law
    (B) building a structure that extends over someone else's land
    (C) selling property for less than the asking price
    (D) selling real estate without a license

77. Mortgage loans guaranteed by agencies of the federal government include
    I. FHA loans   II. VA loans
    (A) I only   (C) both I and II
    (B) II only   (D) neither I nor II

78. In a settlement statement, accrued interest on an assumed loan is a credit to the
    I. buyer   II. seller
    (A) I only   (C) both I and II
    (B) II only   (D) neither I nor II

79. Sam wants to build a patio 60 ft. by 20 ft. and 4 in. thick. How many cu. yd. of concrete will he need?
    (A) 12.4   (C) 120
    (B) 14.8   (D) 400

80. A real estate license may be revoked for
    I. failing to account for money belonging to others
    II. submitting an offer for much less than the asking price
    III. representing both buyer and seller without the consent of both
    (A) I only   (C) III only
    (B) I and II only   (D) I and III only

Model Examination 5

Broker (ACT)

The following examination is for use by broker license examinees in states that use the ACT examination. Note also that this examination may be useful for those taking broker license examinations in states that prepare their own exams and that use the multiple-choice format. However, examinations in such states may have more or fewer questions than the 100 that appear on the general portion of the ACT broker examination.

If your state uses the Rectangular Survey *anywhere* in the state, be sure also to take Supplemental Examination 4 found in the next chapter. Although the ACT examination does not use questions that require you to fill out contracts or settlement forms, you may also want to take Supplemental Examinations 1, 2, and 3 in the next chapter for practice.

Directions: Select the choice, marked A, B, C, or D, that best answers the question or completes the thought. Mark your answers clearly on the answer sheet.

1. Will openly occupied Ward's land for a period of time, without interference from Ward, and then received fee simple title to the land. This was an example of
   (A) an easement in gross   (C) estoppel
   (B) adverse possession   (D) subrogation

2. Joe has Fred's power of attorney. Fred is called a(an)
   (A) agent in place   (C) lawyer
   (B) real estate broker   (D) attorney-in-fact

3. If the state takes title to real estate for which no legal owner can be found it is called
   (A) police power
   (B) tenancy
   (C) eminent domain
   (D) escheat

4. Which of the following types of deeds has no warranty?
   (A) executor's deed
   (B) quit claim
   (C) general warranty deed
   (D) trustee's deed

5. Sam does work on Joe's house, but is not paid. He may file a
   (A) mechanic's lien
   (B) satisfaction piece
   (C) notice of foreclosure
   (D) sheriff's auction

6. What is the cash-on-cash ratio for a property having a cash flow of $8360 and an initial investor's cash equity of $76,000?
   (A) 0.10%
   (B) 0.105
   (C) 0.11
   (D) 0.12

7. What percent of a square mile is 96 acres?
   (A) 21%
   (B) 19.6%
   (C) 15%
   (D) 12%

8. Which claim is paid first at a foreclosure?
   (A) tax lien
   (B) first mortgage
   (C) second mortgage
   (D) mechanic's lien

9. In an agency relationship, the principal is the
   (A) seller
   (B) buyer
   (C) broker
   (D) employer

10. In a lease contract, the landlord is the
    (A) leasee
    (B) leasor
    (C) lessee
    (D) lessor

11. If consideration has value only to the person receiving it, it is
    (A) personal consideration
    (B) good consideration
    (C) valuable consideration
    (D) good and valuable consideration

12. A lease that requires the landlord to pay operating expenses of the property is a _____ lease.
    (A) gross
    (B) flat
    (C) net
    (D) step

13. Taxes are due on June 1 of the year in which they are assessed. Tax rate is 41 mills. Assessed value is $53,250. If a sale of the property is closed on August 15, then at settlement (using the statutory year)
    (A) seller owes buyer $818.72
    (B) buyer owes seller $818.72
    (C) buyer owes seller $1364.53
    (D) seller owes buyer $1364.53

14. A properly done appraisal is a(an)
    (A) authentication of value
    (B) estimate of value
    (C) prediction of value
    (D) statement of exact value

15. If Murphy defaults on the payments to his mortgagee, under which clause may the lender demand immediate payment in full of the entire remaining loan balance?
    (A) defeasance clause
    (B) subrogation clause
    (C) acceleration clause
    (D) due-on-sale clause

16. Which of the following does not have the right of survivorship?
    (A) joint tenant
    (B) tenant in severalty
    (C) tenant by the entirety
    (D) all of the above

17. An easement can be
    (A) the right to cross someone else's land to get to the road
    (B) a variety of fraud exclusive to real estate
    (C) the right to inherit if there is no will
    (D) none of the above

18. A broker's license is revoked. The broker's salespeople
    (A) also have their licenses revoked
    (B) may continue to operate the broker's business
    (C) may, upon proper application, transfer their licenses to another broker
    (D) must place their licenses on inactive status for a year

19. In an exclusive right-to-sell listing,
    (A) only one broker is authorized to act as the seller's agent
    (B) if the seller finds the buyer, he/she still must pay the broker a commission
    (C) the broker must use his/her best efforts to solicit offers
    (D) all of the above

20. Among the broker's functions, he/she may
    (A) accept an offer on behalf of the seller
    (B) solicit offers for the seller's listed property
    (C) try to negotiate better terms before submitting an offer
    (D) work to get the buyer the best possible price

21. Which of the following is an "improvement" to land?
    (A) rezoning
    (B) driveway
    (C) orchard
    (D) all of the above

22. One of the following is a nonfreehold estate. Which is it?
    (A) fee simple estate
    (B) leasehold estate
    (C) life estate
    (D) dower estate

23. The rent for Sam's store is based at least in part upon Sam's gross business revenues. Sam's lease is a _____ lease.
    (A) reappraisal
    (B) net
    (C) step
    (D) percentage

24. What is usury?
    (A) collecting more interest than that allowed by law
    (B) building a structure that extends over someone else's land
    (C) selling property for less than the asking price
    (D) selling real estate without a license

25. Joe wants to build a patio 20 yd. by 20 ft. and 6 in. thick. How many cu. yd. of concrete will he need?
    (A) 22.2
    (B) 40.0
    (C) 20.0
    (D) 400

26. The number of sq. ft. in one acre is
    (A) 640
    (B) 43,560
    (C) 45,360
    (D) 53,460

27. How is the *gross rent multiplier* calculated?
   (A) market value/market rental
   (B) monthly payment/market rental
   (C) market rental/market price
   (D) sales price/market price

28. Minimum allowable construction standards are established by
   (A) building codes
   (B) zoning codes
   (C) environmental laws
   (D) condemnation laws

29. An allowed land use which is not normally permitted by the property's zoning classification is a(an)
   (A) dispensation
   (B) zone change
   (C) variance
   (D) restrictive covenant

30. Peeling paint and loose floorboards are examples of
   (A) physical deterioration
   (B) functional obsolescence
   (C) economic obsolescence
   (D) A and B only

31. The market approach would generally be most suitable for appraising
   (A) commercial and investment property
   (B) single-family homes
   (C) heavily mortgaged property
   (D) heavily insured property

32. A feature of a freehold estate is that it is
   (A) acquired without paying anything for it
   (B) always acquired by adverse possession
   (C) an estate of uncertain duration
   (D) any leasehold estate

33. One who has the appearance of owning land, but does not own it, has
   (A) good title
   (B) recorded title
   (C) constructive notice
   (D) color of title

34. A contract entered into by a minor can be
   (A) void
   (B) voidable by the minor
   (C) voidable by all parties
   (D) voidable by non-minor parties

35. One of the following will not terminate a lease. Which is it?
   (A) surrender
   (B) performance
   (C) vacancy
   (D) breech

36. In mortgage lending, one discount point is equal to
   (A) 1% of the sale price
   (B) 1% of the loan amount
   (C) 1% of the interest rate
   (D) 1% of the commission

37. Hooper's offer to purchase Looper's real estate stated that the offer would become void if it were not accepted within five days. The day after the offer was made, having heard nothing from Looper, Hooper wanted to withdraw his offer to Looper.
   (A) Hooper had to wait until the seven days had passed.
   (B) Hooper was required to notify Looper of his desire to withdraw the offer, and to give Looper "reasonable time" to accept or reject it.
   (C) Hooper could withdraw the offer immediately.
   (D) none of the above

38. In a real estate transaction, title to land passes
   (A) on the date shown on the deed
   (B) upon recordation of the deed
   (C) upon notarization of the deed
   (D) upon delivery of the deed

39. A fixture is
    (A) anything that cannot be removed from the real estate without leaving a hole larger than 6 inches.
    (B) anything the seller says is a fixture
    (C) anything needed for the proper use of the real estate
    (D) none of the above

40. The law that requires that all transfers of ownership rights to real estate be in writing is the
    (A) contract act
    (B) statute of limitations
    (C) statute of recordation
    (D) statute of frauds

41. All of the following should be recorded except
    (A) deed of trust
    (B) 20-year lease
    (C) executor's deed
    (D) contract of sale

42. In a typical mortgage loan transaction, the mortgagor is the
    (A) lender
    (B) borrower
    (C) appraiser
    (D) closing agent

43. A salesperson sold a property for $106,000. If the broker received 50% of the commission, and the salesperson's 60% share of that amount was $2544, what was the commission rate charged on the sale?
    (A) 7%
    (B) 7.5%
    (C) 7.75%
    (D) 8%

44. An estate that any party can terminate at any time is an estate
    (A) for years
    (B) at will
    (C) in possession
    (D) leasehold entailed

45. A listing contract says that the seller receives $32,000, and the broker receives all of the purchase price over $32,000 as his/her commission. This is a(an)_____ listing
    (A) open
    (B) net
    (C) multiple
    (D) exclusive

46. Jones leases a building that is damaged by a storm. Under common law,
    (A) the lease is no longer enforceable
    (B) Jones needn't pay rent until the building is repaired
    (C) Jones must repair the building, but may deduct the cost from rent
    (D) Jones must continue to pay rent until the lease expires

47. In each locality, real estate brokerage commissions are determined by
    (A) the local board of REALTORS®
    (B) the laws of the state
    (C) the board of estimate
    (D) agreement between property owner and broker

48. A lot sold for $98 a front ft. If the lot was 132 ft. deep and had an area of 6468 sq. ft., how much did the lot sell for?
    (A) $6468
    (B) $5771
    (C) $4800
    (D) $3900

49. Which of the following is required of "mutual agreement" in a contract?
    (A) offer and acceptance
    (B) proper consideration
    (C) description of the land
    (D) legal form

50. In most states, a six-month lease
    (A) must be in writing
    (B) need not be written
    (C) may not be in writing
    (D) ought not to be written

51. The expenses of settlement are
    (A) paid by the broker
    (B) paid by the seller
    (C) negotiated between buyer and seller
    (D) paid by the buyer

52. In most states a primary source of revenue for local government is
    (A) income taxes
    (B) sales taxes
    (C) property taxes
    (D) severance taxes

53. The purpose of real estate licensing laws is to protect
    (A) salespersons
    (B) lawyers and legislators
    (C) developers
    (D) the general public

54. In most states, an unlicensed person who collects a real estate commission is
    (A) subject to duress
    (B) guilty of a misdemeanor
    (C) guilty of a felony
    (D) inactivated

55. Salesperson Jones pockets an earnest money deposit and is found out. Jones's broker must
    I. report the incident to the state real estate authorities
    II. repay the money if Jones cannot do so
    III. pay to defend Jones in court, if necessary
    (A) I only
    (B) I and II only
    (C) II only
    (D) I and III only

56. Listed real estate should be advertised in the name of the
    (A) owner
    (B) salesperson
    (C) broker
    (D) closing agent

57. A 2.6-acre lot sold for $188,000. What was the price per sq. ft.?
    (A) $1.19
    (B) $1.55
    (C) $1.66
    (D) $1.82

58. Hamilton's broker license is revoked by the real estate commission. Hamilton may
    (A) apply for a salesperson's license
    (B) appeal the revocation to the courts
    (C) wait six months and apply for reinstatement
    (D) continue to operate his business until his existing listings are sold or have expired

59. Commissions from the sale of real estate
    (A) must be divided equally between broker and salesperson
    (B) must be divided equally among all participating brokers
    (C) are not taxable income
    (D) none of the above

60. Which is the superior lien?
    (A) tax lien
    (B) first mortgage
    (C) junior mortgage
    (D) mechanic's lien

61. A tenancy in severalty exists when
    (A) one person owns real estate
    (B) husband and wife own real estate together
    (C) any related persons own real estate together
    (D) none of the above

62. Which of the following is not a test of a fixture?
    (A) manner of attachment
    (B) intent of person who put it there
    (C) cost of the item
    (D) custom in the community

63. During the life of the life tenant, the remainderman has a(an)
    (A) easement in gross
    (B) reversionary interest
    (C) fee simple estate
    (D) renewing leasehold estate

64. At settlement, the seller paid the buyer $351.00 toward the annual tax bill of $972.00. If taxes are assessed for the calendar year and must be paid by July 15, what was the date of the settlement?
    (A) May 10
    (B) August 20
    (C) July 15
    (D) can't be determined

65. When parties to a contract agree to amend the contract, the document they prepare and sign is called a
    (A) deed amendment
    (B) satisfaction piece
    (C) novation
    (D) relinquishment

66. What kind of estate is received if the deed states that the grantor grants to the grantee "and his heirs and assigns forever"?
    (A) fee simple
    (B) leasehold
    (C) life estate
    (D) nonfreehold

67. A deed that conveys only the interest of the grantor is a
    (A) general warranty deed
    (B) bargain and sale deed
    (C) quit claim
    (D) special warranty deed

68. Real estate licenses should be
    (A) carried in the licensees' wallets
    (B) posted at the Real Estate Commission
    (C) posted in a public place in the broker's office
    (D) posted in the licensees' homes

69. The usefulness of the cost approach in appraisal may be limited if the subject property is
    (A) a new structure
    (B) functionally obsolescent
    (C) in an inactive market
    (D) proposed construction

70. A tenant paid rent at the beginning of the month; the property sold in the middle of the month. To prorate rent at settlement,
    (A) credit the buyer
    (B) credit the seller
    (C) both A and B
    (D) neither A nor B

71. Which of the following are considered "finance charges" for purposes of Regulation Z?
    (A) title insurance fee
    (B) deed preparation fee
    (C) monthly payment
    (D) none of the above

72. One who is employed by a broker to rent property but not to sell it
    (A) must be licensed
    (B) need not be licensed
    (C) must have a special rent-only license
    (D) must be a licensed broker

73. The process whereby someone may have real estate sold to pay a debt or claim is called
    (A) lien
    (B) foreclosure
    (C) covenant
    (D) defeasance

74. One who owns an undivided interest in real estate with at least one other person, and has the right of survivorship, is called a
    (A) tenant in severalty
    (B) life tenant
    (C) tenant in common
    (D) joint tenant

75. Which is not considered real estate?
    (A) fixtures
    (B) trees
    (C) chattels
    (D) sidewalk

76. One who dies and leaves no will is said to have died
    (A) without heirs
    (B) intestate
    (C) unbequeathed
    (D) unherited

77. A broker must keep funds entrusted to him, but belonging to others, in a(an)
    (A) office safe to which only he/she has the combination
    (B) savings account in the name of the person whose money it is
    (C) trust or escrow account
    (D) special account managed by the state

78. When a party to a contract has deliberately lied in order to mislead the other party(ies) into agreeing to the contract, it is an example of
    (A) fraud
    (B) misrepresentation
    (C) duress
    (D) defeasance

79. If a party to a contract acts so as to make performance under the contract impossible, it is an example of
    (A) discharge of contract
    (B) performance of contract
    (C) abandonment of contract
    (D) breach of contract

80. A minor may be bound by the courts to contracts for
    (A) personal property
    (B) realty only
    (C) necessaries
    (D) rent

81. Edgar purchases a house costing $77,500. The loan requires a 15% down payment, an origination fee of 0.75%, 2.25 points discount, and a 0.5% PMI fee. How much money does Edgar need for this?
    (A) $7750
    (B) $9665.25
    (C) $13,930.63
    (D) $14,337.50

82. A makes an offer to buy B's real estate. B makes a counteroffer to A.
    (A) A is bound by his original offer
    (B) A must accept the counteroffer
    (C) A's original offer no longer exists
    (D) A may not counteroffer back to B

83. A contract of sale of real estate must be signed by
    (A) buyer and seller
    (B) broker, buyer, and seller
    (C) buyer only
    (D) broker only

84. In a contract of sale, the seller is the
    (A) grantor
    (B) vendee
    (C) grantee
    (D) vendor

85. Which of the following statements is true?
    (A) To be valid, a contract of sale must be signed by the broker, if a broker assists in the transaction.
    (B) A corporation may be a party to a contract of sale.
    (C) A contract of sale need not be written if it is closed within one year.
    (D) One who is an attorney-in-fact must also be an attorney-at-law.

86. Which of the following must be included in a deed?
    (A) proper description of the real estate
    (B) street address, if the real estate is a house
    (C) area of the land ("more or less")
    (D) all of the above

87. A deed is recorded
    (A) to give public notice
    (B) to insure title
    (C) because it is the law
    (D) to avoid extra taxes

88. The part of a deed that defines or limits the quantity of estate granted is the
    (A) habendum
    (B) premises
    (C) equity
    (D) consideration

89. A final payment larger than the intermediate payments to a note is called a(an)
    (A) escalator
    (B) amortization
    (C) balloon
    (D) reappraisal

90. The interest rate on a loan is 11.5%. The interest for the month of July was $456.41. What was the loan balance at the beginning of July?
    (A) $55,173
    (B) $51,394
    (C) $47,625
    (D) $45,641

91. A conventional mortgage loan is
    (A) self-amortizing
    (B) not government insured/guaranteed
    (C) approved by FHA
    (D) uninsurable

92. The mortgage with the highest priority is usually the one
    (A) with the highest unpaid balance
    (B) with the highest original loan amount
    (C) with the highest interest rate
    (D) recorded first

93. The seller of real estate takes a note secured by a mortgage on the real estate as partial payment. The mortgage is
    (A) sale financed
    (B) a purchase-income mortgage
    (C) a secondary mortgage
    (D) a first lien

94. An *ad valorem* tax is one based upon
    (A) taxpayer's income
    (B) sale price of article taxed
    (C) size and/or weight
    (D) value of article taxed

95. One who is too young to be held to a contract is called
    (A) minority-impaired
    (B) youthful
    (C) unavailable in law
    (D) incompetent

96. A contract in which rights to use and occupy real estate are transferred for a specified period of time is a(an)
    (A) deed
    (B) easement
    (C) life estate
    (D) lease

97. Whenever all parties agree to the terms of a contract, there has been
    (A) mutual agreement
    (B) legality of object
    (C) consideration
    (D) competency

98. Recording a deed
    (A) passes title
    (B) gives constructive notice
    (C) insures title
    (D) removes liens

99. The multiple listing
    (A) causes lost commissions
    (B) is a listing-sharing organization of brokers
    (C) is illegal in some states
    (D) is a violation of anti-trust law

100. A contract that gives someone the right to buy during a specified time, but carries no obligation to do so, is a(an)
    (A) sale contract
    (B) land contract
    (C) option
    (D) bargain and sale

Model Examination 6

Broker (ASI)

The following examination is for use by broker license examinees in states that use the ASI examination. Note also that this examination may be useful for those taking broker license examinations in states that prepare their own exams and that use the multiple-choice format. However, examinations in such states may have more or fewer questions than the 80 that appear on the general portion of the ASI REAL (Real Estate Assessment for Licensure) broker examination.

If your state uses the Rectangular Survey *anywhere* in the state, be sure also to take Supplemental Examination 4 found in the next chapter. Although the ASI examination does not use questions that require you to fill out contracts or settlement forms, you may also want to take Supplemental Examinations 1, 2, and 3 in the next chapter for practice.

Directions: Select the choice, marked A, B, C, or D, that best answers the question or completes the thought. Mark your answers clearly on the answer sheet.

1. Jack wants to buy a house costing $111,500. The loan requires a down payment of $17,250, plus 1.5% origination fee, 2 points discount, and an 0.75% PMI fee. How much money does he need for this?
    (A) $17,250
    (B) $19,665.25
    (C) $21,988.75
    (D) $21,255.63

2. The interest rate on a loan is 10.5%. The interest for the month of April was $496.56. What was the loan balance at the beginning of April?
    (A) $49,656
    (B) $56,750
    (C) $60,000
    (D) $62,500

3. Usury is defined as
    (A) selling listed property for less than the seller's asking price
    (B) selling real estate without a license
    (C) collecting more interest than that allowed by law
    (D) acquiring an easement by adverse possession

4. Simpson's broker license is revoked by the real estate commission. Simpson may
   (A) apply for a salesperson's license
   (B) appeal the revocation to the courts
   (C) wait six months and apply for reinstatement
   (D) continue to work his existing listings

5. Real estate commission payments
   (A) must be divided equally among all participating brokers
   (B) must be paid directly to the salesperson
   (C) must be divided equally between broker and salesperson
   (D) none of the above

6. Which is the superior lien in the event of foreclosure?
   (A) tax lien   (C) junior mortgage
   (B) first mortgage   (D) home equity loan

7. A tenancy in severalty exists when
   (A) husband and wife own real estate together
   (B) any related persons own real estate together
   (C) one person owns real estate
   (D) the tenant has the right to sublet

8. One of the following is not a test of a fixture. Which is it?
   (A) manner of attachment   (C) time of attachment
   (B) intent of person who put it there   (D) custom in the community

9. Joe wants to build a driveway 70 ft. by 12. ft. and 5 in. thick. How many cu. yd. of concrete will he need?
   (A) 9.6   (C) 13
   (B) 11.8   (D) 84

10. So long as the life tenant is alive, the remainderman has a(an)
    (A) easement in gross   (C) fee simple estate
    (B) reversionary interest   (D) renewing leasehold estate

11. A deed conveying only the grantor's interest is a
    (A) general warranty deed   (C) quit claim
    (B) absolute deed   (D) special warranty deed

12. A real estate license should be
    (A) posted in the licensee's home
    (B) carried in the licensee's car
    (C) posted at the Real Estate Commission
    (D) posted in a public place in the broker's office

13. The usefulness of the cost approach in appraisal may be limited if the subject property is
    (A) a new building   (C) in an inactive market
    (B) functionally obsolescent   (D) under construction

14. A landlord receives rent at the beginning of the month. The property is sold ten days later. To prorate rent at settlement,
    (A) credit the buyer   (C) both A and B
    (B) credit the seller   (D) neither A nor B

15. Which of the following are considered "finance charges" for purposes of Regulation Z?
    (A) title insurance fee
    (B) deed preparation fee
    (C) monthly payment
    (D) prepaid interest

16. Which method of advertising do real estate brokers use the most?
    (A) radio and TV
    (B) magazines
    (C) newspapers
    (D) billboards

17. Which of the following is a nonfreehold estate?
    (A) fee simple estate
    (B) leasehold estate
    (C) life estate
    (D) qualified fee simple

18. A lease that spells out specific increases in rent during the term of the lease is a _____ lease.
    (A) reappraisal
    (B) net
    (C) step
    (D) percentage

19. A clause in a percentage lease that allows the lessor to cancel the lease if the lessee's revenues are not at least a minimum amount is a _____ clause.
    (A) nonperformance
    (B) net
    (C) defeasance
    (D) recapture

20. Zoning laws are usually not enacted by _____ government.
    (A) federal
    (B) state
    (C) county
    (D) city

21. A court appoints a(an) _____ to settle and manage the estate of a person who dies intestate.
    (A) trustee
    (B) executor
    (C) administrator
    (D) attorney-in-fact

22. A lot 59 ft. 6 in. wide contains 535.5 sq. yd. How deep is it?
    (A) 5.33 rods
    (B) 88 ft.
    (C) 27 yd.
    (D) 0.03 mile

23. A broker's license is suspended for six months. Salespersons whose licenses are held by this broker
    (A) may apply to transfer their licenses to another broker
    (B) must place their licenses on inactive status for six months
    (C) also lose their licenses for six months
    (D) may continue to operate the broker's business

24. The largest "bundle of rights" to real estate is a _____ estate.
    (A) remainder
    (B) fee simple
    (C) life
    (D) homestead

25. One of broker Mack's salespeople sold a house for $82,000. Mack received 48% of the commission and paid his salesperson 55% of that amount. How much did Mack keep, if the commission rate was 7%?
    (A) $1239.84
    (B) $1515.36
    (C) $2583.00
    (D) $3157.00

26. A 1.6-acre lot sold for $25,100. What was the price per sq. ft.?
    (A) $3.61
    (B) $0.36
    (C) $1.88
    (D) $2.29

27. A broker receives two offers on the same property at the same time. He/she should
    (A) reject both offers
    (B) submit both offers to the property owner
    (C) submit the better offer while trying to improve the other one
    (D) submit the better offer and reject the other one

28. As the seller's agent a broker may
    (A) reject an offer on behalf of the seller
    (B) work to get the buyer the best possible price
    (C) solicit offers for the seller's listed property
    (D) try to negotiate better terms before submitting an offer

29. Which of the following is not an "improvement" to land?
    (A) building   (C) corn crop
    (B) sidewalk   (D) flower bed

30. Unlicensed persons who receive shares of real estate commission payments may be in violation of
    (A) federal law   (C) zoning law
    (B) license law   (D) common law

31. A person who is employed by a broker to rent property but not to sell it
    (A) must be licensed   (C) must have a special rent-only license
    (B) need not be licensed   (D) must be a licensed broker

32. Which of the following statements is true?
    (A) One who is an attorney-in-fact must also be an attorney-at-law.
    (B) To be valid, a contract of sale must be signed by the broker.
    (C) A corporation may be a party to a contract of sale.
    (D) A contract of sale need not be written if it is closed within one year.

33. Which of the following must be included in a deed?
    (A) street address, if the real estate is a house
    (B) area of the land ("more or less")
    (C) proper description of land and improvements
    (D) proper description of land

34. A deed is recorded
    (A) to give public notice   (C) because it is the law
    (B) to insure title   (D) to avoid extra taxes

35. The clause that defines or limits the quantity of estate granted in a deed is the
    (A) habendum   (C) addendum
    (B) premises   (D) consideration

36. In a mortgage, the contract specifies payments of $200 a month, and a final payment of $6,000 at the end of 30 years. The final payment is called a(an)
    (A) escalator   (C) balloon
    (B) amortization   (D) parachute

37. The process by which real estate is sold to pay debts or claims is known as
    (A) lien   (C) covenant
    (B) foreclosure   (D) defeasance

38. One who owns an undivided interest in real estate with at least one other person, without the right of survivorship, is called a
    (A) tenant in severalty   (C) tenant in common
    (B) life tenant   (D) joint tenant

39. Brokers often hold funds belonging to others. They must keep these funds in a(an)
    (A) office safe to which only the broker has the combination
    (B) savings account in the name of the person whose money it is
    (C) trust or escrow account
    (D) special account managed by the state

40. When a party to a contract unintentionally misleads the other party(ies) into agreeing to the contract, it is an example of
    (A) fraud   (C) duress
    (B) misrepresentation   (D) defeasance

41. If a party to a contract is responsible for making performance under it impossible, it is an example of
    (A) specific performance   (C) abandonment of contract
    (B) breach of contract   (D) nonperformance of contract

42. At settlement, the buyer took over the seller's one-year property insurance policy which had been purchased on February 1 for $324.00. If the seller was credited for $63.00 at settlement, what was the settlement date?
    (A) May 10   (C) July 19
    (B) November 20   (D) can't be determined

43. A minor may be bound by the courts to contracts for
    (A) personalty only   (C) rent only
    (B) realty only   (D) necessaries

44. Fred makes a counteroffer in response to Joe's offer to buy Fred's lot.
    (A) Joe may not counteroffer back to Fred.
    (B) Joe is bound by his original offer.
    (C) Joe must accept the counteroffer as is, reject it, or let it expire.
    (D) If Joe makes a counteroffer, Fred may accept Joe's original offer.

45. A contract of sale of real estate must be signed by
    (A) buyer only   (C) buyer and seller
    (B) broker, buyer, and seller   (D) broker only

46. In a quit claim, the seller is the
    (A) grantor   (C) grantee
    (B) vendee   (D) vendor

47. If a property has more than one mortgage on it, the one with the highest priority is usually the one
    (A) with the highest interest rate
    (B) recorded first
    (C) with the highest upaid balance
    (D) with the highest original loan amount

48. The seller of real estate takes a note secured by a mortgage on the real estate as partial payment. The mortgage is
    (A) sale financed   (C) a secondary mortgage
    (B) a purchase-money mortgage   (D) a first lien

49. The market value of a house is $86,000. If property is assessed at 35% of market value and the annual tax rate is 42 mills, how much is the tax?
    (A) $1264.20   (C) $3511.00
    (B) $2102.40   (D) $3612.00

Questions 50 to 53 refer to the following situation:

May buys a house from Ray. The price is $77,900. May gets a VA loan for 90% of the purchase price. The loan discount is 2.5 points. The broker's commission on the sale is 6%. The contract interest rate on the VA loan is 9.75%.

50. What is the dollar amount of the discount?
    (A) $759.53
    (B) $1182.20
    (C) $1752.75
    (D) $1947.50

51. What is the lender's effective rate of return on the loan?
    (A) 12.25%
    (B) 7.25%
    (C) 10.0625%
    (D) 9.6225%

52. Who pays the discount on the VA loan?
    (A) May
    (B) Ray
    (C) broker
    (D) VA

53. To whom is the discount paid?
    (A) broker
    (B) lender
    (C) VA
    (D) May

54. An ad valorem taxes are based upon
    (A) size and/or weight
    (B) value of article taxed
    (C) taxpayer's income
    (D) sale price of article taxed

55. Whenever all parties agree to the terms of a contract, there has been
    (A) reality of consent
    (B) legality of object
    (C) consideration
    (D) competency

56. A contract that gives someone the right to buy during a specified time, but carries no obligation to do so, is a(an)
    (A) sale contract
    (B) land contract
    (C) option
    (D) bargain and sale

57. The amount remaining each year after deducting expenses from rent receipts and other property income is
    (A) cash-on-cash
    (B) cash depletion
    (C) cash amortization
    (D) cash flow

58. A property in a run-down neighborhood may lose value due to
    (A) physical deterioration
    (B) functional obsolescence
    (C) economic obsolescence
    (D) red lining

59. Which of the following is realty?
    (A) 1-year lease
    (B) equitable title
    (C) land contract
    (D) life estate

60. Which of the following can adequately describe the consideration in a deed?
    (A) "for ten dollars and other valuable consideration"
    (B) "for natural love and affection"
    (C) the actual amount of consideration paid
    (D) all of the above

61. Which type of depreciation generally is not curable?
    (A) physical deterioration
    (B) functional obsolescence
    (C) economic obsolescence
    (D) all of the above

62. What is the cash-on-cash ratio for a property that has a cash flow of $32,300 and an initial investor's cash equity of $222,750?
    (A) 7.05%   (C) 0.145
    (B) 0.0705   (D) 0.113

63. What percent of a sq. mi. is a lot 1085 ft. by 900 ft.?
    (A) 28.5%   (C) 3.5%
    (B) 18.494%   (D) 1.57%

64. Max has a six-month lease that says the rent is $100 per week. The lease does not say when the rent shall be paid. When does Max have to pay?
    (A) at the end of each month   (C) at the end of the lease period
    (B) at the beginning of each month   (D) at the end of each week

65. Miller got fee simple title to land that had belonged to Payne by using and occupying it openly for a certain time, unknown to and unmolested by Payne. This is an example of
    (A) estoppel   (C) an easement in gross
    (B) subrogation   (D) adverse possession

66. Baker gives Able his power of attorney. Able is called a(an)
    (A) agent in place   (C) lawyer
    (B) real estate broker   (D) attorney-in-fact

67. When the state takes title to real estate for which no legal owner can be found, it is called
    (A) police power   (C) eminent domain
    (B) tenancy   (D) escheat

68. Moe receives title to Zoe's real estate after Zoe dies without a will. Moe has received
    (A) title by descent   (C) an easement
    (B) clouded title   (D) legacy title

69. A parcel of land is 1077 ft. by 607 ft. How many acres does it contain?
    (A) 14.9   (C) 13.22
    (B) 9.88   (D) more than 15

70. Of the following instruments, the one with no warranty is the
    (A) executor's deed   (C) general warranty deed
    (B) quit claim   (D) trustee's deed

71. A workman who is not paid for work that improved real estate may file a
    (A) labor judgment   (C) mechanic's lien
    (B) novation   (D) lis pendens

72. When a property is foreclosed, which of the following claims takes first priority?
    (A) mechanic's lien   (C) general lien
    (B) mortgage dated June 11, 1979   (D) mortgage dated July 22, 1987

73. In an agency relationship, the employer is called the
    (A) seller   (C) principal
    (B) agent   (D) broker

74. If consideration in a deed has value only to the person receiving it, it is
    (A) no consideration   (C) valuable consideration
    (B) good consideration   (D) good and valuable consideration

75. A lease that does not require the tenant to pay any of the operating expenses of the property is a _____ lease.
    (A) gross
    (B) flat
    (C) net
    (D) step

76. Sam's contractor quotes "per square foot" costs of $51.10 for the first 1600 sq. ft. of house, $42.25 for square footage over 1600, $22.50 for basements, $29.20 for attached garages. Sam wants a 2100 sq. ft., 2-story house, with a basement, and a 420-sq. ft. attached garage. What price (to nearest $1000) will the contractor quote for the entire job?
    (A) $127,000
    (B) $139,000
    (C) $146,000
    (D) $162,000

77. A house is valued at $81,225 for tax purposes. This is the
    (A) assessed value
    (B) appraised value
    (C) market value
    (D) replacement value

78. Simmy buys a house and gets a mortgage loan for $128,000 to pay for it. Simmy becomes a
    (A) vendor
    (B) mortgagor
    (C) lessee
    (D) mortgagee

79. A function of Regulation Z is to
    (A) determine discounts on VA loans
    (B) set maximum interest rates on mortgage loans
    (C) allow borrowers to repay loans ahead of time without penalty
    (D) require that borrowers be informed of the cost of credit

80. An investor purchased 3 lots. Lot A cost $11,000, Lot B cost 2.5 times the cost of A, and lot C cost half the cost of B. She then sold lots A and B for 25% more than the cost of all 3 lots. If she then sold lot C for twice its cost, what is her total profit (to the nearest $100)?
    (A) $19,100
    (B) $26,800
    (C) $33,800
    (D) none of the above

Model Examination 7
True-False, Fill-In State Questions.

The following examination is for the use of examinees in states that write their own examinations, and that may make use of the true-false or fill-in format. This examination has 140 questions. Questions 1–80 are true-false (numbers 74-80 concern arithmetic); questions 81–140 are fill-ins (numbers 134-140 concern arithmetic).

Note that states that use either or both of these kinds of questions may use other kinds as well — especially multiple-choice — so be sure to take and study the other model examinations as well.

PART A: TRUE-FALSE (80 questions)

Directions: In the space provided before each statement, mark *T* if the statement is true or *F* if it is false.

_____ 1. The parties to a lease are the lessor and the lessee.

_____ 2. "Permanent" loans are loans with terms in excess of thirty years.

_____ 3. A mortgage that covers more than one real property is called a blanket mortgage.

_____ 4. The object of a novation is to effect a substitution of an item in a contract.

_____ 5. It is possible to exchange real estate for real estate without paying a capital gains tax.

_____ 6. Some properties may be subject to real property taxes levied by more than one jurisdiction.

_____ 7. A part-time real estate salesperson is not required to abide by the Fair Housing Act.

_____ 8. If lenders fail to make required disclosures, they may be sued for actual damages, plus twice the amount of the finance charge, as well as court costs and attorney's fees.

_____ 9. One who discovers that he has entered into a contract with a minor may void the contract.

_____ 10. A contract of sale is invalid if it is not signed by a licensed real estate broker.

_____ 11. A lease of one year or less need not necessarily be written.

_____ 12. The warranty in a deed guarantees that the real estate will be in good condition for a certain length of time.

_____ 13. A licensee who has had his license revoked for violating the license law may continue to operate his business if he has no other means of support.

_____ 14. If an adult discovers that he has signed a contract of sale with a minor, he can refuse to grant title until the minor reaches the age of majority.

_____ 15. The Fair Housing Act does not apply to an owner selling his own home, which is the home he owns.

_____ 16. If a listed property is destroyed by fire, the listing contract is terminated.

_____ 17. If a borrower misses a payment on his mortgage loan, he will be evicted immediately.

_____ 18. Under common law, the broker earns his commission only after the sale has been closed and title has been transferred to the buyer.

_____ 19. A tax lien takes priority over all other liens.

_____ 20. The capitalization approach attempts to place a value on the right to receive the income a property will generate in the future.

_____ 21. A contract has the "force of law" among the parties to it.

_____ 22. A minor can disaffirm all of his contracts and incur no penalty at all for doing so regardless of the damage it may cause other parties.

_____ 23. Today over 90% of all housing is subject to the Fair Housing Act.

_____ 24. No license is required for someone who sells no more than two properties per year for a commission.

_____ 25. An executor's deed would contain a full and general warranty.

_____ 26. It is a violation of license law for a broker to charge consistently lower commissions than his competitors.

_____ 27. An object cannot have market value if it cannot be transferred from someone who has it to someone who does not have it.

_____ 28. It is illegal for someone to intimidate someone else into violating the Fair Housing Act.

_____ 29. All leases of six months or longer must be in writing to be enforceable.

_____ 30. Licensed real estate brokers must make full accounting for all trust monies that have come into their care, if requested to do so by the proper state authorities.

_____ 31. A warranty deed is the best kind of deed for a grantee to receive.

_____ 32. Charges or premiums for credit life insurance required by the lender are considered finance charges.

_____ 33. A restrictive covenant is a clause in a lease that prevents the tenant from doing certain things with or on the leased premises.

_____ 34. After a contract of sale is entered into, it is possible that if the building burns down, the loss will be the buyer's.

_____ 35. The sale price and conditions of the sale should be clearly stated in the contract of sale.

_____ 36. An agency relationship is one of employment.

_____ 37. The Fair Housing Act would not apply to a building containing three dwelling units, one of which is occupied by the owner.

_____ 38. A lease of more than one year must be in writing to be enforceable.

_____ 39. Sellers must pay discount, or points, on FHA/VA loans because it is illegal for these fees to be charged to borrowers.

_____ 40. A quitclaim deed does not include a description of the warranty to the grantee.

_____ 41. A contract for the exchange of real estate may have no more than two parties.

_____ 42. A corporation may be a party to a contract.

_____ 43. Real estate owners benefit from many of the services provided by local government with the money collected from real property taxes.

_____ 44. A satisfaction piece is a document that states that FHA or VA is satisfied with the fairness of the price being charged for a particular property.

_____ 45. A net lease is one that requires the tenant to pay operating expenses.

_____ 46. License laws prohibit discrimination by licensees with regard to race.

_____ 47. There is no way that a property owner can appeal an assessment he considers incorrect.

_____ 48. The value of real estate can fall as well as rise.

_____ 49. Every option must have consideration.

_____ 50. A deed must show consideration, though it is usually permissible to state a nominal amount, i.e., less than the true amount.

_____ 51. All states have real estate licensing laws.

_____ 52. Appraisal fees are not considered as finance charges in real estate credit transactions.

_____ 53. Tenancy in severalty refers to land ownership by one person.

_____ 54. Things such as friendship, love, etc., are called "good consideration" if they are used as the consideration in a contract.

_____ 55. In a contractual arrangement it is not required that equal consideration accrue to all the parties.

_____ 56. A tenancy at will may be terminated at any time by either tenant or landlord.

_____ 57. If an agent brings an offer that exactly conforms to the requirements spelled out in the listing, the employer may reject it without incurring any liability to the third party who made the offer.

_____ 58. An easement is the right to use property of another upon payment of rent.

_____ 59. Federal law prohibits the sale of real estate without a license.

_____ 60. A lease that calls for a level amount of rent throughout the lease period is called a "straight" or "flat" lease.

_____ 61. GRM stands for Great Reproduction Method.

_____ 62. Loan discounts are considered a finance charge in real estate credit transactions.

_____ 63. One who has permission to use land, but no lease, is said to have license.

_____ 64. All real estate credit transactions, except agricultural credit, are covered under the Truth in Lending Act.

_____ 65. It is against licensing law for a licensee to collect commission from more than one party to a transaction.

_____ 66. A suit in court that asks that a party to a contract be required to do what he agreed upon is not valid.

_____ 67. A real estate broker may delegate his responsibilities to licensed salespersons in his employ.

_____ 68. The property tax rate is always applied to the market value of the property.

_____ 69. A deed must be in writing, and if it is to be recorded it must be acknowledged as well.

_____ 70. Functional obsolescence is exemplified by a building becoming out-of-date or out of style.

_____ 71. A contract of sale need not be written if it is closed within one year.

_____ 72. Tenancy at sufferance occurs when a tenant stays on after the expiration of a lease.

_____ 73. To completely free yourself of a debt, merely assign that debt to another.

_____ 74. If Harrison rents a 35 ft. × 15 ft. office for $8.40 per sq. ft. per year, his monthly rental is $367.50.

_____ 75. A tract bought for $50,000 two years ago has increased in value by 10% per year in each of the two years (compounded). It is now worth $60,000.

_____ 76. Simmons borrowed $17,000.00. He pays $155.83 per month interest. His annual interest rate is 11%.

_____ 77. An apartment is 60 ft. × 24 ft. and has 9 ft. high walls. It contains 480 cu. yd.

_____ 78. The amount of $2000 is borrowed for 3 years and 9 months at an annual interest rate of 12%. The total amount of interest due is $800.

_____ 79. Excavation for the foundation of a new building measured 90 ft. by 50 ft. and was 12 ft. deep. At a price of $17.75 per cu. yd., the total cost of the excavation was $35,500.

_____ 80. $82 is 8% of $1025.

PART B: FILL-INS (60 questions)

Directions: In the space provided, fill in the missing word or phrase that best completes the thought or statement.

81. The value that the appraiser usually seeks is _____.

82. _____ rights in some states determine that a wife shall receive at least a certain portion of her deceased husband's real estate.

83. When an agency expires because all parties have done what was agreed upon, it is said to have been terminated by _____ .

84. In an agency relationship, the employer is called the _____ .

85. A loan that requires periodic payments that will pay the loan partly or fully by the time the loan term ends is called a(n) _____ loan.

86. _____ is defined as land and all attachments to it.

87. A mortgage loan payable by a buyer of property to the seller of that same property is called a(n) _____ .

88. A listing in which the broker receives a commission only if he actually secures the buyer himself is called a(n) _____ listing.

89. Ownership by more than one person, with each owner having an undivided interest that he may dispose of as he wishes, is called _____ .

90. If the capitalization rate is raised, the resultant value will _____ .

91. Rights to use leased property may be transferred through a(n) _____ .

92. When mortgaged real estate is being exchanged and mortgages will be assumed by new owners, the _____ for both properties should be evaluated to determine whether it is a fair trade.

93, 94, 95. The three kinds of depreciation that appraisers recognize in real estate are _____ , _____ , and _____ .

96, 97, 98. The three approaches to appraisal are _____ , _____ , and _____ .

99. When a tenant leases all or part of his rented premises to a third party, this new lease is called a _____ .

100. Unpaid and overdue property taxes become a _____ on the property.

101. If, after foreclosure, the proceeds from the sale of foreclosed property are not enough to pay the debt owed, the lender may secure a _____ for the unpaid balance, which requires the borrower to pay the unrecovered amount.

102. Upon final payment of an installment land contract, the buyer should receive a _____ .

103. A state in which a mortgage is considered to be a transfer of title to the lender is called a _____ state.

104. A lease that requires the landlord to pay all operating expenses of the property is a _____ .

105. The lender of a mortgage loan is called the _____ .

106. The best way to free oneself of an assumed obligation is to obtain a _____ from the lender.

107. A claim entered by one who has done work to improve real estate, but who has not been paid for it, is a _____ .

108. A *mill* is an amount of money equal to _____ .

109. The contract whose parties are the grantor and the grantee is the _____ .

110. A lease that requires the tenant to pay part of his business revenue taken in on the leased property as all or part of the rent is a _____ .

111. At the time a contract of sale is created, _____ title passes to the buyer.

112. The Federal Fair Housing Act was enacted in the year _____.

113. A broker who solicits listings in a transitional area by trying to convince owners that values will decline because of the influx of people of another race, creed, color, or national origin is guilty of _____.

114. The Truth in Lending Act is enforced through application of Regulation _____.

115. A contract in which A agrees to give B the right to buy A's property at a specific price, during a specific time, is a(n) _____.

116. If a residence is used as collateral for a loan that is *not* a first mortgage loan used to purchase one's dwelling, the borrower has _____ business days in which he can cancel the transaction.

117. A lease in which the rent is automatically raised periodically during the lease period is a _____ lease.

118. The law that requires that most real estate contracts be written is _____.

119. The parties to a contract of sale are called the _____.

120. The _____ rule prevents oral testimony from being introduced when it conflicts with written evidence.

121. Minors have the right to _____ their transactions.

122. The part of the deed that contains the warranty(ies), if any, is called the _____.

123. A deed that conveys only the interest of the grantor is a _____.

124. With an option goes the right but not the _____ to buy.

125. The property tax is based on the value of the thing taxed, so it is a form of _____ tax.

126. A millage rate can also be expressed as so many dollars per _____.

127. The term APR stands for _____.

128. The parties to a deed are called the _____ and _____.

129, 130, 131, 132, 133. The five essential parts to a contract are _____, _____, _____, _____, and _____.

134. If the assessed valuation is $40,000, and the tax rate is 77 mills based on 28% of assessed value, the tax is _____.

135. Four equally sized lots contain a total of 1.77 acres. What is the size of each lot? _____

136. A house measuring 40 ft. × 28 ft. was on a 71.2 ft. × 100 ft. lot. An addition measuring 20 ft. × 24 ft. was put on the house. What percentage of the *uncovered* area of the lot was used by the addition? _____

137. A specific parcel of real estate has been assessed at a value of $6500. The local tax rate is 30 mills. What is the amount of the tax? _____

138. A loan of $35,000 carrying an annual interest rate of 9% will have a quarterly interest charge of _____.

139. A tract of 3.8 acres contains _____ sq. ft.

140. The loan on a property is 80% of the sale price. The interest rate is 9½%; the first monthly payment is $285. What is the sale price? _____

Chapter 25 / Supplemental Examinations: Contracts, Settlement Statements, Rectangular Survey

The examinations in this section are designed to meet the special requirements of certain states.

Supplemental Examinations 1 and 2 concern listing and sales contracts respectively. All states require knowledge of these contracts of *broker* examinees; many will require them of sales examinees as well. Check with your state agency to see if you have to study such material. When taking these examinations, you will first read a narrative, which describes a certain situation; from that information you must fill out a contract, a form for which is provided. Then, *using the completed filled-out form as a reference,* you are asked to answer questions. The exam keys in this book include correctly made-out forms.

Supplemental Examination 3 considers settlement statements (called *closing statements* in some states). Normally, knowledge of these is required *only* of broker applicants. You will read a narrative, from which you will get the information to fill out the blank settlement sheet provided. Then, *using only the filled-out form as a reference,* you are asked to answer questions. A correctly filled-out settlement statement is included as part of the key to this examination.

Supplemental Examination 4 concerns the Rectangular Survey (or Government Survey) method of property description. Take this examination if it applies to your state.

Supplemental Examination 1
(Listing Contract)

LISTING CONTRACT NARRATIVE

On June 16, 1983, you contact Mr. Sydney Purvis, whose two-story brick house has a "For Sale by Owner" sign in front. The home is a two-story brick house with four bedrooms (one downstairs) and three baths (one downstairs also). It is federal colonial in styling. The address is 8811 Quagmire Place, being Lot 18, Block G, Quagmire Estates Addition, Benedictine County, Utah. You have done some checking and know that Mr. Purvis has bought a new home. The house he is selling has natural gas heat and hot water, central air conditioning, no basement, a breakfast area in the kitchen, a 98 ft. × 155 ft. lot, is 12 years old, has an entrance foyer and a center hall plan, and an attic with pull-down stairs. It is assessed for $26,550 and the tax rate is 88 mills. Mr. Purvis is moving in a week, so you can offer immediate possession.

The next morning you call him at his home (555-1116) and get no answer, so you call his office (555-2822) and he agrees to see you immediately to sign a listing agreement. At that time you find out that his current mortgage loan is not assumable, and that he will include all appliances (refrigerator, dishwasher, and dryer). He prefers to show the home only by appointment and will give you a key to keep handy at your office. The home has 2510 sq. ft. Nearby schools are Dimbulb Elementary, Nitwit Junior High, Ignoramus High School, and

St. Vitus Parochial. You and Mr. Purvis agree on a 90-day listing, at $54,500, with a 7½% commission, and your broker signs it.

Fill out the accompanying contract ("Exclusive Authorization to Sell" form) according to this information.

EXCLUSIVE AUTHORIZATION TO SELL

SALES PRICE: _____ TYPE HOME _____ TOTAL BEDROOMS ____ TOTAL BATHS ____

ADDRESS: _____ JURISDICTION OF ____

AMT. OF LOAN TO BE ASSUMED $ _____ AS OF WHAT DATE: _____ TAXES & INS. INCLUDED ____ YEARS TO GO ____ AMOUNT PAYABLE MONTHLY $ ____ @ __ % TYPE LOAN

MORTGAGE COMPANY _____ 2nd TRUST $ _____

ESTIMATED EXPECTED RENT MONTHLY $ _____ TYPE OF APPRAISAL REQUESTED _____

OWNER'S NAME _____ PHONES: (HOME) _____ (BUSINESS) _____

TENANTS NAME _____ PHONES: (HOME) _____ (BUSINESS) _____

POSSESSION _____ DATE LISTED: _____ EXCLUSIVE FOR _____ DATE OF EXPIRATION _____

LISTING BROKER _____ PHONE _____ KEY AVAILABLE AT _____

LISTING SALESMAN _____ HOME PHONE _____ HOW TO BE SHOWN _____

(1) ENTRANCE FOYER □ CENTER HALL □	(18) AGE	AIR CONDITIONING	(32) TYPE KITCHEN CABINETS
(2) LIVING ROOM SIZE FIREPLACE □	(19) ROOFING	TOOL HOUSE	(33) TYPE COUNTER TOPS
(3) DINING ROOM SIZE	(20) GARAGE SIZE	PATIO	(34) EAT-IN SIZE KITCHEN
(4) BEDROOM TOTAL: DOWN UP	(21) SIDE DRIVE □	CIRCULAR DRIVE □	(35) BREAKFAST ROOM
(5) BATHS TOTAL: DOWN UP	(22) PORCH □ SIDE □ REAR □	SCREENED □	(36) BUILT-IN OVEN & RANGE
(6) DEN SIZE FIREPLACE □	(23) FENCED YARD	OUTDOOR GRILL □	(37) SEPARATE STOVE INCLUDED
(7) FAMILY ROOM SIZE FIREPLACE □	(24) STORM WINDOWS □	STORM DOORS □	(38) REFRIGERATOR INCLUDED
(8) RECREATION ROOM SIZE FIREPLACE □	(25) CURBS & GUTTERS □	SIDEWALKS □	(39) DISHWASHER INCLUDED
(9) BASEMENT SIZE	(26) STORM SEWERS □	ALLEY □	(40) DISPOSAL INCLUDED
NONE □ 1/4 □ 1/3 □ 1/2 □ 3/4 □ FULL □	(27) WATER SUPPLY		(41) DOUBLE SINK SINGLE SINK
(10) UTILITY ROOM SIZE	(28) SEWER □	SEPTIC □	STAINLESS STEEL PORCELAIN
TYPE HOT WATER SYSTEM:	(29) TYPE GAS: NATURAL □	BOTTLED □	(42) WASHER INCLUDED DRYER INCLUDED
(11) TYPE HEAT	(30) WHY SELLING		(43) PANTRY EXHAUST FAN
(12) EST. FUEL COST			(44) LAND ASSESSMENT $
(13) ATTIC □	(31) DIRECTIONS TO PROPERTY		(45) IMPROVEMENTS $
PULL DOWN STAIRWAY □ REGULAR STAIRWAY □ TRAP DOOR □			(46) TOTAL ASSESSMENT $
(14) MAIDS ROOM □ TYPE BATH			(47) TAX RATE
LOCATION			(48) TOTAL ANNUAL TAXES $
(15) NAME OF BUILDER			(49) LOT SIZE
(16) SQUARE FOOTAGE			(50) LOT NO. BLOCK SECTION
(17) EXTERIOR OF HOUSE			

NAME OF SCHOOLS: ELEMENTARY: _____ JR. HIGH _____

HIGH _____ PAROCHIAL _____

PUBLIC TRANSPORTATION: _____

NEAREST SHOPPING AREA: _____

REMARKS: _____

Date: _____

In consideration of the services of _____ (herein called "Broker") to be rendered to the undersigned (herein called "Owner"), and of the promise of Broker to make reasonable efforts to obtain a Purchaser therefor, Owner hereby lists with Broker the real estate and all improvements thereon which are described above (all herein called "the property"), and Owner hereby grants to Broker the exclusive and irrevocable right to sell such property from 12:00 Noon on _____, 19____ until 12:00 Midnight on _____, 19__ (herein called "period of time"), for the price of _____ Dollars ($ _____) or for such other price and upon such other terms (including exchange) as Owner may subsequently authorize during the period of time.

It is understood by Owner that the above sum or any other price subsequently authorized by Owner shall include a cash fee of _____ per cent of such price or other price which shall be payable by Owner to Broker upon consummation by any Purchaser or Purchasers of a valid contract of sale of the property during the period of time and whether or not Broker was a procuring cause of any such contract of sale.

If the property is sold or exchanged by Owner, or by Broker or by any other person to any Purchaser to whom the property was shown by Broker or any representative of Broker within sixty (60) days after the expiration of the period of time mentioned above, Owner agrees to pay to Broker a cash fee which shall be the same percentage of the purchase price as the percentage mentioned above.

Broker is hereby authorized by Owner to place a "For Sale" sign on the property and to remove all signs of other brokers or salesmen during the period of time, and Owner hereby agrees to make the property available to Broker at all reasonable hours for the purpose of showing it to prospective Purchasers.

Owner agrees to convey the property to the Purchaser by warranty deed with the usual covenants of title and free and clear from all encumbrances, tenancies, liens (for taxes or otherwise), but subject to applicable restrictive covenants of record. Owner acknowledges receipt of a copy of this agreement.

WITNESS the following signature(s) and seal(s):

Date Signed: _____ _____ (SEAL) (Owner)

Listing Broker _____

Address _____ Telephone _____ _____ (SEAL) (Owner)

_____

QUESTIONS ON LISTING CONTRACT

Answer these questions *only* by referring to the listing contract form you have filled out.

1. This contract is a(n)
   (A) exclusive right to sell listing
   (B) exclusive agency listing
   (C) open listing
   (D) net listing

2. If the property is sold at the listed price, the broker's commission will be
   (A) $3270.00
   (B) $3815.00
   (C) $4087.50
   (D) $4400.00

3. This listing will expire on
   (A) September 15, 1983
   (B) September 16, 1983
   (C) September 17, 1983
   (D) September 18, 1983

4. The annual tax bill on the property is
   (A) $233.64
   (B) $2336.40
   (C) $2398.00
   (D) $4796.00

5. The date of the listing is
   (A) June 16, 1983
   (B) June 17, 1983
   (C) June 18, 1983
   (D) September 15, 1983

6. Which of the following is *false*?
   I. The parochial school is St. Vitus.
   II. The home has three bathrooms.
   (A) I only
   (B) II only
   (C) Both I and II
   (D) Neither I nor II

7. Which of the following is *true*?
   I. The home will be shown only by appointment.
   II. The key to the home is under the doormat.
   (A) I only
   (B) II only
   (C) Both I and II
   (D) Neither I nor II

8. Which of the following is *true*?
   I. The home is assessed for $26,550.
   II. The kitchen has a breakfast area.
   (A) I only
   (B) II only
   (C) Both I and II
   (D) Neither I nor II

9. Which of the following telephone numbers can be used to contact the seller?
   (A) 555-1717
   (B) 555-2282
   (C) 555-1116
   (D) None of the above

10. Which of the following is *false*?
    (A) The lot size is 98 ft. × 155 ft.
    (B) The house is 21 years old.
    (C) The home has natural gas heat.
    (D) All of the above

11. Which is *false*?
    I. Immediate possession is possible.
    II. The listing price was $54,500.
    (A) I only
    (B) II only
    (C) Both I and II
    (D) Neither I nor II

12. Which of the following is *true*?
    (A) The home is in Benedictine County.
    (B) The address is 8811 Quagmire Place.
    (C) The home telephone number is 555-1116.
    (D) All of the above

13. The home is Lot _____ of Block _____ of Quagmire Estates Subdivision.
    (A) 17, F
    (B) 18, G
    (C) 16, G
    (D) 18, F

14. Which features does the house have?
    I. Four bedrooms
    II. Central air conditioning
    (A) I only
    (B) II only
    (C) Both I and II
    (D) Neither I nor II

15. Which of the following is *true*?
    I. The tax rate is 88 mills.
    II. The home has four bedrooms on the second floor.
    (A) I only
    (B) II only
    (C) Both I and II
    (D) Neither I nor II

Supplemental Examination 2 _____
(Contract of Sale)

SALES CONTRACT NARRATIVE

On August 14, 1988, you show the home belonging to Sydney Purvis (refer to the listing contract narrative for details) to a prospective purchaser, Mr. Marvin Jardin.

Three days later Mr. Jardin informs you that he wishes to offer $52,000 for the house, subject to his getting a mortgage loan for at lease 80% of the sale price, with a term of 30 years and at the currently prevailing rate of interest. Closing will be at the broker's office no later than September 18, 1988. Mr. Jardin leaves his personal check for $1000 as a deposit. Mr. Purvis will receive all cash at the closing, from the proceeds of Mr. Jardin's loan, his deposit, and additional cash necessary to make up the purchase price.

The next day your broker draws up the contract and Mr. Purvis and Mr. Jardin sign it.

Fill out the accompanying contract form ("Offer to Purchase Agreement") according to this information.

QUESTIONS ON OFFER TO PURCHASE CONTRACT

When answering these questions, refer *only* to the completed purchase contract form you have filled out.

1. The broker's commission will be
   (A) $2650.00
   (B) $3875.00
   (C) $3900.00
   (D) $4087.50

2. The purchaser requires a loan of at least
   (A) $43,600
   (B) $41,600
   (C) $40,000
   (D) $39,700

3. The contract allows how many days until closing?
   (A) 29
   (B) 30
   (C) 31
   (D) 32

4. After allowing for the deposit he has made and a mortgage loan of 80% of the purchase price, how much additional cash must the purchaser pay at closing?
   (A) $10,400
   (B) $9,400
   (C) $8,400
   (D) $8,250

5. The date of the contract is
   (A) August 14, 1983
   (B) August 17, 1983
   (C) August 18, 1988
   (D) August 20, 1988

OFFER TO PURCHASE AGREEMENT

This AGREEMENT made as of_____, 19_____,

among_____(herein called "Purchaser"),

and_____(herein called "Seller"),

and_____(herein called "Broker"),
provides that Purchaser agrees to buy through Broker as agent for Seller, and Seller agrees to sell the following described real estate, and all improvements
thereon, located in the jurisdiction of_____
(all herein called "the property"):_____

_____
_____, and more commonly known as_____
_____(street address).

1. The purchase price of the property is_____
Dollars ($_____), and such purchase price shall be paid as follows:
_____
_____

2. Purchaser has made a deposit of_____ Dollars ($_____)
with Broker, receipt of which is hereby acknowledged, and such deposit shall be held by Broker in escrow until the date of settlement and then applied
to the purchase price, or returned to Purchaser if the title to the property is not marketable.

3. Seller agrees to convey the property to Purchaser by Warranty Deed with the usual covenants of title and free and clear from all encumbrances,
tenancies, liens (for taxes or otherwise), except as may be otherwise provided above, but subject to applicable restrictive covenants of record. Seller further
agrees to deliver possession of the property to Purchaser on the date of settlement and to pay the expense of preparing the deed of conveyance.

4. Settlement shall be made at the offices of Broker or at_____on or before
_____, 19_____, or as soon thereafter as title can be examined and necessary documents prepared, with allowance of
a reasonable time for Seller to correct any defects reported by the title examiner.

5. All taxes, interest, rent, and F.H.A. or similar escrow deposits, if any, shall be prorated as of the date of settlement.

6. All risk of loss or damage to the property by fire, windstorm, casualty, or other cause is assumed by Seller until the date of settlement.

7. Purchaser and Seller agree that Broker was the sole procuring cause of this Contract of Purchase, and Seller agrees to pay Broker for services
rendered a cash fee of_____per cent of the purchase price. If either Purchaser or Seller defaults under such Contract, such defaulting party shall
be liable for the cash fee of Broker and any expenses incurred by the non-defaulting party in connection with this transaction.

Subject to:_____
_____
_____
_____

8. Purchaser represents that an inspection satisfactory to Purchaser has been made of the property, and Purchaser agrees to accept the property in
its present condition except as may be otherwise provided in the description of the property above.

9. This Contract of Purchase constitutes the entire agreement among the parties and may not be modified or changed except by written instrument
executed by all of the parties, including Broker.

10. This Contract of Purchase shall be construed, interpreted, and applied according to the law of the jurisdiction of_____ and shall
be binding upon and shall inure to the benefit of the heirs, personal representatives, successors, and assigns of the parties.

All parties to this agreement acknowledge receipt of a certified copy.

WITNESS the following signatures and seals:

_____(SEAL)   _____(SEAL)
Seller   Purchaser

_____(SEAL)   _____(SEAL)
Seller   Purchaser

_____(SEAL)
Broker

Deposit Rec'd $

Personal Check   Cash

Cashier's Check   Company Check

Sales Agent:

6. The deposit paid by the buyer is
    I. $1,000
    II. paid in cash
(A) I only
(B) II only
(C) Both I and II
(D) Neither I nor II

7. The parties to the contract are
    I. Mr. Purvis, the seller
    II. Mr. Jardin, the buyer
(A) I only
(B) II only
(C) Both I and II
(D) Neither I nor II

8. The purchaser's loan must
    I. be at an interest rate of 9%
    II. be for a term of 30 years
(A) I only
(B) II only
(C) Both I and II
(D) Neither I nor II

9. In this deal,
    I. the purchase price is $52,000
    II. the buyer will assume the seller's mortgage loan
(A) I only
(B) II only
(C) Both I and II
(D) Neither I nor II

10. With respect to the closing,
    I. it will be at the broker's office
    II. it will be no later than September 18, 1988
(A) I only
(B) II only
(C) Both I and II
(D) Neither I nor II

Supplemental Examination 3
(Settlement Statement)

SETTLEMENT STATEMENT NARRATIVE

On September 18, 1988, you close a sale between Sydney Purvis (seller) and Marvin Jardin (buyer). The sale price is $52,000.00, and your commission is 7½% of the sale price. Mr. Jardin receives a mortgage loan for 90% of the sale price and has paid a deposit of $1000.00. The property is assessed at $26,550.00 and the tax rate is 88 mills. Taxes are on a calendar year basis but must be paid by June 15 each year. Mr. Jardin will assume a three-year fire insurance policy, which Mr. Purvis took out on October 22, 1986, paying the full three-year premium of $888.75 at that time. Mr. Purvis's existing mortgage loan of $32,331.70 will be paid off at closing from the proceeds of the sale.

Mr. Purvis must pay attorney fees of $175.00, a deed preparation fee of $80.00, and miscellaneous fees of $356.55. Mr. Jardin must pay attorney fees of $325.00, an appraisal fee of $100.00, a mortgage insurance premium of 2½% of the loan amount, and a title insurance premium of 0.85% of the purchase price.

Fill out the accompanying settlement statement worksheet according to this information.

QUESTIONS ON SETTLEMENT STATEMENT

Answer the questions *only* by referring to the settlement statement sheet you have filled out.

1. The buyer will owe what amount of cash at closing?
(A) $6,237.03
(B) $6,560.44
(C) $6,898.98
(D) $7,222.39

SETTLEMENT STATEMENT
WORKSHEET

SETTLEMENT DATE:	BUYER'S STATEMENT		SELLER'S STATEMENT	
	DEBIT	CREDIT	DEBIT	CREDIT

2. The seller will receive what amount of cash at closing?
   (A) $16,142.14
   (B) $16,465.55
   (C) $16,804.12
   (D) $17,127.53

3. With regard to the property taxes, which of the following is (are) true?
   I. The prorated amount is $661.98.
   II. The seller pays this amount to the buyer.
   (A) I only
   (B) II only
   (C) Both I and II
   (D) Neither I nor II

4. The buyer's mortgage insurance premium is
   (A) $297.50
   (B) $887.50
   (C) $1170.00
   (D) $1300.00

5. The buyer's title insurance premium is
   (A) $397.80
   (B) $398.80
   (C) $411.80
   (D) $442.00

6. The buyer's loan will be
   (A) $52,000
   (B) $46,800
   (C) $44,200
   (D) $41,600

7. The broker's commission is
   (A) $390
   (B) $3221
   (C) $3510
   (D) $3900

8. With regard to the prorated insurance policy, which of the following is (are) true?
    I. The prorated amount is $565.34.
    II. The seller pays this amount to the buyer.
    (A) I only
    (B) II only
    (C) Both I and II
    (D) Neither I nor II

9. The purchaser's earnest money deposit being held by the broker until closing is shown as a
    I. credit to the purchaser
    II. debit to the seller
    (A) I only
    (B) II only
    (C) Both I and II
    (D) Neither I nor II

10. The seller will pay a broker's commission. The commission would be shown as
    (A) a credit to the seller
    (B) a debit to the seller
    (C) a debit to the buyer
    (D) A and C only

11. The buyer will pay for an appraisal and title insurance at closing. These items are shown as
    (A) a credit to the buyer
    (B) a debit to the buyer
    (C) a credit to the seller
    (D) A and C only

12. The buyer will take over the unexpired portion of the seller's insurance policy, for which the seller has paid the full premium. The unexpired premium is a
    I. debit to the buyer
    II. credit to the seller
    (A) I only
    (B) II only
    (C) Both I and II
    (D) Neither I nor II

13. The seller's mortgage insurance premium is a
    I. credit to the seller
    II. credit to the buyer
    (A) I only
    (B) II only
    (C) Both I and II
    (D) Neither I nor II

14. The purchase price is
    (A) shown on seller's statement as a debit
    (B) shown on seller's statement as a credit
    (C) not shown on statement for seller
    (D) shown on seller's statement as both credit and debit

15. The payoff of the existing mortgage is
    (A) a credit to the buyer
    (B) a credit to the seller
    (C) a debit to the seller
    (D) none of the above

Supplemental Examination 4
(Rectangular Survey)

QUESTIONS ON RECTANGULAR SURVEY

Answer these questions if your state uses the U.S. Government Rectangular Survey method of property description *anywhere in the state.*

1. Which of the following is correct?
    I. A section is one square mile.
    II. One square mile contains 840 acres.
    (A) I only
    (B) II only
    (C) Both I and II
    (D) Neither I nor II

2. How many acres are in N½ NW¼ SE¼ of a given section?
   (A) 20   (C) 160
   (B) 40   (D) 180

3. What is the description of a section whose eastern boundary is 25 mi. *west* of the principal meridian and whose northern boundary is 42 mi. *north* of the base line?
   (A) Section 35, T7N, R5W   (C) Section 2, T7N, R5W
   (B) Section 35, T8N, R5W   (D) None of the above

4. How far must a rabbit hop in a straight line from the western boundary of NE¼, NW¼ to the eastern boundary of NE¼, NE¼ of the same section?
   I. ¾ mi.
   II. 3960 ft.
   (A) I only   (C) Both I and II
   (B) II only   (D) Neither I nor II

Questions 5–14 refer to the following figure.

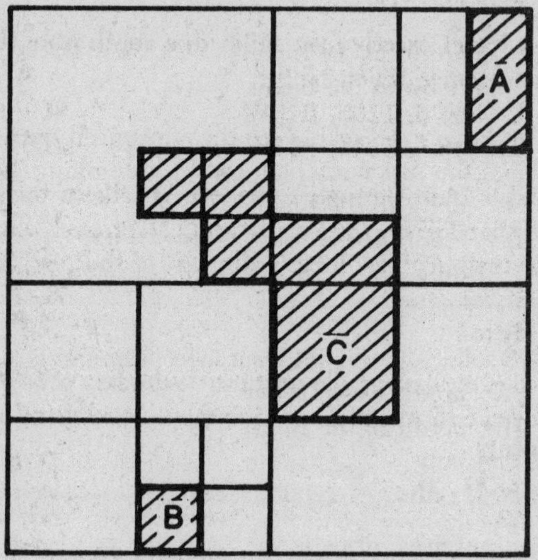

Section 20, T 14 S, R 16 W

5. What is the description of the shaded area marked A?
   (A) NE¼, NW¼, NE¼   (C) E½, NE¼
   (B) E¼, NE¼   (D) E½, NE¼, NE¼

6. How many acres are there in the shaded tract marked A?
   (A) 20   (C) 80
   (B) 40   (D) 160

7. What is the description of the shaded tract marked B?
   (A) SE¼, SW¼, SE¼   (C) SE¼, SW¼, NE¼
   (B) SW¼, SE¼, SW¼   (D) S¼, SE¼, S¼

8. What is the area of the shaded tract marked B?
   (A) 5 acres   (C) 20 acres
   (B) 10 acres   (D) 40 acres

9. What is the description of the irregular shaded area marked C?
   I. NW¼, SE¼ and S½, SW¼, NE¼ and SE¼, SE¼, NW¼ and N½, SE¼, NW¼
   II. NW¼, SE¼ and S½, SW¼, NE¼ and E½, SE¼, NW¼ and NW¼, SE¼, NW¼
   (A) I only   (C) Both I and II
   (B) II only   (D) Neither I nor II

10. What is the area of the irregular shaded area marked C?
    I. 80 acres
    II. 0.125 sq. mi.
    (A) I only
    (B) II only
    (C) Both I and II
    (D) Neither I nor II

11. What is the area of that portion of the irregular shaded tract marked C that is located in the NW¼ of the section?
    (A) 20 acres
    (B) 30 acres
    (C) 40 acres
    (D) 80 acres

12. How far is the *center* of the illustrated section from the base line?
    (A) 86½ mi. north
    (B) 87½ mi. south
    (C) 24½ mi. south
    (D) 23½ mi. north

13. How far is the *center* of the illustrated section from the principal meridian?
    (A) 65½ mi. east
    (B) 65½ mi. west
    (C) 17½ mi. west
    (D) None of the above

14. If you travel exactly *four* miles due south from the center of the illustrated section, what section will you be in?
    (A) Section 5, T15S, R16W
    (B) Section 5, T14S, R17W
    (C) Section 8, T15S, R16W
    (D) Section 32, T14S, R16W

15. A road is built through a section. It follows the line dividing E½, SE¼ from W½, SE¼; then follows the line dividing N½ from S½ until it reaches the western boundary of the section. How long is the part of the road inside the section?
    (A) ½ mi.
    (B) ¾ mi.
    (C) 1 mi.
    (D) 1¼ mi.

16. A road is built along the northern boundary of SW¼, SE¼ of a given section. The road extends 66 ft. in width into the tract. How many acres in this tract are not covered by the road?
    (A) 27.81
    (B) 33
    (C) 38
    (D) 38.80

17. A man owns SW¼, SW¼ of a section. He purchases the remainder of the SW¼. By what percentage has he increased his holding of acreage?
    (A) 100%
    (B) 200%
    (C) 300%
    (D) 400%

18. Helen Smith purchases S½, NW¼, NE¼ of a section. What *percentage* of the total area of the section has she purchased?
    (A) $1^7/_{16}$%
    (B) $3^1/_8$%
    (C) 5%
    (D) $31^1/_4$%

Chapter 26/ *Answer Keys And Explanations*

Following are answer keys to all the model and supplemental examinations in the previous two chapters. Also included are contract forms for Supplemental Examinations 1 and 2, and the settlement statement for Supplemental Examination 3.

A final section contains explanations of all the arithmetic questions in all the examinations.

Model Examination 1

1.	D	17.	A	33.	A	49.	C	65.	B
2.	B	18.	A	34.	B	50.	C	66.	B
3.	C	19.	C	35.	A	51.	B	67.	A
4.	D	20.	A	36.	A	52.	C	68.	A
5.	D	21.	C	37.	B	53.	B	69.	A
6.	A	22.	B	38.	C	54.	A	70.	D
7.	B	23.	B	39.	B	55.	A	71.	B
8.	C	24.	B	40.	B	56.	B	72.	D
9.	B	25.	D	41.	B	57.	B	73.	C
10.	C	26.	C	42.	A	58.	C	74.	B
11.	A	27.	C	43.	D	59.	C	75.	C
12.	A	28.	C	44.	D	60.	D	76.	C
13.	C	29.	A	45.	C	61.	C	77.	A
14.	C	30.	B	46.	C	62.	C	78.	D
15.	B	31.	B	47.	C	63.	C	79.	B
16.	B	32.	A	48.	D	64.	C	80.	A

Model Examination 2

1.	B	6.	B	11.	C	16.	A	21.	D
2.	D	7.	B	12.	C	17.	B	22.	A
3.	D	8.	B	13.	D	18.	B	23.	C
4.	B	9.	C	14.	B	19.	C	24.	A
5.	D	10.	D	15.	C	20.	A	25.	C

26. D	41. C	56. D	71. B	86. D
27. D	42. B	57. D	72. B	87. B
28. D	43. A	58. B	73. B	88. C
29. C	44. D	59. A	74. B	89. D
30. D	45. D	60. D	75. D	90. D
31. B	46. D	61. A	76. C	91. C
32. A	47. B	62. C	77. D	92. C
33. D	48. C	63. B	78. C	93. A
34. B	49. D	64. A	79. D	94. A
35. B	50. A	65. C	80. C	95. C
36. B	51. A	66. C	81. A	96. D
37. C	52. D	67. C	82. C	97. C
38. B	53. A	68. A	83. B	98. B
39. A	54. A	69. C	84. B	99. A
40. C	55. C	70. C	85. C	100. B

Model Examination 3

1. C	17. B	33. B	49. A	65. A
2. C	18. C	34. A	50. B	66. B
3. A	19. C	35. D	51. C	67. A
4. D	20. D	36. D	52. B	68. D
5. C	21. C	37. D	53. B	69. B
6. A	22. B	38. D	54. A	70. A
7. B	23. C	39. B	55. B	71. B
8. A	24. D	40. B	56. C	72. C
9. C	25. C	41. A	57. D	73. A
10. A	26. A	42. C	58. C	74. C
11. A	27. C	43. C	59. D	75. C
12. B	28. B	44. B	60. B	76. A
13. A	29. C	45. D	61. B	77. A
14. B	30. A	46. A	62. C	78. C
15. A	31. C	47. D	63. C	79. B
16. C	32. B	48. D	64. D	80. C

Model Examination 4

1. D	17. A	33. B	49. C	65. B
2. A	18. A	34. C	50. A	66. A
3. C	19. C	35. D	51. C	67. B
4. C	20. B	36. A	52. D	68. C
5. D	21. D	37. B	53. A	69. C
6. C	22. D	38. B	54. C	70. D
7. B	23. A	39. C	55. C	71. A
8. B	24. A	40. A	56. B	72. C
9. C	25. D	41. A	57. C	73. B
10. C	26. B	42. C	58. B	74. B
11. B	27. C	43. D	59. A	75. D
12. A	28. D	44. A	60. A	76. A
13. B	29. C	45. C	61. A	77. C
14. A	30. A	46. B	62. B	78. A
15. D	31. B	47. B	63. D	79. B
16. B	32. B	48. D	64. B	80. D

Model Examination 5

1. B	21. B	41. D	61. A	81. C
2. D	22. B	42. B	62. C	82. C
3. D	23. D	43. D	63. B	83. A
4. B	24. A	44. B	64. A	84. D
5. A	25. A	45. B	65. C	85. B
6. C	26. B	46. D	66. A	86. A
7. C	27. A	47. D	67. C	87. A
8. A	28. A	48. C	68. C	88. A
9. D	29. C	49. A	69. B	89. C
10. D	30. A	50. B	70. A	90. C
11. B	31. B	51. C	71. D	91. B
12. A	32. C	52. C	72. A	92. D
13. B	33. D	53. D	73. B	93. B
14. B	34. B	54. B	74. D	94. D
15. C	35. C	55. B	75. C	95. D
16. B	36. B	56. C	76. B	96. D
17. A	37. C	57. C	77. C	97. A
18. C	38. D	58. B	78. A	98. B
19. D	39. D	59. D	79. D	99. B
20. B	40. D	60. A	80. C	100. C

Model Examination 6

1. D	17. B	33. D	49. A	65. D
2. B	18. C	34. A	50. C	66. D
3. C	19. D	35. A	51. C	67. D
4. B	20. A	36. C	52. B	68. A
5. D	21. C	37. B	53. B	69. D
6. A	22. C	38. C	54. B	70. B
7. C	23. A	39. C	55. A	71. C
8. C	24. B	40. B	56. C	72. A
9. C	25. A	41. B	57. D	73. C
10. B	26. B	42. B	58. C	74. B
11. C	27. B	43. D	59. D	75. A
12. D	28. C	44. C	60. D	76. B
13. B	29. C	45. C	61. C	77. A
14. A	30. B	46. A	62. C	78. B
15. D	31. A	47. B	63. C	79. D
16. C	32. C	48. B	64. D	80. B

Model Examination 7

PART A

1. T	9. F	17. F	25. F	33. F
2. F	10. F	18. F	26. F	34. T
3. T	11. T	19. T	27. T	35. T
4. T	12. F	20. T	28. T	36. T
5. T	13. F	21. T	29. F	37. T
6. T	14. F	22. F	30. T	38. T
7. F	15. T	23. T	31. T	39. T
8. T	16. T	24. F	32. T	40. T

41.	F	49.	T	57.	T	65.	F	73.	F
42.	T	50.	T	58.	F	66.	F	74.	T
43.	T	51.	T	59.	F	67.	T	75.	F
44.	F	52.	T	60.	T	68.	F	76.	T
45.	T	53.	T	61.	F	69.	T	77.	T
46.	T	54.	T	62.	T	70.	T	78.	F
47.	F	55.	T	63.	T	71.	F	79.	T
48.	T	56.	T	64.	F	72.	T	80.	T

PART B

81. market value
82. dower
83. performance
84. principal
85. amortizing
86. real estate
87. purchase money mortgage
88. open
89. tenancy in common
90. decrease
91. assignment
92. equities
93, 94, 95. physical deterioration; functional obsolescence; economic deterioration
96, 97, 98. market; replacement (cost); capitalization (or income)
99. sublease
100. lien
101. deficiency judgment
102. deed
103. title theory
104. gross lease
105. mortgagee
106. novation
107. mechanic's lien
108. ¹/₁₀ cent
109. deed
110. percentage lease
111. equitable
112. 1968
113. blockbusting
114. Z
115. option
116. three
117. step, or graduated
118. Statute of Frauds
119. vendor and vendee
120. parol evidence
121. disaffirm
122. testimonium
123. quitclaim
124. obligation
125. ad valorem
126. thousand
127. annual percentage rate
128. grantor, grantee
129—133. mutual agreement, *or* reality of consent, *or* meeting of the minds, *or* offer and acceptance; consideration; competent parties; legal purpose; legal form
134. $862.40
135. 19,275.3 sq. ft.
136. 8%
137. $195
138. $787.50
139. 165,528
140. $45,000

Supplemental Examinations

1 — LISTING CONTRACT QUESTIONS

1.	A	4.	B	7.	A	10.	B	13.	B
2.	C	5.	B	8.	C	11.	D	14.	C
3.	A	6.	D	9.	C	12.	D	15.	A

2 — OFFER TO PURCHASE CONTRACT QUESTIONS

1. C	3. C	5. C	7. C	9. A
2. B	4. B	6. A	8. B	10. C

3 — SETTLEMENT STATEMENT QUESTIONS

1. D	4. C	7. D	10. B	13. D
2. A	5. D	8. D	11. B	14. B
3. A	6. B	9. A	12. C	15. C

The properly filled-out contract and settlement statement forms are shown on the next pages.

4 — RECTANGULAR SURVEY QUESTIONS

1. A	5. D	9. C	13. D**	16. C
2. A	6. A	10. D*	14. C	17. C
3. C	7. B	11. B	15. D	18. B
4. C	8. B	12. B		

*The correct answer to #10 is 90 acres.
**The correct answer to #13 is 100½ mi. *west*.

EXCLUSIVE AUTHORIZATION TO SELL

SALES PRICE: **$54,500.00** TYPE HOME **2-STORY** TOTAL BEDROOMS **4** TOTAL BATHS **3**

ADDRESS **6811 QUAGMIRE PLACE** JURISDICTION OF **BENEDICTINE COUNTY**

AMT. OF LOAN TO BE ASSUMED $ **NOT ASSUMABLE** AS OF WHAT DATE ____ TAXES & INS. INCLUDED ____ YEARS TO GO ____ AMOUNT PAYABLE MONTHLY $ ____ @ ____ % TYPE LOAN ____

MORTGAGE COMPANY ____ 2nd TRUST $ ____

ESTIMATED EXPECTED RENT MONTHLY $ ____ TYPE OF APPRAISAL REQUESTED ____

OWNER'S NAME **SYDNEY PURVIS** PHONES (HOME) **555-1116** (BUSINESS) **555-2822**

TENANTS NAME ____ PHONES (HOME) ____ (BUSINESS) ____

POSSESSION **IMMEDIATE** DATE LISTED **6/17/83** EXCLUSIVE FOR **90 DAYS** DATE OF EXPIRATION **9/15/88**

LISTING BROKER **YOUR BROKER** PHONE **-** KEY AVAILABLE AT **OFFICE**

LISTING SALESMAN **YOUR NAME** HOME PHONE **YOURS** HOW TO BE SHOWN **APPOINTMENT**

(1) ENTRANCE FOYER ✓ CENTER HALL ✓	(18) AGE **12 YRS** AIR CONDITIONING ✓	(32) TYPE KITCHEN CABINETS
(2) LIVING ROOM SIZE ___ FIREPLACE ☐	(19) ROOFING ___ TOOL HOUSE ☐	(33) TYPE COUNTER TOPS
(3) DINING ROOM SIZE	(20) GARAGE SIZE ___ PATIO ☐	(34) EAT-IN SIZE KITCHEN
(4) BEDROOM TOTAL **4** DOWN **1** UP **3**	(21) SIDE DRIVE ☐ CIRCULAR DRIVE ☐	(35) BREAKFAST ROOM ✓
(5) BATHS TOTAL **3** DOWN **1** UP **2**	(22) PORCH ☐ SIDE ☐ REAR ☐ SCREENED ☐	(36) BUILT-IN OVEN & RANGE ✓
(6) DEN SIZE ___ FIREPLACE ☐	(23) FENCED YARD ☐ OUTDOOR GRILL ☐	(37) SEPARATE STOVE INCLUDED ☐
(7) FAMILY ROOM SIZE ___ FIREPLACE ☐	(24) STORM WINDOWS ☐ STORM DOORS ☐	(38) REFRIGERATOR INCLUDED ✓
(8) RECREATION ROOM SIZE ___ FIREPLACE ☐	(25) CURBS & GUTTERS ✓ SIDEWALKS ☐	(39) DISHWASHER INCLUDED ✓
(9) BASEMENT SIZE	(26) STORM SEWERS ☐ ALLEY ☐	(40) DISPOSAL INCLUDED
NONE ☐ 1/4 ☑ 1/3 ☐ 1/2 ☐ 3/4 ☐ FULL ☐	(27) WATER SUPPLY **CITY**	(41) DOUBLE SINK ___ SINGLE SINK
(10) UTILITY ROOM SIZE	(28) SEWER ☐ SEPTIC ☐	STAINLESS STEEL ___ PORCELAIN ☐
TYPE HOT WATER SYSTEM **GAS**	(29) TYPE GAS: NATURAL ✓ BOTTLED ☐	(42) WASHER INCLUDED ✓ DRYER INCLUDED ✓
(11) TYPE HEAT **GAS**	(30) WHY SELLING **BOUGHT ANOTHER HOME**	(43) PANTRY ___ EXHAUST FAN
(12) EST. FUEL COST		(44) LAND ASSESSMENT $
(13) ATTIC	(31) DIRECTIONS TO PROPERTY	(45) IMPROVEMENTS $
PULL DOWN STAIRWAY ✓ REGULAR STAIRWAY ☐ TRAP DOOR ☐		(46) TOTAL ASSESSMENT $ **26,550**
(14) MAIDS ROOM ☐ TYPE BATH		(47) TAX RATE **88 MILS**
LOCATION		(48) TOTAL ANNUAL TAXES $ **2336.40**
(15) NAME OF BUILDER		(49) LOT SIZE **98' X 155'**
(16) SQUARE FOOTAGE **2510**		(50) LOT NO. **18** BLOCK **Q** SECTION
(17) EXTERIOR OF HOUSE **BRICK**		**QUAGMIRE ESTATES ADDITION**

NAME OF SCHOOLS: ELEMENTARY **DIMBULB** JR HIGH **NITWIT**

HIGH **IGNORAMUS** PAROCHIAL **ST. VITUS**

PUBLIC TRANSPORTATION ____

NEAREST SHOPPING AREA ____

REMARKS ____

Date: **6/17/83**

In consideration of the services of **YOUR BROKER** (herein called "Broker") to be rendered to the undersigned (herein called "Owner"), and of the promise of Broker to make reasonable efforts to obtain a Purchaser therefor, Owner hereby lists with Broker the real estate and all improvements thereon which are described above (all herein called "the property"), and Owner hereby grants to Broker the exclusive and irrevocable right to sell such property from 12:00 Noon on **JUNE 17**, 19 **88** until 12:00 Midnight on **SEPT. 15**, 19 **88** (herein called "period of time"), for the price of **FIFTY FOUR THOUSAND FIVE HUNDRED** Dollars ($ **54,500.00**) or for such other price and upon such other terms (including exchange) as Owner may subsequently authorize during the period of time.

It is understood by Owner that the above sum or any other price subsequently authorized by Owner shall include a cash fee of **7½** per cent of such price or other price which shall be payable by Owner to Broker upon consummation by any Purchaser or Purchasers of a valid contract of sale of the property during the period of time and whether or not Broker was a procuring cause of any such contract of sale.

If the property is sold or exchanged by Owner, or by Broker or by any other person to any Purchaser to whom the property was shown by Broker or any representative of Broker within sixty (60) days after the expiration of the period of time mentioned above, Owner agrees to pay to Broker a cash fee which shall be the same percentage of the purchase price as the percentage mentioned above.

Broker is hereby authorized by Owner to place a "For Sale" sign on the property and to remove all signs of other brokers or salesmen during the period of time, and Owner hereby agrees to make the property available to Broker at all reasonable hours for the purpose of showing it to prospective Purchasers.

Owner agrees to convey the property to the Purchaser by warranty deed with the usual covenants of title and free and clear from all encumbrances, tenancies, liens (for taxes or otherwise), but subject to applicable restrictive covenants of record. Owner acknowledges receipt of a copy of this agreement.

WITNESS the following signature(s) and seal(s):

Date Signed: **June 17, 1988** **Sydney Purvis** _____ (SEAL) (Owner)

Listing Broker **Your Broker**

Address ____ Telephone ____ _____ (SEAL) (Owner)

OFFER TO PURCHASE AGREEMENT

This AGREEMENT made as of _____ *August 18* _____, 19 *88* ,

among _*MARVIN JARDIN*_____ (herein called "Purchaser"),

and _*SYDNEY PURVIS*_____ (herein called "Seller"),

and _*YOUR BROKER*_____ (herein called "Broker"),

provides that Purchaser agrees to buy through Broker as agent for Seller, and Seller agrees to sell the following described real estate, and all improvements thereon, located in the jurisdiction of _*BENEDICTINE COUNTY*_____

(all herein called "the property"): _*LOT 18, BLOCK G, QUAGMIRE ESTATES ADDITION*_____

_____ , and more commonly known as _*8811 QUAGMIRE PLACE*_____ (street address).

1. The purchase price of the property is *FIFTY TWO THOUSAND*_____
Dollars ($ *52,000.—*), and such purchase price shall be paid as follows:
CASH AND PROCEEDS OF MORTGAGE LOAN TO BE OBTAINED BY PURCHASER, ALL PAYABLE AT CLOSING.

2. Purchaser has made a deposit of _*ONE THOUSAND*_____ Dollars ($ *1,000.00*)
with Broker, receipt of which is hereby acknowledged, and such deposit shall be held by Broker in escrow until the date of settlement and then applied to the purchase price, or returned to Purchaser if the title to the property is not marketable.

3. Seller agrees to convey the property to Purchaser by Warranty Deed with the usual covenants of title and free and clear from all encumbrances, tenancies, liens (for taxes or otherwise), except as may be otherwise provided above, but subject to applicable restrictive covenants of record. Seller further agrees to deliver possession of the property to Purchaser on the date of settlement and to pay the expense of preparing the deed of conveyance.

4. Settlement shall be made at the offices of Broker or at _____ on or before
*SEPTEMBER 18*_____, 19 *88* , or as soon thereafter as title can be examined and necessary documents prepared, with allowance of a reasonable time for Seller to correct any defects reported by the title examiner.

5. All taxes, interest, rent, and F.H.A. or similar escrow deposits, if any, shall be prorated as of the date of settlement.

6. All risk of loss or damage to the property by fire, windstorm, casualty, or other cause is assumed by Seller until the date of settlement.

7. Purchaser and Seller agree that Broker was the sole procuring cause of this Contract of Purchase, and Seller agrees to pay Broker for services rendered a cash fee of _*7 1/2*_ per cent of the purchase price. If either Purchaser or Seller defaults under such Contract, such defaulting party shall be liable for the cash fee of Broker and any expenses incurred by the non-defaulting party in connection with this transaction.

Subject to: *PURCHASER OBTAINING 30-YEAR MORTGAGE LOAN FOR AT LEAST $41,600 AT CURRENTLY PREVAILING RATE OF INTEREST.*

8. Purchaser represents that an inspection satisfactory to Purchaser has been made of the property, and Purchaser agrees to accept the property in its present condition except as may be otherwise provided in the description of the property above.

9. This Contract of Purchase constitutes the entire agreement among the parties and may not be modified or changed except by written instrument executed by all of the parties, including Broker.

10. This Contract of Purchase shall be construed, interpreted, and applied according to the law of the jurisdiction of _*UTAH*_ and shall be binding upon and shall inure to the benefit of the heirs, personal representatives, successors, and assigns of the parties.

All parties to this agreement acknowledge receipt of a certified copy.

WITNESS the following signatures and seals:

Sydney Purvis _____ (SEAL) Seller   *Marvin Jardin* _____ (SEAL) Purchaser

_____ (SEAL) Seller   _____ (SEAL) Purchaser

_____ *YOUR BROKER* _____ (SEAL) Broker

Deposit Rec'd $ *1,000.—*

(Personal Check)   Cash

Cashier's Check   Company Check

Sales Agent: *YOUR NAME*

SETTLEMENT STATEMENT WORKSHEET

SETTLEMENT DATE:	BUYER'S STATEMENT		SELLER'S STATEMENT	
	DEBIT	CREDIT	DEBIT	CREDIT
SALE PRICE	52,000.00			52,000.00
BROKER'S COMMISSION			3,900.00	
MORTGAGE LOAN PROCEEDS		46,800.00		
DEPOSIT		1,000.00		
PRORATED TAXES	661.98			661.98
PRORATED INSURANCE	323.41			323.41
ATTORNEY FEES	325.00		175.00	
DEED PREPARATION FEE			80.00	
MISCELLANEOUS FEES			356.55	
APPRAISAL FEE	100.00			
MORTGAGE INSURANCE	1170.00			
TITLE INSURANCE	442.00			
MORTGAGE LOAN PAYOFF			32,331.70	
SUB-TOTALS	55,022.39	47,800.00	36,843.25	52,985.39
DUE FROM BUYER		7,222.39		
DUE TO SELLER			16,142.14	
TOTALS	55,022.39	55,022.39	52,985.39	52,985.39

Answer Explanations — Arithmetic Questions

MODEL EXAMINATION 1

6. If the tax is based on 20% of the appraised value of $25,000, then the tax is based on
$$0.2 \times \$25,000 = \$5000$$
City tax is 50 mills, or 5%, so
$$\$5000 \times 0.05 = \$250 \text{ city tax}$$
County tax is 40 mills, or 4%, so
$$\$5000 \times 0.04 = \$200 \text{ county tax}$$
Therefore, (I) is true but (II) is false.

7. This is a sidewalk question; remember not to count the corners twice. The total sidewalk area is 320 ft. × 5 ft. = 1600 sq. ft. Since it is 6 in., or half a foot deep, the cubic measure is 800 cu. ft. A cu. yd. contains 27 cu. ft. (3 ft. × 3 ft. × 3 ft.), so the total number of cu. yd. is
$$800 \text{ cu. ft.} \div 27 \text{ cu. ft.} = 29.63 \text{ cu. yd.}$$

21. After depreciating eight years at 3% per year, the building has lost 24% of original value (8 × 0.03 = 0.24). This means that it is now worth the remaining 76% of its original value. If that sum is $19,000, then the original value is
$$\$19,000 \div 0.76 = \$25,000$$

22. 9% of $40,000.00 is $0.09 \times \$40,000.00 = \$3600.00$. Interest for a single month would be $\$3600.00 \div 12$, or $300.00. Therefore, of the $340.00 *first* payment, $300.00 goes to interest, leaving $40.00 to reduce the principal. This means that Smith will pay interest on $39,960.00 the second month. Figuring the same way, we get a monthly interest charge of $299.70 for the second month on that amount; this will leave $40.30 by which the second monthly payment will reduce the principal.

38. Annual rent is $850 \times 12 = \$10,200$. Taxes are based on 40% of appraisal of $47,000, or $0.4 \times \$47,000 = \$18,800$. The tax rate is 75 mills, or $7\frac{1}{2}\%$, so the tax is
$$0.075 \times \$18,800 = \$1410$$
This represents 13.8% of the annual rent ($1410 ÷ $10,200).

39. Total appreciation is $\$59,900 - \$42,000 = \$17,900$. Total percent appreciation is $\$17,900 \div \$42,000 = 42.619\%$. Average over four years is
$$42.619\% \div 4 = 10.65\%$$

45. The 11 lots originally cost a total of $11 \times \$2100 = \$23,100$; he sells 7 lots for $2800 more than that, or a total of $\$23,100 + \$2800 = \$25,900$. The average sale price would be
$$\$25,900 \div 7 = \$3700$$

50. The house is a combination of two rectangles: one is 50 ft. × 24 ft. (1200 sq. ft.) and the other smaller part jutting out to the bottom is 24 ft. × 16 ft. (384 sq. ft.). You get the 16 ft. measurement by subtracting the 24 ft. of the short side of the house from the 40 ft. of the long side.
$$1200 \text{ sq. ft.} + 384 \text{ sq. ft.} = 1584 \text{ sq. ft.}$$

51. The lot is 120 ft. × 75 ft. = 9000 sq. ft. The area taken by the house is
$$1584 \text{ sq. ft.} \div 9000 \text{ sq. ft.} = 0.176 = 17.6\%$$

59. This figure is a trapezoid. The top (T) and bottom (B) are of unequal lengths, while the height (H) does not change. The formula for this figure is
$$\text{AREA} = \frac{1}{2} \times (T + B) \times H$$
The area of the lot, then, is
$\frac{1}{2} \times (110 \text{ ft.} + 160 \text{ ft.}) \times 200 \text{ ft.} = \frac{1}{2} \times 270 \text{ ft.} \times 200 \text{ ft.} = 27,000 \text{ sq. ft.}$
If the lot is sold for $78,300.00, then the price per sq. ft. is
$$\$78,300.00 \div 27,000.00 = \$2.90$$

60. The salesperson's $3024 was 60% of total commission. So
$$\$3024 \div 0.6 = \$5040 \text{ total commission}$$
Since the sale price was $63,000, the *rate* of commission was
$$\$5040 \div \$63,000 = 0.08 = 8\%$$

65. First find the value of the house alone. Land is 15% of the total value, which means that the house is 85% of the total ($100\% - 15\% = 85\%$). So, the house is worth
$$0.85 \times \$47,000 = \$39,950$$
If the house has 1733 sq. ft., the cost per sq. ft. is
$$\$39,950.00 \div 1733 \text{ sq. ft.} = \$23.05251, \text{ which rounds to } \$23.05.$$

66. First find the amount of the total commission:
$$0.065 \times \$46,900.00 = \$3048.50$$
If Jones gets to keep 42% of this, then the broker must get to keep the remaining 58%. Therefore, the broker's share is:
$$0.58 \times \$3048.50 = \$1768.13$$

67. 90 ft. × 60 ft. = 5400 sq. ft. $630 × 12 mo. = $7560 per yr. Annual rent per sq. ft. is
$$\$7560 \div 5400 \text{ sq. ft.} = \$1.40$$

70. The lot value has increased by 800%. Don't forget to include the fact that the lot was originally worth 100% of its value at that time, so if it has gone up by 800%, then today it is worth 900% or 9 times its original value.
$$9 \times \$2000 = \$18,000 \text{ lot value today}$$
Similarly, since the house is worth 40% more, today it is worth 140% of its original value:
$$1.4 \times \$13,000 = \$18,200 \text{ house value today}$$
House and lot together are worth $18,000 + $18,200 = $36,200 today.

74. There are two ways of answering this question.
   (A) You can figure the commissions on $35,000 and $31,500 and subtract.
$$0.06 \times \$35,000 = \$2100$$
$$0.06 \times \$31,500 = \$1890$$
$$\$2100 - \$1890 = \$210, \text{ the correct answer}$$
   (B) You can subtract $31,500 from $35,000 and get $3500, which is the difference in price. The broker will lose the commission on that amount, so
$$0.06 \times \$3150 = \$210, \text{ also the correct answer}$$

75. One acre contains 43,560 sq. ft., so
$$1\tfrac{1}{4} \times 43,560 \text{ sq. ft.} = 54,450 \text{ sq. ft.}$$

MODEL EXAMINATION 2

91. The millage rate of 32.5 is 3.25%, so tax on $60,000 is
$$0.0325 \times \$60,000 = \$1950$$

92. Let the price of the *third* lot be P. The price of the second lot, then, will be $2 \times P$. The price of the first lot will be $1\tfrac{1}{2} \times 2 \times P$. All three cost $9000, so
$$P + (2 \times P) + (1\tfrac{1}{2} \times 2 \times P) = \$9000, \text{ or } 6 \times P = \$9000$$
Therefore, $P = \$9000 \div 6 = \$1500$. The price of the second lot was twice that, or $3000. The third lot was 1½ times the second lot, or $4500.

93. If he uses 10% of the 44 acres for parks, he will use 4.4 acres. Add that to the 6.6 other acres that must be used for streets, etc., and you get a total of 11 acres not devoted to lots. This leaves 33 acres, or 33 acres × 43,560 sq. ft. = 1,437,480 sq. ft. for lots. If each lot must be at least 7500 sq. ft., then the maximum number of lots is
$$1,437,480 \text{ sq. ft.} \div 7500 \text{ sq. ft.} = 191.664, \text{ or } 191 \text{ full lots}$$

94. Smith paid $2700 interest over four years; this comes to $675 per year ($2700 ÷ 4). The annual interest rate was
$$\$675 \div \$7500 = 0.09 = 9\%$$

95. If Jim made a profit of 43%, then he sold the land for 143% of its purchase price. The purchase price was
$$\$164,450 \div 1.43 = \$115,000$$

96. Bill's $390.60 was 12% of Joe's commission, which must have been $390.60 ÷ 0.12 = $3255.00. If the sale price was $46,500.00, the rate of commission was
$$\$3255.00 \div \$46,500.00 = 0.07 = 7\%$$

97. 11% of $210,000 is $23,100.
$$\$23,100 \div 12 = \$1925 \text{ monthly}$$

98. How long will it take $1000.00 to compound to $3000.00 at 25% per year?
One year: 1.25 × $1000 = $1250.00
Two years: 1.25 × $1250.00 = $1562.50
Three years: 1.25 × $1562.50 = $1953.13
Four years: 1.25 × $1953.13 = $2441.41
Five years: 1.25 × $2441.41 = $3051.76
It will take about five years.

99. 1700 ft. × 2100 ft. = 3,570,000 sq. ft.

$$3,570,000 \text{ sq. ft.} \div 43,560 \text{ sq. ft.} = 81.96 \text{ acres}$$

100. The backyard is 100 ft. + 80 ft. + 100 ft. + 80 ft. = 360 ft. around. From this we subtract the 40 ft. taken up by the house, to get 320 lineal ft. of fence needed. If the fence is 4 ft. high, it will have 320 ft. × 4 ft. = 1280 sq. ft. of fence fabric. 1280 sq. ft. is 142.222 sq. yd.

$$142.222 \text{ sq. yd.} \times \$1.80 = \$256.00 \text{ total cost}$$

MODEL EXAMINATION 3

4. 10.6 acres is

$$10.6 \times 43,560 \text{ sq. ft.} = 461,736 \text{ sq. ft.}$$

If one side is 181 ft., the other must be

$$461,736 \text{ sq. ft.} \div 181 \text{ ft.} = 2551.0276 = 2551 \text{ ft., rounded off}$$

5. 17.1 acres is

$$17.1 \text{ acres} \times 43,560 \text{ sq. ft.} = 744,876 \text{ sq. ft.}$$

If 19% must be set aside, that leaves 81% for lots, or

$$0.81 \times 744,876 \text{ sq. ft.} = 603,349.56 \text{ sq. ft.}$$

If each lot must have at least 8000 sq. ft., the maximum number of lots is

$$603,399.56 \text{ sq. ft.} \div 8000 \text{ sq. ft.} = 75.4, \text{ or a maximum of 75 full lots}$$

10. 400 ft. × 665 ft. = 266,000 sq. ft.
266,000 sq. ft. ÷ 43,560 sq. ft. = 6.1065 acres
$17,100.00 ÷ 6.1065 acres = $2800.29, or $2800 per acre

11. $42,500.00 × 0.30 = $12,750.00 taxable value
71 mills is the same as a tax rate of 7.1%, so the tax is

$$0.071 \times \$12,750.00 = \$905.25$$

17. A building that is 40 ft. × 22 ft. is 124 ft. around (40 + 22 + 40 + 22). The total wall area would be 124 ft. × 10 ft., or 1240 sq. ft. From this we subtract the 52 sq. ft. of windows (4 sq. ft. × 13) and the 48 sq. ft. of door to get 1140 sq. ft. of wall area needing paint. One gal. of paint covers 400 sq. ft. To get one coat of paint we need 1140 sq. ft. ÷ 400 sq. ft. = 2.85 gal., so two coats will require twice as much, or 5.7 gal.

18. $330 per quarter is $1320 per yr. (4 × $330). The interest rate is

$$\$1320 \div \$12,000 = 0.11 = 11\%$$

24. Smith will pay $50 less rent per mo. if he pays the utility bills himself. Average bills are $480 per yr., which is $40 per mo. ($480 ÷ 12). Smith thinks he can reduce this by 35%, which means that he expects to pay only 65% of the $40 per mo. average, or 0.65 × $40 = $26. He saves $50 on rent and expects to pay $26 of that for utilities, so he expects to save $24 per month.

25. 7% × $1,100,000 = $77,000 total commissions brought in by Jones. He gets 50% of the first $20,000 (or $10,000) *plus* 60% of the rest. In his case, the rest is $57,000.

$$0.6 \times \$57,000 = \$34,200$$

To this we add his $10,000 share of the first $20,000 to get a total income for him of $44,200.

42. If Jackson paid a 6½% commission, then the $33,613.25 he has left represents the remaining 93½% of the sale price. The sale price then must be

$$\$33,613.25 \div 0.935 = \$35,950.00$$

48. Anderson paid out a total of 12% of the selling price in fees, so his $176,000 is the 88% of the sale price that he has left. Therefore, his sale price was
$176,000 \div 0.88 = $200,000

49. The 9-in. thick walls are ¾ ft. thick. Therefore, the interior dimensions of the floor are 50½ ft. × 34½ ft. (remember, the walls are at *both* ends):
50.5 × 34.5 = 1742.25 sq. ft. gross,
from which we subtract the area taken up by the pillars. They are each ½ ft. × ½ ft., or ¼ sq. ft. Their total area is
13 × ¼ sq. ft. = 3¼ sq. ft.
Subtracting this amount from the 1742¼ leaves a net of 1739 sq. ft.

62. The lots contain 10,500 sq. ft. each and must each have 1380 sq. ft. additional amenity. Therefore, Smith will need a minimum of 11,880 sq. ft. for each lot (10,500 sq. ft. + 1380 sq. ft.). Since he wants 55 lots, he will need at least 55 × 11,880 sq. ft. = 653,400 sq. ft. 653,400 sq. ft. ÷ 43,560 sq. ft. = 15 acres exactly.

70. Interior gross dimensions are 41 ft. × 27 ft. = 1107 sq. ft. (Remember to subtract 6 in. of outside wall from each end. Interior wall area is ⅓ ft. × 135 ft. = 45 sq. ft. Each bathroom is 54 sq. ft. The kitchen is 144 sq. ft. This is a total area of 297 sq. ft. *not* to be carpeted, leaving 810 sq. ft. A sq. yd. contains 9 sq. ft. (3 ft. × 3 ft.); the total number of sq. yd. to be carpeted is 810 sq. ft. ÷ 9 sq. ft. = 90 sq. yd. At $13.95 per sq. yd., the total cost is $1255.50 (90 sq. yd. × $13.95).

71. To determine how much Fred still needs, we subtract from the $55,000 purchase price the $1500 earnest money payment and the 75% loan. The loan is 75% of $55,000, or $55,000 × 0.75 = $41,250. $55,000 less $1500 is $53,500. Subtracting the $41,250 loan leaves $12,250 still needed.

74. A lot 100 ft. × 100 ft. contains 100 × 100 = 10,000 sq. ft. 3 acres contain 43,560 × 3 = 130,680 sq. ft. 130,680 ÷ 10,000 = 13.068, or 13 full lots.

75. The width of the lot is 6336 ÷ 96 = 66 ft. At $225 a front ft. the lot would sell for 66 × $225 = $14,850.

MODEL EXAMINATION 4

2. Assessed value is 20% of $70,000 × 0.2 = $14,000. 80 mills is 8%.
$14,000 × 0.08 = $1120.00

9. We must subtract the broker's commission and the loan discount from the $50,000 sale price, since seller (Freddy) must pay both.
6% of $50,000 is $50,000 × 0.06 = $3000 commission.
Loan is 80% of $50,000. $50,000 × 0.80 = $40,000 loan. Discount is 3 points, or 3% of $40,000. $40,000 × 0.03 = $1200
Total payments by Freddy are $3000 commission + $1200 loan discount, or $4200. $50,000 − $4200 = $45,800

10. Same problem as question #9, where we found the loan discount to be $1200.

11. We figure the *effective* rate to the lender of a mortgage loan by adding *1/8 of one percent* to the *contract* interest rate for each *one* point of discount paid on the loan. The contract interest rate is 10%; there are 3 points discount. Thus, the effective rate is 10% + ⅜%, or 10⅜% (10.375%).

28. Cash-on-cash ratio is annual cash return received, divided by the cash spent (original equity) to acquire the investment.
$$\$16,900 \div \$130,000 = 0.13$$

29. A sq. mi. contains 640 acres.
$$200 \div 640 = 0.3125, \text{ or } 31.25\%$$

31. An acre contains 43,560 sq. ft. The tract in this problem is 440 ft. × 817 ft. = 359,480 sq. ft. 359,480 ÷ 43,560 = 8.253, or 8.25 rounded

41. The sale closed July 15, but the taxes aren't due until October 15. Therefore, the taxes haven't been paid; the buyer will have to pay the full year's tax bill on October 15. So, *seller pays buyer* at closing.
Assessed value is $48,500, tax rate is 38 mills (which is 3.8%, or 0.038). So, the year's tax is 48,500 × 0.038 = $1843.00
Seller owned property for exactly 6½ mo. (January through June, and half of July). So, the seller owes the buyer 6.5 mo. of taxes. One mo. of taxes is $1843 ÷ 12 = $153.583. 6.5 × $153.583 = $998.29

47. In this problem we have to determine how long the buyer owned the property. We know the buyer owned it at the end of the yr. We calculate time from his tax payment, and then figure backwards from December 31 to determine the date of settlement. Remember, the settlement date is considered a day that the *seller* owned the property. The total tax bill is $763.20. $763.20 ÷ 12 = $63.60 per mo. $63.60 ÷ 30 = $2.12 per day.
First we determine how many *whole mo.* the buyer owned the property by dividing the buyer's share of taxes ($250.16) by the monthly tax share of $63.60. $250.16 ÷ $63.60 = 3.93333. Thus, the buyer owned the property for 3 whole mo. (October, November, and December) and then some. So now we know that the settlement occurred sometime in September.
Now we subtract the 3 whole mo. worth of taxes from the buyer's share 3 × $63.60 = $190.80. $250.16 − $190.80 = $59.36. So the buyer also owned the property for $59.35 "worth" of September.
$59.36 ÷ $2.12 = 28 of September's 30 days. Thus, the closing had to be on 30 − 28 = 2 of September.

53. A sq. yd. is 3 ft. × 3 ft. = 9 sq. ft. 825 sq. yd. is 825 × 9 = 7425 sq. ft. 7425 ÷ 75 = 99 ft. None of the answers says "99 ft", but 3 choices are expressed in measures other than ft. 1$\frac{1}{16}$ mile is 5280 ÷ 16 = 330 feet, which is *not* 99 ft. 32 yards is 32 × 3 = 96 feet; *not* 99, 6 rods is 16.5 × 6 = 99 ft., the correct answer.

55. 4840 sq. yd. ÷ 9 sq. ft. = 43,560 sq. ft. A sq. chain is 66 ft. × 66 ft. = 4356 sq. ft. 10 sq. chains are 43,560 sq. ft. Both answers are correct.

58. First we find the amount of the total commission. Lois's share of $1158.30 was 45% of the total her firm received. $1158.30 × 0.45 = $2574, Lois's firm's share, which was 60% of the total. $2574 ÷ 0.6 = $4290 total commission.
The house sold for $66,000. $4290 ÷ $66,000 = 0.065, or 6.5%

59. ¼ acre contains 43,560 ÷ 4 = 10,890 sq. ft.
$$\$12,000 \div 10,890 = \$1.102 \text{ or } \$1.10 \text{ rounded}$$

74. We have to calculate the down payment, the origination fee, the discount, and the PMI fee. We add all of these to get the answer.
Down Payment is 10%. $73,500 × 0.10 = $7350 down payment

Origination fee, discount, and PMI fee all are calculated as part of the *loan amount* (not the sales price). The loan will equal the sales price less the down payment, or $73,500 − $7350 = $66,150 loan amount.

$$\text{Origination fee } (1\%) \text{ is } \$66,150 \times 0.01 = \$661.50$$
$$\text{Discount } (2\%) \text{ is } \$66,150 \times 0.02 = \$1323.00$$
$$\text{PMI fee } (0.5\%, \text{ or } \tfrac{1}{2}\%) \text{ is } \$66,150 \times 0.005 = \$330.75$$
$$\$7350 + \$661.50 + \$1323 + \$330.75 = \$9665.25$$

75. We have to calculate the monthly interest rate, because we are given a monthly interest payment. $9\% \div 12 = 0.75\% = 0.0075$. The interest payment of $468.75 is 0.75% of the loan amount.

$$468.75 \div 0.0075 = \$62,500$$

79. We have to determine the number of cu. yd. in the patio. First we determine the number of cu. ft. The patio is 60 ft. × 20 ft. = 1200 sq. ft. It is 4 in. thick = $\tfrac{4}{12}$ ft. or $\tfrac{1}{3}$ ft. So, 1200 ÷ 3 = 400 cu. ft. is the *volume* of the patio. A cu. yd. is 3 × 3 × 3 = 27 cu. ft.

$$400 \div 27 = 14.82 \text{ cu. yd., or } 14.8 \text{ rounded}$$

MODEL EXAMINATION 5

6. Cash-on-cash ratio is annual cash return received, divided by the cash spent (original equity) to acquire the investment.
$$\$8360 \div \$76,000 = 0.11$$

7. A sq. mi. contains 640 acres. 96 ÷ 640 = 0.15, or 15%

13. The sale closed August 15, but the taxes were due on June 1. Therefore, the taxes have already been paid by the seller. So, *buyer pays seller* at closing, to reimburse the taxes already paid.
Assessed value is $53,250, tax rate is 41 mills (which is 4.1%, or 0.041). So, the year's tax is 53,250 × 0.041 = $2183.25
Seller owned property for exactly 7½ mo. (January through July, and half of August). So, the buyer owes the seller the taxes for the remaining 4.5 mo. of the yr. that the buyer will own the property. One mo. of taxes is $2183.25 ÷ 12 = $181.9375. 4.5 × $181.9375 = $818.719, or (rounded) $818.72 that buyer owes seller.

25. 20 yd. is 20 × 3 = 60 ft. The area of the patio is 60 × 20 = 1200 sq. ft. The patio is 6 in., or half a ft. thick. 1200 × 0.5 = 600 cu. ft., the *volume* of the patio. A cu. yd. is 3 × 3 × 3 = 27 cu. ft. Therefore, Joe will need 600 ÷ 27 = 22.22, or (rounded) 22.2 cu. yd. of concrete.

43. First we find the amount of the total commission. Salesperson's share of $2544 was 60% of the total the firm received. $2544 ÷ 0.6 = $4240 for the firm's share, which was 50% of the total. $4240 ÷ 0.5 = $8480 total commission.
The house sold for $106,000. $8480 ÷ $106,000 = 0.08, or 8%

48. We have to determine the number of front ft. in the lot, and multiply that number × $98 to determine the price the lot sold for.
$$6468 \div 132 = 49 \text{ front ft. } 49 \times 98 = \$4802, \text{ or } \$4800 \text{ rounded}$$

57. $188,000 ÷ 2.6 acres = $72,307.69 per acre
$$\$72,307.69 \div 43,560 = \$1.65997, \text{ or } \$1.66 \text{ rounded}$$

64. In this problem we have to determine how long the seller owned the property. We know the seller owned it at the beginning of the yr. We calculate time from his tax payment, and then figure from January 1 to determine the date of settlement. Remember, the settlement date is considered a day that the *seller* owned the property. The total tax bill is $972. $972 ÷ 12 = $81 per month

$$\$81 \div 30 = \$2.70 \text{ per day}$$

First we determine how many *whole mo.* the seller owned the property by dividing the seller's share of taxes ($351) by the monthly tax share of $81. $351 ÷ $81 = 4.33333. Thus, the seller owned the property for 4 whole mo. (January through April) and part of May, the mo. in which settlement must have occurred.

Now we subtract the 4 whole mo. worth of taxes from the seller's share. 4 × $81 = $324. $351 − $324 = $27. So, the seller also owned the property for $27 "worth" of May. $27 ÷ $2.70 = 10 of May's 31 days (statutory yr.). Thus, the closing had to be on May 10.

81. We have to calculate the down payment, the origination fee, the discount, and the PMI fee. We add all of these to determine the answer.

Down payment is 15%. $77,500 × 0.15 = $11,625 down payment

Origination fee, discount, and PMI fee all are calculated as part of the *loan amount* (not the sales price). The loan will be the sales price less the down payment, or $77,500 — $11,625 = $65,875 loan amount

Origination fee (0.75%) is $65,875 × 0.0075 = $494.06
Discount (2.25%) is $65,875 × 0.0225 = $1482.19 (rounded)
PMI fee (0.5%, or ½%) is $65,875 × 0.005 = $329.38 (rounded)
$11,625 + $494.06 + $1482.19 + $329.38 = $13,930.63

90. We have to calculate the monthly interest rate, because we are given a monthly interest payment. 11.5% ÷ 12 = 0.95833% = 0.0095833. The interest payment of $468.75 is 0.95833% of the loan amount.

$$456.41 \div 0.0095833 = \$47,625 \text{ rounded}$$

MODEL EXAMINATION 6

1. We know the down payment and must calculate the origination fee, the discount, and the PMI fee. We add all of these to determine the answer.

Origination fee, discount, and PMI fee all are calculated as part of the *loan amount* (not the sales price). The loan will be the sales price less the down payment, or $111,500 − $17,250 = $94,250 loan amount

Origination fee (1.5%) is $94,250 × 0.015 = $1413.75
Discount (2%) is $94,250 × 0.02 = $1885.00
PMI fee (0.75%) is $94,250 × 0.0075 = $706.88 (rounded)
$17,250 + $1413.75 + $1885.00 + $706.88 = $21,255.63

2. We have to calculate the monthly interest rate, because we are given a monthly interest payment. 10.5% ÷ 12 = 0.875% = 0.00875. The interest payment of $496.56 is 0.875% of the loan amount.

$$496.56 \div 0.00875 = \$56,750 \text{ rounded}$$

9. The area of the driveway is 70 ft. × 12 ft. = 840 sq. ft. The driveway is 5 in., or 5/12 ft. thick. 5 ÷ 12 = 0.41667 ft. thick. 840 × 0.41667 = 350 cu. ft. (rounded), the *volume* of the driveway. A cu. yd. is 3 × 3 × 3 = 27 cu. ft. Therefore, Joe will need 350 ÷ 27 = 12.96, or (rounded) 13 cu. yd. of concrete.

22. 59 ft. 6 in. is 59.5 ft. 535.5 sq. yd. is 535.5 × 9 = 4819.5 sq. ft. 4819.5 ÷ 59.5 = 81 ft. of depth. This answer is not one of the choices. However, 3 of the answers are expressed in measures other than ft. 0.03 mi. is 0.03 × 5280 = 158.4 ft. 5.33 rods is 5.33

× 16.5 = 87.95 ft. Both of these choices are incorrect. However, 27 yd. is 27 × 3 = 81 ft., which is correct.

25. The commission was 7%. $82,000 × 0.07 = $5740 total commission. Mack's 48% share is $5740 × 0.48 = $2755.20. 55% of that was paid to the salesperson, leaving 1 − 0.55 = 0.45 or 45% for Mack.
$$\$2755.20 \times 0.45 = \$1239.84$$

26. 1.6 acres is 1.6 × 43,560 = 69,696 sq. ft.
$$\$25,100 \div 69,696 = .3601, \text{ or } \$0.36 \text{ rounded}$$

42. In this problem we have to determine how long the seller owned the property, and then figure from February 1 (the day the insurance policy was purchased) to determine the date of settlement. Remember, the settlement date is considered a day that the *seller* owned the property.
$$\text{The total bill was } \$324. \ \$324 \div 12 = \$27 \text{ per mo.}$$
$$\$27 \div 30 = \$0.90 \text{ per day}$$
First we determine how many *whole mo.* of the policy year the buyer owned the property. We divide the buyer's share of the policy cost ($63) by the monthly share of $27. $63 ÷ $27 = 2.33333. Thus, the buyer owned the property for 2 whole mo. and part (0.3333) of a third. 0.3333 × 30 = 10 more days. The policy expires January 31, so the buyer's 2 full mo. are December and January. Since the buyer had already owned the policy for 10 days at the beginning of December, the settlement must have occurred in November. 30 − 10 = 20 of November.

49. 35% of $86,000 is 0.35 × $86,000 = $30,100 assessed value. 42 mills is 4.2%.
$$\text{So, } 0.042 \times \$30,100 = \$1264.20$$

50. **The discount is based on the** *loan amount.* The loan is 90% of $77,900. 0.9 × $77,900 = $70,110. The discount is 2.5 points, or 2.5%.
$$0.025 \times \$70,110 = \$1752.75$$

51. For every 1 point discount paid, we increase the *effective* rate of return to the lender by ⅛%, or 0.125%. The contract interest rate is 9.75%, and there are 2.5 points. 2.5 × 0.1255 = 0.3125%, which we add to the contract rate.
$$9.75\% + 0.3125\% = 10.0625\%$$

62. Cash-on-cash ratio is annual cash return received, divided by the cash spent (original equity) to acquire the investment.
$$\$32,300 \div \$222,750 = 0.145 \text{ rounded}$$

63. 1085 × 900 = 976,500 sq. ft. in the lot. One sq. mi. contains 5280 × 5280 = 27,878,400 sq. ft.
$$976,500 \div 27,878,400 = 0.035, \text{ or } 3.5\% \text{ rounded}$$

69. 1077 × 607 = 653,739 sq. ft. 653,739 × 43,560 = 15.0078 acres. The only acceptable answer, therefore, is "more than 15."

76. This problem isn't difficult, but it requires several calculations. You may find it helpful to leave time-consuming problems such as this one until after you have answered the simpler questions.
We have to calculate the cost of the house, basement, and garage and then add them together.
House: First 1600 sq. ft. costs $51.10 × 1600 = $81,760. There are 2100 − 1600 = 500 additional sq. ft. to pay for. 500 × $42.25 = $21,225 additional. $81,760 + $21,225 = $102,885 for the house.

Basement: Note that this is a two-story house. Therefore, the basement will be only *half* the area of the house, or 2100 ÷ 2 = 1050 sq. ft. 1050 × $22.50 = $23,625 for the basement.

Garage: 420 × $29.20 = $12,264

$102,885 + $23,625 + $12,264 = $138,774, or $139,000 to the nearest $1000

80. First we calculate the cost of the lots. We know A cost $11,000. B cost 2.5 times that amount. 2.5 × $11,000 = $27,500. C cost half the price of B. $27,500 ÷ 2 = $13,750. So, $11,000 + $27,500 + $13,750 = $52,250, the cost of all 3 lots. A and B were sold for 25% more than this amount, or 125% of this amount, or 1.25 × $52,250 = $65,312.50. C was sold for twice its cost: $13,750 × 2 = $27,500. Thus, $65,312.50 + $27,500 = $92,812.50, the amount all 3 lots sold for. $92,812.50 − $52,250 = $40,562.50. However, this is not one of the answer choices. Therefore, "none of the **above**" is correct.

MODEL EXAMINATION 7

74. 35 ft. × 15 ft. = 525 sq. ft. 525 sq. ft. × $8.40 = $4410 rent per yr., which is $367.50 per mo. ($4410 ÷ 12).

75. First year: $50,000 × 1.1 = $55,000
Second year: $55,000 × 1.1 = $60,500. The question statement is false.

76. $17,000.00 × 0.11 = $1870.00
$1870.00 ÷ 12 = $158.83

77. 60 ft. × 24 ft. × 9 ft. = 12,960 cu. ft. There are 27 cu. ft. to a cu. yd., so
12,960 cu. ft. ÷ 27 cu. ft. = 480 cu. yd.

78. 3 yr. 9 mo. is 3¾ yr., so the total interest due is 3¾ × 12% or 45% of the loan amount: 0.45 × $2000 = $900. The question statement is false.

79. Total cubic footage is 90 ft. × 50 ft. × 12 ft. = 54,000 cu. ft. Cubic yardage is 54,000 cu. ft. ÷ 27 cu. ft. = 2000. At $17.75 per cu. yd., the excavation costs $35,500.

80. $1025.00 × 0.08 = $82.00

134. The tax is based on 28% of $40,000.00, or 0.28 × $40,000.00 = $11,200.00. The 77 mill tax rate is 7.7%, so the tax is
0.077 × $11,200.00 = $862.40

135. 1.77 acres × 43,560 sq. ft. = 77,101.2 sq. ft.
77,101.2 sq ft. ÷ 4 = 19,275.3 sq. ft.

136. 71.2 ft. × 100 ft. = 7120 sq. ft. of lot
40 ft. × 28 ft. = 1120 sq. ft. of original house. 7120 sq. ft. − 1120 sq. ft. = 6000 uncovered sq. ft. The new addition is 20 ft. × 24 ft. = 480 sq. ft.
480 sq. ft. ÷ 6000 sq. ft. = 0.08 = 8% of the uncovered area

137. The 30 mill tax rate is 3%.
0.03 × $6500 = $195

138. 0.09 × $35,000.00 = $3150.00 interest per year.
$3150.00 ÷ 4 = $787.50 interest per quarter

139. 3.8 acres × 43,560 sq. ft. = 165,528 sq. ft.

140. The first monthly interest payment is $285, which would be $3420 annually. If this is 9.5% of the loan, then the loan must be

$$\$3420 \div 0.095 = \$36,000$$

If this is 80% of the sale price, then the price is

$$\$36,000 \div 0.8 = \$45,000$$

SUPPLEMENTAL EXAMINATION 1

2. The commission is 7½% of $54,500.00

$$0.075 \times \$54,500.00 = \$4087.50$$

4. The tax rate is 88 mills (8.8%) on $26,550.00

$$0.088 \times \$26,550.00 = \$2336.40$$

SUPPLEMENTAL EXAMINATION 2

1. The commission is 7½% of $52,000.

$$0.075 \times \$52,000 = \$3900$$

2. The mortgage loan is at least 80% of the price.

$$0.8 \times \$52,000 = \$41,600$$

4. $52,000 − $41,600 = $10,400 cash that the buyer must provide. Since he already has paid $1000 in earnest money, he must pay an additional $9400 at closing.

SUPPLEMENTAL EXAMINATION 3

3. The annual property taxes are $2336.40 (see question 4, Supplemental Examination 1). The closing date is September 18, and the seller has already paid the full year's tax bill. The buyer will own the house for the remaining 12 days of September and the three months of October, November, and December.

$$\$2336.40 \div 12 = \$194.70 \text{ taxes per month}$$
$$\$194.70 \div 30 = \$6.49 \text{ tax per day}$$
$$3 \text{ months @ } \$194.70 = \$584.10$$
$$12 \text{ days @ } \$6.49 \quad = \quad \underline{77.88}$$

Total tax proration $661.98, paid by buyer to seller

(I) is true, but (II) is false.

4. The mortgage insurance premium is 2½% of the mortgage amount. The mortgage is 90% of $52,000.

$$0.9 \times \$52,000 = \$46,800$$
$$0.025 \times \$46,800 = \$1170$$

5. The title insurance premium is 0.85% of the sale price.

$$0.0085 \times \$52,000 = \$442$$

6. $0.9 \times \$52,000 = \$46,800$

7. $0.075 \times \$52,000 = \$3900$

8. The three-year premium is $888.75, which is $296.25 annually, $24.6875 monthly, and $0.8229 daily. The policy expires on October 21, 1984, leaving the buyer with one year, one month, and three days of insurance.

1 year	$296.25
1 month	24.6875
3 days @ 0.8229	2.4687

Total prorated amount $323.41 paid by buyer to seller

Both (I) and (II) are false.

SUPPLEMENTAL EXAMINATION 4

16. The northern boundary of SW¼, SE¼ is ¼ mi., or 1320 ft. 1320 ft. × 66 ft. = 87,120 sq. ft.; 87,120 sq. ft. ÷ 43,560 sq. ft. = 2 acres. Since SW¼, SE¼ contains 40 acres, the part uncovered by the road is 38 acres.

17. He owns ¼ of the total, and he buys the rest which is ¾ of the total, or 3 times as much (300%) as he started with.

18. S½, NW¼, NE¼ contains 20 acres. A section contains 640 acres. Therefore, she has bought

$$20 \div 640 = 0.03125 = 3.125\% = 3\frac{1}{8}\%$$

Appendix:
State Real Estate Licensing Offices

ALABAMA
   Real Estate Commission
   State of Alabama
   562 State Office Building
   Montgomery, Alabama 36130
   (205) 832-3266

ALASKA
   Real Estate Commission of Alaska
   Division of Occupational Licensing
   Department of Commerce and
      Economic Development
   Pouch D, Juneau, Alaska 99811
   (907) 465-2500

ARIZONA
   Arizona Department of Real Estate
   1645 W. Jefferson Street
   Phoenix, Arizona 85007
   (602) 271-4345

ARKANSAS
   Arkansas Real Estate Commission
   Suite 600, TCB Building
   1 Riverfront Place
   North Little Rock, Arkansas 72214
   (501) 371-1247

CALIFORNIA
   Department of Real Estate
   State of California
   714 P Street
   Sacramento, California 95814
   (916) 445-8645

COLORADO
   Colorado Real Estate Commission
   110 State Services Building
   1525 Sherman Street
   Denver, Colorado 80203
   (303) 892-2633

CONNECTICUT
   Connecticut Real Estate Commission
   90 Washington Street
   Hartford, Connecticut 06115
   (203) 566-5130

DELAWARE
   Delaware Real Estate Commission
   Division of Business and
      Occupational Regulations
   Department of Administrative Services
   State House Annex
   Dover, Delaware 19901
   (302) 678-4186

DISTRICT OF COLUMBIA
   Real Estate Commission of the
      District of Columbia
   Department of Economic Development
   614 H Street, N.W.
   Washington, D.C. 20001
   (202) 629-4543

FLORIDA
   Florida Real Estate Commission
   400 West Robinson Avenue
   Orlando, Florida 32801
   (305) 423-6053

GEORGIA
   Georgia Real Estate Commission
   40 Pryor Street, S.W.
   Atlanta, Georgia 30334
   (404) 656-3916

HAWAII
   Professional & Vocational Licensing Division
   Department of Regulatory Agencies
   State of Hawaii
   P.O. Box 3469
   Honolulu, Hawaii 96801
   (808) 548-7464

IDAHO

Idaho Real Estate Commission
633 North Fourth Street
State Capital Building
Boise, Idaho 83720
(208) 384-3285

ILLINOIS

Department of Registration & Education
628 East Adams Street
Springfield, Illinois 62786
(217) 782-8024

INDIANA

Indiana Real Estate Commission
1022 State Office Building
100 North Senate Avenue
Indianapolis, Indiana 46204
(317) 633-5386

IOWA

Iowa Real Estate Commission
1223 East Court
Des Moines, Iowa 50319
(515) 281-3183

KANSAS

Kansas Real Estate Commission
Room 1212
535 Kansas Avenue
Topeka, Kansas 66603
(913) 296-3411

KENTUCKY

Kentucky Real Estate Commission
100 E. Liberty Street, Suite 204
Louisville, Kentucky 40202
(502) 588-4462

LOUISIANA

Real Estate Commission
Department of Occupational Standards
P.O. Box 44517
Baton Rouge, Louisiana 70804
(504) 389-7755

MAINE

Maine Real Estate Commission
Department of Business Regulation
State Office Annex
Augusta, Maine 04333
(207) 289-3735

MARYLAND

Maryland Real Estate Commission
Department of Licensing and Regulation
1 South Calvert Street
Baltimore, Maryland 21202
(301) 383-2130

MASSACHUSETTS

Massachusetts Department of Civil Service
    and Registration
Board of Registration of Real Estate Brokers
    & Salesmen
Leverett Saltonstall Building
100 Cambridge Street
Boston, Massachusetts 02202
(617) 727-3055

MICHIGAN

Michigan Department of Licensing and
    Regulation, Real Estate Division
808 Southland
P.O. Box 30018
Lansing, Michigan 48909
(517) 373-0490

MINNESOTA

Commissioner of Securities
Department of Commerce
State of Minnesota
Metro Square Building, 5th Floor
St. Paul, Minnesota 55101
(612) 296-6319

MISSISSIPPI

Mississippi Real Estate Commission
Busby Building
754 North President
Jackson, Mississippi 39202
(601) 354-7093

MISSOURI

Missouri Real Estate Commission
3253 North 10 Mile Drive
P.O. Box 1339
Jefferson City, Missouri 65101
(314) 751-2334

MONTANA

Montana Real Estate Commission
La Londe Building
42½ North Main Street
Helena, Montana 59601
(406) 449-2961

NEBRASKA
Nebraska Real Estate Commission
2300 State Capital Building
Lincoln, Nebraska 68509
(402) 471-2004

NEVADA
Administrator
Real Estate Division
Department of Commerce
Capitol Complex
201 South Fall Street, Room 129
Carson City, Nevada 89710
(702) 885-4280

NEW HAMPSHIRE
New Hampshire Real Estate Commission
3 Capitol Street
Concord, New Hampshire 03301
(603) 271-2701

NEW JERSEY
New Jersey Real Estate Commission
Department of Insurance
P.O. Box 1510
201 East State Street
Trenton, New Jersey 08625
(609) 292-7656

NEW MEXICO
New Mexico Real Estate Commission
600 Second, N.W., Suite 608
Albuquerque, New Mexico 87102
(505) 842-3226

NEW YORK
Secretary of State
Department of State
Division of Licensing Services
162 Washington Avenue
Albany, New York 12231
(518) 474-2121

NORTH CAROLINA
North Carolina Real Estate Licensing Board
115 Hillsborough Street
P.O. Box 266
Raleigh, North Carolina 27602
(919) 833-2771

NORTH DAKOTA
North Dakota Real Estate Commission
410 East Thayer Avenue
P.O. Box 727
Bismarck, North Dakota 58505
(701) 224-2749

OHIO
Department of Commerce
Real Estate Commission
180 East Broad Street
Columbus, Ohio 43215
(616) 466-4100

OKLAHOMA
Oklahoma Real Estate Commission
Suite 100
4040 North Lincoln Boulevard
Oklahoma City, Oklahoma 73105
(405) 521-3387

OREGON
Department of Commerce
Real Estate Division
158 12th Street, N.E.
Salem, Oregon 97310
(503) 378-4170

PENNSYLVANIA
Commissioner of Professional &
  Occupational Affairs
State Real Estate Commission
Commonwealth of Pennsylvania
Box 2649
Harrisburg, Pennsylvania 17120
(717) 787-2100

RHODE ISLAND
Department of Business Regulation
Real Estate Division
State of Rhode Island
100 North Main Street
Providence, Rhode Island 02903
(401) 277-2255

SOUTH CAROLINA
South Carolina Real Estate Commission
2221 Devine Street, Suite 530
Columbia, South Carolina 29205
(803) 758-3981

SOUTH DAKOTA
South Dakota Real Estate Commission
P.O. Box 638
Pierre, South Dakota 57501
(605) 224-3600

TENNESSEE
Tennessee Real Estate Commission
556 Capitol Hill Building
Nashville, Tennessee 37219
(615) 741-2273

TEXAS

Texas Real Estate Commission
P.O. Box 12188
Capitol Station
Austin, Texas 78711
(512) 475-4250

UTAH

Real Estate Division
Department of Business Regulation
State of Utah
330 East 4th South Street
Salt Lake City, Utah 84111
(801) 533-5661

VERMONT

Vermont Real Estate Commission
7 East State Street
Montpelier, Vermont 05602
(802) 828-3228

VIRGINIA

Department of Professional &
    Occupational Regulation
Virginia Real Estate Commission
2 South 9th Street, 2nd Floor
P.O. Box 1-X
Richmond, Virginia 23202
(804) 786-2161

WASHINGTON

Business and Professions Administration
Real Estate Division
P.O. Box 247
Olympia, Washington 98504
(206) 753-6681

WEST VIRGINIA

Real Estate Commission of West Virginia
402 State Office Building No. 3
1800 East Washington Street
Charleston, West Virginia 25305
(304) 348-3555

WISCONSIN

Department of Regulation and Licensing
Real Estate Examining Board
1400 East Washington Avenue
Madison, Wisconsin 53702
(608) 266-5450

WYOMING

Wyoming Real Estate Commission
Supreme Court Building
Cheyenne, Wyoming 82002
(307) 777-7660

VIRGIN ISLANDS

Virgin Islands Real Estate Commission
P.O. Box 925
Charlotte Amalie, St. Thomas 00801
(809) 774-2991

Answer Sheets

MODEL EXAMINATION 1

NAME _____

LAST   FIRST   MIDDLE

SOC. SEC. # _____ / _____ / _____

SESSION _____ AM ☐   PM ☐

Enter your IDENT. NUMBER ↓

EXAM CODE # _____

DATE _____

PLACE OF EXAM _____

TITLE OF EXAM _____ SALESMAN ☐   BROKER ☐

BOOK # _____

IMPORTANT: IN MARKING YOUR ANSWERS FILL IN THE ANSWER BOX COMPLETELY.

1 ::A:: ::B:: ::C:: ::D::	4 ::A:: ::B:: ::C:: ::D::	8 ::A:: ::B:: ::C:: ::D::	12 ::A:: ::B:: ::C:: ::D::
2 ::A:: ::B:: ::C:: ::D::	5 ::A:: ::B:: ::C:: ::D::	9 ::A:: ::B:: ::C:: ::D::	13 ::A:: ::B:: ::C:: ::D::
3 ::A:: ::B:: ::C:: ::D::	6 ::A:: ::B:: ::C:: ::D::	10 ::A:: ::B:: ::C:: ::D::	14 ::A:: ::B:: ::C:: ::D::
	7 ::A:: ::B:: ::C:: ::D::	11 ::A:: ::B:: ::C:: ::D::	15 ::A:: ::B:: ::C:: ::D::
16 ::A:: ::B:: ::C:: ::D::	19 ::A:: ::B:: ::C:: ::D::	23 ::A:: ::B:: ::C:: ::D::	27 ::A:: ::B:: ::C:: ::D::
17 ::A:: ::B:: ::C:: ::D::	20 ::A:: ::B:: ::C:: ::D::	24 ::A:: ::B:: ::C:: ::D::	28 ::A:: ::B:: ::C:: ::D::
18 ::A:: ::B:: ::C:: ::D::	21 ::A:: ::B:: ::C:: ::D::	25 ::A:: ::B:: ::C:: ::D::	29 ::A:: ::B:: ::C:: ::D::
	22 ::A:: ::B:: ::C:: ::D::	26 ::A:: ::B:: ::C:: ::D::	30 ::A:: ::B:: ::C:: ::D::
31 ::A:: ::B:: ::C:: ::D::	34 ::A:: ::B:: ::C:: ::D::	38 ::A:: ::B:: ::C:: ::D::	42 ::A:: ::B:: ::C:: ::D::
32 ::A:: ::B:: ::C:: ::D::	35 ::A:: ::B:: ::C:: ::D::	39 ::A:: ::B:: ::C:: ::D::	43 ::A:: ::B:: ::C:: ::D::
33 ::A:: ::B:: ::C:: ::D::	36 ::A:: ::B:: ::C:: ::D::	40 ::A:: ::B:: ::C:: ::D::	44 ::A:: ::B:: ::C:: ::D::
	37 ::A:: ::B:: ::C:: ::D::	41 ::A:: ::B:: ::C:: ::D::	45 ::A:: ::B:: ::C:: ::D::
46 ::A:: ::B:: ::C:: ::D::	49 ::A:: ::B:: ::C:: ::D::	53 ::A:: ::B:: ::C:: ::D::	57 ::A:: ::B:: ::C:: ::D::
47 ::A:: ::B:: ::C:: ::D::	50 ::A:: ::B:: ::C:: ::D::	54 ::A:: ::B:: ::C:: ::D::	58 ::A:: ::B:: ::C:: ::D::
48 ::A:: ::B:: ::C:: ::D::	51 ::A:: ::B:: ::C:: ::D::	55 ::A:: ::B:: ::C:: ::D::	59 ::A:: ::B:: ::C:: ::D::
	52 ::A:: ::B:: ::C:: ::D::	56 ::A:: ::B:: ::C:: ::D::	60 ::A:: ::B:: ::C:: ::D::
61 ::A:: ::B:: ::C:: ::D::	64 ::A:: ::B:: ::C:: ::D::	68 ::A:: ::B:: ::C:: ::D::	72 ::A:: ::B:: ::C:: ::D::
62 ::A:: ::B:: ::C:: ::D::	65 ::A:: ::B:: ::C:: ::D::	69 ::A:: ::B:: ::C:: ::D::	73 ::A:: ::B:: ::C:: ::D::
63 ::A:: ::B:: ::C:: ::D::	66 ::A:: ::B:: ::C:: ::D::	70 ::A:: ::B:: ::C:: ::D::	74 ::A:: ::B:: ::C:: ::D::
	67 ::A:: ::B:: ::C:: ::D::	71 ::A:: ::B:: ::C:: ::D::	75 ::A:: ::B:: ::C:: ::D::
76 ::A:: ::B:: ::C:: ::D::	79 ::A:: ::B:: ::C:: ::D::	83 ::A:: ::B:: ::C:: ::D::	87 ::A:: ::B:: ::C:: ::D::
77 ::A:: ::B:: ::C:: ::D::	80 ::A:: ::B:: ::C:: ::D::	84 ::A:: ::B:: ::C:: ::D::	88 ::A:: ::B:: ::C:: ::D::
78 ::A:: ::B:: ::C:: ::D::	81 ::A:: ::B:: ::C:: ::D::	85 ::A:: ::B:: ::C:: ::D::	89 ::A:: ::B:: ::C:: ::D::
	82 ::A:: ::B:: ::C:: ::D::	86 ::A:: ::B:: ::C:: ::D::	90 ::A:: ::B:: ::C:: ::D::
91 ::A:: ::B:: ::C:: ::D::	94 ::A:: ::B:: ::C:: ::D::	98 ::A:: ::B:: ::C:: ::D::	
92 ::A:: ::B:: ::C:: ::D::	95 ::A:: ::B:: ::C:: ::D::	99 ::A:: ::B:: ::C:: ::D::	
93 ::A:: ::B:: ::C:: ::D::	96 ::A:: ::B:: ::C:: ::D::	100 ::A:: ::B:: ::C:: ::D::	
	97 ::A:: ::B:: ::C:: ::D::		

MODEL EXAMINATION 2

NAME _____

LAST   FIRST   MIDDLE

SESSION   AM ☐   PM ☐

SOC. SEC. # _____ / _____ / _____

Enter your IDENT. NUMBER ↓

EXAM CODE # _____

DATE _____

BOOK # _____

PLACE OF EXAM _____

TITLE OF EXAM _____

SALESMAN ☐   BROKER ☐

IMPORTANT: IN MARKING YOUR ANSWERS FILL IN THE ANSWER BOX COMPLETELY.

::0:: ::1:: ::2:: ::3:: ::4::   ::5:: ::6:: ::7:: ::8:: ::9::
::0:: ::1:: ::2:: ::3:: ::4::   ::5:: ::6:: ::7:: ::8:: ::9::
::0:: ::1:: ::2:: ::3:: ::4::   ::5:: ::6:: ::7:: ::8:: ::9::
::0:: ::1:: ::2:: ::3:: ::4::   ::5:: ::6:: ::7:: ::8:: ::9::

	4 ::A:: ::B:: ::C:: ::D::	8 ::A:: ::B:: ::C:: ::D::	12 ::A:: ::B:: ::C:: ::D::
1 ::A:: ::B:: ::C:: ::D::	5 ::A:: ::B:: ::C:: ::D::	9 ::A:: ::B:: ::C:: ::D::	13 ::A:: ::B:: ::C:: ::D::
2 ::A:: ::B:: ::C:: ::D::	6 ::A:: ::B:: ::C:: ::D::	10 ::A:: ::B:: ::C:: ::D::	14 ::A:: ::B:: ::C:: ::D::
3 ::A:: ::B:: ::C:: ::D::	7 ::A:: ::B:: ::C:: ::D::	11 ::A:: ::B:: ::C:: ::D::	15 ::A:: ::B:: ::C:: ::D::
	19 ::A:: ::B:: ::C:: ::D::	23 ::A:: ::B:: ::C:: ::D::	27 ::A:: ::B:: ::C:: ::D::
16 ::A:: ::B:: ::C:: ::D::	20 ::A:: ::B:: ::C:: ::D::	24 ::A:: ::B:: ::C:: ::D::	28 ::A:: ::B:: ::C:: ::D::
17 ::A:: ::B:: ::C:: ::D::	21 ::A:: ::B:: ::C:: ::D::	25 ::A:: ::B:: ::C:: ::D::	29 ::A:: ::B:: ::C:: ::D::
18 ::A:: ::B:: ::C:: ::D::	22 ::A:: ::B:: ::C:: ::D::	26 ::A:: ::B:: ::C:: ::D::	30 ::A:: ::B:: ::C:: ::D::
	34 ::A:: ::B:: ::C:: ::D::	38 ::A:: ::B:: ::C:: ::D::	42 ::A:: ::B:: ::C:: ::D::
31 ::A:: ::B:: ::C:: ::D::	35 ::A:: ::B:: ::C:: ::D::	39 ::A:: ::B:: ::C:: ::D::	43 ::A:: ::B:: ::C:: ::D::
32 ::A:: ::B:: ::C:: ::D::	36 ::A:: ::B:: ::C:: ::D::	40 ::A:: ::B:: ::C:: ::D::	44 ::A:: ::B:: ::C:: ::D::
33 ::A:: ::B:: ::C:: ::D::	37 ::A:: ::B:: ::C:: ::D::	41 ::A:: ::B:: ::C:: ::D::	45 ::A:: ::B:: ::C:: ::D::
	49 ::A:: ::B:: ::C:: ::D::	53 ::A:: ::B:: ::C:: ::D::	57 ::A:: ::B:: ::C:: ::D::
46 ::A:: ::B:: ::C:: ::D::	50 ::A:: ::B:: ::C:: ::D::	54 ::A:: ::B:: ::C:: ::D::	58 ::A:: ::B:: ::C:: ::D::
47 ::A:: ::B:: ::C:: ::D::	51 ::A:: ::B:: ::C:: ::D::	55 ::A:: ::B:: ::C:: ::D::	59 ::A:: ::B:: ::C:: ::D::
48 ::A:: ::B:: ::C:: ::D::	52 ::A:: ::B:: ::C:: ::D::	56 ::A:: ::B:: ::C:: ::D::	60 ::A:: ::B:: ::C:: ::D::
	64 ::A:: ::B:: ::C:: ::D::	68 ::A:: ::B:: ::C:: ::D::	72 ::A:: ::B:: ::C:: ::D::
61 ::A:: ::B:: ::C:: ::D::	65 ::A:: ::B:: ::C:: ::D::	69 ::A:: ::B:: ::C:: ::D::	73 ::A:: ::B:: ::C:: ::D::
62 ::A:: ::B:: ::C:: ::D::	66 ::A:: ::B:: ::C:: ::D::	70 ::A:: ::B:: ::C:: ::D::	74 ::A:: ::B:: ::C:: ::D::
63 ::A:: ::B:: ::C:: ::D::	67 ::A:: ::B:: ::C:: ::D::	71 ::A:: ::B:: ::C:: ::D::	75 ::A:: ::B:: ::C:: ::D::
	79 ::A:: ::B:: ::C:: ::D::	83 ::A:: ::B:: ::C:: ::D::	87 ::A:: ::B:: ::C:: ::D::
76 ::A:: ::B:: ::C:: ::D::	80 ::A:: ::B:: ::C:: ::D::	84 ::A:: ::B:: ::C:: ::D::	88 ::A:: ::B:: ::C:: ::D::
77 ::A:: ::B:: ::C:: ::D::	81 ::A:: ::B:: ::C:: ::D::	85 ::A:: ::B:: ::C:: ::D::	89 ::A:: ::B:: ::C:: ::D::
78 ::A:: ::B:: ::C:: ::D::	82 ::A:: ::B:: ::C:: ::D::	86 ::A:: ::B:: ::C:: ::D::	90 ::A:: ::B:: ::C:: ::D::
	94 ::A:: ::B:: ::C:: ::D::	98 ::A:: ::B:: ::C:: ::D::	
91 ::A:: ::B:: ::C:: ::D::	95 ::A:: ::B:: ::C:: ::D::	99 ::A:: ::B:: ::C:: ::D::	
92 ::A:: ::B:: ::C:: ::D::	96 ::A:: ::B:: ::C:: ::D::	100 ::A:: ::B:: ::C:: ::D::	
93 ::A:: ::B:: ::C:: ::D::	97 ::A:: ::B:: ::C:: ::D::		

MODEL EXAMINATION 3

NAME _____

LAST   FIRST   MIDDLE

SOC. SEC. # _____

DATE _____

PLACE OF EXAM _____

TITLE OF EXAM _____

SALESMAN ☐   BROKER ☐

IMPORTANT: IN MARKING YOUR ANSWERS FILL IN THE ANSWER BOX COMPLETELY.

Enter your IDENT. NUMBER

SESSION   AM ☐   PM ☐

EXAM CODE # _____

BOOK # _____

MODEL EXAMINATION 4

NAME _____

LAST   FIRST   MIDDLE

SESSION   AM ☐   PM ☐

SOC. SEC. # _____/_____/

Enter your IDENT. NUMBER ↓

EXAM CODE # _____

DATE _____
PLACE OF EXAM _____
TITLE OF EXAM _____   SALESMAN ☐   BROKER ☐

BOOK # _____

IMPORTANT: IN MARKING YOUR ANSWERS FILL IN THE ANSWER BOX COMPLETELY.

1 ::A:: ::B:: ::C:: ::D::
2 ::A:: ::B:: ::C:: ::D::
3 ::A:: ::B:: ::C:: ::D::

4 ::A:: ::B:: ::C:: ::D::
5 ::A:: ::B:: ::C:: ::D::
6 ::A:: ::B:: ::C:: ::D::
7 ::A:: ::B:: ::C:: ::D::

8 ::A:: ::B:: ::C:: ::D::
9 ::A:: ::B:: ::C:: ::D::
10 ::A:: ::B:: ::C:: ::D::
11 ::A:: ::B:: ::C:: ::D::

12 ::A:: ::B:: ::C:: ::D::
13 ::A:: ::B:: ::C:: ::D::
14 ::A:: ::B:: ::C:: ::D::
15 ::A:: ::B:: ::C:: ::D::

16 ::A:: ::B:: ::C:: ::D::
17 ::A:: ::B:: ::C:: ::D::
18 ::A:: ::B:: ::C:: ::D::

19 ::A:: ::B:: ::C:: ::D::
20 ::A:: ::B:: ::C:: ::D::
21 ::A:: ::B:: ::C:: ::D::
22 ::A:: ::B:: ::C:: ::D::

23 ::A:: ::B:: ::C:: ::D::
24 ::A:: ::B:: ::C:: ::D::
25 ::A:: ::B:: ::C:: ::D::
26 ::A:: ::B:: ::C:: ::D::

27 ::A:: ::B:: ::C:: ::D::
28 ::A:: ::B:: ::C:: ::D::
29 ::A:: ::B:: ::C:: ::D::
30 ::A:: ::B:: ::C:: ::D::

31 ::A:: ::B:: ::C:: ::D::
32 ::A:: ::B:: ::C:: ::D::
33 ::A:: ::B:: ::C:: ::D::

34 ::A:: ::B:: ::C:: ::D::
35 ::A:: ::B:: ::C:: ::D::
36 ::A:: ::B:: ::C:: ::D::
37 ::A:: ::B:: ::C:: ::D::

38 ::A:: ::B:: ::C:: ::D::
39 ::A:: ::B:: ::C:: ::D::
40 ::A:: ::B:: ::C:: ::D::
41 ::A:: ::B:: ::C:: ::D::

42 ::A:: ::B:: ::C:: ::D::
43 ::A:: ::B:: ::C:: ::D::
44 ::A:: ::B:: ::C:: ::D::
45 ::A:: ::B:: ::C:: ::D::

46 ::A:: ::B:: ::C:: ::D::
47 ::A:: ::B:: ::C:: ::D::
48 ::A:: ::B:: ::C:: ::D::

49 ::A:: ::B:: ::C:: ::D::
50 ::A:: ::B:: ::C:: ::D::
51 ::A:: ::B:: ::C:: ::D::
52 ::A:: ::B:: ::C:: ::D::

53 ::A:: ::B:: ::C:: ::D::
54 ::A:: ::B:: ::C:: ::D::
55 ::A:: ::B:: ::C:: ::D::
56 ::A:: ::B:: ::C:: ::D::

57 ::A:: ::B:: ::C:: ::D::
58 ::A:: ::B:: ::C:: ::D::
59 ::A:: ::B:: ::C:: ::D::
60 ::A:: ::B:: ::C:: ::D::

61 ::A:: ::B:: ::C:: ::D::
62 ::A:: ::B:: ::C:: ::D::
63 ::A:: ::B:: ::C:: ::D::

64 ::A:: ::B:: ::C:: ::D::
65 ::A:: ::B:: ::C:: ::D::
66 ::A:: ::B:: ::C:: ::D::
67 ::A:: ::B:: ::C:: ::D::

68 ::A:: ::B:: ::C:: ::D::
69 ::A:: ::B:: ::C:: ::D::
70 ::A:: ::B:: ::C:: ::D::
71 ::A:: ::B:: ::C:: ::D::

72 ::A:: ::B:: ::C:: ::D::
73 ::A:: ::B:: ::C:: ::D::
74 ::A:: ::B:: ::C:: ::D::
75 ::A:: ::B:: ::C:: ::D::

76 ::A:: ::B:: ::C:: ::D::
77 ::A:: ::B:: ::C:: ::D::
78 ::A:: ::B:: ::C:: ::D::

79 ::A:: ::B:: ::C:: ::D::
80 ::A:: ::B:: ::C:: ::D::
81 ::A:: ::B:: ::C:: ::D::
82 ::A:: ::B:: ::C:: ::D::

83 ::A:: ::B:: ::C:: ::D::
84 ::A:: ::B:: ::C:: ::D::
85 ::A:: ::B:: ::C:: ::D::
86 ::A:: ::B:: ::C:: ::D::

87 ::A:: ::B:: ::C:: ::D::
88 ::A:: ::B:: ::C:: ::D::
89 ::A:: ::B:: ::C:: ::D::
90 ::A:: ::B:: ::C:: ::D::

91 ::A:: ::B:: ::C:: ::D::
92 ::A:: ::B:: ::C:: ::D::
93 ::A:: ::B:: ::C:: ::D::

94 ::A:: ::B:: ::C:: ::D::
95 ::A:: ::B:: ::C:: ::D::
96 ::A:: ::B:: ::C:: ::D::
97 ::A:: ::B:: ::C:: ::D::

98 ::A:: ::B:: ::C:: ::D::
99 ::A:: ::B:: ::C:: ::D::
100 ::A:: ::B:: ::C:: ::D::

MODEL EXAMINATION 5

NAME _____   SESSION _____   AM ☐   PM ☐
          LAST   FIRST   MIDDLE

SOC. SEC. # _____ / _____ / _____   EXAM CODE # _____

                                                    Enter your
                                                    IDENT.
                                                    NUMBER
                                                        ↓

DATE _____   BOOK # _____

PLACE
OF EXAM _____

TITLE
OF EXAM _____

        SALESMAN ☐   BROKER ☐

**IMPORTANT: IN MARKING YOUR ANSWERS
FILL IN THE ANSWER BOX COMPLETELY.** ━━

1 ::A:: ::B:: ::C:: ::D::
2 ::A:: ::B:: ::C:: ::D::
3 ::A:: ::B:: ::C:: ::D::

4 ::A:: ::B:: ::C:: ::D::
5 ::A:: ::B:: ::C:: ::D::
6 ::A:: ::B:: ::C:: ::D::
7 ::A:: ::B:: ::C:: ::D::

8 ::A:: ::B:: ::C:: ::D::
9 ::A:: ::B:: ::C:: ::D::
10 ::A:: ::B:: ::C:: ::D::
11 ::A:: ::B:: ::C:: ::D::

12 ::A:: ::B:: ::C:: ::D::
13 ::A:: ::B:: ::C:: ::D::
14 ::A:: ::B:: ::C:: ::D::
15 ::A:: ::B:: ::C:: ::D::

16 ::A:: ::B:: ::C:: ::D::
17 ::A:: ::B:: ::C:: ::D::
18 ::A:: ::B:: ::C:: ::D::

19 ::A:: ::B:: ::C:: ::D::
20 ::A:: ::B:: ::C:: ::D::
21 ::A:: ::B:: ::C:: ::D::
22 ::A:: ::B:: ::C:: ::D::

23 ::A:: ::B:: ::C:: ::D::
24 ::A:: ::B:: ::C:: ::D::
25 ::A:: ::B:: ::C:: ::D::
26 ::A:: ::B:: ::C:: ::D::

27 ::A:: ::B:: ::C:: ::D::
28 ::A:: ::B:: ::C:: ::D::
29 ::A:: ::B:: ::C:: ::D::
30 ::A:: ::B:: ::C:: ::D::

31 ::A:: ::B:: ::C:: ::D::
32 ::A:: ::B:: ::C:: ::D::
33 ::A:: ::B:: ::C:: ::D::

34 ::A:: ::B:: ::C:: ::D::
35 ::A:: ::B:: ::C:: ::D::
36 ::A:: ::B:: ::C:: ::D::
37 ::A:: ::B:: ::C:: ::D::

38 ::A:: ::B:: ::C:: ::D::
39 ::A:: ::B:: ::C:: ::D::
40 ::A:: ::B:: ::C:: ::D::
41 ::A:: ::B:: ::C:: ::D::

42 ::A:: ::B:: ::C:: ::D::
43 ::A:: ::B:: ::C:: ::D::
44 ::A:: ::B:: ::C:: ::D::
45 ::A:: ::B:: ::C:: ::D::

46 ::A:: ::B:: ::C:: ::D::
47 ::A:: ::B:: ::C:: ::D::
48 ::A:: ::B:: ::C:: ::D::

49 ::A:: ::B:: ::C:: ::D::
50 ::A:: ::B:: ::C:: ::D::
51 ::A:: ::B:: ::C:: ::D::
52 ::A:: ::B:: ::C:: ::D::

53 ::A:: ::B:: ::C:: ::D::
54 ::A:: ::B:: ::C:: ::D::
55 ::A:: ::B:: ::C:: ::D::
56 ::A:: ::B:: ::C:: ::D::

57 ::A:: ::B:: ::C:: ::D::
58 ::A:: ::B:: ::C:: ::D::
59 ::A:: ::B:: ::C:: ::D::
60 ::A:: ::B:: ::C:: ::D::

61 ::A:: ::B:: ::C:: ::D::
62 ::A:: ::B:: ::C:: ::D::
63 ::A:: ::B:: ::C:: ::D::

64 ::A:: ::B:: ::C:: ::D::
65 ::A:: ::B:: ::C:: ::D::
66 ::A:: ::B:: ::C:: ::D::
67 ::A:: ::B:: ::C:: ::D::

68 ::A:: ::B:: ::C:: ::D::
69 ::A:: ::B:: ::C:: ::D::
70 ::A:: ::B:: ::C:: ::D::
71 ::A:: ::B:: ::C:: ::D::

72 ::A:: ::B:: ::C:: ::D::
73 ::A:: ::B:: ::C:: ::D::
74 ::A:: ::B:: ::C:: ::D::
75 ::A:: ::B:: ::C:: ::D::

76 ::A:: ::B:: ::C:: ::D::
77 ::A:: ::B:: ::C:: ::D::
78 ::A:: ::B:: ::C:: ::D::

79 ::A:: ::B:: ::C:: ::D::
80 ::A:: ::B:: ::C:: ::D::
81 ::A:: ::B:: ::C:: ::D::
82 ::A:: ::B:: ::C:: ::D::

83 ::A:: ::B:: ::C:: ::D::
84 ::A:: ::B:: ::C:: ::D::
85 ::A:: ::B:: ::C:: ::D::
86 ::A:: ::B:: ::C:: ::D::

87 ::A:: ::B:: ::C:: ::D::
88 ::A:: ::B:: ::C:: ::D::
89 ::A:: ::B:: ::C:: ::D::
90 ::A:: ::B:: ::C:: ::D::

91 ::A:: ::B:: ::C:: ::D::
92 ::A:: ::B:: ::C:: ::D::
93 ::A:: ::B:: ::C:: ::D::

94 ::A:: ::B:: ::C:: ::D::
95 ::A:: ::B:: ::C:: ::D::
96 ::A:: ::B:: ::C:: ::D::
97 ::A:: ::B:: ::C:: ::D::

98 ::A:: ::B:: ::C:: ::D::
99 ::A:: ::B:: ::C:: ::D::
100 ::A:: ::B:: ::C:: ::D::

MODEL EXAMINATION 6

NAME _____

SOC. SEC. # _____

DATE _____

PLACE
OF EXAM _____

TITLE
OF EXAM _____   SALESMAN ☐   BROKER ☐

IMPORTANT: IN MARKING YOUR ANSWERS
FILL IN THE ANSWER BOX COMPLETELY.

Enter your
IDENT.
NUMBER

SESSION   AM ☐   PM ☐

EXAM CODE # _____

BOOK # _____